BASEBALL

100 Classic Moments in the History of the Game

BASEBALL

100 Classic Moments in the History of the Game

THE NATIONAL BASEBALL HALL OF FAME AND MUSEUM

JOSEPH WALLACE

NEIL HAMILTON · MARTY APPEL

DORLING KINDERSLEY
LONDON, NEW YORK, DELHI, JOHANNESBURG, MUNICH, PARIS, and SYDNEY

DORLING KINDERSLEY

LONDON, NEW YORK, DELHI, JOHANNESBURG, MUNICH, PARIS, and SYDNEY

www.dk.com

Produced by The Moschovitis Group, Inc.
95 Madison Avenue, New York, New York 10016
www.mosgroup.com

Chapter introductions by Neil Hamilton
Text by Joseph Wallace with contributions from Marty Appel

Executive Editor: Valerie Tomaselli
Senior Editor: Jill Pope
Art Director and Designer: Annemarie Redmond
Director of Photo Research and Rights: Pat Kelly
Library Director: Jim Gates
Director of Research: Tim Wiles
Editorial Coordinator: Stephanie Schreiber
Editorial Assistant: Renée Miller
Copyediting: Paul Scaramazza
Factchecking and Proofreading: Dan Bennett, Bill Burdick, Eric Enders, Bill Francis,
Greg Harris, Jeremy Jones, Amy Kaiman, Bruce Markusen, Scot Mondore, Helen Stiles
Production Assistant: Yolanda Pluguez
Index: AEIOU, Inc.

First American Edition, 2000
2 4 6 8 10 9 7 5 3 1

Published in the United States by
Dorling Kindersley Publishing, Inc.
95 Madison Avenue, New York, New York 10016

Dorling Kindersley offers special discounts for bulk purchases for sales promotions or premiums.
Specific, large-quantity needs can be met with special editions, including personalized covers, excerpts of
existing guides, and corporate imprints. For more information, contact Special Markets Department,
Dorling Kindersley Publishing, Inc., 95 Madison Avenue, New York, NY 10016 Fax: 800-600-9098

Library of Congress Cataloging-in-Publication Data
Baseball: 100 classic moments in the history of the game / Joseph Wallace, Neil Hamilton, Marty Appel.—1st American ed.
p.   cm.
Includes index.
1. Baseball—United States—History—20th century. I. Hamilton, Neil A., 1949- II. Appel, Martin. III. Title.
GV863.A1 W357 2000   796.357'0973—dc21   99-047606
ISBN 0-7894-5121-2

Reproduced by Colourpath, London
Printed and bound in the United States by Quebecor.

CONTENTS

FOREWORD

by Nolan Ryan

A line from one of my favorite movies, *Field of Dreams,* says that sometimes we don't recognize the most significant moments in our lives as they're happening. Though I was involved in a couple of the moments described in this book, and witnessed a few more, I never thought at the time about their significance in baseball history. Sometimes when you're playing the game you have to try and ignore the big picture to concentrate on the moment at hand, and it's only afterward that you realize what a moment truly means.

A good example is my seven no-hitters (the first is shown at left). I'd entered games throughout my 27-year big league career with what I thought was great stuff while warming up in the bullpen, only to find I had lost it somewhere between there and the mound. But on those rare occasions, usually when you least expect it, you toss one of those games when everything turns out right—and those are the ones everybody remembers. I've pitched what I thought were better games, either where I had great control or my fastball was really popping, but the no-hitters simply get more attention because of the rarity of them. I pitched 12 one-hitters, 19 two-hitters, 31 three-hitters, and lost five no-hitters with hits in the ninth inning, but the moments for which I'm probably best remembered are those seven special occasions when everything fell into place. That's something I never imagined when I began my big league career as a 19-year-old with the New York Mets in 1966.

Also, you never know how fleeting these moments are until time passes and you realize that you will never experience such a feeling again. In retrospect, when I look back upon my long career, I never would have guessed that being part of the "Amazing Mets" that won the 1969 World Series would end up being my only experience in the Fall Classic. We were all so young—Tom Seaver, Jerry Koosman, Tug McGraw, and myself—and the Mets had been perennial losers since their inception in 1962, but we were able to overcome the odds by defeating the heavily favored Orioles for the championship. Little did I know at the time that I would play another 24 years without competing for the game's ultimate prize.

This book does a wonderful job of reliving some great moments from major league history, but there are many other moments worth remembering that happened outside of big league stadiums. Some of the best memories I have of my life in baseball are of when I was growing up in Texas. I couldn't get enough of the game, and every so often, I'd just go play with a group of my childhood friends all day long. Their enthusiasm rubbed off on me and, I think, contributed to the love of the game that kept me in baseball for more than 20 years. As I look back now on my life in baseball, many of my fondest memories are not of major league games, but of things like playing catch with my children in the back yard.

I had the good fortune of being inducted into the National Baseball Hall of Fame in Cooperstown, New York, in 1999. What a thrill that was. And walking through the museum just reinforces how the "moment" in baseball is critical and how the outcome of a game can be changed without a moment's notice. In Cooperstown and in this book you will not only see the great accomplishments attained by the true stars of the game, such as the recent home run race between Mark McGwire and Sammy Sosa that captivated the nation, but also those achievements that came from lesser known players whose careers will forever be defined in an instant, like Bobby Thomson's "Shot Heard 'Round the World."

I consider myself one of the lucky ones. I've spent most of my adult life making a living doing something I love. I always remembered when I went out to the mound, how fortunate I was to be there. Then I'd look out in the stands and see the fans who came to that game, like the father who worked all day and brought his young son out to see me pitch, and I'd do my best to make it a memory that would last them a lifetime. I'd like to think I made that possible more times than not, because it's really the fans' game, a game that comes alive in the memories of those that love it.

Being a fan of the national pastime myself, I'm thankful that my career was long enough that I was active during a number of the moments mentioned in this book. It's a special feeling thumbing through the book and recalling old teammates, former opponents, and fierce rivalries, while also having a chance to read about events before my time. Every page brought about a rush of excitement, a new revelation, and a sense of wonder. I hope the reader enjoys it as much as I did.

PREFACE

Baseball: 100 Classic Moments in the History of the Game was born from a photographic exhibit that the Hall of Fame created in 1997. Our idea was to present the story of baseball, through a series of memorable moments and to illustrate those moments in photographs. The exhibit toured the country to great response, and, very quickly, we knew that the exhibit should become a book.

The translation of the photo exhibit to book form allowed us a variety of unique opportunities. While a touring exhibit limited the space and time we could devote to the subject, a book would offer more flexibility and the advantage of timelessness. So we took up the challenge. We expanded the text from short captions, which briefly summarized the important facts of each moment, to a full story, presenting not just the highlights of the moment, but background, context, and wide-ranging detail. Further, we greatly increased the number of photos to more fully depict the events, and added statistical tables that would further enhance each story. (We included some images, whose photographhic quality may not be perfect, for the sake of the historical value they bring to the book.)

Selecting the moments from the exhibit, and reassessing them for inclusion in the book, were not easy tasks. First of all, we wanted to focus the story we were telling, so we chose to concentrate on the Major Leagues. This, of course, excluded many interesting and compelling stories—such as events in the Negro Leagues, All-American Girl's Professional Baseball League, and the minor leagues, to name a few. Further, we had to somehow define what constituted a "moment." When all was said and done, we agreed that a moment could happen in the blink of an eye, or take an entire career to unfold. Finally, our intention was to cover the most memorable moments in the game—classic moments that shaped the history of the national pastime, for good or bad. Hence, we have included the lows as well as the highs, the great mistakes as well as the great achievements, the defeats as well as the victories.

We do not anticipate that our list of one hundred classic moments will match up exactly with yours. In fact, there were many spirited arguments among our staff as to which moments to include, and which would have to be left out. Of course, this is part of what makes baseball great. The game touches every fan in a different way and leaves us each with our own unique memories. These are the memories of our staff.

Baseball is organized into five eras, each of which is presented in its own chapter. Each chapter opens with an essay that gives a broad historical overview to the period, what it meant for baseball, and how baseball helped to characterize the era. The moments flow from the introductory essays to highlight the most memorable moments for each era, thereby detailing the history of baseball not only in broad strokes but also in great detail.

The volume closes with a detailed index, meant to help all readers—the serious researcher, the avid fan, the casual spectator—locate the players, teams, and events they are most interested in. It includes entries on teams, players, awards, major contests (the LCS, World Series, All-star games, etc.), stadiums, owners, and mangers, among other items. Use the index for targeted reading and research, to make your use of the book more meaningful and complete. More importantly, read through the entire book for the pleasure that it will bring, the details it will illuminate, and the awe of the sport it will inspire.

Our hope is that Baseball: 100 Classic Moments in the History of the Game will offer an enduring record of the history of the game and a timeless keepsake for baseball enthusiasts to enjoy. We hope that fans, young and old, will treasure the stories it tells, and will take pleasure in the recollections it inspires. As the years go by, and other events unfold, we hope to publish new expanded editions to insure that all the great moments are captured. For now, enjoy Baseball, the story of 100 classic moments in the history of this great game.

ECSTATIC FANS OF THE UNDERDOG NEW YORK METS poured onto the field after their team defeated the Baltimore Orioles in the 1969 World Series.

A SPORT...AND A SCANDAL

The ball took off with such force it belied the ease with which it had been launched. When it landed in the upper right field stands of New York City's Polo Grounds on a spring day cleansed by recent rains, it announced a great baseball player in the making and a new era for baseball itself. Babe Ruth, then a pitcher with the Boston Red Sox, had hit the ball in 1915 against the New York Yankees, the very club he would soon become synonymous with. That his exploit occurred while playing for a big-city team against a big-city team underscored baseball's crucial ties to urban America in an era when the farm and the village were rapidly receding into the past.

Historian Arthur Schlesinger, Sr., has described the small town's fate as society passed from the nineteenth to the twentieth century: "In the Middle West and the North Atlantic states, rural America, like a stag at bay, was making its last stand." With that development, Americans struggled to embrace the modern era—its factories, cities, and resulting materialism—while heavily influenced by their pastoral heritage and longing for the past.

As baseball grew into a professional sport, it tapped into this nostalgia and created an image of itself— based partly in fact, mostly in myth—that was opposed to that of the city . . . its own field of dreams. The image, fashioned like so many pictures stitched on a country quilt—cornfields, farmhouses, bandstands—portrayed baseball as all-American, as representing honesty, community, and individualism.

Thus, in a report issued by a blue ribbon commission in 1907, professional baseball said that Abner Doubleday, a Civil War general, had invented the game in idyllic Cooperstown,

BASEBALL FOUND ITS PLACE in American cities early in its history. Above, a game is being played on Boston Common, circa 1834.

New York, in 1839. With its report, the commission rejected evidence to the contrary and denied that baseball had evolved from the English game of rounders and other similar games played years before Doubleday's time.

Despite the village imagery, from its inception as a highly organized sport, baseball depended on the city. Way back in 1845 a group of New York City gentlemen founded the Knickerbocker Base Ball Club. They treated it as a game for the elite but, in the urban environment with its diverse population, young men from the working classes soon embraced the sport and organized their own clubs.

While baseball developed, the nation's urban population increased from 10 million in 1870 to 54 million in 1920—nearly 550 percent! During the same era, the number of cities with more than 100,000 people increased from 15 to 68, and those with more than 500,000 from two to 12. Where did all these people come from? For the most part, the numbers represent migration—Americans moving from farms and villages to the cities, and arrivals from foreign countries. About 26 million immigrants entered the United States between 1870 and 1920. Seeking leisure activities, the teeming masses soon jammed ball parks in New York, Boston, Philadelphia, and other cities; attendance figures rose and professional baseball prospered.

Cities attracted people because they offered employment in factories. Whereas only about 25 percent of Americans worked in manufacturing or transportation in 1860, more than 50 percent did so by 1900. The machine had taken over, hammering out steel girders and leather shoes, filling cans with processed foods, sewing textiles into clothes. Americans seemed destined to be driven by the machine, and shackled to it.

As machines required mainly unskilled labor and as factory owners looked for cheap workers, they hired more women and children. In 1900, a record 18.2 percent of children aged 10 to 15 occupied the work force. Women filled the growing clerical ranks as well, totaling nearly 50 percent of such workers by the early 1900s as they learned to use a new invention, the typewriter. As the years progressed, working conditions changed. Average workweeks in manufacturing shortened from over 60 hours in the late 1800s to just under 50 in 1920, with more people having entire weekends free. The proportion of children in the work force dropped to about 11 percent in that year (although their total number continued to rise).

This combination of repetitive, mechanized labor and decreasing work hours affected baseball. Workers sought release from the factory through recreation—either as participants or spectators. An entire philosophy argued they should. Numerous books and articles warned that urban life differed from rural life, with its farms and manual labor, and made people sedentary and weak, prone to poor health; in short, Americans needed to exercise or they would deteriorate.

Riding the recreational wave, baseball and a related sport, softball, attracted more and more young participants. Businesses, unions, churches, civic groups—all formed baseball teams. Churches in New York City organized the Sunday School Athletic League. In Chicago there was a women's softball team as early as 1895, and by 1924 there were softball clubs in 161 cities with over 74,000 players.

Urban growth went hand in hand with changes in transportation, as far-reaching in their effect in the early twentieth-century as the computer has been in our own day. By the 1880s cable cars jangled through Chicago, San Francisco, and several other cities, and in the 1890s electric-powered streetcars, or trolleys, began transporting urbanites. Subways and elevated trains added to the transportation revolution. All told, these devices spread cities out by enabling residents to live farther from their workplaces. For baseball, they provided a way for fans scattered about the metropolis to travel to games—and in one instance lent a colorful nickname to a team: "Dodgers" for the Brooklyn club, a reference, legend has it, to those who "dodged" streetcars while scurrying through city streets. And existing railway connections between cities provided baseball teams with the means to travel long distances to play on the road.

The automobile added another dimension. By 1910 middle-class Americans were buying these affordable vehicles from

As CITIES GREW, people flocked to retail department stores like those on Washington Avenue in St. Louis, Missouri, for ready-made material goods.

Henry Ford's assembly line, and by 1920 the number of registered cars had exceeded 10 million. Spectators pulled their autos right up to the outfields, while club owners incorporated land for parking spaces into their plans for new ballparks.

Great changes in communication came from the cities. There appeared mass-circulation newspapers such as the *New York Journal* and *New York World*, and magazines such as *McClure's, Saturday Evening Post,* and *Ladies' Home Journal*, all of which by the early 1900s carried substantial advertising. Spending on advertising, primarily in print form, increased from $95 million in 1900 to $500 million in 1919. Specialized magazines and periodicals, such as the *Spalding* and *Reach* guides, dedicated themselves solely to sports. These guides were published annually for a nationwide audience. Others appealed mainly to kids. *Tip Top Weekly*—"an ideal publication for the American youth"—carried Frank Merriwell's widely popular fictional stories about baseball and other sports heroes.

In pursuit of greater circulation to generate more advertising revenue, publications boosted readership by expanding their news and sports coverage. Newspapers, in particular, latched on to baseball. The sport provided a different story

AFFORDABLE AUTOMOBILES HELPED SPECTATORS get to ballparks. Above, a traffic jam at 42nd Street and Madison Avenue in New York City, circa 1917.

nearly every day and allowed for player profiles, game summaries, and the latest scores. Pitching duels, home runs, and last-minute victories jumped from stories written with flare.

General economic growth meant more money for baseball. Industrialization benefited the wealthy more than any other class, as the richest five percent of the population obtained nearly 25 percent of all earned income. But middle-class incomes rose too; for example, the average pay for clerical workers increased 36 percent between 1890 and 1910. On the downside, from 1889 to 1913 prices went up 47 percent for an average wage-earning family of four. Nevertheless, in an era when department stores reached such dimensions that they carried the label "consumers' palaces," middle-class Americans spent more, notably on recreation. In 1905 the Sears catalog contained an entire two pages devoted to baseballs and baseball equipment, and by 1919, the value of sporting goods manufactured in the United States neared $40 million.

Attendance at games within the splendor of new major league parks revealed the surge for spectator sport in America's consumer-based economy. Of the 16 big league clubs in 1919, a full 14 played in recently-built facilities that replaced old wooden stands with concrete and steel. In 1909, the Philadelphia Athletics christened Shibe Park, with its double-decker grandstand. Soon after, Forbes Field opened in Pittsburgh, a triple-decker with elevators, electric lights, telephones, ramps rather than stairs and, in an ultimate luxury statement, box seats renting at $100 for the season—complete with personalized brass nameplates. Although attendance for the American and National leagues fluctuated, it went up from nearly five million in 1903 to over seven million in 1909, and then over nine million in 1920.

In a nation kicking the rural dust from its heels and embracing a modern economy, the competitive instinct that ruled the business world dominated society and, with it, baseball. Obviously teams competed on the baseball field and players competed for positions on clubs. But it went deeper than that: Clubs competed with one another for the best players. To control the latter, in an atmosphere where quality ballplayers were at a premium, professional baseball established the reserve clause in 1883. Historian Harold Seymour notes in *Baseball: The Early Years* that the owners' general labor policies were necessary to stabilize baseball as a business and that "the players had no voice; the owner decided everything." This was equally true of the reserve clause.

The clause stated that once a player signed for a team, he was to stay there for the rest of his career—"reserved" for subsequent seasons—unless the club traded him or released him. Thus 20th-century baseball inherited a system that governed the game's labor relations for nearly a century until free agency changed the rules in the mid-1970s.

When ballplayers competed as individuals to make it to the Majors and excel there, they reflected the value society placed on individualism and the related success ethic that said a person could advance through hard work. Newspapers extolled individual accomplishments in the sport and encouraged admiration of players' achievements. When the great Christy Mathewson pitched flawlessly, or when Honus Wagner won eight National League batting titles, or when Cy Young amazed everyone by earning 511 career victories, or when Ty Cobb stole 96 bases in 1915, they captured the competitive passion that tapped society's inner core.

In addition to competition and individualism, baseball reflected America's social and cultural prejudices. Although immigrants, including Jewish players, found success in the Major Leagues, they also experienced harassment and discrimination. African Americans faced an even more dismal condition. While no official barrier existed, organized baseball, in effect, barred black players, and discrimination ruled the stands as ballparks in the South segregated African-American spectators from whites at games played by minor league teams, and by touring major league teams.

Urban society often measured success by material gain; so too did baseball—both the players and the owners. Around 1900, when the National League and American League veered away from the reserve clause and competed for players on the open market, the athletes' salaries more than doubled. But the two leagues quickly realized such competition could affect profits, and so in 1902 they reached a peace pact whereby they agreed to respect the reserve clause.

When the owners of the American League champion Boston Pilgrims (later Red Sox) and the National League champion Pittsburgh Pirates agreed in 1903 to hold a World Series, they did so in part to satisfy fans who demanded such an inter-league match-up, but also to gain profits from the competition and, most importantly, to generate more interest in the sport. Although New York Giants owner John Brush and team manager John McGraw refused to have their N.L. championship team play the World Series the following year—against what they labeled an inferior A.L. team—they came around in 1905. The plan worked beautifully. Newspapers presented the World Series as the ultimate athletic competition, the crown for a truly American sport, and fans formed team booster clubs and paraded to the games. The Series did much to make baseball an integral part of American culture, profits and all.

America's entry into World War I affected baseball only slightly. The draft and enlistments in 1918 pulled some players from the sport and convinced the Major Leagues to shorten the season, but within two years normal play had resumed. The war helped baseball, however, by accelerating the nation's industrial expansion and the growth of its cities.

While war clouds dissipated, a sensational scandal shook baseball to its very core. Evidence strongly indicates that in 1919 several Chicago White Sox players accepted money to throw the World Series against the Cincinnati Reds. Rumors had circulated for a long time that earlier games may have been fixed, and gambling surrounded the sport as many fans placed bets and some athletes associated with suspicious characters. At one point, several players charged that a former Cincinnati Reds' player, Hal Chase, had offered them money to throw games. Evidence indeed shows that on several occasions Chase threw games himself.

In an attempt to protect baseball's clean image, the club owners covered up reports of such misdoing. White Sox owner Charles Comiskey did likewise after learning about the alleged 1919 fix; the following year, seven of the eight players involved returned to the team at double salary in a strategy to keep them quiet. But in 1920 a newspaper broke the story about the fix, and a grand jury in Cook County, Illinois, investigated. In 1921, all eight players and several gamblers were indicted in what was labeled the Black Sox scandal. Five of the players had confessed, with "Shoeless" Joe Jackson claiming he had moved slowly to retrieve balls hit to him. But the players withdrew their confessions before the trial. On August 2, 1921, a jury acquitted all the players, and the jurors carried them about on their shoulders in celebration.

The players, however, never returned to baseball. Shortly before the verdict, the club owners had appointed Kenesaw Mountain Landis as baseball's first commissioner. Headstrong and opinionated, Landis was a federal judge known for his controversial decisions that oftentimes defied legal logic. His first act as commissioner was to ban the eight Black Sox players from organized baseball.

Critics of Landis's action in the Black Sox scandal say that he cared more about appearing to clean up baseball than actually doing it, that by expelling the Black Sox players he made it seem as if the scandal was entirely their fault, with the owners and the larger gambling environment blameless. Landis' defenders, however, say that his firm action projected baseball as a clean sport intolerant of anyone who would sully it. As it turned out, the expulsion of the Black Sox proved less important to saving baseball than did Babe Ruth and the home run era. When Ruth's shots began clearing the fences, they thrilled fans throughout the nation. At any moment a game could be changed by one big swing of a bat. Ruth won new loyalties to baseball. He attracted new fans to the game, changed its entire style of play, and created a new public persona at a time when the shape of America itself was changing from rural to urban.

NEWSPAPERS BEGAN EXPANDING THEIR baseball coverage in the early 1900s. Vendor Simon Mellitto, age 10, stood in front of a Woolworth store in Philadelphia in 1910.

PERFECTION

In baseball it's defined as retiring all 27 batters in a nine inning game, and it's only happened
16 times since 1876. One of the most exciting pitted Cleveland's future Hall-of-Famer Addie Joss against the White Sox'
future Hall-of-Famer Ed Walsh on October 2, 1908. Joss retired all 27 hitters, while Walsh struck out 15 "Naps," as
the Indians were then known. The only run in Joss' 1-0 victory scored on a passed ball. The 16 perfect hurlers:
John Lee Richmond, John Montgomery Ward, Cy Young, Addie Joss, Charlie Robertson, Don Larsen, Jim Bunning, Sandy
Koufax, Catfish Hunter, Len Barker, Mike Witt, Tom Browning, Dennis Martinez, Kenny Rogers, David Wells, and David Cone.

MOST DIFFICULT OF ALL

O f all the single-game accomplishments in baseball, the most difficult
may be pitching a perfect game.
Since the arrival of organized professional
baseball, only 15 men have faced 27 opposing
hitters in a nine-inning regular-season game
and gotten all 27 hitters out: Lee Richmond,
John Montgomery Ward, Cy Young, Addie Joss,
Charlie Robertson, Jim Bunning, Sandy Koufax,

Catfish Hunter, Len Barker, Mike Witt, Tom
Browning, Dennis Martinez, Kenny Rogers,
David Wells, and, most recently, David Cone.
In 1956, Don Larsen pitched the only perfect
game in World Series history.

Perhaps the most exciting of all perfect
games took place more than 90 years ago, on
October 2, 1908, when two future Hall of
Famers faced off. The Cleveland Naps' Addie
Joss and the Chicago White Sox' Ed Walsh
were both pitching aces at the top of
their form—Walsh would end the
season with an astounding 40 wins,
while Joss would win 24—and on
October 2 their teams were fighting it out as part of a furious
four-team pennant race. They

"A THOUSAND
FINGERNAILS HIT
THE FLOOR AS
JOSS HAD TO BE
CAREFUL NOW."

On October 2, 1908, pitchers Addie Joss
(right) and Ed Walsh faced each other.
At the end of the day, Joss had pitched a
perfect game, and Walsh had struck
out 15, the record at the time.

At Right, Joss of the
Cleveland Naps in fine
pitching form.

couldn't have confronted each other in a more important game.

THE GREAT GAME

It was a cool, clear fall day at Cleveland's League Park as the Naps and Sox took the field. The Sox were a bare half-game behind the Naps in the pennant race, and both Joss and Walsh had come equipped with

IN A GAME AGAINST THE MINNESOTA TWINS on May 17, 1998, left-handed Yankee pitcher David Wells threw a perfect game, making him the 15th man to do so in baseball history. He was also the first Yankee to pitch a regular-season perfect game at Yankee Stadium.

their best stuff. For Joss, this meant that his "fadeaway" breaking pitch was moving and his fastball was hopping. Meanwhile, Walsh had complete control of his best pitch: the spitball, which was legal at the time.

Through two innings, neither team had come close to getting a hit. But then, in the bottom of the third, the Naps' Joe Birmingham led off with a single. He moved to second on a delayed steal (edging far enough off first base to draw a throw from Walsh, then scooting down to second before the Sox first baseman could throw him out). When the throw to second hit him in the back and rolled to the outfield, Birmingham ran to third.

Here he stood while Walsh got the next two men out. Then, with two strikes on the Naps' Wilbur Goode, Walsh and Sox catcher Ossie Shreck got mixed up on the signs. Shreck thought he'd asked for an inside pitch, and wasn't expecting Walsh's outside fastball. He stuck out his hand in an attempt to grab the ball, but all he got for his efforts was a torn and bleeding hand that caused him to leave the game. The ball rolled all the way to the backstop, and Birmingham came in to score.

So the score was 1–0 after three innings, and there it stayed. Cleveland's second baseman-manager Nap "Larry" Lajoie (the team was named the Naps in his honor) saved the no-hitter several times with great plays on slow ground balls. By the sixth inning, the noisy crowd, knowing they were watching history in the making, had fallen silent, respecting the tradition that says that you never mention a potential no-hitter in progress.

In the seventh inning, Joss almost gave away his perfect game, going to a three balls, two strikes count on Chicago's player-manager Fielder Jones. "A thousand fingernails hit the floor as Joss had to be careful now," recalled writer Franklin Lewis. Joss threw a sinking fastball, a borderline pitch. Jones took it, and then everyone waited to see what umpire Tommy Connolly would call. He said, "Strike three!" and the perfect game was still on track.

PRESSURE

Now it was the ninth inning, still 1–0. The Naps had done nothing with the three other hits they'd managed to scratch out against Walsh, who'd struck out 15. By now the crowd was so silent that, as one writer said, "A mouse working his way along the grandstand floor would have sounded like a shovel scraping over concrete."

The Sox sent three pinch hitters to the plate in the ninth. Doc White grounded out, and then Jiggs Donahue fanned on three pitches. Now there were two outs, but a strong hitter named John Anderson was coming to the plate. Though at the end of his career, the "Terrible Swede" (as he was called) had home run power. He could ruin Joss' perfect game and tie the score with just one swing.

Joss threw his first pitch, trying to get it inside, on Anderson's hands. Perhaps he'd break Anderson's bat, get him to roll an easy grounder to the infield. But the pitch wasn't a good one. Anderson slammed it high and far...and foul.

Everyone, players and fans alike, took a deep breath. Joss reared back and threw, and again Anderson swung, this time hitting a hard ground ball to third base. The Naps' third base-man, Bill Bradley, fielded the ball cleanly behind the bag, but then threw the ball low to first base.

Luckily, first baseman George Stovall was wielding a nimble glove that day, and he made a fine pickup of Bradley's low throw. It was a close play at the base, but the umpire called Anderson out. The fans flooded across the field, celebrating both the perfect game and a win that they thought might bring the pennant.

Unfortunately, not even this perfect game could guarantee a perfect ending to the season for Cleveland's fans. Neither the Naps nor the White Sox would win the pennant in 1908. The Detroit Tigers, led by Ty Cobb, edged out the Naps by a half-game for the flag, while the White Sox fell just a game-and-a-half short.

ON JULY 18, 1999 AT YANKEE STADIUM, David Cone pitched a perfect game in interleague play against the Montreal Expos. As it was "Yogi Berra Day," former Yankee Don Larsen, who pitched the only perfect game ever in a World Series (1956), threw out the day's first pitch and was in attendance, along with Berra.

Perfect Nine-Inning Games Since 1876

Year	Pitcher	Team	Opposing Team
1880	J.L. Richmond	Worcester	Cleveland (N)
1880	J.M. Ward	Providence	Buffalo (N)
1904	Cy Young	Boston	Philadelphia (A)
1908	Addie Joss	Cleveland	Chicago (A)
1922	Charlie Robertson	Chicago	Detroit (A)
1956	Don Larsen	New York (A)	Brooklyn (N)*
1964	Jim Bunning	Philadelphia	New York (N)
1965	Sandy Koufax	Los Angeles	Chicago (N)
1968	Catfish Hunter	Oakland	Minnesota (A)
1981	Len Barker	Cleveland	Toronto (A)
1984	Mike Witt	California	Texas (A)
1988	Tom Browning	Cincinnati	Los Angeles (N)
1991	Dennis Martinez	Montreal	Los Angeles (N)
1994	Kenny Rogers	Texas	California (A)
1998	David Wells	New York	Minnesota (A)
1999	David Cone	New York (A)	Montreal (N)**

*World Series, **Interleague game

THE FIRST WORLD SERIES

It seems so natural today, the champions of both Major Leagues meeting in a post-season World Series to decide it all. But in 1903, it was a new idea. The National League had been around since 1876, but the upstart American League was only three years old! The N.L.'s Pittsburgh Pirates faced the A.L.'s Boston Pilgrims in a best-of-nine game Series. 36-year-old Cy Young, along with Bill Dinneen, led the Bostons to the championship in eight games. Though John McGraw's pennant-winning New York Giants refused to play Boston the next year, by 1905 the World Series was here to stay.

THE SERIES STARTS

"IT'S A MINOR LEAGUE," MCGRAW SAID, "AND THE GIANTS WOULD OUTCLASS THEM."

Although championship series had been held during the nineteenth-century, there had been no season-ending competition since 1897, and there seemed no hope for one after the American League was born in 1901.

While fans would have loved games between the National League and American League champions, the leagues were at war over player contracts, each seeking to sign their rival's biggest stars. For the American League, there was no bigger prize than Cy Young, the game's best pitcher, who jumped to the A.L. from St. Louis, joined the Boston Pilgrims, and took his 286 N.L. victories with him.

So there would be no postseason championship until 1903, when a peace agreement was reached and contract raiding ended, would postseason title games resume.

With Honus Wagner, baseball's biggest star, it was perhaps no surprise that Pittsburgh would win the National League pennant in 1903. They had won in '01 and '02, and the "Flying Dutchman" was at his peak. Just 29 years old in 1903, he was in his seventh season, his first spent almost exclusively at shortstop. He would win his second of eight batting titles that year, hitting .355, stealing 46 bases, and leading the league with 19 triples. Bow-legged and wide-bodied, he did not look graceful or fleet, but he was baseball's most celebrated performer.

Young had pitched in the big leagues for more than a decade, and his 28 victories in 1903, while enough to lead the league, was

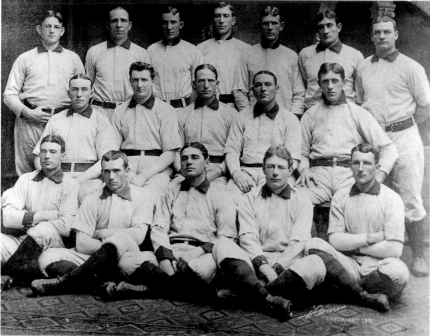

THE 1901 PITTSBURGH PIRATES. The team won the National League pennant in 1901, 1902 and 1903. The first World Series took place in 1903 when Barney Dreyfuss, the Pirates' owner, invited the Boston Pilgrims, the A.L. champs, to play.

FANS POURED ONTO THE FIELD at Boston's Huntington Avenue Base Ball Grounds after the first World Series.

ON OCTOBER 13, 1903, an over-flow crowd of eager Boston fans filled the stands inside the Huntington Avenue Base Ball Grounds for the final game of the first World Series.

The 1903 Boston Pilgrims, victors in the first World Series.

hardly his high-water mark. He had topped 30 victories five times in the past. But by the turn of the century a more modern game had been created than the baseball he knew when he broke in. He had weathered many rule changes, and still dominated pitching statistics. His durability—which would lead to a record 511 career victories—is even more remarkable today.

With a peace settlement between the leagues at hand, Boston met Pittsburgh in a best-of-nine World Series, initiated at the invitation of Pittsburgh owner Barney Dreyfuss. The Series began on October 1 in Boston's Huntington Avenue Base Ball Grounds. The Pirates pitching staff was beset by injuries, forcing Deacon Phillippe to start five of the eight games that would be played.

Phillippe would win three—but it took five to carry home the title, and Boston was not only formidable, but also inspired by the challenge of bringing honor and added legitimacy to the new league.

A SUBPAR PERFORMANCE FROM WAGNER

As it would happen, the great Wagner was not the factor many expected. Hobbled by a bad right leg, he was reduced to batting only .222 with one extra-base hit. He made six errors and went 1-for-14 in the final three games. With Wagner limping and two of their pitchers sidelined, this was not a Pirates team in top, contending form.

Cy Young was also surprisingly ineffective at times, getting pounded in Game One for four runs in the first inning, and losing the game. Both teams were weary from the long season and were fighting for a championship at less than full strength.

Boston won the second game behind two home runs from left fielder Patsy Dougherty, and Phillippe beat Long Tom Hughes in Game Three to put Pittsburgh up, two games to one.

A rain delay gave the pitchers an extra day of rest, and enabled Phillippe to pitch—and win—Game Four, giving him three wins in four games. But he would not win again, and the Pirates' lead of three games to one would soon fade. Boston won the next two, to tie the series at three games a piece, setting up a seventh game repeat matchup between Young and Phillippe. Young won it, 7–3, helped by playing manager Jimmy Collins' first inning triple. Boston then made it four straight victories—and a world championship— finishing off the Pirates in the eighth game behind the four-hit pitching of Bill Dinneen.

The celebration took place on the field, fans mingling with players, toasting their success. Bragging rights resided in Boston, and the American League received a terrific boost from meeting the challenge.

"A Minor League" Says McGraw of A.L.

Was this the start of the great October tradition of the modern World Series? Well, not quite. The war between the leagues was not over for the Giants' John McGraw, and when his team won the 1904 pennant, New York declined a postseason championship. As far as Giant owner John T. Brush and McGraw were concerned, postseason play was voluntary, and they would not be a party to games against an inferior, upstart league. "It's a minor league," McGraw said, "and the Giants would outclass them."

Not until 1905 would the World Series resume on an annual basis, McGraw having accepted the inevitable. But 1903 is recognized as the first of the modern Series, and for that, baseball owes a debt to Barney Dreyfuss, and to the Pittsburgh and Boston players who came together to begin baseball's championship tradition.

A FORMIDABLE STRATEGIST, John McGraw, nicknamed "Little Napoleon," managed the New York Giants for 30 years, from 1902 to 1932, but originally resisted the idea of a World Series. He was also a tough infielder with a lifetime .334 batting average.

THREE FOR BIG SIX

McGraw's Giants won their second consecutive pennant in 1905, and unlike the previous year, consented to play the A.L.-champion Philadelphia Athletics, managed by Connie Mack. The Giants were led by Christy "Big Six" Mathewson, who did the unbelievable. After winning 31 games that season, Mathewson pitched games One, Three, and Five of the World Series over a six-day span, hurling three complete-game shutouts, striking out 18 and walking just one. The Giants Team ERA for the Series was 0.00. The A's, who won just one game, had a team ERA of 0.84, due to fine pitching by Chief Bender and Eddie Plank.

THE WORLD SERIES THAT WASN'T

The 1903 World Series, pitting the National League's Pittsburgh Pirates against the Boston Pilgrims of the upstart American League, had been a big success with the public. But it was less popular among N.L. owners, who still resented the arrival in 1901 of the new major league. They were especially annoyed because the Pilgrims had won that first Series, putting the lie to their theories that the A.L. couldn't hold a candle to the more established league.

So, when the time came for the 1904 Series, between the N.L champion New York Giants and the Pilgrims, Giants' owner John T. Brush and manager John McGraw had second thoughts about the whole World Series concept. They didn't want to risk jeopardizing the league championship by losing to the powerful Pilgrims.

As an excuse, Brush pointed out that no rule required his Giants to play against a team from a "minor" league, which the A.L. had been until 1901. The team that defeated all others in the National League was, he said, "entitled to the honor of champions of the United States without being called upon to contend with or recog-

ONE OF THE PHILADELPHIA ATHLETICS' STAFF ACES, Eddie Plank, pitched against the New York Giants' Christy Mathewson in the 1905 World Series.

nize clubs from minor league towns." It took a lot of gumption to call the league that had won the last World Series "minor league," but Brush had gumption to spare.

Unfortunately for him, the public didn't buy Brush's rationale. The reaction across the country was so loud, so critical, and so unanimous, that it must have stunned Brush. *The Sporting News* put the matter succinctly in an editorial in October 1904: "There is a public demand for a world's series and the owner of one club stands between the game's patrons and their wishes."

By this time it was too late to reschedule the canceled 1904 Series. But when the Giants won the pennant again in 1905, there was no way that Brush was going to duck the forthcoming Series against the A.L. champion Philadelphia A's.

A PITCHERS' SERIES

Pitchers had dominated the 1905 regular season, especially in the A.L., where the league as a whole batted only .241. The A's, led by 18-game-winner Andy Coakley and future Hall of Famers Rube Waddell, Eddie Plank, and Chief Bender, had been so overpowering during the regular season that *The Sporting News* writer Joseph Vila scoffed at the Giants' chances. Calling them the "so-called Giants," he even shrugged off the presence of 31-game-winner Christy Mathewson on New

York's pitching staff. "The big collegian has been the team's mainstay all the year," Vila wrote of Mathewson, "but look what a lot of weak-hitting teams he has been opposed to."

But Vila and other experts underestimated the brilliance of "Big Six," as Mathewson was nicknamed. Facing off against Plank in the first game (the unpredictable Waddell was unavailable for the Series, due to an injured shoulder), Mathewson was almost flawless, allowing only four hits in a complete-game 3–0 victory. The closest thing to a run that the A's scored came when a batter tried to "squeeze" home a run from third base with a bunt in the sixth inning. Mathewson fielded

> "THERE IS A PUBLIC DEMAND
>
> FOR A WORLD'S SERIES."

the bunt and threw the runner out at the plate. Little did the A's know that this would be the closest that they would ever come to scoring off Mathewson.

Chief Bender evened the Series in Game Two, shutting out the Giants on four hits in a 3–0 A's victory over hard-luck loser Joe McGinnity. But then it was Mathewson's turn again in Game Three, and again he was unhittable, scattering four singles in an easy 9–0 win.

By this time it was obvious that this was a pitchers' Series, and Joe McGinnity did nothing to dispel that impression in Game Four, shutting out the A's on five singles in a 1–0 win. The only Giants run was scored following an A's error, making Eddie Plank the unlucky loser.

MAGNIFICENT MATHEWSON

Riding his hottest hand, John McGraw sent Mathewson out to the mound again for Game Five, despite the fact that Big Six had had only a single day's rest. The Giants' ace, however, didn't seem the least bit tired. Again he was virtually unhittable, scattering six hits and retiring the last 10 A's for his third straight shutout and a Series victory for the Giants.

The hitters on both teams would have been forgiven if they left this World Series off their records. Every game was a shutout, and since the only runs scored by the A's resulted from Giants' errors, the Giants' pitchers' earned run average for the whole Series was a stunning 0.00.

The Sporting News' Joseph Vila, who had scoffed at New York's chances, changed his tune. "So-called Giants no longer!" he wrote. "Christopher Mathewson, one of the greatest pitchers that ever slung a curve, did it!"

GIANTS' PITCHER CHRISTY MATHEWSON pitched three complete-game shutouts over the course of six days in the 1905 World Series.

PLAYER-MANAGER JOHN MCGRAW (right) decided to send Mathewson (left) to pitch in Game Five of the 1905 World Series on just one day's rest. The move paid off: Mathewson pitched a shut-out, winning the game and the series for the Giants.

THE HITLESS WONDERS PREVAIL

The 1906 Chicago Cubs won 116 games while losing only 36, a record which has never been bested. The squad was led by Frank Chance, and featured his fellow infielders Joe Tinker and Johnny Evers, along with pitcher "Three-Finger" Brown, whose 26-6 record and 1.04 E.R.A. led the team. The Highest E.R.A. on the team was 2.21. Amazingly, the Cubs dropped the World Series in six games to their cross-town rivals, the White Sox, who were known as the "Hitless Wonders," because their team batting average hovered around the .230 mark during the season.

"EVERY TIME SOMETHING WENT WRONG ON THE FIELD...THERE WOULD BE A FIGHT IN THE CLUBHOUSE AFTER THE GAME."

THE BEST EVER?

The 1906 Chicago Cubs may have been the best baseball team of all time. Playing just 152 games during the regular season, the Cubs won an astounding 116 of them, more than any other team in major league history. (By comparison, the mighty 1998 Yankees, playing 162 games, won "only" 114.)

The Cubs were powerful in all facets of the game, but they shone especially bright in fielding and pitching. Their infield was anchored by the most famous double-play combination in baseball history: player/manager Frank Chance at first base, Johnny Evers at second, and Joe Tinker at shortstop, all of whom ended up in the Hall of Fame. Add in third baseman Harry Steinfeldt, who led the team in runs batted in, and the Cubs were strong at every infield position.

Amazingly, the Tinker-to-Evers-to-Chance combination thrived for many seasons in spite of the fact that the three men fought constantly, sometimes going for years without exchanging a word off the field. Evers and Tinker in particular couldn't tolerate each other. "Every time something

MORDECAI "THREE FINGER" BROWN, the Cubs' ace pitcher, whose curve balls swerved and dipped like no other pitchers' could. An accident as a child led to the loss of one finger and severely damaged two others.

Teams Wins in a Season—Top 13		
Team	Year	Wins
Chicago (N)	1906	116
New York (A)	1998	114
Cleveland (A)	1954	111
Pittsburgh (N)	1909	110
New York (A)	1927	110
New York (A)	1961	109
Baltimore (A)	1969	109
Baltimore (A)	1970	108
Cincinnati (N)	1975	108
New York (N)	1986	108
Chicago (N)	1907	107
Philadelphia (A)	1931	107
New York (A)	1932	107

went wrong on the field, we would be at each other and there would be a fight in the clubhouse after the game," Evers recalled.

Evers, whose prickly personality gained him the nickname "The Crab," weighed in at just 135 pounds, but that didn't keep him from taking on Tinker and other much larger teammates, opposing players, and umpires. In fact, it might have helped keep him alive. "That was one nice thing about being a little guy," he said. "Somebody was always sure to hold the big guys when they wanted to hit me."

Along with its fiery infield stars, the Cubs boasted a tremendously strong pitching staff, anchored by the extraordinary Mordecai

"Three Finger" Brown. As a child, Brown got his throwing hand caught in a corn chopper and had half of his index finger amputated and two other fingers badly damaged. This injury gave him a unique grip on the ball, allowing his curveballs to twist and drop in a way no other pitcher's did. Brown had perhaps his finest season in 1906, going 26–6 with an amazing earned run average of 1.04. Brown was not the only star pitcher on the Cubs' staff. Jack Pfiester, Ed Reulbach, Orval Overall, and others all contributed to a team ERA of just 1.75. These were pitchers who were extremely stingy during the regular season.

AND IN THE OTHER CORNER

Facing the Cubs in the 1906 Series were their crosstown rivals, the Chicago White Sox. In contrast to the mighty Cubs, the Sox were seen as a fluke winner, a mediocre team that had stolen a pennant. Somehow they had put together a 19-game winning streak in August that had carried them to a 93–58 record and a victory in a tight pennant race.

The White Sox held on, despite being dubbed "The Hitless Wonders" by the press during the season. That cutting nickname was warranted: Not a single everyday player hit as high as .280. Lee Tannehill, their regular third baseman, hit just .183 for the season. The team as a whole hit a meager .230 average. Despite the Sox' fine pitching, the coming Chicago versus Chicago World Series was shaping up as a mismatch.

As it turned out, the Series was the furthest thing from a runaway. The first game, played through intermittent snowfall, was just what could be expected in a contest between Three

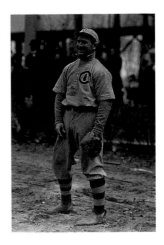

CUBS' PLAYER-MANAGER Frank Chance, at the heart of the famous Tinkers-Evers-Chance double play combo: Chance at first base, Johnny Evers at second, and Joe Tinker at shortstop. Off the field, the trio fought doggedly but, on the field, their cooperation was impeccable.

THE CHICAGO WHITE SOX LOAD THE BASES in the sixth inning of the third game of the 1906 World Series. Known as the "Hitless Wonders," the White Sox parlayed this rally to a 3-0 win, and 2-1 game edge, over the highly-favored Cubs, their cross-town rivals.

Finger Brown and the Sox' 20-game-winner Nick Altrock. An unearned run gave the White Sox a tense 2–1 victory and a 1–0 Series lead.

The *Chicago Tribune*, which had persisted in calling the Cubs "the Spuds" (in honor of their Irish owner) during the season, headlined its story about the defeat "Mashed Potatoes!" But no one really thought that the Sox would be able to hold the Cubs down for long.

In Game Two, two Sox errors led to five unearned runs and an easy Cubs victory, 7–1. But Game Three saw the Sox' spitball pitcher Ed Walsh completely shut down the Cubs on two hits. The Hitless Wonders' unlikely hitting star was George Rohe, forced into the lineup at third base due to an injury to the Sox' starting shortstop and a resulting reshuffle. As Rohe came to bat with the bases loaded in the sixth inning of a scoreless game, Cubs' catcher Johnny Kling said, "You're the guy who likes fastballs. Well, you won't see any more."

Rohe shrugged off the free advice. "I figured Kling was trying to confuse me," he said. "I looked for the fast one and got it. The ball was a fast inside pitch, shoulder high, and I hit it right on the line." His triple cleared the bases, giving Walsh and the Sox a 3–0 win and a 2–1 Series lead.

But again the Cubs bounced back as Brown and Altrock faced off in another nailbiter, with Altrock giving up the only run in a 1–0 Sox defeat. After four games, the Series was knotted at 2–2. This, most baseball writers and fans agreed, was the moment at which the powerful Cubs would finally assert their dominance and run roughshod over their weaker rivals.

ATTACK OF THE HITLESS WONDERS

But, as Yogi Berra reportedly said, and as players and fans have learned throughout the game's long history: In baseball, you don't know nothin'. The last two games were, in fact,

THE TINKER-EVERS-CHANCE double play combo was the legendary centerpiece of the Cubs' infield. It was immortalized in the above poem, which began, "These are the saddest of possible words, Tinker to Evers to Chance."

decisive wins—but the winning team was the supposedly inferior Sox. The White Sox erupted for eight runs in Game Five, hanging on for an 8–6 victory. And then, shockingly, they buried Three Finger Brown in Game Six, driving him from the game in the second inning en route to an 8–3 victory and the Series championship.

Even after the Series was over, baseball pundits still seemed shocked by the result.

"Who would have thought that the Sox would show up the Cubs the way they did?" wondered *The Sporting News*. Added *The Sporting Life*: "By this remarkable crowning triumph . . . the White Sox have proven themselves the most wonderful major league ball team on record." In the nearly 100 years since then, the cross-town rival Cubs and Sox have not met again in a World Series.

A TEAM SHOT of the unassailable favorites in the 1906 World Series, the Chicago Cubs. The club's stunning defeat, at the hands of the underdog Chicago White Sox team, eclipsed the Cubs' brilliant performance during the year: they garnered 116 wins in the season, a record yet to be bested.

ETERNAL REPLAY

Fred Merkle played 16 years in the Major Leagues but he never lived down what happened to him on September 23, 1908. With Merkle's Giants and the Cubs locked in a tight pennant race, the two teams battled to a 1-1 tie in the bottom of the ninth. The Giants had Harry McCormick on third and the 19-year-old Merkle on first. Al Bridwell singled, scoring McCormick, and the game was over. Or was it? Cub second baseman Johnny Evers called for the ball and tagged second, declaring that Merkle had been forced out and thus the run did not count. Later that evening, umpire Hank O'Day declared that the game had ended in a tie. The Giants and the Cubs finished the season tied, and the directors of the National League ordered the game be replayed. This time, "Three-Finger" Brown beat Christy Mathewson, and the Cubs won the pennant.

HEAD-TO-HEAD

A s the 1908 season approached its final days, it was fitting that the New York Giants and the Chicago Cubs, the two best teams in the National League, should be battling head-to-head for the pennant. Sometimes, schedule makers could seem like prophets, but, of course, it was just good luck.

On September 23, the Giants were in first place, just six percentage points ahead of the Cubs. The two teams were to meet at the Polo Grounds in New York, with the great Christy Mathewson on the mound for John McGraw's Giants, and Jack Pfiester his opponent for the Cubs. Chicago was managed by Frank Chance, the first baseman of the famous Joe Tinker to Johnny Evers to Chance double-play combo.

A large crowd of some 20,000 filed in, knowing that the winning team would be in sole possession of first place. As pre-game warm-ups were held, the fans were surprised to see 19-year-old Fred Merkle working out at first for the Giants. The team's regular, Fred Tenney, was suffering from an attack of

> "NEXT TIME," UMPIRE HANK O'DAY TOLD EVERS, "I'LL CALL IT OUT."

lumbago. It would be the only game he would miss all season. Merkle, who spent the year sitting at McGraw's side and learning from one of the game's great teachers, had played little. He had gotten 10 hits all season. And now, he was in the lineup in this enormously important contest.

Merkle was a big kid from Wisconsin who had made his major league debut in 1907 at the age of 18. He was a bridge player (McGraw liked how that sharpened his mind) and a golfer (McGraw hated how that affected his swing). It was considered a privilege to sit by McGraw, and it was clear that Merkle was being groomed for bigger things.

This game against the Cubs was certainly a big one for the kid to start. And, as one might expect, it became a pitching duel. Tinker hit an inside-the-park homer off Mathewson in

FRED MERKLE WAS A YOUNG New York Giants' player, in only his second year in the Majors, when he made a costly "mistake" in the 1908 pennant race. Following the custom of the day, he never touched second base when the tie-breaking run was driven home from third in the bottom of the ninth. His team's pennant victory was reversed after umpire Hank O'Day called Merkle out, negating the winning run.

FRED MERKLE CARRIED his alleged mistake with him throughout his 16-year career in the Major Leagues. Even six years later, when still on the New York Giants' roster, Merkle was referred to as "jinx."

the fifth to break a scoreless tie, taking advantage of the long, center field power alleys at the Polo Grounds to leg out his sixth homer of the year, tops on the team.

With one man on in the last of the sixth, Turkey Mike Donlin singled over Evers' head at second to tie the score, 1–1.

A NINETY-MINUTE CONTEST

As was the style of the day, the game moved quickly—it would take only 90 minutes. Pfiester did not strike anyone out, and walked only two. Mathewson was recording nine strikeouts, no walks. Three Giant rallies were felled by Cub double plays, although none went Tinker to Evers to Chance.

In the last of the ninth, with the score still knotted at 1–1 and tension rising, Art Devlin singled to center to get the Giants going. The winning run was on first. Moose McCormick got a hit but forced Devlin out at second, and Merkle came to the plate.

Pfiester studied the young right-hand hitter, and delivered. Base hit, right field! McCormick raced to third, Merkle was on at first, and the winning run was 90 feet away. If Merkle felt like smiling, he thought better of it, kept his game face, and took his lead off first as Al Bridwell came to bat.

What happened next became baseball history. Bridwell took Pfiester's first pitch and lined it to center for the game-winning single. It was, wrote McGraw, "the greatest hit I ever saw, because it was the most timely." McCormick raced home with the winning run, and the fans poured onto the field. But wait! Merkle, according to the custom of the day, never did reach second base. As soon as McCormick scored, Fred turned and headed for the clubhouse.

CUBS' SECOND BASEMAN Johnny Evers challenged umpire Hank O'Day to call the unusual out that negated the Giants' pennant victory.

Just 19 days earlier, the same second baseman, Johnny Evers, and the same umpire, Hank O'Day, were on the field when the same play happened in Pittsburgh. Then, Evers got the ball and stepped on second, asking O'Day to call the runner out. O'Day agreed in principle, but wouldn't call the out. "Next time," he told Evers, "I'll call it out."

BONEHEAD

Next time was here, nineteen days later. Evers tried to get his center fielder to throw the ball in, but it never got there. The Giants' Joe McGinnity, who had run onto the field, retrieved it and tossed it into the stands. Somehow, Evers got another ball and stepped on second. O'Day, remembering his earlier promise, called Merkle out for failing to touch second.

McGraw, furious, made Merkle return to the Polo Grounds that night to touch second, so that he could swear he did in fact do it on September 23, 1908. But it was to no avail. The game was ruled a tie, to be replayed if necessary after the season. On October 8, there they were again, the Cubs with Pfiester and the Giants with Mathewson, replaying the game. This time, the Cubs won 4–2, to win the National League pennant.

Forever after, Merkle would be known as the Bonehead. He would go on to play 16 seasons and produce over 1,500 hits, but baseball can be a cruel game. Think of Fred Merkle today and one word comes to mind. Bonehead.

UMPIRE HANK O'DAY had already spent a decade calling games for the National League before the 1908 season. He would spend another 17 years as an umpire following his notorious call.

THE COMPLETE CY YOUNG

Records are made to be broken, they say, but will anyone ever win more games than Cy Young, who recorded his 500th win on July 19, 1910, and finished his career with 511? In order to break Young's record, a pitcher would have to win 20 games each year, for 25 years, and then win 12 more for good measure. Cy Young's 316 losses are also tops for all-time.

FEW PLAYERS DEFINE their position in the game the way Denton True "Cy" Young defined pitching.

MADE TO BE BROKEN

The history of baseball is filled with supposedly unbreakable records. When Babe Ruth hit 29 home runs in 1919, pundits assured the public that this was a fluke, that neither Babe nor anyone else was likely to hit 29 ever again. In a way, they were right: Babe didn't hit 29 round-trippers again in 1920. He hit 54.

Similarly, Ty Cobb's 4,191 career hits was considered to be far beyond the capabilities of modern players, until Pete Rose surpassed his record. Lou Gehrig's 2,130-consecutive-game streak was so much longer than anyone else's that the conventional wisdom said it was untouchable; Cal Ripken, however, didn't listen to the conventional wisdom. Someday some great player is likely to surpass even Joe DiMaggio's 56-game hitting streak.

However, there are some baseball records that truly are unlikely ever to be broken—and many of them are held by the great right-handed pitcher Denton True Young, better known as Cy. Perhaps most amazingly, during his career (1890–1911), Cy Young completed a record 749 games out of 815. Starting as many as 49 games in a single

season, he averaged more than 34 complete games each year for his entire career. In fact, between 1891 and 1909, Young completed fewer than 30 games in a season only once (1906, when he finished "only" 28).

Today, even the best starting pitchers complete only about five or 10 games a season, and very few pitch for 20 years. This doesn't mean

Pitchers Winning 300 or More Games in their Career

Pitcher	Pitching Career	Wins
Cy Young	1890-1911	511
Walter Johnson	1907-1927	417
Grover C. Alexander	1911-1930	373
Christy Mathewson	1900-1916	373
Warren Spahn	1942-1965	363
Pud Galvin	1875-1892	361
Kid Nichols	1890-1906	361
Tim Keefe	1880-1893	342
Steve Carlton	1965-1988	329
John Clarkson	1882-1894	328
Eddie Plank	1901-1917	326
Nolan Ryan	1966-1993	324
Don Sutton	1966-1988	324
Phil Niekro	1964-1987	318
Gaylord Perry	1962-1983	314
Tom Seaver	1967-1986	311
Charley Radbourn	1881-1891	309
Mickey Welch	1880-1892	307
Lefty Grove	1925-1941	300
Early Wynn	1939-1963	300

that today's pitchers are "worse" than Young. What the difference demonstrates is how much baseball has changed since Young's day.

IN THE OLDEN DAYS

Back at the turn of the century, most teams had only two or three starting pitchers, which meant that starters got to pitch in 50 or even 60 games each year (compared to 30 or so today). And these old-time pitchers were expected to complete their starts, unlike today, when relief pitchers are groomed for the job and can throw 95-mile-per-hour fastballs. Knowing that he'd have to pitch so many innings each season, Young was careful to preserve his arm. "My arm would get weak and tired at times, but never sore," he said. "I worked hard all winter on my farm, from sun-up to sundown."

Despite this fitness regimen, Cy Young did not cut a very forbidding figure on the mound. With his creased face and thick (even portly) body, he looked more like a pitcher in a week-end softball game than a major league Hall of Famer. His nicknames, "Uncle" and "Foxy Grandpa," reflected his mild-mannered look.

Young's careful tending of his precious pitching arm continued on into the games themselves. Young believed that his arm had only a certain number of pitches in it, so he never took more than about a dozen warm-up tosses before he was ready to start the game.

Young didn't throw nearly as hard as today's hurlers, but he had pinpoint control, leading the league in fewest walks allowed per nine innings many times during his career. In 1904,

for example, he pitched 380 innings and walked 29 men, an amazing average of one walk every 13 innings. It's no surprise that Young completed 40 of the 41 games he started that season, with an earned run average of just 1.97. What is remarkable is that he somehow managed to lose 16 games, going 26–16 for the year.

MANY ACCOMPLISHMENTS built Young's legendary career. He started in 49 games in a single season; he completed 749 games out of a total of 815. And, in 1911, he won his 511th game, which was to be the last he pitched. The pitcher to come closest to Young's career wins is Walter Johnson , who won 417 games, nearly 100 games less than Young's career win figure.

A MOMENT OF GLORY

Cy Young pitched most of his career before the creation of the World Series in 1903. Fittingly, though, the 36-year-old Young got the chance to pitch in the very first Series. As the ace pitcher for the Boston Pilgrims of the new American League, he'd gone 28–9 and helped lead the Pilgrims to the pennant.

In the Series against the Pittsburgh Pirates, Young was equally impressive. He won two games (losing one) and was an important reason why the Pilgrims defied all predictions and beat the Pirates 5–3 in a best-of-nine World Series.

In 1911, at the age of 44, Cy Young won his 511th and final game. Uncle Cy was elected to the Hall of Fame in 1937, and in 1956 the award for the leagues' best pitchers for each season was named after him. From 1956–66, one Cy Young Award was given; it wasn't until 1967 that separate awards for each league were given out. It was a suitable honor for the pitcher who holds what may be the most unbreakable records of all.

FANS, YOUNG AND OLD, honored Young at the 1955 Hall of Fame induction ceremonies. Young was inducted years earlier, in 1937. Mrs. Ford Frick, the wife of baseball's then–commissioner, looked on as Young signed this ball.

TWICE THE ICE

There's nothing quite like a no-hitter for adding drama and weight to each pitch. Unless, of course, both starting pitchers throw a no-hitter, as happened on May 2, 1917. Lefty Jim "Hippo" Vaughn of the Cubs started at home against righty Fred Toney of the Reds. After nine full innings, both teams were hitless. The Reds won it in the top of the 10th, on a hit by Olympic immortal Jim Thorpe, while Toney stifled the Cubs one more inning to complete a ten-inning gem.

NEVER BEFORE, NEVER SINCE

One of the most amazing things about baseball is that it's still capable of producing something that's never happened before. Despite all the millions of innings in all the tens of thousands of games played since professional baseball began in 1869, it's still possible to go to a game and witness something unique.

No-hit games are rare, but not incredibly so. (There were seven in the American League in 1990 alone.) Perfect games are far rarer, but even so, there have been 15 regular-season perfect games in major league history. Fifteen in 123 years equals about one every eight years—making the perfect game an unexpected, but not unheard of, treat. Still, it's hard to imagine a pitching performance even rarer than a game in which the pitcher faces 27 opposing hitters and gets

"HE COULDN'T HAVE DOCTORED THE BALL BETTER IF HE'D USED A PENKNIFE."

FRED TONEY, of the Cincinnati Reds, the winner in an amazing pitching duel against the Cubs' ace Jim "Hippo" Vaughn. Each hurled a no-hitter through the initial nine innings and forced the game into the 10th, and final, inning of play.

them all out. On May 2, 1917, a pair of pitchers named Fred Toney and Jim "Hippo" Vaughn did the almost unimaginable: They pitched no-hitters against each other.

A PAIR OF ACES

If any pitchers in 1917 might be expected to throw no-hitters, Vaughn and Toney were strong candidates. Vaughn went 23–13 for the Chicago Cubs that season, with five shutouts and a stingy 2.01 earned run average. Meanwhile, Toney was just as good, winning 24 games for the Cincinnati Reds, posting a 2.20 ERA, and tossing seven shutouts.

Both pitchers also cut impressive figures on the mound: Vaughn (called Hippo because of his strange, lumbering gait on the basepaths) stood six feet four inches and weighed about 215 pounds. Meanwhile, Toney was a towering six feet six inches (he was one of the tallest players in the Major Leagues), weighed in at 245, and was called "the man who walked like a bear." They both threw hard and had excellent control.

Fans in Chicago that day had every reason to expect a pitchers' duel, but they never could have expected what actually did happen. As the innings rolled past, the fans began to realize that neither pitcher had allowed a single hit.

Neither Vaughn nor Toney was perfect. The Cubs' Cy Williams had always hit Toney hard, so the big right-hander pitched him very carefully, walking him the first two times Williams came to the plate. Meanwhile, the left-handed

Vaughn walked Heinie Groh twice—also a good idea, since Groh was a .300 hitter.

That was it for the offense. No one came close to getting a hit until Cy Williams came to the plate for the third time and slammed a pitch from Toney down the left-field line. Players and fans alike watched helplessly until, at the last moment, the ball caromed off the grandstand seats, just foul.

As writer Arthur Daley recalled in the *New York Times,* that long foul actually helped Toney keep his no-hitter going. For some reason, the umpire chose not to take the ball out of play, despite its violent encounter with the grandstand. "Toney's eyes bulged when he saw it," Daley wrote. "There was a scuff mark on it as big as a silver dollar. He couldn't have doctored the ball better if he'd used a penknife."

As every pitcher knows, a scuffed ball won't rotate evenly as it flies toward home plate. Instead, it will dart and dive in unpredictable ways as the air encounters the scuffmark. It's very hard to hit a scuffed ball, which is why, even today, pitchers get caught with nail files, emery boards, and other illegal scuffing objects.

Equipped with his heaven-sent doctored ball, Toney stopped nibbling at the corners of the plate against the dangerous Williams. Instead, he just reared back and threw as hard as he could. "The scuffed ball danced away from Williams' bat," Daley wrote. "Cy fanned. The worst was over."

Now, somehow, nine innings had passed, and still neither team had gotten a hit. The score remained 0–0. Both starting pitchers were still in the game; what manager would risk removing a huge man nicknamed Hippo and another who "walked like a bear" from a no-hitter?

THE TURNING POINT

The double no-hitter didn't last much past the ninth inning. Vaughn retired the first man to face him in the top of the 10th, but then Larry Kopf hit a grounder that snuck between first and second base. It was a clean hit, the first of the game.

With two men out, Hal Chase came to the plate, and promptly hit a long fly ball to Williams in center field. Williams got both hands on it. But then, as the crowd gasped in dismay, Cy dropped the ball. Kopf raced all the way to third on the error.

The next man up was Jim Thorpe, the world-famous football star and Olympic athlete who also played major league baseball for six years. Vaughn threw hard and Thorpe swung hard—but the result was a chopper up the third base line, just a few feet from home plate.

Kopf raced toward the plate from third and Vaughn came rushing in from the mound to field the ball. "I knew the minute it was hit that I couldn't get Thorpe at first. He was as fast as a racehorse," Vaughn recalled. "So I went over to the line, fielded the ball, and scooped it toward the plate as Kopf was running in." The only way to preserve the shutout and the tie game was if the Cubs' catcher, Art Wilson, grabbed the toss and tagged Kopf out.

Vaughn made a good throw, but Wilson wasn't expecting it. The ball bounced away, and Kopf scored easily. The score was now 1–0, Cincinnati, and there it stayed as Vaughn got the last out.

Fred Toney was not to be denied. He retired the Cubs' hitters in order in the bottom of the inning. Vaughn had pitched nine no-hit innings, but Toney had outdone even that great achievement. He'd pitched a complete game, a 10-inning no-hitter, and won the game.

JIM "HIPPO" VAUGHN, whose no-hit battle against Fred Toney was broken by a grounder up the middle by the Reds' Larry Kopf.

ALREADY A MAJOR FOOTBALL and Olympic track and field star, Jim Thorpe of the Reds helped win the game. His 10th-inning chopper hit toward third base might have been an easy out for pitcher Jim Vaughn, who fielded the play, had it not been Thorpe who hit it. Thorpe's speed forced Vaughn to make the play at home, but the runner from third beat the tag to score the only run.

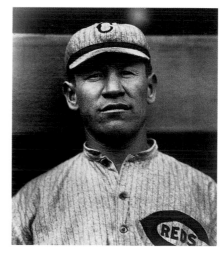

EXIT, STAGE LEFT

Before he became a legendary home run hitter, Babe Ruth was a standout pitcher for the Boston Red Sox. On June 23rd, 1917, the Red Sox hosted Washington, with Ruth on the mound. After walking leadoff hitter Ray Morgan, Ruth was ejected by umpire Brick Owens for arguing the calls too vigorously. Ernie Shore relieved Ruth, and after Morgan was caught stealing, retired the next 26 men in order, beating the Senators 4-0. Ruth and Shore's no-hitter was the subject of perennial debate until it was officially declared a no-hitter by a baseball rules committee in 1991.

THE ROOKIE

From the moment he joined the Boston Red Sox as a pitcher in 1914, Babe Ruth cut an outsized figure on the baseball diamond. "All eyes were turned on Ruth, the giant lefthander, who proved a natural ball player and went through his act like a veteran of many wars," wrote an admiring correspondent for the *Boston Globe*.

The Babe's teammates noticed him too. As Hall of Fame outfielder Harry Hooper told the writer Lawrence Ritter in *The Glory of Their Times* (1966), Ruth was like any other rookie in 1914, except for two things: "he could eat more than anyone else, and he could hit a baseball further."

Despite his size, the Babe was a naive and poorly educated young man when he joined the Red Sox, and this left him open to

vicious teasing. Nor was all the abuse verbal. As Ruth recalled years later, one day he accidentally hit teammate Joe Wood with a ball during a game of catch. Wood then purposely threw the ball back as hard as possible when Ruth wasn't looking, hitting the Babe in the shin.

Before the Red Sox' next game, Ruth called a team meeting—something unheard of for a rookie to do. But he had things he wanted to tell his teammates. "I told them I was a green kid of 20, just a few months out of a home, with little experience and knowledge of the world. I said I wanted to make good in baseball, wanted to mind my own business and sit back and learn something."

Clearly, though, there were some players who didn't like having him around. "So I suggested that we be permitted to fight it out," Ruth

"I SUGGESTED THAT WE BE PERMITTED TO FIGHT IT OUT"

STAR PITCHING STAFF of the Boston Red Sox from 1915 to 1917. From left to right, Ernie Shore, Dutch Leonard, George Foster, and Babe Ruth.

recalled. "I said: 'If they lick me, all right, and if I lick them, all right, but let it end there.'"

The veterans were smart: Not one of them offered to fight the Babe. They could tell right away that he had a hot temper and—even more importantly—the strength to back it up.

EXCITABLE BOY

Especially in his early years, Ruth had trouble keeping his temper under control. In fact, it was Ruth's temper that led to one of the oddest records and most memorable moments in the history of baseball: a no-hit perfect game by the Red Sox in which the Babe was the starting pitcher, but didn't record a single out!

Here's what happened on Saturday, June 23, 1917. The Red Sox were playing the Washington Senators in a double-header, with Ruth starting the first game. The Babe was facing Ray Morgan, Washington's lead-off hitter. By the time Brick Owens, the home plate umpire, called "Ball three!" it was clear that he and Ruth weren't seeing eye to eye on the dimensions of the strike zone.

Ruth threw another pitch and Owens called it ball four, sending Morgan to first. Ruth was furious and came stalking in from the mound. He and Owens spent a few seconds exchanging loud opinions, but then the Babe committed an unforgivable sin: He hauled off and punched the umpire, hitting him either in the jaw or left ear. Owens, who wasn't injured, tossed Ruth from the game immediately.

Now Black Jack Barry, the Red Sox' second baseman and manager, was in a jam. He'd been counting on a complete game— or at least lots of innings—from Ruth, and instead the Babe hadn't gotten a single man out during his brief stint. Someone else was going to have to step in.

WHAT A RELIEF

Then Barry's gaze settled on Sox right-hander Ernie Shore. "He asked me if I'd pitch until he could get someone else warmed up," Shore

told *Sports Illustrated* years later. "In those days you were only allowed five practice pitches."

Apparently, Shore's five warm-up tosses were enough. On his first pitch, Ray Morgan tried to steal second, but the Sox catcher threw him out. When the next two batters also made outs, the manager asked Shore if he'd like to stay in the game. "I told him sure," Shore said.

Shore had his best stuff that day. He relied on a sinking fastball, which the Washington hitters kept hammering on the ground straight at Boston infielders. No one had even come close to a hit as Shore stepped to the mound to start the ninth inning, with the Sox leading 4–0. Nor had he walked a batter.

The first man up for Washington, Hank Shanks, was retired easily. But then John Henry hit a screaming liner that luckily streaked right toward Sox left fielder Duffy Lewis. Lewis caught it without taking a step.

Now there was just one out to go. Speedy Mike Menosky came to the plate as a pinch hitter, and immediately bunted. Bunting to break up a no-hitter is considered poor sportsmanship, but, as Shore said, Washington manager Clark Griffith "never gave the opponents a thing."

Shore tried to field the bunt, but it rolled past him. Black Jack Barry raced in from second base, grabbed the ball, and flipped it to first. The umpire's hand flew up: Out!

Ernie Shore had finished the most remarkable perfect game in baseball history. After Babe Ruth walked the first man he faced, Shore came in, faced 26 batters, and got 27 outs. No one has ever pitched a more efficient ballgame.

RELIEVING RUTH following his ejection from the game—after pitching to just one batter— Ernie Shore pitched a no-hitter.

HOME-PLATE UMPIRE Brick Owens. Ruth disagreed with the walk Owens called against Ruth on the game's lead-off batter, and let Owens have it, literally, with a punch in the face. Needless to say, Owens ejected him on the spot.

BABE RUTH, PITCHER

Babe Ruth was not only one of the game's most feared sluggers, but also a standout pitcher. He compiled a lifetime mark of 94-46 and surpassed 20 wins in 1916 and 1917. He was also a great World Series pitcher, winning all of his three starts for Boston in 1916 and 1918, and compiling a 29⅔ inning scoreless streak in the process. In his only 1916 Series start, Ruth allowed only one run in a 14-inning complete game. His 0.87 career ERA for the World Series still ranks third on the all-time list.

THE YOUNG LEFT-HANDER

When Babe Ruth arrived from Baltimore to join the Boston Red Sox in 1914, he was little more than a boy. "He had never been anywhere, didn't know anything about manners or how to behave among people—just a big overgrown green pea," as teammate Harry Hooper put it.

But Ruth, then a left-handed pitcher, did know how to do one thing: He could throw the ball over the plate and past opposing hitters. Even as a "green pea," he knew what to do with a baseball. "As soon as I got out there I felt a strange relationship with the pitcher's mound," he said. "It was as if I'd been born out there."

As a 19-year-old in 1914, he pitched in only four games with the Red Sox. But by 1915 he was already putting up solid numbers, going 18–8 with a 2.44 earned run average. (He also hit .315 with four home runs, leading the team in round-trippers.)

Behind the pitching of Ruth, Rube Foster, Dutch Leonard, and others, the Red Sox won the American League pennant in 1915, edging out the Detroit Tigers. But the Sox's pitching staff was so strong that Ruth didn't get to pitch even a single inning in the World Series, which was won by the Sox in five games over the Philadelphia Phillies.

Ruth had an even better year in 1916, winning 23 games and leading the league with a 1.75 ERA. Again the Red Sox prevailed in a tight A.L. pennant race—but this time Ruth wasn't going to take a seat on the sidelines in the World Series, which pitted the Sox against the Brooklyn Robins.

Starting Game Two, Ruth gave up an inside-the-park home run to the Robins' Hy Myers in the first inning, but drove in the tying run himself off of Brooklyn's Sherry Smith in the third. That was it for the offense, as the game stayed at 1–1 through nine innings, then 12, all the way to the bottom of the 14th, when the Red Sox finally pushed across the winning run. What was most remarkable about this

BABE RUTH shown as a pitcher for the Boston Red Sox in 1919.

Babe Ruth's Pitching Record

Year	Team	Wins	Losses	Win%	ERA
1914	Boston (A)	2	1	.667	3.91
1915	Boston (A)	18	8	.692	2.44
1916	Boston (A)	23	12	.657	1.75
1917	Boston (A)	24	13	.649	2.01
1918	Boston (A)	13	7	.650	2.22
1919	Boston (A)	9	5	.643	2.97
1920	New York (A)	1	0	1.000	4.50
1921	New York (A)	2	0	1.000	9.00
1930	New York (A)	1	0	1.000	3.00
1933	New York (A)	1	0	1.000	5.00
Total	10 seasons	94	46	.671	2.28

game was not the final score, but the fact that both starting pitchers threw complete games. After giving up that first-inning run, Ruth had strung together 13 straight scoreless innings in his first Series start.

The Red Sox didn't win the A.L. pennant in 1917, but they were back on top in 1918, going to the World Series for the third time in four years. Ruth had had another good year as a pitcher, going 13–7 with a 2.22 ERA. But the handwriting was on the wall: The Babe was simply too good a hitter to come to the plate only one game out of four or five. Ruth himself was already beginning to realize that his future lay in socking the ball. "I am a pitcher myself and I like to pitch," he said in a 1918 issue of *Baseball Magazine*. "But if there is

> "IT WAS AS IF I'D BEEN
>
> BORN OUT THERE."

any one thing that appeals to me more than winning a close game from a tough rival, it's knocking out a good clean three-bagger with men on bases."

BABE RULES THE MOUND

Still, the Babe had one more moment of glory during his pitching career: his performance in the 1918 World Series. The Red Sox were pitted against the Chicago Cubs, who'd run away with the N.L. pennant. Despite his gradual turn away from pitching during the regular season, Ruth was chosen to start Game One against the Cubs ace Hippo Vaughn.

Vaughn and Ruth were both superb, but the Babe was just a bit better. He gave up six singles to the Cubs, while the Sox managed only five. But Boston managed to bunch two of their singles and a walk to score a run in the fourth inning, and Ruth made it stand up for a thrilling 1–0 win. His World Series scoreless-inning streak had now reached 22.

Ruth didn't start again until Game Four, by which time the Red Sox had a 2-1 Series

lead. Though he wasn't as overpowering as he'd been in Game One, Ruth was good enough to hold the Cubs scoreless until the eighth inning, when the Cubs tied the game 2–2. Ruth's World Series consecutive-inning scoreless streak, which began in 1916 and stretched over three games, had finally come to an end after 29 ²/₃ innings.

The Red Sox won that game, and went on to defeat the Cubs for the World Series crown. But Babe Ruth's pitching career was almost over. Though he started 17 games in 1919, it was his slugging (an unprecedented 29 home runs) that grabbed the public's attention. Moving to the Yankees in 1920, he became an everyday outfielder—and, of course, the greatest home run hitter anyone had ever seen.

Ruth missed the thrill of pitching more than most people realize. In a 1920 interview with *Baseball Magazine*, he contradicted his earlier claim that hitting was more fun than pitching. "There is one thing better than knocking a home run," he said. "That one thing is pitching and winning a World's Series game. That's the truth."

So which was his real opinion? Ruth himself answered that question, in an interview given shortly before his death in 1948. Asked what the highlight of his career was, he didn't choose his 60 home run season, his 714 career home runs, or any other of his spectacular achievements as a hitter. No, Babe Ruth said that his proudest moment came when he hurled 29 ²/₃ consecutive scoreless innings as a pitcher with the Boston Red Sox.

RUTH'S LEGENDARY CAREER included not only a slugging record that helped define the history of the game. He was also a pitcher to be reckoned with. He compiled a 94-46 career record along with a 2.28 ERA.

RUTH CUT A FAMILIAR FORM on the pitcher's mound, no matter what ballpark he played in. He pitched for a total of six years with Boston and then occasionally for the Yankees following his move to New York in 1920.

THE CURSE

Harry Frazee owned the Boston Red Sox from 1916 to 1923. His first love, however, was the New York stage, where he produced many shows. In order to keep cash pouring in to finance more plays, Frazee developed the habit of selling talented Red Sox players to the Yankees. Ernie Shore, Duffy Lewis, and Carl Mays went south before Frazee sold Babe Ruth to the Yankees in late 1919 for $125,000 and a $300,000 loan, using Fenway Park as collateral. The Red Sox won their last World Series in 1918, leading to speculation that shipping Ruth to the Yanks brought the fabled "Curse of the Bambino" on Boston. Said Ruth, "They'll never build any monuments to Harry Frazee in Boston."

STAR OF STARS

As the 1919 season drew to a close, Boston's Babe Ruth seemed like the one ballplayer most likely to remain with his club for years to come. After years as a brilliant pitcher, the Babe had undergone an unprecedented transition to become the most feared slugger in baseball. In 1919 he'd gone 9–5 with a 2.97 earned run average in 17 pitching appearances—but as a hitter he'd belted 29 home runs, a major league record at the time. He'd also scored and driven in more than 100 runs, leading the Majors in both of those categories as well.

HARRY FRAZEE, OWNER of the Boston Red Sox from 1916 to 1923. He will forever live in infamy as the person who sold Babe Ruth to the New York Yankees and introduced the fabled "Curse of the Bambino."

Perhaps most importantly, Babe Ruth was only 24 years old in 1919. His best years were ahead of him. It was clear even then that the Babe was a once-in-a-lifetime crown jewel of a player, the kind of superstar that any owner would thank the fates for having on his team. Unless, of course, that owner's name was Harry Frazee.

HARRY FRAZEE'S FIRST LOVE

Harry Frazee owned the Red Sox from 1916 to 1923. He inherited a championship-quality team, and during the early years of his ownership the team stayed strong. But there was something that Frazee enjoyed even more than owning a great ball club. Above all, he loved being a Broadway producer, putting on expensive shows on New York's Great White Way.

Then as now, producing Broadway shows was a costly business, and Frazee was more enthusiastic than wise in his choices of which shows to back. As a result, regardless of the Red Sox success, he was almost always in need of money. The best way to raise cash, he decided, was to sell his best players to the highest bidder.

The highest bidder usually turned out to be the New York Yankees. Colonels Jacob Ruppert and T. L. Huston, the Yankees' owners, ran their successful franchise with a combination of deep pockets and great baseball sense. They were more than willing to pay good prices for the players Frazee was offering—especially when the players included such fine talents as Ernie Shore, Duffy Lewis, Carl Mays, Wally Schang, Joe Dugan, and Herb Pennock.

Almost all of these players were either .300 hitters or 20-game-winning pitchers, still at the height of their powers. And almost all of them contributed to the great Yankee teams of the 1920s. "The Yankee dynasty of the twenties was three-quarters the Red Sox of a few years before. All Frazee wanted was the money," Hall of Famer Harry Hooper, still bitter decades later, told writer Lawrence Ritter. "What a way to end a wonderful ballclub!"

But the bitterest pill of all to Red Sox players and fans alike was the sale of Ruth to the Yankees for $125,000 cash and a low-interest personal loan. As might be imagined, the reaction in Boston was loud, angry, and prolonged. To these fans, this move was the one that brought down the Curse of the Bambino on the Red Sox. Somehow, they believe, the sale of Ruth provoked a drastic change in the alignment of the baseball planets, guaranteeing that the Yankees would win, and the Red Sox lose, in perpetuity.

WRONG ON ALL COUNTS

Frazee, who had managed to shrug off criticism of his previous moves, felt the need to respond to the outcry raised by the sale of the Babe. He defended

himself in an article in *Baseball Magazine* in April 1920. This article, a masterpiece of self-justification, sought to blame Ruth, who had asked for a raise to $20,000 a year following his record-setting 1919 season.

"To my mind, no individual player in so uncertain a profession as baseball is worth any such sum of money," Frazee opined. "Ruth made twenty-nine home runs last year, but no one knows what he will do next year." This was undeniable: No one in their right mind would have predicted that the Babe would hit .376, slug 36 doubles, 9 triples, and 54 home runs, or drive in 137 runs with the Yankees in 1920. But that's what he did.

"I BELIEVE THAT THE SALE OF RUTH WILL ULTIMATELY STRENGTHEN THE TEAM."

By the time Frazee sold Ruth to the New York Yankees, Ruth was already of legendary status. His performance for Boston, where he started his major league career, dominated the team, and when the transfer to New York took place, Boston fans were up in arms.

"The value of an individual player, however great, may well be exaggerated," Frazee went on. "If one member of a club dominates public interest to the exclusion of the other members of that club, he may well do more injury than good." This may well be true in general, but the Yankees were certainly willing to put up with Ruth's dominating presence while he led the league in home runs 10 times in the next 12 years (with a high of 60 in one season) and compiled a lifetime .342 batting average.

"My sole object, since coming to Boston, has been to give the public a winning team," Frazee concluded. "And, personally, I think this latest deal will take its place along with the rest for I believe that the sale of Ruth will ultimately strengthen the team."

It's safe to say that in this final, self-confident statement, Harry Frazee landed on a point 180 degrees removed from the truth. In 1920, Ruth's first season with the team, the Yankees won 95 games, missing first place by only three games. (The Red Sox went 72–81.) In 1921 and '22, the Yankees won the American League pennant, while the Sox slipped further and further behind. And in 1923, Ruth led the Yankees to their first-ever World Series victory, while the Sox finished in last place with a 61–91 record.

To Boston fans, the "Curse of the Bambino" has lasted far beyond the infuriating events of the 1920s. Prior to the sale of Ruth, the Red Sox had won three World Series in five years. In the 80 years since that dark day, the Sox have won a total of zero world championships. It's one of the longest dry spells in the history of professional sports.

And the Yankees? Since they acquired Ruth, the Yankees have won a World Series or two . . . 25, to be exact. This is one of the greatest records of success in the history of professional sports.

Harry Frazee is long gone, but the "Curse of the Bambino" lives on.

As if to add insult to injury, not only did Babe Ruth become baseball's biggest star after the Red Sox sold him to the Yankees, he even attracted Hollywood's attention. He is shown here signing a $100,000 movie contract with W.A. Shea and T.W. Walsh, two film studio executives.

BLACK SOX

In September 1920, the faith of baseball fans everywhere was shaken. Eight members of the Chicago White Sox confessed to a plot to deliberately lose the 1919 World Series to the Cincinnati Reds. Though they were acquitted in a grand jury trial, the eight players were banned from baseball by new Commissioner Kenesaw Mountain Landis, whose appointment as baseball's first absolute czar was a direct result of the scandal. The fall from grace set the stage for Babe Ruth to save the game with his fabulous home run heroics of the 1920s.

THE RUMOR MILL GRINDS

As the 1919 World Series between the Chicago White Sox and Cincinnati Reds approached, dark rumors began to swirl. Whispers told of gangsters in the locker room, secret payments, games to be lost on purpose. The upcoming Series was fixed, the whispers said. Star outfielder Joe Jackson, pitching ace Eddie Cicotte, and other White Sox players had taken cash to throw the Series. Just watch the Sox (considered by far the stronger team) lose to the Reds.

Yet, though many heard the rumors about the fixing of the 1919 World Series, only a few believed them. One was Christy Mathewson, former great pitcher and Reds' manager, who in past years had spoken out openly against seemingly crooked play. Another was sportswriter Hugh Fullerton, who almost alone among the press took the rumors seriously, and was ridiculed by other magazines and newspapers as a result.

Still, as the Series got underway, the whispers refused to die down.

THE SERIES THAT DIDN'T SMELL RIGHT

Baseball writer Fred Lieb covered the 1919 Series, and got a whiff that something might not be on the level when he learned that the betting odds were on the Reds, not the Sox. He wondered if Cicotte had come up with a lame arm, and his wondering only increased when the Sox ace lost the first game in Cincinnati, 9–1.

SPORTS WRITER FRED LIEB knew something was wrong when he found out the betting odds were on the Reds to win the Series. And the performance of White Sox pitching star Eddie Cicotte in Game One provoked Lieb's suspicion even more.

After the game, Chicago's catcher, Ray Schalk (who was not one of the tainted

players) told the press that Cicotte had paid no attention to his signals, instead throwing whatever pitches he wanted to. Even then, few writers allowed themselves to guess what was going on.

The Reds also won the second game, 4–2, as Sox pitcher Lefty Williams suffered an uncharacteristic burst of wildness in the fourth inning, walking three before giving up a triple to weak-hitting Larry Kopf.

The Sox, behind honest Dickie Kerr, won Game Three, but it was back to business as usual in Game Four, as Cicotte interfered with a throw that would have nailed a runner at the plate in a 2–0 White Sox loss. The next day Lefty Williams lost again, and now the Sox trailed four games to one in the best-of-nine Series.

Surprisingly, the Sox came back to win Games Six and Seven. Though rumors circulated at the time that a counter-fix was in, the truth seems to be that the crooked Sox players were angry because they hadn't received all of the money they were owed, and some of them (including Cicotte, who won Game Seven) were now trying to win.

But Lefty Williams was slated to start the eighth game for the Sox, and new rumors

TEAM SHOT of the 1919 Chicago White Sox. The eight tainted players: Joe Jackson, Chick Gandil, and Fred McMullin are in the back row starting from the left; in the first row are Swede Risberg, second from the left, and Eddie Cicotte and Lefty Williams, the first two players at the right. Buck Weaver, who knew about the scandal but played well, is in the middle row at the end on the right.

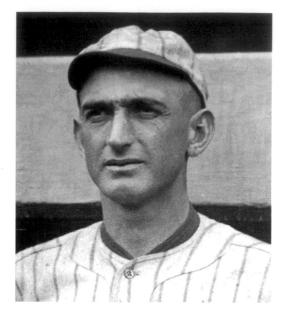

Outfielder Joe Jackson, while hitting .375 for the Series, confessed that, when good hits were needed, he batted poorly, either popping up or grounding softly.

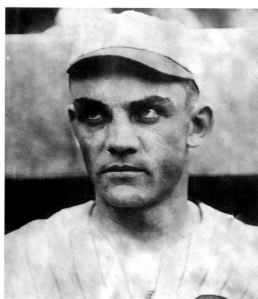

First baseman Chick Gandil hit poorly throughout the Series, squeezing out a batting average of only .233.

Buck Weaver played the Series to win but, because he knew about the conspiracy and said nothing, he was forever tainted by it.

swirled that he was comfortably in the gamblers' pocket. Williams may also have felt he had no choice. Wrote Fred Lieb: "According to what I heard later, some Chicago gangsters had threatened to kill the left-hander if he pitched a victory; they said he would be shot right in the pitcher's box."

True or not, Williams didn't get out of the first inning, giving up four runs to the Reds. Sox manager Kid Gleason quickly replaced Williams, but it was too late. The Reds won the game, 10–5, and took the Series.

A CONSPIRACY UNRAVELS

Hugh Fullerton was a lonely voice in the press after the Series ended. "Professional baseball has reached a crisis," he wrote in the winter of 1919. But all his warnings did was bring the wrath of the establishment down on his head. "Who is Hugh Fullerton anyway?" *Baseball Magazine* replied in an editorial, calling his suggestions that the Series was fixed "vicious" and "inexcusable."

But too many people knew about the fix for it to be buried under the rug forever. American League president Ban Johnson, who had at first discounted the rumors, began an investigation. Meanwhile, an even more serious investigation was begun before a grand jury in Chicago. And the press at last turned from attacking the messengers to focusing on the real story.

Finally, on September 27, 1920, a Philadelphia newspaper printed an interview with a mysterious gambler named Billy Maharg, and the cover-up came to an end. The story described how seven players—Eddie Cicotte, Lefty Williams, Joe Jackson, Chick Gandil, Happy Felsch, Swede Risberg, and Fred McMullin—had accepted money to throw the Series. An eighth player, Buck Weaver, had known about the conspiracy; though he had played hard and to win, he had not told anyone what he knew.

Now, at last, the players confessed, and the full story came out. Cicotte admitted that, in Game One, he threw the ball so softly that "you could read the trademark on it." Jackson, meanwhile,

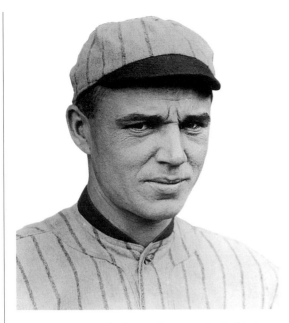

WHITE SOX CATCHER RAY SCHALK, who was not involved in the scandal, delivered a veiled clue to the press after the first game. He told reporters that the pitcher Eddie Cicotte had ignored his signals, choosing to throw any pitch he wanted.

Landis, the new commissioner who had been given almost czar-like powers to police the game. Landis immediately stepped forward and banned all eight players from baseball for life.

Landis' words are worth repeating, for they are a major reason why baseball has seen so few betting scandals since the dark days of the Black Sox. "Regardless of the verdict of juries," he said, "no player that throws a ball-game, no player that entertains proposals or promises to throw a game, no player that sits in a conference with a bunch of crooked players and gamblers where the ways and means of throwing games are discussed, and does not promptly tell his club about it, will ever play professional baseball."

CICOTTE ADMITTED THAT...HE THREW THE BALL SO SOFTLY THAT "YOU COULD READ THE TRADEMARK ON IT."

had hit .375 in the Series, a fact that leads his defenders to say that he actually played to win. But in his confession he said that he either struck out or hit weak grounders or pop-ups when hits would have plated important runs. Most of the others hadn't been even that subtle and creative: Williams lost three games, Gandil hit .233, and Felsch managed just five hits in 26 at bats.

JUDGE LANDIS DECREES

The players were immediately suspended by Judge Kenesaw Mountain Landis, who had recently been named the first commissioner of baseball. They were also indicted by the Chicago grand jury—but before their trial, witnesses and important evidence disappeared, and the players recanted their confessions. Then, in the trial itself, the players were acquitted of all charges, after which the jury and the players met at an Italian restaurant for a celebratory dinner.

But they had celebrated too soon. The players hadn't taken into account Judge

BASEBALL'S FIRST COMMISSIONER, THE IRON-HANDED KENESAW MOUNTAIN LANDIS, swiftly suspended the players involved in the scandal and just as swiftly overruled the jury verdict, which had acquitted the players, by banning them from baseball for life.

THE HOME RUN SAVES THE GAME

It was quite a ride. In the 1920s, hitting defined baseball. Not so much the strategic hitting of a decade earlier, but the big hits, the towering home runs and in-the-park smashes from Babe Ruth, Lou Gehrig, and others. More fans than ever followed the game, and with John Philip Sousa leading a marching band, the New York Yankees, then baseball's dominant team, opened their impressive stadium, christened, appropriately enough, by a Ruth homer. The economy scored big too, with an expansion as bold and impressive as the batters slugging away. Then came the collapse. Following the 1929 stock market crash, America's economy plunged drastically. Although baseball players kept the hitting game alive, for a while they did so in near-empty parks as attendance fell, starting in 1931, and several teams neared bankruptcy. The good times had been replaced by the trying times.

Historian Guy Lewis has labeled the 1920s "the Golden Age of Sport." Americans spent ever greater money on amusement and recreation, 300 percent more at the end of the decade than at the beginning. Spectator sports boomed; in 1921 about 60,000 fans watched Jack Dempsey fight Georges Carpentier. Many more than that listened on the radio when Dempsey fought Gene Tunney in 1927. Colleges built big stadiums for their football teams—64,000 seats at Ohio State, for example. At the same time, major league baseball enlarged its audience; attendance topped 9.5 million in 1924 and 10 million in 1930. Fifteen of the 16 clubs operated in the black from 1920 through 1930, and often handsomely so. The Yankees surpassed all others by far at the gate—and on the field—when they earned $3.5 million during the decade. Several developments

FUN FILLED FADS *marked the Roaring Twenties, such as marathon dance contests like the one shown above.*

stimulated this sports mania. During World War I the federal government built baseball and football fields on military bases to keep soldiers occupied and healthy. This advocacy of physical activity was spurred further when one-third of the men who reported for duty proved unfit. After the war, these men took their interest in sports back home with them.

But more than anything else, economic prosperity boosted sports. With good reason observers attached the phrase "Roaring Twenties" to the decade. The economy roared onward and upward, its unbridled strength seemingly ready to pull everyone out of poverty and provide national prosperity forever. Between 1922 and 1927, the economy grew at seven percent per year—the longest peacetime expansion up to then. For the decade, manufacturing output increased 64 percent and output per work hour increased 40 percent—an economic grand slam.

Millions of Americans threw thrift out the window. Encouraged by advertisers to spend more, they spent beyond their means with installment buying. When Robert and Helen Lynd undertook research for their book *Middletown: A Study in American Culture* (1929), they found that nearly all the families in Muncie, Indiana, had debts. Nationally, personal debt increased more than twice as fast as income.

The automobile rolled through the decade. Nationally, where there had been 6.7 million passenger cars in 1919, there were over 23 million in 1929. Cars pumped money through the economy faster than blacktop could be laid down. Gas stations, hot dog stands, camp sites—all provided goods, services, and jobs.

Radio added another big economic boost. In 1922, the sales of radio sets, parts, and accessories reached $60 million; in 1929 they reached $842 million. Excitement generated from the coverage of sports events and politics—treated as a sport when the 1924 Democratic National Convention deadlocked stronger than a wrestler's head hold—stirred more Americans to buy radios.

Baseball joined the radio act. In 1921, the World Series was broadcast by a reporter sitting in a box seat at the Polo Grounds in New York City and relaying the play-by-play via telephone to an announcer, who repeated the developments over the air at the WJZ studio in Newark, New Jersey. Some major league club owners worried that radio would keep people from ballparks, and newspapers complained that broadcasts would reduce their readership. But over the next two decades the owners gradually adopted radio after they realized it stimulated a greater interest in the game.

"Ev'ry morning, ev'ry evening, ain't we got fun," blared a popular song, and as Americans reveled in prosperity, fads swept the entire nation, the result of an increasingly integrated national media that made America smaller. Frederick Lewis Allen observed in *Only Yesterday* that "it was now possible . . . for more people to enjoy the same good show at the same time than in any other land on earth or at any previous time in history." Flagpole sitting, goldfish swallowing, marathon dance contests, all received extensive coverage from newspapers that were now part of large consolidated chains. The chains used many of the same news wires and syndicated features, such as Heywood Broun's column "It Seems to Me," about the 1923 World Series, which appeared across the country.

As Broun's reporting indicated, sports shared in the media attention. Newspapers heaped enormous coverage on University of Illinois football player Red Grange, on golf—which attracted men and women to the point that two million players were spending $500 million a year on the game—on prizefights, and on reports from baseball spring training camps and during the regular season.

The nation's economic boom seemed so invincible that Americans expressed as much faith in it as they had in the *Titanic* before it started its ill-fated voyage from England back in 1912. The structure would never fail, even given attack by an external force, and its captain, the business leaders, had the knowledge to guide it to a glorious future. It would be no exaggeration to say that Americans worshipped the businessman. President Calvin Coolidge declared: "The business of America is business. The man who builds a factory builds a temple. The man who works there worships there." Bruce Barton made comparisons to religion, too, with his book, *The Man Nobody Knows,* which topped the best-seller lists in 1925

RADIO COVERAGE OF ALL KINDS of sporting events increased in the 1930s. CBS announcer Ted Husing interviews Joe Louis after a 1936 fight.

and 1926 by presenting Jesus Christ as the world's most successful businessman. His parables, Barton said, were "the most powerful advertisements of all time." Everything in the 1920s seemed transformed—rural America faded into memory and events moved faster as the economy grew bigger. But tradition proved powerful and progress bypassed some people. Millions found hope in old-time revivalist religion, while others expressed hatred and discomfort with change by joining racist or anti-immigrant groups, such as the Ku Klux Klan. Economically, many suffered. Farmers generally shared little of the decade's prosperity; certain industries such as textiles suffered from high unemployment; two-thirds of all homes lacked washing machines and vacuum cleaners; half lacked phones; more than nine-tenths lacked refrigerators. Many small towns saw few automobiles and had yet to pave their main streets.

Baseball tied into this split personality, progress and tradition, and even thrived on it. As speed consumed society—faster communications, action-packed movies, frenetic dances and jazz music—baseball shifted into high gear. The Major Leagues used a livelier ball, phased out the spitball—which had given pitchers an advantage—and glorified the heavy hitters. "Baseball was a changed game," historian Harold Seymour has said, "and it was the increased power of the offense that revolutionized it."

Thus fans watched in awe and reacted with excitement as Rogers Hornsby, second baseman for the St. Louis Cardinals, achieved a hitting average above .400 from 1921 through 1925 (his .424 average in 1924 ranks as the highest for the 20th century). In 1927, Lou Gehrig hit .373 with 47 homers, and the Babe continued his offensive attack. When he sent home run number 60 sailing fair by six inches in Yankee Stadium, *New York Herald* reporter W. B. Hanna announced: "The home-run record for the season and for the major leagues went into the discard . . . when Babe Ruth lined the ball, sprouting wings as it does when he hits it, into the right-field bleachers . . . ." Major league teams taken together averaged 2.5 runs more per game in 1925 than in 1915, and home runs increased from 384 in 1915 to 1,167 in 1925 and 1,565 in 1930.

Branch Rickey, vice president of the St. Louis Cardinals, mimicked big-business's efforts to bring production and supply together under single ownership when he began the major league farm system. Rickey believed that if the Cardinals owned several minor league clubs, he could use them to develop players who would then be ready for the big leagues, both for St. Louis and for other clubs to whom they could be sold for a profit. Under that system, the Cardinals won their first National League pennant in 1926. By 1928, St. Louis owned five minor league teams, among them Houston and Syracuse, while other clubs owned additional ones. Critics, however, likened the farm system to the expansion of retail chain stores—much as Woolworth's and other companies seemed to be destroying local businesses, the farm system seemed to be destroying locally-owned clubs.

For all these changes, baseball still appealed as a traditional sport. Major league teams had been in their cities for

years, and there seemed little likelihood they would leave. And the game itself, played in the open on pastoral fields, symbolized a quieter, pre-urban era.

Despite such idyllic surroundings, materialism touched organized baseball in much the same way it did society at large. Stock market fever infected Charles A. Stoneham, one of the owners of the New York Giants. Stoneham ran an office that took orders for stocks from clients, but he invested their money in stocks he chose. Although no federal laws prohibited the practice, local ones did. Stoneham made $10 million from the business, left it, and then helped fund another office that eventually went bankrupt.

In 1929, such speculative activities contributed to the stock market crash that marked the start of the Great Depression. The economic collapse devastated Americans and presented a grave threat to baseball. To this day, no one knows for sure what caused the collapse, but its origins went well beyond problems with stocks. Indeed, there were several warning signs, among them a consumer debt that had risen 250 percent. In time, consumers decided they could no longer expand their installment buying, and this damaged large parts of the economy, particularly markets for big ticket items such as automobiles and appliances. Consumer demand began slipping in 1928, leaving the auto industry with too many cars, and during the last 10 months of that year building permits dropped 65 percent. Unemployment rose dramatically weeks before the market crashed, with three million out of work by early fall of 1929.

If the Twenties seemed destined for great heights, the Thirties seemed doomed to great depths. From 1929 to 1930 alone, Gross National Product decreased 46 percent, employment 20 percent, and industrial production 25 percent. By 1933, national income had dropped 50 percent, and 5,000 banks had collapsed, taking with them nine million dollars in savings accounts. The tune "Ain't We Got Fun" was replaced with "Buddy Can You Spare A Dime?"

As the economic crisis worsened, people doubted the ethic that said hard work leads to success. Farmers watched helplessly as commodity prices plummeted; former office workers sold apples on sidewalks to earn pennies; unemployed factory workers took to railroad cars, riding as hobos from town to town, looking for the one job that, as it turned out, 4,000 other men were looking for at the same time. So it seemed "the dark fields of the republic," as F. Scott Fitzgerald once called America's heartland, no longer held opportunity, but mocked it.

As the 1930s began, America sank into the Great Depression. In July 1934, farmers in Kaufman County, Texas picked up benefit checks.

Yet recreation remained strong, especially games that required little money to play, such as softball and baseball. "Sometimes we'd go on playing with the [baseball] after the cover came off," said journalist Robert W. Creamer about his childhood. "The end of the tightly wound string of the ball's inside was glued down. . . . Inevitably the glued end would work loose and the string would unwind. I have clear memories of baseballs hit past the infield with a thin white line of string trailing behind."

Although sporting goods manufacturing declined between 1929 and 1933, companies produced more softballs and baseballs than ever, particularly cheaper or lower-end ones. In 1930, about 240,000 Americans played in amateur baseball leagues and over 300,000 boys in American Legion junior baseball tournaments. At the end of the decade, Carl Stotz founded Little League baseball in Williamsport, Pennsylvania.

President Franklin Roosevelt's New Deal programs to ease the Depression benefited recreation. The national government helped build 3,000 athletic facilities between 1935 and 1940, on which the Works Progress Administration spent one billion dollars. Historian William Baker later claimed that with this spending, the New Deal "produced a kind of quiet revolution in the relation of American government to the sports and recreation of its citizenry."

Ultimately, the widespread participation in recreation helped major league baseball by maintaining popular interest in organized sports. At first, however, the Depression nearly ruined several teams. Attendance plummeted as fans could no longer afford tickets; in 1932, it dropped nearly 70 percent from two years earlier. The St. Louis Browns averaged fewer than 1,500 spectators per game; the Cincinnati Reds, Boston Braves, and Philadelphia Phillies almost folded.

Nor did the big leagues stand alone. Minor league teams offered all kinds of promotions to attract fans—from raffles to cow-milking contests. After the Negro National League collapsed in 1931, black teams resorted to barnstorming in order to stay active and earn a living.

Despite its problems, big league baseball continued to offer diversion from the difficulties of the Depression. The All Star Game began in 1933 in Chicago as part of the Century of Progress Exhibition, and the Majors copied the minor and Negro Leagues in offering night games, with Cincinnati playing the first one in 1935. That same year, the economy improved slightly and attendance picked up.

As Babe Ruth aged (and retired in 1935), other players came to the fore. Hack Wilson hit a National League-record 56

THE WORKS PROGRESS ADMINISTRATION *employed people in public works. Here, workers in Fairbault, Minnesota repair a sidewalk in 1936.*

home runs for the Chicago Cubs in 1930. Pitching for the St. Louis Cardinals, Dizzy Dean won 30 games in 1934. In his first start with the Cleveland Indians in 1936, Bob Feller struck out 15 St. Louis Browns. Joe DiMaggio—the son of an Italian-born fisherman, and a testimony to the arrival of players from immigrant families—hit 29 homers that year as a rookie for the Yankees while driving in 125 runs. Another Yankee, Lou Gehrig, was named the A.L.'s most valuable player for 1936 with 49 home runs and 152 RBI. In 1939, a rookie for the Boston Red Sox stirred fans: Ted Williams, a right fielder, hit .327 with 31 homers and 145 RBI.

By the close of the decade, all major league teams were broadcasting at least some of their games on radio. At the same time, radio brought into homes a more sobering event: the crisis in Europe leading to World War II. As tension mounted, European nations turned to the United States for armaments and other supplies, and the resulting demand lifted the economy and ended the Depression.

As the war and the economic revival in 1939 carried America into a new era, the National Baseball Hall of Fame opened in Cooperstown, New York. About 10,000 people attended the induction of players and viewed museum exhibits. When fans entered the Hall, they could see in photographs and artifacts past glories and historic moments that conjured up Ruth, Cobb, and even John Philip Sousa's marching band. But while the Hall of Fame spoke of history, its creation pointed baseball confidently toward the future by proclaiming its faith in new players, new records, and new moments that would create more inductees, lead to more exhibits, and declare that baseball and American culture would survive World War II and prosper together.

DO IT YOURSELF

In Game Five of the 1920 World Series between the Cleveland Indians and the Brooklyn Dodgers, Indian's shortstop Bill Wambsganss (known as "Wamby"), completed an unassisted triple play. With men on first and second, pitcher Clarence Mitchell lined to short. Wamby snared the drive and stepped on second to erase Pete Kilduff, then tagged the incoming Otto Miller to complete the rare play. Only 11 unassisted triple plays have occurred in baseball history. Like Don Larsen's perfect game, Wamby's gem is the only one to happen in the World Series. Later in the game, Cleveland outfielder Elmer Smith hit the first grand slam in World Series history. The Indians went on to win the game and the Series.

A NAME IN THE CROWD

Until the 1920 World Series, the most famous thing about Cleveland infielder Bill Wambsganss was his name. A mediocre hitter (career average .259) with no power and moderate speed, he played regularly with the Indians primarily because he was a competent fielder at both second base and shortstop.

But it was impossible to ignore that name. In 1914 Wambsganss was bought by the Indians (then called the Naps) to compete for the shortstop job with Ray Chapman, a fine player whose possible Hall of Fame career was tragically interrupted when he was killed by a pitch in

CLEVELAND INDIANS' SHORTSTOP Bill Wambsganss. A capable infielder and an average hitter, he may never have earned a spot in baseball history, if it wasn't for the unassisted triple play he completed in Game Five of the 1920 World Series.

a 1920 game. The writer Ring Lardner took a look at Wambsganss and decided that his name provided an irresistible poetic challenge. Lardner wrote:

The Naps bought a shortstop named
> *Wambsganss*
Who is slated to fill Ray Chapman's pants
But when he saw Ray,
And the way he could play
He muttered, "I haven't a clam's chance!"

Wambsganss himself agreed, and moved to second base. His career continued in a quiet way until 1920, when the Indians, led by Tris Speaker, held off a pair of challengers to win the American League pennant. Their opponents in the World Series were the Brooklyn Robins, starring future Hall of Famers Zack Wheat, Burleigh Grimes, and Rube Marquard.

A MEDIOCRE SEASON

That season of 1920 was the first year of what is now called the Lively Ball Era. Stricter pitching rules had begun to prohibit "trick" pitches: spitballs, emery balls (balls scuffed with an emery board), shine balls, and other pitches that used doctored balls. In addition, umpires had become more diligent about removing dirty or scuffed balls from play and replacing them with new, clean, white ones. In the past, pitchers and infielders had purposely discolored baseballs to make them harder for the batter to see, but this was no longer permitted.

Hitters thrived as never before as a result of these changes. In the American League alone, 1920 saw St. Louis' George Sisler hit .407 and the Indians' Tris Speaker hit .388, while Babe Ruth slugged 54 home runs, nearly doubling his previous record of 29.

Unfortunately, Wambsganss hadn't benefited from the lively ball in 1920. In fact, he had suffered through a subpar season, batting just .244 with one home run. Nor did the early games of the World Series provide him with any sort of showcase.

But, unique name or no, Bill Wambsganss would not be remembered today if something hadn't happened to reverse his waning fortunes. In the fifth game, with the Series tied 2–2, he got his opportunity.

ONE CHANCE AT GLORY

With the Indians leading 7–0 in the fifth inning, Pete Kilduff led off for Brooklyn and promptly singled to left field. Catcher Otto Miller followed with a single to center. Up next was Clarence Mitchell, Brooklyn's pitcher. Mitchell was a good hitter and was allowed to hit for himself.

Cleveland pitcher Jim Bagby threw a fastball, which Mitchell smacked on a line over Wambsganss's head. That is—*almost* over his head. Wambsganss leaped and snagged the ball out of the air. One out.

His leap had taken him toward second base, and when he landed on his feet the quick-witted

WAMBSGANSS tags Brooklyn Dodger Otto Miller as he is running from first to second on a line-drive, the third out in his unassisted triple play.

Wambsganss immediately saw that Kilduff, the runner on second, was so sure the ball would be a hit that he'd headed to third without a backward glance. "There I was with the ball in my glove, and him with his back to me," Wambsganss told Lawrence Ritter in *The Glory of Their Times,* "so I just kept right on going and touched second with my toe." Two out.

Next, Wambsganss looked to his left, and saw that the runner on first, Otto Miller, had also taken off at the crack of the bat, sure that Mitchell's blow was going to be a hit. Now he stood just a few feet away from the second-base bag, his mouth open. "I intended to throw to [first baseman Doc] Johnston to nail Miller after I'd stepped on second," Wambsganss said after the game, "but when I saw Miller so close, I instinctively tagged him for the third out." In just a few moments, Wambsganss had completed one of the rarest plays in baseball: an unassisted triple play.

Cleveland went on to defeat Brooklyn in the 1920 World Series, Wambsganss hitting only .154 in the Series. In a flash, his name had become immortal. As soon as he'd tagged out Otto Miller, *Baseball Magazine* said, "the busy telegraph was flashing Wambsganss' curious name East and West and North and South to the farthest hamlet in this broad land . . . Somewhere in the remote recesses of Asia, the swift electric currents traveling East met the equally swift aerial couriers from the West and the marvelous exploits of this player had circled the Globe."

Unassisted Triple Plays

Player, Team	Date	Position
Paul Hines, Providence (N)	May 8, 1878	Outfield
Neal Ball, Cleveland (A)	July 19, 1909	Shortstop
Bill Wambsganss, Cleveland (A)	Oct. 10, 1920	2nd base
George Burns, Boston (A)	Sept. 14, 1923	1st base
Ernie Padgett, Boston (N)	Oct. 6, 1923	Shortstop
Glenn Wright, Pittsburgh (N)	May 7, 1925	Shortstop
Jimmy Cooney, Chicago (N)	May 30, 1927	Shortstop
Johnny Neun, Detroit (A)	May 31, 1927	1st base
Ron Hansen, Washington (A)	July 29, 1968	Shortstop
Mickey Morandini, Philadelphia (N)	Sept. 23, 1992	2nd base
John Valentin, Boston (A)	July 15, 1994	Shortstop

JOHN VALENTIN, THE LAST PLAYER to complete an unassisted triple play. Playing for the Red Sox on July 15, 1994, against the Minnesota Twins, Valentin retired batter Marc Newfield and base runners Mike Blowers and Keith Mitchell. Valentin opened the bottom of the six with a home run.

THE HOUSE THAT RUTH BUILT

Folklore has it that the Yankees built their mammoth new stadium to accommodate all the fans who wanted to see Babe Ruth's prodigious home run hitting. Along with Boston's Braves Field and Cleveland's Municipal Stadium, Yankee Stadium was a concrete and steel monument to the home run. Ruth brought down the house on April 18th, 1923, hitting the first home run in Yankee Stadium history, and incidentally, winning the game against the Red Sox.

"I'D GIVE A YEAR OF MY LIFE IF I CAN HIT A HOME RUN IN THIS FIRST GAME IN THIS NEW PARK."

WITH 197 HOME RUNS as the 1923 season opened, already over one-quarter of his lifetime home run record of 714, Babe Ruth delivered on expectations for the opening day of Yankee Stadium. His home run was not only the first in the new stadium; it also won the game against the Red Sox, the team that had sold him four years earlier to the Yankees.

THE ONE AND ONLY BAMBINO

No professional athlete has ever had an impact on his sport to match the effect Babe Ruth had on baseball after he joined the New York Yankees in 1920. Slamming home runs in unprecedented numbers, making the front page of the New York papers as often as he appeared in the sports section, posing for innumerable photo opportunities in whatever outlandish costume he chose. The Babe was exactly what the game needed at the time.

At the vanguard of the Lively Ball Era, which saw hitting reach heights not attained again until the 1990s, Ruth (the highest paid player in baseball) was so popular that he also meant more money in the pockets of owners and other players alike. As Hall of Famer Waite Hoyt, a teammate of Ruth's, put it, "Every big leaguer and his wife should teach their children to pray, 'God bless Mommy, God bless Daddy, and God bless Babe Ruth.'"

But during Ruth's early glory years with the Yankees, there was just one problem: The team was playing in the Polo Grounds, home to the arch-rival New York Giants. And in 1921, the Giants announced that the Yankees would no longer be welcome after the 1922 season. Suddenly, the team with the greatest attraction in baseball needed a new home.

FIT FOR A KING

In a cunning move, the Yankees' owners, Colonels Jacob Ruppert and T. L. Huston, chose to buy a parcel of land directly across the Harlem River from the Polo Grounds. Fans watching Giant games, the owners implied, could also look up and watch an even more exciting ballgame—albeit at a great distance.

In prior years, the site had been considered too far from New York City's hub. Who would want to travel to the sticks to see a game? But with the building of the Lexington Avenue subway, fans could now travel from midtown Manhattan to the ballpark in just

minutes. There was no reason not to build on this prime site.

From the start, Ruppert and Huston thought big. This would be no rickety wooden ballpark, no halfhearted showcase for a team on the verge of dynasty status. First 45,000 cubic yards of dirt were brought in to grade the property, and then 25,000 cubic yards were removed to lay the park's concrete foundation. The framework was built out of 2,200 tons of structural steel, 28,000 cubic yards of concrete, and another 800 tons of steel reinforcements. The bleachers

AN AERIAL VIEW of the new stadium shows how deep the center field, known as "Death Valley," extended (top). The lot chosen, across the river from the Polo Grounds where the New York Giants played, was the site of a farm granted to John Lion Gardiner before the Revolutionary War (bottom).

required 950,000 board-feet of Pacific fir, brought to the East Coast through the Panama Canal, while the 58,000 individual seats were built from 400,000 pieces of maple, 135,000 steel casings, and more than a million brass screws.

In designing the park, Ruppert and Huston were canny in another way. Yankee Stadium's original dimensions favored left-handed hitters who could pull the ball to right field, while penalizing those who hit the ball to the vast and cavernous centerfield, otherwise known as "Death Valley." As *The Sporting News's* Joe Vila put it in an article two weeks before the new park opened, "I doubt if a fly ball will ever be driven into the left and center field bleachers, but the right field seats fairly yawn for the home run hitters."

Babe Ruth, of course, was a left-handed hitter who pulled the ball to right field, and the new ballpark was built with him in mind. Even so, he said, "I cried when they took me out of the Polo Grounds." Who could blame him? All he'd done in his three years with the Polo Grounds as his home park was hit 148 home runs and accumulate 407 runs batted in!

THE GREATEST DAY

Yankee Stadium—the first ballpark grand enough to be called a stadium—opened on

CARS LINED UP OUTSIDE Yankee Stadium on opening day, April 18, 1923. Dignitaries from beyond the baseball world attended, including New York State Governor Al Smith.

Wednesday, April 18, 1923, before the largest crowd that had ever watched a baseball game. There were, the *New York Times* reported, 74,200 paying customers (some of whom must have been sitting on each other's laps, given that the stadium had about 64,000 seats), along with 25,000 more who went home "convinced that baseball parks are not nearly as large as they should be."

The hubbub in and around the stadium was a sight to behold. John Philip Sousa marched the Seventh Regiment band to the center field flagpole, where the rival managers, the Yankees' Miller Huggins and the Boston Red Sox' Frank Chance, hoisted the American flag. Then everyone, including New York's Governor Al Smith, baseball

comissioner Kenesaw Mountain Landis, and many other dignitaries, took their seats, and the first game at Yankee Stadium began.

All that was left to make it a perfect day was for Babe Ruth to strike the first dramatic blow in the stadium's history. Before the game, he'd told a reporter, "I'd give a year of my life if I can hit a home run in this first game in this new park." And with his phenomenal sense of timing, that's what he did, breaking a scoreless tie with a blast into the inviting rightfield stands.

"The moment Ruth's drive landed among the bleacher spectators, the crowd went mad," reported Joe Vila. "Hats, canes, and umbrellas were thrown up and a tremendous volley of cheers greeted the smiling Bambino as he trotted around the circuit." As the *Times* put it, the home run was "the real baptism of Yankee Stadium."

That day, in a moment of inspiration, the great baseball writer Fred Lieb dubbed the new ballpark "The House that Ruth Built." More than 75 years later, it remains a living testament to the greatest star the game has ever known.

FANS PACKED THE STANDS on opening day. According to some reports, the sell-out crowd numbered over 74,000. Given a capacity of 64,000, the stadium was overflowing with people.

THE FESTOONED FRONT FAÇADE of the stadium welcomed fans to the big event. With a convenient connection to New York's subway system behind the right-center bleachers, New Yorkers poured in for opening day.

BOTTOMLEY'S UP

Future Hall of Famer "Sunny" Jim Bottomley cleaned up his plate on September 16, 1924. Bottomley went 6-for-6 with a record 12 RBI and two home runs as the Cardinals overwhelmed the Dodgers 17-3. Bottomley's record RBI total was equaled by another St. Louis Cardinal, outfielder Mark Whiten, in 1993. Whiten exploded for four home runs and 12 RBI in Game Two of a doubleheader at Cincinnati.

JAMES LEROY BOTTOMLEY, also known as "Sunny Jim," came to baseball from the coal-mining region of Illinois and worked as blacksmith and mechanic in the off-season.

A FLOOD OF IMMORTALS

No era in baseball's history has sent more players to the Hall of Fame than the 1920s and 1930s, the game's first "golden age." This was the time when a behemoth named Babe Ruth dominated the game, but he was just one of a passel of great players from the time who have been honored with a plaque in Cooperstown.

The list includes Ty Cobb, Rogers Hornsby, Lou Gehrig, Jimmy Foxx, Hank Greenberg, Al Simmons, Tris Speaker, Paul Waner, Kiki Cuyler, Bill Dickey, and Mickey Cochrane. Even in this hitter's era, pitchers were not neglected in the Hall of Fame voting: Carl Hubbell, Dizzy Dean, and the two Leftys (Grove and Gomez) were among those who survived the batting onslaught and ascended to the Hall.

In an era blessed with such an abundance of all-time superstars, it's understandable that some great players—Hall of Famers themselves—might find themselves nearly forgotten today. And that's a shame: After all, any player with a lifetime average of .310 (including seasons in which he batted .371, .367, and .348), seasons with 137, 136, and 128 RBI, and as many as 31 home runs, deserves to be remembered.

That player was James LeRoy "Sunny Jim" Bottomley, one of the Hall of Fame's forgotten men.

THE LIFE OF A BALLPLAYER

In the 1920s, Sunny Jim Bottomley played well enough with the St. Louis Cardinals to be the subject of several articles in *Baseball Magazine,* the leading sports publication of its time. But even then, the general opinion was that Bottomley was condemned to labor in comparative anonymity. "One of the best natural hitters who has broken into baseball for a decade, his talents were, nevertheless, thrown into the shade by the transcendent abilities of [teammate] Rogers Hornsby," was how writer F. C. Lane put it.

Bottomley always shrugged off any sense that he wasn't getting the credit he deserved. Like many ballplayers of every era, he saw baseball as a ticket away from a hard life at home. He'd been born and raised in a coal-mining region of Illinois, and worked as a blacksmith and mechanic before playing baseball.

With a lifetime average of .310, Bottomley was as accomplished as many other Hall of Famers, even though his name is much less well-known than some.

It was dangerous work, as Bottomley told F. C. Lane. "Just before I reported to [Cardinals' owner] Branch Rickey, I got hit on the side of the head with a sledgehammer," he recalled. "It closed up one eye and when Branch first looked at me, he asked if I'd been fighting again. I had, but I had been fighting to make a living and it was some fight in those days."

In the course of his 16-year career, Bottomley did have a few moments in the sun. One was during the Cardinals' World Series victory over the powerful Yankees in 1926. Sunny Jim collected 10 hits in 29 at bats in that seven-game Series, driving in five runs. But even in this moment of glory, he had to hand over center stage. The 1926 World Series will always be

remembered for the sight of ancient Grover Cleveland Alexander slogging in from the bullpen to strike out Tony Lazzeri with the bases loaded and save the Cardinals' Game Seven victory.

But no one can diminish the brilliance of Bottomley's other famous accomplishment: On September 16, 1924, he drove in 12 runs in a single game.

THE RBI MACHINE

To drive in 12 runs in a nine-inning game, you have to have a lot of opportunities—and make the most of all of them. When Bottomley came to bat against the Brooklyn Robins in the first inning, the bases were loaded. He singled to drive in two runs.

Sunny Jim came to bat again in the second, and this time he doubled to drive in another run (number three). Then, in the fourth inning, Robins' pitcher Art Decatur intentionally walked Rogers Hornsby to pitch to Bottomley. This was not a good idea: Sunny Jim slammed the ball over the right field fence for a grand slam home run, bringing his RBI total to seven.

He was up next in the sixth inning, and this time he hit a two-run home run. He followed this with a two-run single in the seventh, giving him 11 RBI. This tied the existing record, ironically held by Robins' manager Wilbert Robinson, watching from the opposing dugout that day.

Bottomley had one opportunity to set a new record. In the ninth, Rogers Hornsby tripled, and Bottomley finished his onslaught with another single and his twelfth RBI in the Cardinals' 17–3 win. Overall, he'd gone 6–6, with three singles, a double, and two home runs.

Sunny Jim Bottomley was elected to the Hall of Fame in 1974. But he was destined to share center stage one more time: On September 7, 1993, the Cardinals' Mark Whiten drove in 12 runs in a game, joining Sunny Jim in the record books.

"ONE OF THE BEST NATURAL HITTERS WHO HAS BROKEN INTO BASEBALL FOR A DECADE."

In 1993, nearly 70 years after Bottomley achieved his record of 12 RBIs in a single game, Mark Whiten, outfielder for the St. Louis Cardinals, matched the record.

WALTER JOHNSON AT LAST

In 1924, after pitching 18 years and winning 354 games, Walter Johnson finally got a chance to pitch for his Washington Senators in the World Series. Johnson lost a heartbreaker in Game One, going 12 innings only to lose 4-3. He was roughed up in Game 5, losing again 6-2. However, when called upon to relieve in the ninth inning of the seventh game, "The Big Train" rose to the occasion, holding the Giants scoreless through the 12th, when the Senators finally managed to push across a run and win 4-3. The Senators had won their first World Series title.

THE BIG TRAIN

B y 1924, only the Washington Senators and St. Louis Browns had failed to win a pennant in the American League. They were two franchises destined to spend most of their histories in the second division, the bottom half of the standings.

There was always sentiment on the side of the hapless Senators. They were, after all, the team representing the nation's capital. The president of the United States regularly threw out the first ball of the season. The owner, Clark Griffith, was a respected pioneer from the game's humble beginnings. And they had one of the game's most beloved players—Walter "The Big Train" Johnson, perhaps the hardest throwing pitcher in baseball history. They called him "The Big Train" because of his durability, and the way his fastball arrived like a locomotive.

ONLY CY YOUNG WON MORE GAMES

He came up in 1907, out of Humboldt, Kansas, and by 1910 had established himself as the best pitcher in the league. He was 25–17 with a 1.36 earned run average (ERA) that year. It was his first of 12 20-victory seasons—including two in which he won over 30. He would lead the league in strikeouts 12 times, twice topping 300. He won five ERA titles, six times coming in under 2.00. Nine times he exceeded 300 innings pitched. He won 417 games, bettered only by Cy Young. One hundred and ten of them were shutouts—necessary for a man backed with little offensive support. His 3,509 career strikeouts were a major league record that stood for 56 years

WASHINGTON SENATORS' PITCHER Walter "The Big Train" Johnson's achievements were legion: he ended 12 seasons with over 20 victories and he led the American League in strikeouts 12 times.

"ANYONE WHO THOUGHT WALTER WAS THROUGH WAS A FOOL."

JOHNSON LED THE SENATORS to their first World Series in 1924. Here the team is pictured in September in front of the White House with President Calvin Coolidge, who is standing to the left of Johnson in the center wearing a light-colored jacket and a black arm band.

after his retirement, until Nolan Ryan and Steve Carlton finally passed him in 1983.

But his Senators were never contenders. A World Series was never in their sights. Not until 1924, at least, when their playing manager, Bucky Harris, led them to the promised land. Imagine! A World Series in Washington!

Walter Johnson was already 36 years old. He hadn't won 20 games since 1919, but he delivered in the pennant season with a 23–7 record, cranking up the arm for another six shutouts in his 38 starts. And now, after 18 big league campaigns, he was there. His Senators edged the Yankees on the next-to-last day of the season. Walter won 13 straight down the stretch. Now, he stood on the mound in Griffith Stadium, with President and Mrs. Coolidge in the stands, to face John McGraw's Giants. Eighteen long seasons—half his life— had brought him at last to this moment.

He was surely the sentimental favorite of the nation, but the script took an odd turn. He lost the first game 4–3 in 12 innings. His head hung low in the clubhouse. He blamed himself for letting down the fans.

A VICTORY AT LAST

Johnson came back to start Game Five with the Series tied at two each, but he allowed 13 hits, struck out only three, and lost again, 6–2. He was now 0–2, and the Senators were a game from elimination. He might not pitch again.

After the Giants lost Game Six and sent the series to a Game Seven—October 10, 1924, in Washington—the Senators went with Curly Ogden as their starting pitcher. Again, President and Mrs. Coolidge were in Griffith Stadium. This time, the game was tied 3–3 in the ninth, when Harris summoned the Big Train from the bullpen on just two days' rest. The roar of the crowd surely pumped up Johnson's adrenaline level, for devoid of his best stuff, he gamely pitched out of trouble, inning after inning. When he needed a double play grounder, he got it. When he needed to strike out Frankie Frisch and George Kelly— two future Hall of Famers—he did it.

Finally, in the last of the 12th, the Senators scored on a bad-hop single past 19-year-old third baseman Freddie Lindstrom, and they had their first and only World Championship. The winning pitcher? Walter Johnson, the toast of the town!

"Anyone who thought Walter was through was a fool," said celebrating manager Harris. "I knew he was all right!"

The Senators would repeat their pennant in 1925, giving Walter another chance at the World Series in his final 20-win season. He was 2–1 against the Pirates that year, but lost the deciding game. He retired after the 1927 season, and was among the first five players elected to the Hall of Fame nine years later.

The First Five Players Elected to the Hall of Fame (1936)

Ty Cobb
Honus Wagner
Babe Ruth
Christy Mathewson
Walter Johnson

"DON'T COME HOME A FAILURE"

His father's parting words were, "Don't come home a failure," when Ty Cobb left his hometown in Georgia to become a ballplayer. Young Ty took them to heart, racking up over 4,000 hits and at one point, nine batting titles in a row! On May 5th, 1925, Cobb had a banner day, going 6-for-6, with three homers and 16 total bases. Cobb added two more homers the next day for good measure.

BASEBALL GIANT TY COBB, who owns the game's top lifetime batting average of .366.

THE BATTLEGROUND

I have observed that baseball is not unlike a war," Ty Cobb told the *New York Tribune* in 1914, "and when you come right down to it, we batters are the heavy artillery."

This simple sentence reveals much about what drove this angry, intelligent, supremely competitive man throughout his extraordinary 24-year career. Cobb's offensive numbers are astounding. Between 1905, when he joined the Detroit Tigers as an 18-year-old country boy out of small-town Georgia, and his retirement in 1928, Cobb batted below .300 only once (his rookie season, when he hit .240 in 150 at bats). He hit over .400 three times, and over .350 16 times. He led the American League in hitting nine years in a row (1907–15) and 12 years out of 13. The one year he didn't lead the league he hit "only" .371.

Ty Cobb's career batting average was .366, the highest of all time. His 4,189 career hit total has been surpassed only once, by Pete Rose—who required 2,619 more at bats to get 67 more hits.

But with all these batting feats, Cobb was probably most famous for his base-running. He was fast (fast enough to steal 892 bases), but, even more importantly, he was absolutely fearless, hurling his body around with no regard for his own well-being.

LESSONS IN BASERUNNING

"The great secret, to my mind, of being a good baserunner is to hit the dirt with the feeling that you like the sensation," he said. "In the early months of a championship race, I am always covered with sliding blisters. . . . It is hardest to get going in the

DRIVEN TO SUCCEED from a young age, Ty Cobb is shown here at 18 years of age. This is one of the first press photos taken of him in his professional career.

NOTORIOUS for his aggressive sliding technique—feet first and spikes high—Cobb is pictured here sliding into home plate for his Detroit Tigers in the 1908 World Series against the Chicago Cubs.

early weeks of the race when the sliding sores are bad."

Cobb may have been most notorious for the way he would slide into a base with his spikes high. Many a fielder came out of an encounter with Cobb on the basepaths with bleeding feet or legs. As the great pitcher Smoky Joe Wood recalled: "Cobb always told me and the other fellows he played against, 'All you've got to do is give me room to get in there and it'll be all right, but if you don't give me room, I'll cut my way in.'"

DRIVEN TO SUCCEED

What made Ty Cobb run? If you looked at him, you'd see an average-looking man, 6 feet 1 inch tall and about 175 pounds. He didn't have the great physical presence of Babe Ruth, the obvious strength of Lou Gehrig. What he had was a mind that was always several steps ahead of everyone else's, and a spirit that was completely fearless.

Cobb brought these qualities with him when he joined the Tigers. After being released by a minor league team when he was 17, young Ty (away from home for the first time) wrote a disappointed letter home to his parents. His father, whom Cobb described as "cold" and "austere," sent back a devastating reply: "Don't come home a failure." All his

career, Cobb kept that message in mind. No one ever worked harder, or possessed a more insatiable desire to succeed, than Ty Cobb.

Cobb's greatest years came during the "dead ball" era, when home runs were scarce and base-running and strategy were extremely important. After the arrival of Babe Ruth and other sluggers in the 1920s, Cobb felt baseball had lost some of its depth. He also often said that, had he been a rookie during the 1920s, he too could have been a home run hitter.

This might seem like an idle claim, impossible to prove—except that in a pair of games in 1925, Cobb showed what he was capable of. On May 5, the 40-year-old Cobb went 6-for-6, with three home runs. The next day, he slugged two more round-trippers. Maybe he could have hit 60 home runs in a season, if he'd been younger when the Lively Ball Era began, and if he'd wanted to!

After he retired, Cobb explained why he'd always driven himself so hard. "I never thought I was any genius," he said, "so I gave up my life to the game for twenty-five years."

Hall of Fame pitcher Walter Johnson, who faced Cobb dozens of times, had another appraisal. "Cobb was the smartest player that I ever saw by so wide a margin," he said, "that I won't even bother to think who was second best."

Top 10 Lifetime Batting Averages

Name	Average
Ty Cobb	.366
Rogers Hornsby	.358
Joe Jackson	.356
Ed Delahanty	.346
Tris Speaker	.345
Ted Williams	.344
Billy Hamilton	.344
Dan Brouthers	.342
Babe Ruth	.342
Harry Heilmann	.342

GO ASK ALEX

After throwing complete game victories for the Cardinals in Games 2 and 6 of the 1926 World Series, grizzled veteran Grover Cleveland "Pete" Alexander figured he had earned a day off for the seventh game. Cardinal player-manager Rogers Hornsby thought otherwise, and signaled for "Old Pete" to relieve with the bases loaded and two outs in the bottom of the seventh at Yankee Stadium. In one of the most dramatic confrontations in World Series history, the aging veteran proceeded to strike out rookie Tony Lazzeri to end the threat. Alexander stifled the Yanks for two more innings, but walked Babe Ruth with two outs in the ninth. With cleanup hitter Bob Meusel at the plate, Ruth lit out for second and was caught stealing to end the Series.

OL' PETE

"I THOUGHT HE WAS JUST AS ANXIOUS AS I WAS, AND THEN SOME."

Grover Cleveland "Pete" Alexander was one of the greatest pitchers of all time. He pitched for 20 years (1911–30) and won 373 games, tied for third most ever. From 1915 through 1917 he won 30 or more games three years in a row, a stretch that included an astounding 36 shutouts.

Yet Alexander's prickly personality and well-publicized off-the-field exploits—including an ongoing battle with alcoholism—kept the fans at a distance. It also contributed to his being traded several times in his career, rare for such a great talent at that time. In fact, today he might be remembered more for his failings than for his successes, if not for his spectacular performance with the St. Louis Cardinals during the 1926 World Series, when no one expected anything from him.

A CHANCE AT REDEMPTION

Alexander, nearing the end of his career at age 39, found a kindred spirit in Cardinals second baseman-manager Rogers Hornsby in 1926. While others whispered that ol' Pete was through, Hornsby was willing to give him another chance. And Alexander came through, winning nine games for the Cardinals during the regular season and helping the team capture its first National League pennant since 1888.

The Cardinals' opponent in the 1926 World Series was a fearsome one: Babe Ruth's New York Yankees. Accompanying Ruth were Hall of Famers Lou Gehrig, Tony Lazzeri, Earle Combs, Waite Hoyt, and Herb Pennock—one of the greatest accumulations of ballplayers in history. It seemed a lot to expect of Pete Alexander and the Cinderella Cardinals to match the Yankees' lineup.

Surprisingly, the teams split the first six games, with a rejuvenated Alexander winning both Games Two and Six with superb pitching. Fans and the press alike were astounded by Alex' performance, but no one could have predicted that, in Game Seven, he would take a step into baseball immortality.

UNEXPECTED GLORY

Alexander himself thought it highly unlikely that he would pitch again in the seventh game. After all, he'd thrown a complete game just one day earlier.

This fact, coupled with Alexander's checkered past, led to the rumor that he'd spent the night after his Game Six win celebrating in local taverns. But he denied such rumors for the rest of his life, saying that he'd promised manager Hornsby that he'd stay sober.

Rogers Hornsby, player-manager for the Cardinals in 1926, who put pitcher Pete Alexander in with bases loaded, bottom of the seventh, in the World Series against the Yankees.

Game Seven started quietly on a cool afternoon under drizzly skies, with both the Cardinals' Jesse Haines and the Yankees' Waite Hoyt pitching well. Then, in the seventh, with the Cardinals clinging to a 3–2 lead, Haines developed a blister on his finger and loaded the bases with two out. With the Yankee Stadium crowd roaring, Tony Lazzeri strode to the plate, knowing that one hit would put the Yankees in the lead. Who would Hornsby choose to save the game?

To everyone's surprise, Hornsby called for Alexander one more time. Not expecting to be used, Alex had been relaxing in the bullpen. Now he took a few hurried warm-up tosses, and walked slowly out to the mound.

Legend has it that Alex paused to pick a four-leaf clover on the way, but he denied it.

YANKEES' BATTER Tony Lazzeri. Alexander broke the Yankees' hold on the 1926 World Series by striking out Lazzeri in the bottom of the seventh with bases loaded.

He didn't deny taking his time, though, and letting Lazzeri stew for a while at home plate. "Well, I didn't see any reason why I should run," he said later. "I thought he was just as anxious as I was, and then some."

Alexander had gotten Lazzeri out four times in Game Six by throwing him a steady diet of curveballs. Now

he and catcher Bob O'Farrell stayed with what had worked, throwing two breaking pitches in a row. The count went to one ball, one strike.

On his next pitch, Alexander tried a fastball. Lazzeri swung and hit the ball high and far. "I spun around to watch the ball and all the Yankees on base were on their way," Alexander said. "But the ball had a tail-end fade and landed foul by eight-ten feet in the left-field bleachers."

After that, Alexander threw nothing but curveballs. It took only two more. Lazzeri swung and missed at both of them for a strikeout. Somehow, Alex had preserved the 3–2 lead.

Today, many people believe that the Series ended with that dramatic strikeout. But the game still had two innings to go—and Hornsby was going to let Alexander pitch both of them. It was Ol' Pete's game to save or lose.

Alex breezed through the eighth and the first two outs of the ninth. Then, still nursing a one-run lead, he walked Babe Ruth. This put the tying run on first, and brought Bob Meusel (a .315 hitter during the regular season) to the plate. The crowd, which had grown quiet as the innings passed, began to buzz.

What happened next, though, stunned everyone into silence. On Alex' first pitch to Meusel, Babe Ruth broke for second. O'Farrell caught the pitch and fired the ball toward the second base bag.

"I wheeled around, and there was one of the grandest sights of my life," Alexander said. "Hornsby, his foot anchored on the bag and his gloved hand outstretched was waiting for Ruth to come in." The Babe was out by a mile, and just like that the Series was over. The improbable Cardinals, led by their equally improbable aging pitcher, were champions of the world.

VETERAN PITCHER Grover Cleveland "Pete" Alexander played most of his remaining years with St. Louis.

63

SIXTY

When Babe Ruth started hitting home runs in the late 'teens, no one had ever hit more in a season than Ned Williamson, who whacked 27 in 1884. In 1919, outfielder-pitcher Ruth launched 29 homers for the Red Sox, establishing a new all-time record. He broke his own record each of the next two seasons as a Yankee, hitting the unheard of totals of 54 followed by 59. In the stellar season of 1927, when he hit .356 with 164 RBI, Ruth on September 30 broke the record for the fourth time, hitting his 60th home run of the season.

SETTING THE PACE

Beginning in 1919, Babe Ruth broke the baseball mold in ways that no one has replicated before or since. He simply hit home runs in such mind-boggling abundance that he revolutionized the game.

Prior to Ruth's arrival as a hitter, the average home run champion sometimes didn't even break into double digits in round-trippers. In 1917, for example, the leading slugger in the American League had nine home runs, while two National Leaguers made it all the way to 12.

The first time Babe Ruth led the Majors in home runs, in 1918, he did so with 11, tied with Philadelphia's Tilly Walker. Of course, Ruth was still a part-time pitcher with the Boston Red Sox that year, and had only 317 at bats.

In 1919 he began to show what he was made of. Pitching less and playing in the outfield more, he accumulated 432 at bats and slugged an unprecedented 29 home runs. Tilly Walker was next with 10, while the National League champion, Gavvy Cravath, managed 12.

Ruth's 29 home runs were more than were hit by 10 of the 15 other *teams* in the Majors.

THE BEHEMOTH

But more was yet to come. In 1920 the Babe moved to the Yankees, who were then playing in the cozy Polo Grounds. At the same time, baseball officials had begun to ban what they called "freak" pitches: spitballs and others that involved doctoring the ball.

These rule changes marked the birth of the Lively Ball Era, and Babe Ruth took full advantage of them. In 1920 he nearly doubled his previous year's home run total, slugging an unheard-of 54. He also hit 36 doubles and 9 triples and drove in 137 runs—all in just 458 at bats.

No one had ever seen a batter hit balls harder than the Babe did. When pitching great Walter Johnson was asked later if Ruth hit the longest home runs he'd ever seen, the Big Train had to think. Finally, he replied, "I don't know who hit the longest ball, but I can tell you one thing I always noticed—the balls Ruth hit always got smaller faster than anybody else's, on their way out of the park."

Ruth upped his record again in 1921, to 59, but after that his totals began to settle down. In the five seasons spanning 1922–26, his highest total was 47—still enough to win the home run race most years, but no longer breathtakingly beyond what others were hitting.

THE PINNACLE

As the 1927 season dawned, the Yankees had something to prove. They'd lost a heartbreaking World Series to St. Louis in 1926—and despite the presence of Ruth and other stars, the team had just one World Series victory (in 1923) to show for four A.L. pennants since 1921.

The Babe himself had a lot to prove as well. He was coming off of a great season, in which he'd batted .372 with 47 home runs. But he'd also attempted an ill-advised steal in

"THE BALLS RUTH HIT ALWAYS GOT SMALLER FASTER THAN ANYBODY ELSE'S."

Ned Williamson set the last record for single-season home runs at 27 in 1884, before Ruth started setting his own records in 1919.

the ninth inning of the final game of the 1926 World Series, with the Yankees down by a run. When he was thrown out, the Series was over, and Ruth had had the whole winter to think about it.

Ruth found himself in the midst of what may have been the most powerful lineup in baseball history in 1927. Leadoff hitter Earl Combs hit .356. Bob Meusel hit .337, and he and Tony Lazzeri each knocked in more than 100 runs. And then there was Lou Gehrig, who reached his full potential that season. Gehrig hit an astounding .373 in 1927, but his other totals were even more amazing: 52 doubles, 18 triples, 47 home runs, and 175 runs batted in.

In this gaudy lineup, even Babe Ruth had to do something extraordinary to earn the limelight. And so he did. Entering the last month of the season with 43 home runs, he went on a torrid tear, seemingly slamming another one almost every game.

On September 30, 1927, the Yankees' next-to-last game of the year, the Babe's home run total had reached 59, matching his career high. Stepping to the plate in the eighth inning of a tied game at Yankee Stadium, he took two pitches and then swung.

From all accounts, the ball got small very quickly, ending up far into the right field bleachers for home run number 60. The Babe,

showman to the end, then took a slow and triumphant tour around the bases.

Babe Ruth, a legend even while he played, had done it again.

MOMENTS AFTER Ruth launched his record 60th home run in 1927. This record stood until Roger Maris hit his 61st in 1961.

Babe Ruth's Home Run Record

Year	Team	Number of Home Runs
1914	Boston (A)	0
1915	Boston (A)	4
1916	Boston (A)	3
1917	Boston (A)	2
1918	Boston (A)	11
1919	Boston (A)	29
1920	New York (A)	54
1921	New York (A)	59
1922	New York (A)	35
1923	New York (A)	41
1924	New York (A)	46
1925	New York (A)	25
1926	New York (A)	47
1927	New York (A)	60
1928	New York (A)	54
1929	New York (A)	46
1930	New York (A)	49
1931	New York (A)	46
1932	New York (A)	41
1933	New York (A)	34
1934	New York (A)	22
1935	Boston (N)	6
Total		714

RUTH'S HOME RUN PERFORMANCE peaked at 60 in 1927, but six years earlier, in 1921, he scored one homer short of that record, closing the season with 59.

THE MAN THEY CALLED HACK

1930 was a good year for hitters all around. In fact, the National League's overall batting average was .303. But the undisputed leader was Hack Wilson, who clubbed an N.L. record 56 homers, while hitting .356 and driving in an all-time record 191 runs. He also led the league in walks with 105, and slugging average with .723. He had 208 hits, 35 doubles, and scored 146 runs. The portly Wilson even hit six triples. Despite these heroics, Wilson's Cubs finished in second place behind the Cardinals.

THE AMAZING SEASON

The Lively Ball Era, which began in 1920, was in full flower throughout the '20s. Every year, it seemed, someone would set a new modern-era hitting record: George Sisler's 257 hits in 1920, Babe Ruth's 119 extra-base hits in 1921, Rogers Hornsby's .424 batting average in 1924—all set new marks. So did Ruth's 54 home runs in 1920, followed by 59 in 1921, and 60 in 1927.

Even fans got used to endless hitting exploits during the 1920s, they couldn't have been prepared for 1930, the height of the sluggers' era.

HACK WILSON COMPLETED five of his 12 seasons with a batting average over .300. He finished his career with a lifetime average of .307 and a single-season record of 191 RBI.

In 1930, the National League *as a whole* hit .303. Take a moment to think about that: The average player in the National League that year hit over .300—and this included pitchers, who then as now went to the plate in the N.L.

The hitters' dominance in 1930 was widespread. The New York Yankees had a pitcher, Red Ruffing, who hit .374, with four home runs. Across the river, the New York Giants' team batting average was .319. Giants' shortstop Travis Jackson hit .339, but was just fourth on his team in batting average, behind Bill Terry (.401), Fred Lindstrom, and Mel Ott.

But despite such hitting heroics, the Giants finished third in 1930. Every member of the starting lineup of the first place St. Louis

RBI in a Year—Top 10

Name	Year	Number of RBI
Hack Wilson	1930	191
Lou Gehrig	1931	184
Hank Greenberg	1937	183
Lou Gehrig	1927	175
Jimmie Foxx	1938	175
Lou Gehrig	1930	174
Babe Ruth	1921	171
Chuck Klein	1930	170
Hank Greenberg	1935	170
Jimmie Foxx	1932	169

Cardinals hit over .300. And on the bench they had players who hit .396, .374, and .366. The Cardinals scored 1,004 runs, more than six and a half a game.

In other words, it was a year when anything could happen. Still, no one predicted that a short, squat outfielder named Hack Wilson would be the man who would step forward and set two remarkable hitting records—one of which lasted for 68 years, and the other of which remains unbroken today.

A MAN CALLED HACK

At just 5 feet 6 inches tall and 190 pounds or more, Hack Wilson may have been the most oddly proportioned player in the Major Leagues. "One's first impression is of the amazing immensity of this man, the compact bulk of him," one writer marveled in 1929. "The barrel-like chest, huge powerful shoulders, long, thick arms, short, thick neck, broad face and large head make him appear dangerously top-heavy, because from the waist down, he has the figure of a dancer."

Wilson had built his physique through years of hard manual labor. He quit school at age 14 and went to work in his father's print shop. He worked 12 hours a day, with only a half-hour break for lunch. "I crammed my lunch in five minutes and used the other 25 for playing baseball," he recalled later. "Even in those days I pictured myself as a big leaguer."

His dream took a while to come true, as he took a winding course through a variety of minor league towns. Everywhere he went—Martinsburg, West Virginia, Portsmouth, Virginia—he hit with power. In 1923, his hitting exploits became impossible for the Major Leagues to ignore, and Wilson was signed by the big-league New York Giants.

In 1926 he moved to the Cubs, and here his great years began. He hit over .300 for five straight seasons, and consistently slugged more than 30 home runs and drove in more than 100 runs. He was not the greatest player of his era, but he was a

THE POWER behind Wilson's form can be seen in this swing from his record-breaking 1930 season with Chicago.

consistently strong hitter, until 1930. In 1930 he became something more.

THE BIGGEST YEAR

In 1930 Hack Wilson slugged 56 home runs, a National League record that would not be bested until Mark McGwire and Sammy Sosa staged their thrilling home run chase in 1998. Ironically, it was a record that lasted far longer than Babe Ruth's more famous American League record of 60 in 1927, which was overtaken by Roger Maris 34 years later.

But if he had to surrender the home run crown after nearly seven decades, Hack Wilson still holds a record that no one else in the Majors has yet reached. He drove in an astounding 191 runs in 1930. Amusingly, Wilson's record stood at 190 RBI until 1999, when researchers uncovered one RBI that hadn't been properly tallied. The last thing modern record-seekers needed to hear was that Wilson was extending his lead decades after the fact!

Wilson never had another year that matched his monster 1930 performance, and by 1934 poor conditioning had driven him from the game. But his string of fine seasons, and one transcendent one, gained him a place in the Hall of Fame in 1979.

DID HE OR DIDN'T HE?

When is a moment not a moment? Babe Ruth allegedly pointed to the bleachers in the fifth inning of Game Three of the 1932 World Series between the Yankees and the Cubs at Wrigley Field, as if to predict a home run. Cubs pitcher Charlie Root insisted that, had Ruth called his shot, Root would have dusted him. But Lou Gehrig, who followed Ruth's homer with a clout of his own, said "What do you think of the nerve of that big monkey calling his shot and getting away with it?" Baseball's most legendary controversy notwithstanding, the Yankees won the next day to sweep the Series.

RUTH'S MOMENT AT WRIGLEY

Of all the home runs hit by Babe Ruth—714 in the regular season, 15 in the World Series, the first ever in an All-Star Game, and countless exhibition blasts—none so made his legend as the "Called Shot Home Run" at Wrigley Field, Chicago, during the 1932 World Series.

The Babe was already the most celebrated player in the game. He would have been no less without this home run. But it would nevertheless become one of the most celebrated moments of his extraordinary career. And amazingly, it may never even have happened.

The 1932 pennant was the only one the Yankees would win between 1928 and 1936. It was the Babe's last. Murderer's Row, the slugging line-up of the 1927 season, had moved on. Joe McCarthy had replaced Miller Huggins as Yankee manager.

Mark Koenig, the fine Yankee shortstop of the roaring '20s, was now in a Cubs uniform, as luck would have it, preparing to face his former teammates in the World Series.

Ruth was older, heavier, and slower by 1932, but still the game's ultimate gate attraction. The return of the Babe and the Yankees to the World Series convinced the Cubs to erect a temporary second deck over the Wrigley Field bleachers, permitting the stadium's attendance to reach nearly 50,000.

RUTH'S "CALLED SHOT HOME RUN" became legendary almost immediately after it happened. It has been immortalized in paintings, like the one shown above.

Everyone who had a ticket for Game Three, October 1, 1932, would have an opinion on the event they were about to see. The spectators included Governor Franklin D. Roosevelt of New York, who was running for president, and 14-year old Little Ray Kelly, the Babe's own personal mascot, who, with his father, were guests of the Babe at the Series.

The Chicago pitcher was 15-game-winner Charlie Root—which was, coincidentally, how Yankee owner Jacob Ruppert pronounced "Ruth" in his German accent. Ruth vs. Root.

PLAYERS VOTE KOENIG A HALF-SHARE

The Yanks had won the first two games of the Series in New York, but there was an unpleasant edge to the competition. Koenig, their old friend, had not been treated well by the Cubs, in dividing up World Series shares. (The players vote on the division before the World Series is played.) Although he had been there for only six weeks, and was awarded a half-share, this was considered cheap by the Yankees. As a result, a good many insulting remarks were being hurled across the dugouts. Some of it was directed at the Babe, some questioning his ancestry. That was always a sure way to get his temper cooking.

In the first inning, the 37-year-old Bambino popped a home run to put the Yankees in the lead 3–0. When he came up in the fifth, the score was 4–4. What happened next came to be known as the "Called Shot Home Run."

The first pitch was a called strike. At that point, Ruth apparently pointed. Some felt he was pointing at Root, as though to say "that's only one." Some felt he was pointing to the bleachers, as though predicting a home run. Twice more, following pitches, he gestured.

The count went to two and two, and again, apparently for a fourth time, Ruth pointed. This time, as he would later say, "the good Lord was with me," and the ball again reached the bleachers for his 15th and last World Series home run.

He laughed and waved as he circled the bases, the homer leading to a 7–5 Yankee win, and a 3–0 lead in games, with a World Series sweep in line for the next day.

A MOMENT FOR THE AGES

What really happened?

Root said if Ruth had pointed at the bleachers, he would have hit him with the next pitch. But his catcher, Gabby Hartnett, swore he pointed at the bleachers. Lou Gehrig, on deck, said he pointed at the bleachers. (Gehrig followed with a home run himself.) Cubs' manager Charlie Grimm said he pointed at the mound. Little Ray Kelly, with a good seat near the Yankee dugout, swore it was the bleachers.

It hardly mattered. It took on a life of its own and became one of the great moments in baseball history. Only the Babe ever really knew, and by his own admission, he was a lucky man that day.

Of course, with more than 700 career home runs, he had more going for him than luck.

CHICAGO CUBS' PITCHER Charlie Root who delivered the pitch that Ruth launched into the bleachers. Root suggested that, had he seen Ruth call the home run, his next pitch would have knocked Ruth down.

RUTH CROSSES HOME PLATE and is congratulated by Lou Gehrig, who was on deck when Ruth hit the "called shot." Gehrig insisted that Ruth pointed to the bleachers. Others said differently, and the controversy goes on.

THE FIRST ALL-STAR GAME

Chicago Tribune sportswriter Arch Ward dreamed of an All-Star Game, and, as sometimes happens, his dream came true. The first major league All-Star Game was held at Comiskey Park in Chicago on July 6, 1933 in conjunction with the Century of Progress Exposition. The National League was managed by John McGraw, while the American League reins were held by Connie Mack. The A.L. prevailed, 4-2, on the strength of a home run by who else, Babe Ruth.

A GATHERING OF GREATS

THE MANAGERS for the first all-star teams. Connie Mack (left) managed the American League, and John McGraw (right) managed the National League.

In 1911, following the sudden and shocking death of pitcher Addie Joss from tuberculosis, many of baseball's superstars gathered in Cleveland for an impromptu benefit for Joss's family. One famous photograph shows a line-up that included future Hall of Famers Ty Cobb (wearing a Cleveland uniform because his Detroit uniform was lost in transit), Tris Speaker, Sam Crawford, Frank Baker, Joe Wood, and Walter Johnson. The game they played against the Cleveland Naps that day was, in many ways, the first All-Star Game.

After that, the idea of an official All-Star Game, pitting the best players of the National and American Leagues against each other, kicked around for a while, but no one ever took the steps needed to make it a reality. That is, until 1933, when *Chicago Tribune* sports editor Arch Ward decided that his city's World's Fair (dubbed the Century of Progress Exposition) needed some livening up. How better to liven up a party than by organizing a true All-Star Game?

Remarkably, Arch Ward's idea gained momentum. Both leagues were willing to give a one-time All-Star Game a try, and baseball fans were ecstatic at the idea. The teams were picked by a nationwide poll—not that much different from the way players are voted in today—and the fans came through. They picked rosters of players who remain legends today, nearly 70 years later.

THE GREATEST LINE-UP EVER?

Imagine sitting in the stands of Chicago's Comiskey Park on July 6, 1933. In the dugout and on the field before you stand the giants of the game. And not just the best players of their time—many of those were among the

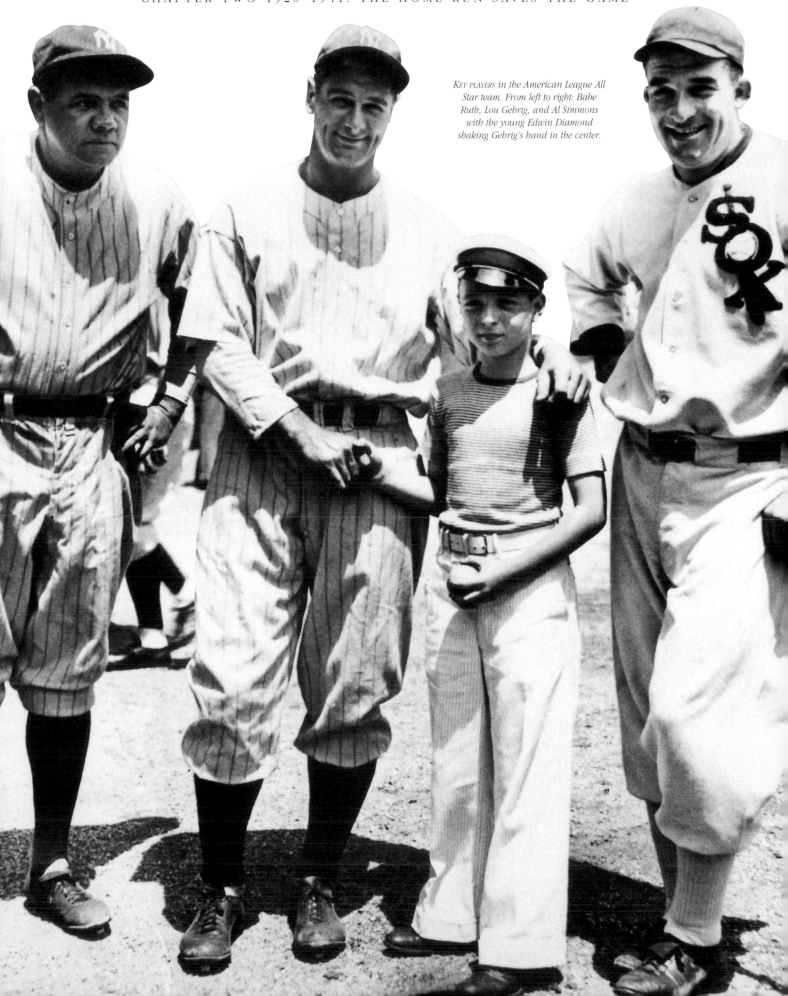

KEY PLAYERS in the American League All Star team. From left to right: Babe Ruth, Lou Gehrig, and Al Simmons with the young Edwin Diamond shaking Gehrig's hand in the center.

"GET 50,000
PEOPLE IN A BALL
PARK AND BABE
RUTH NEVER
DISAPPOINTS."

greatest ever to play baseball during its long
and colorful history.

Who was at Comiskey that day? The
National League team included future Hall of
Famers Frankie Frisch (.316 lifetime batting
average); Bill Terry (.341 lifetime average,
with a high of .401 in 1930); Chuck Klein
(who'd lead the league with a .368 batting
average in '33); Paul Waner (3,152 career
hits); Pie Traynor (.320 career average);
Gabby Hartnett, Chick Hafey, and Carl
Hubbell (253 lifetime wins).

The American League team wasn't anything to scoff at either. At first base it had Lou
Gehrig, still in the glorious prime of his
career. Gehrig's All-Star teammates included
Charlie Gehringer (a brilliant second baseman
who also hit .320 over 19 seasons); Bucketfoot
Al Simmons (.334 lifetime average); Jimmie
Foxx (one of the most feared sluggers of all
time, with 534 career home runs); Joe Cronin
(a brilliant player-manager and career .301
hitter); Bill Dickey (the longtime Yankee backstop, and still considered one of the five best
catchers of all time); Lefty Gomez (a star
Yankee pitcher during their first dynasty); and
Lefty Grove (a 300-game winner despite not
reaching the Majors until he was 25 years old.)

Oh, and the A.L. team had one more drawing
card: an outfielder named Babe Ruth.

THE BABE, OF COURSE

Despite the presence of so much offensive
firepower, the game started out as a pitcher's
duel. Strangely enough, it was A.L. starting
pitcher (and eventual winner) Lefty Gomez
who drove in the first run of the game, singling in Jimmie Dykes in the second inning.

Then, in the third, Ruth came to the plate
with Charlie Gehringer on base. He was facing
St. Louis Cardinals' pitcher Bill Hallahan, and
Hallahan chose to give the Babe a fastball.

Big mistake. Ruth's bat hitting the ball
sounded like a rifle shot. This was no majes-
tic, soaring fly, but a laser beam of a line
drive that disappeared into the stands before
the right fielder could turn around. The Babe
had given the American League a 3–0 lead.

But Ruth wasn't done with his All-Star
heroics. Frankie Frisch homered and the
National League scored two runs in the sixth
inning to draw within 3–2. And though the
A.L. added another run in the bottom of the
sixth to make it 4–2, the game was still very
much in doubt when the N.L. got a man on
base in the eighth.

Team Rosters for First All-Star Game

Comiskey Park, Chicago—July 6, 1933

NATIONAL LEAGUE			AMERICAN LEAGUE		
Player	Team	Position	Player	Team	Position
Jimmie Wilson	St. Louis	Catcher	Rick Ferrell	Boston	Catcher
Gabby Hartnett	Chicago	Catcher	Lou Gehrig	New York	1st base
Bill Terry	New York	1st base	Charlie Gehringer	Detroit	2nd base
Frankie Frisch	St. Louis	2nd base	Joe Cronin	Washington	Shortstop
Dick Bartell	Philadelphia	Shortstop	Jimmy Dykes	Chicago	3rd base
Woody English	Chicago	Shortstop	Babe Ruth	New York	Right field
Pepper Martin	St. Louis	3rd base	Sam West	St. Louis	Center field
Chuck Klein	Philadelphia	Right field	Al Simmons	Chicago	Center field
Paul Waner	Pittsburgh	Right field			and Left field
Wally Berger	Boston	Center field	Ben Chapman	New York	Left field and
Chick Hafey	Cincinnati	Left field			Right field
Bill Hallahan	St. Louis	Pitcher	General Crowder	Washington	Pitcher
Carl Hubbell	New York	Pitcher	Lefty Gomez	New York	Pitcher
Lon Warneke	Chicago	Pitcher	Lefty Grove	Philadelphia	Pitcher
Tony Cuccinello	Brooklyn	Pinch hitter	Earl Averill	Cleveland	Pinch hitter
Lefty O'Doul	New York	Pinch hitter			
Pie Traynor	Pittsburgh	Pinch hitter			

Then Chick Hafey hit a long fly to right field. The ball appeared headed for the stands—or at least seemed guaranteed to bounce around the deepest outfield, setting up a big inning for the N.L. But suddenly, out of nowhere, came Babe Ruth, running like a far younger and svelter man, to pluck the ball out of the air.

That was the National League's last gasp. The final score was 4–2 in favor of the American League. Or should that be 4–2, Babe Ruth? Said National League manager John McGraw, "Ruth's homer won the game and he saved it for 'em with that catch. The old boy came through for them when they needed him.

THE AMERICAN LEAGUE'S first All Star team. Lou Gehrig and Babe Ruth are standing next to each other, third and fourth from the left. Manager Connie Mack is standing also, easily recognized in a suit.

CONSISTENT CARL

In the 1934 All-Star Game, Carl Hubbell of the New York Giants drew the starting nod for the National League, whose manager, Bill Terry, thought that Hubbell's screwball would handcuff the powerful hitters of the American League. Hubbell got off to a shaky start, as Charlie Gehringer's single was followed by a walk to Heinie Manush. The next hitter was Babe Ruth, who took a called third strike. Lou Gehrig followed and went down swinging, as did Jimmie Foxx as Hubbell struck out the side and ended the scoring threat. Al Simmons and Joe Cronin struck out to start the second, before Bill Dickey broke the streak by singling. Hubbell had fanned five future Hall of Famers in succession. The American League went on to win the game 9-7.

A LONG ROAD

Today, Carl Hubbell is remembered as "The Meal Ticket," a pitcher so consistently brilliant for the New York Giants that you could just about pencil him in for a win ahead of time. What isn't so clearly recalled is that Hubbell was 25 years old before he pitched in the big leagues. Few players have ever traveled a more frustrating road to a Hall of Fame career.

The cause of all Hubbell's problems was a pitch he developed in 1925, one that would later make him famous. Released with a sharp twist of the arm and wrist toward his body, the ball would spin and break in the opposite direction from a typical curveball, befuddling hitters. The first catcher to receive one of these odd pitches said, "Well, that's the screwiest damn pitch I ever saw," and the screwball got its name.

The problem was that, despite his tremendous success in the minors, Hubbell had terrible trouble convincing major league coaches and managers that he could throw the screwball without ruining his arm. In spring training with the Detroit Tigers in 1926, he was forbidden to throw the pitch. Deprived of his best weapon, he didn't show much promise—and, though he went to spring training three times with the Tigers, he never pitched a single inning with the club, not even in an exhibition game.

> "I RESPECTED EVERY ONE OF THEM, BUT I HAD NO FEAR OF ANY KIND."

In 1928, he was released. "Hell, I should have had the word 'reject' written over my uniform," he said later. The only team that was interested in him was a minor league club in Beaumont, Texas. There, at least, he was allowed to throw his screwball again, and there his luck finally began to turn.

THE BREAKS

In later years, Carl Hubbell would marvel at how quickly his luck changed. A New York Giants scout named Dick Kinsella happened to be attending the 1928 Democratic National Convention in Houston, and happened to go to a game that pitted Houston against Beaumont—with Hubbell pitching.

Unlike the coaches in Detroit, Kinsella knew what he was seeing as he watched Hubbell's screwball mow down the opposing hitters. The scout hurried to the telephone and told Giants manager John McGraw that the team's pitching problems were solved. "And by God, within about three or four days I was on my way to join the Giants," Hubbell recalled later, still amazed at how fast events had moved after such a long, hopeless wait.

After finally reaching the Major Leagues, Hubbell never looked back. He finished the 1928 season 10–6 with a 2.83 earned run average, one of the best in the league. But that was just a warm-up for his best years. Between 1933 and 1937, he won more than 20 games five seasons in a row, leading the league in both wins and ERA three times in that span. He was so dependable, so consistent, that people began calling him "The Meal Ticket."

In 1933 Hubbell led the Giants to their first World Series victory in 11 years, over the Washington Senators. All he did in that Series was pitch 20 innings in two starts without giving up an earned run.

But it was the following season that saw Hubbell perform the feat that he will always be remembered best for: He struck out a veritable Murderers' Row of batters in the 1934 All-Star Game.

FIVE MEN OUT

Hubbell had pitched in the first All-Star Game, in 1933. After leading the Giants to a World Championship that season, he was tapped to be the starter in the second All–Star Game, held at New York's Polo Grounds, his home turf, on July 10, 1934.

NEW YORK GIANTS' pitching ace Carl Hubbell was pitted against the impressive hitting roster of the American League in the 1934 All-Star Game.

Hubbell never admitted to any nerves over facing the powerful American League line-up. "I respected every one of them, but I had no fear of any kind," he said later. "I didn't think they had ever seen any screwball pitchers before. I figured I had everything to gain and nothing to lose."

The game didn't start promisingly for Hubbell. The first man up, Charlie Gehringer, hit a single, and then Heinie Manush walked. Suddenly there were two men on, no outs, with Babe Ruth coming to the plate. The National League infielders gathered at the mound to give advice, but Hubbell wasn't listening to them. "I was busy having a meeting with myself," he said. "I told myself, 'You're not going to be around here long if you don't settle down.'"

Hubbell decided to rely on his meal ticket, the screwball. With the count at a ball and two strikes, he threw one to Ruth, who could only watch as it broke over the plate for strike three.

Next up was Lou Gehrig, then at the height of his career. Gehrig struck out on a full count. As Gehrig was going down, however, the runners on base pulled off a double steal.

Jimmie Foxx, one of the greatest home run hitters in baseball history, stepped up to the plate. With two strikes, he could do nothing but flail at Hubbell's screwball. Strike three, and the side retired.

In the second inning, the fans knew that Hubbell had begun an amazing streak against the best American League hitters. Now he had to face Al Simmons, on his way to a .344 season. But Simmons had no chance against the screwball, striking out swinging. And so did Joe Cronin, a lifetime .301 hitter.

Bill Dickey broke the remarkable streak with a single, but Hubbell came back to fan the American League's pitcher, Lefty Gomez. In his first two innings, Carl Hubbell had faced nine future Hall of Famers, and struck out six of them—including five in a row. And though the A.L. went on to win the game, 9–7, it was Hubbell's remarkable performance that has become baseball legend.

AFTER THE FIRST TWO MEN GOT ON BASE, Hubbell struck out the next five batters. In order, from top to bottom: Babe Ruth, Lou Gehrig, Jimmie Foxx, Al Simmons, and Joe Cronin.

LET THERE BE LIGHT

President Franklin Delano Roosevelt flipped a switch in the White House at 8:30 p.m. E.S.T. on the night of May 24, 1935 to officially turn on the lights at Cincinnati's Crosley Field, where the Reds defeated the Phillies 2-1 to win the first night game in major league history. The first experiment with night baseball had been conducted in Hull, Massachusetts in 1880, just one year after the invention of the light bulb, but the idea didn't catch on until the early 1930s, when minor league and Negro league teams began using lights with regularity. Negro league owner J. L. Wilkinson prophetically declared that, "What talkies are to movies, lights will be to baseball."

IN THE GLOW OF ELECTRIC LIGHT

Almost as soon as baseball became a moneymaking proposition in the mid-1800s, team owners and town officials tried to figure out ways to play the game at night. It was frustrating that the only times that it was possible to play baseball were on weekdays (when many people were at work or in school) and on weekends. In the Northeast, where baseball was most popular, days grew short by the end of summer, and many a game had to be halted early because the batter and fielders couldn't detect the ball in the encroaching dusk. In addition,

PRESIDENT ROOSEVELT PRESSED a telegraph key to signal the official lighting of Crosley Field. Seconds later, on cue from the President, this man switched on the lights at the park, and initiated night baseball in the Major Leagues.

Sunday baseball was prohibited in many towns, particularly in New England.

What to do? When Thomas Edison unveiled his amazing new invention, the lightbulb, on New Year's Eve, 1879, the solution became obvious: Illuminate the field with electric lights!

Less than a year after Edison introduced his great creation to the public, a pair of Boston-area department stores did just that. On September 2, 1880, teams of employees representing Jordan Marsh & Co. and R. H. White & Co. met at Nantasket Beach in Hull, Massachusetts, for a game beginning after sundown.

Three hundred fans gathered to watch the spectacle, which was illuminated by three towers, each holding 36 lamps powered by an electric generator. "The flood of mellow light, thrown upon the field between 8 and 9:30 p.m., allowed nine innings to be played," one newspaper reported, but this was one of the few positive comments the game, which ended in a 16–16 tie, received in the press. "The light was quite imperfect and there were lots of errors made," the account continued. "The players had to bat and throw with caution."

This particular eyewitness's final judgment on the potential of night baseball was not a kind one: "The showing was far from

impressive. None of the reporters believed the idea to be at all practicable."

ONE STEP FORWARD, TWO STEPS BACK

Despite such comments, in the years that followed the 1880 game, Negro League and minor leagues experimented with games under the lights. Always the results were mixed, but always they were encouraging enough to lead someone else to try it as well.

The first night game ever played in a big league park took place in Cincinnati on June 19, 1909. Although pitting two Elks Lodge teams against each other, this game was organized and watched carefully by Cincinnati Reds president August Herrmann and other baseball officials, who saw it as a test for possible adoption of night games in the Majors.

The game was played under the harsh glare of lights hung from 14 light stands, and was judged a middling success. Hermann, looking on the bright side, said, "Night baseball has come to stay," but others complained

again that the ball was hard to follow. The 4,500 fans in attendance had particular trouble following the flight of outfield flies.

A year later, Chicago White Sox owner Charles Comiskey tried again, sponsoring a night game between two Chicago amateur teams at his new Comiskey Park. According to reports at the time, the lights were plenty bright—so bright, in fact, that they had to be shielded with strips of black cloth, which cast strange shadows across the field. Worse, the lamps dimmed as the game went on, leaving the field in semi-darkness.

Clearly, major league night baseball was not yet here to stay.

LET THERE BE LIGHT, AT LAST

Night baseball finally began to gain in popularity in the 1930s, two decades after the experiment at Comiskey Park. Beginning in 1930, when minor league teams in Independence, Kansas, Decatur, Illinois, and elsewhere, installed permanent lights for use in league games, more and

THE MOISTURE IN THE NIGHT AIR created a pool of haze around the lights in the first night game, played at Crosley Field in Cincinnati.

ACTION UNDER THE LIGHTS could be just as exciting to watch as during day games (above). A fan sitting along the left field line would have had this view of the first night game at Crosley Field (right).

more minor and Negro league teams began playing night games under installed or temporary lights. The innovation increased crowds and brought in more much-needed cash.

The Major Leagues, however, were very cautious about trying night baseball again. It wasn't until May 24, 1935, that the Majors gave lights another chance. What made this attempt so significant was that it would take place during an actual major league game—not an exhibition.

Appropriately, the 1935 experiment was held in Cincinnati, site of the first night game in a major league park back in 1909. More than 20,000 fans packed Crosley Field to watch the Reds play the Philadelphia Phillies; average day game attendance in Cincinnatti in 1935 was between 1,500 and 2,000. The parking lots near the field were packed, as were streetcars.

At 8:30 p.m., President Franklin D. Roosevelt pressed a telegraph key in the White House that officially bathed the field in light. Fireworks filled the sky and bands began to play. Despite the potential for distraction, the game was a clean, well-played affair, with the Reds winning, 2–1.

Or, as *The Sporting News* said: "Furthermore, here's something no baseball owner can laugh off; they filled the park to capacity for a mid-week game and then had to lock the gates."

Negro league owner J.L. Wilkinson put the successful future of night baseball even more succinctly, stating: "What talkies are to movies, lights will be to baseball."

RAPID ROBERT

Hall of Fame pitcher Bob Feller's nickname reflects the speed of his fastball, but could just as easily reflect the speed of his arrival to the Majors. Before his 18th birthday, Feller had already appeared in 14 major league games for the Cleveland Indians. On August 23, 1936, Feller started his first game and struck out 15 St. Louis Browns in the Indians' 4-1 victory. Feller won 266 games despite missing four seasons to serve in the United States Navy. His military service was as impressive as his fastball and "Rapid Robert" was awarded numerous battle citations.

THE SCHOOLBOY

Many great pitchers—from Carl Hubbell to Tom Glavine—are shelled in their first starts, driven from the mound to wonder if they'll ever be able to get big league hitters out.

But not Feller, the one they called "Schoolboy." He was just 17 when he was signed by the Cleveland Indians during the 1936 season, but even before he pitched an inning for them he'd become a legend.

On vacation from high school in Adel, Iowa, Feller journeyed to Cleveland during the summer of 1936 with an eye to earning some money playing semipro ball. As soon as he started playing in the big city, though, word began to spread about the fresh-faced kid pitcher with the blinding speed. The Indians sent a scout to watch him pitch in a sandlot game, and the scout came home raving about "the best fastball" he'd seen in years.

The Indians signed Feller immediately, and brought him to the big league club. But the Indians were a good team that year, with a strong pitching staff, so the phenom got to pitch only in relief here and there. He was impressive even in these spots, and showed a glimpse of what he was capable of in an exhibition game against the St. Louis Browns: He struck out eight of the nine men he faced.

YOUNG PITCHER Bob Feller with his father. Feller started in the Majors when he was only 17, hence his nickname "Schoolboy."

This flashy showing earned him the first start of his career, on August 23, 1936.

UNDER THE SPOTLIGHT

August 23 was a hot midsummer day in 1936, but Feller didn't care. He was getting a chance he couldn't have dreamed of just a few weeks before, when he'd been just another teenage schoolboy playing sandlot ball. The young pitcher was teamed with catcher Charley (Greek) George, another rookie starting his first big league game. "The Greek was four years older than I was, but, in effect, we were just a couple of kids stepping off the deep end together," Feller wrote later in *Now Pitching: Bob Feller* (1990).

The press was surprised that Indians' manager Steve O'Neill would choose to start the untested 17-year-old. Feller overheard reporters asking O'Neill, "Does this mean that you've given up on the pennant?"

O'Neill got annoyed at the question. "We've got to start him sometime, and this is as good a spot as any," he said, not exactly a ringing endorsement.

O'Neill's lack of faith didn't bother him, Feller said. It just made him more determined.

Whether it was determination or luck, Feller was at the top of his game that day. "My control was better than it had ever been," he said. And his fastball was slamming into the catcher's glove. After five innings, Feller had struck out 10 Browns.

Sitting in the dugout, Feller found himself thinking about the major league strikeout record for a single game: 17, held by Dizzy Dean. But then, mature beyond his years, he decided that it was dangerous to start dreaming about such things. He might lose his concentration, and the game. "As I sat there, I decided not to think about a record," he said. "Not to think about anything."

After seven innings, Feller had struck out an amazing 14 men. After that, though, the blistering heat started to get to him. He finished the game with "only" 15 strikeouts—but

also with a 4–1 win, and one of the most remarkable first starts in baseball history.

RAPID ROBERT, HALL OF FAMER

Feller would start seven more times during the 1936 season, and if none of the starts were as stellar as the first, they gave abundant evidence of his extraordinary talent.

From the start, this young man could simply blow his fastball by the best hitters in the game, then freeze them with his deadly curve.

Like many flamethrowers, though, he had to learn to control his pitches. Still, he frequently led the American League in strikeouts. In 1938, for example, he struck out 240 men while walking 208 in 277 innings.

What Feller always did was pitch an enormous number of innings—as many as 371 in a season—and win. He had seasons with 27, 26, 25, 24, and 22 wins, and his lifetime total of 266 would have been far higher if he hadn't missed nearly four entire seasons while performing heroically in World War II.

Bob Feller was elected to the Hall of Fame in 1962, the schoolboy who made good.

IN FELLER'S FIRST major league start he struck out 15 batters, two short of Dizzy Dean's then record of 17 in a single game.

FELLER TRADED one uniform for another to serve in the navy during World War II. Baseball fans still recognized him out of his pinstripes.

LIGHTNING STRIKES TWICE

*Cincinnati Reds pitcher Johnny Vander Meer pitched a no-hitter against the Braves on June 11, 1938.
His next start was on June 15, the first ever night game at Brooklyn's Ebbets Field. Vander Meer was honored before the
game, attended by 700 of his family and friends, and also by Babe Ruth. Despite three wild pitches and three walks
in the ninth inning, Vander Meer notched an unprecedented second no-hitter in a row. In his next start, he lasted
3 2/3 innings before allowing a hit, bringing his remarkable streak to 21 2/3 innings.*

JOHNNY WHO?

Who was the only major league pitcher ever to throw a no-hitter in two consecutive starts?

A few likely candidates leap instantly to mind. Nolan Ryan, he of the seven career no-hitters. Sandy Koufax, who often seemed just an inch away from throwing a perfect game in every start. Perhaps Bob Feller, or Walter Johnson, or Bob Gibson—great pitchers whose overpowering fastballs made them almost unhittable at times.

Nope, none of these. As most fans of baseball history know, the only man to pitch a no-hitter, then come right back and do it again, was a wild left-hander named Johnny Vander Meer. He was a talented pitcher who spent most of his career with the Cincinnati Reds, and tended to mix good seasons (18–12, 16–13) with mediocre ones (15–16, 9–14). His career record, 119–121, defines mediocrity.

But on June 11th and 15th, Johnny Vander Meer pitched no-hitters in two consecutive starts. And that's an accomplishment that neither Ryan, nor Koufax, nor any other pitcher in major league history can claim.

YOUNG MAN WITH FASTBALL

Vandy could always throw hard. His problem, common among those with blazing fastballs,

**"I COULDN'T HIT
THE SIDE OF
A BARN WITH
A HANDFUL
OF PEAS."**

was getting the ball over the plate. The problem was so bad that it almost brought his major league career to a halt even before it started. In the minor leagues in 1936, when he was 21 years old, he found that he "couldn't hit the side of a barn with a handful of peas," he said. Worse, his shoulder was hurting. He lost his first two games of the season, and decided that, if things didn't turn around soon, he would retire.

But things did turn around, in a spectacular way. He won first five, then 10, then 15 in a row. And his stuff was overpowering. In one game, he struck out

82

20 opponents, and 16- or 17-strikeout games weren't rare. He ended the season 19–6, with 295 strikeouts.

These kinds of numbers will get you noticed. Vander Meer was signed by the Reds prior to the 1937 season. It was a learning year for him: He started nine games, relieved in nine others, and finished 3–5, with a 3.84 ERA.

The Reds' only concern was the same one that would bedevil Johnny Vander Meer throughout his career: His control. He pitched 84 innings in 1937, striking out 52 but walking 69, an unacceptable number. Vander Meer returned to the Reds in 1938. He was a member of the starting rotation from the beginning of the season, and though he still walked too many men, he kept his team in almost every game he

Plagued with control problems typical of fastball pitchers, Cincinnati Reds' pitcher Johnny Vander Meer could throw as many balls as he could strikes. The trick, however, was that, when his fastball landed, it was hard to hit and even harder to hit well.

pitched, and won more than his share.

Still, no one looking at the 23-year-old fastball pitcher would have guessed that in this, his first full season, he'd accomplish something no other pitcher ever has.

DOUBLE NO

By June 11, Vander Meer's record stood at 5–2. His opponent in Cincinnati that day was the lowly Boston Bees, managed by Casey Stengel. To the amazement of those who were watching, Vandy shut down the Bees without even a hit.

Four days later, Vander Meer was slated to pitch again, and this time people took notice. The game was against the Dodgers, in Brooklyn, and as it turned out it was the first major league night game ever played at Ebbets

Field. Among the 38,000 fans at the ballpark were 700 of Vander Meer's relatives and friends, there to present him with gifts in a pregame ceremony. Babe Ruth, Vander Meer's boyhood idol, was also in attendance.

This night, Vander Meer's fastball was back with all its speed and movement intact. Unfortunately, so was Johnny's typical lack of control. The Dodgers rarely hit the ball hard off of him, but he went to one 3–2 count after another, walking a total of eight men in the game.

In the ninth, with a 6–0 lead, Vandy still hadn't given up a hit. With one out, he walked Babe Phelps, Cookie Lavagetto, and Dolph Camilli. Suddenly, the bases were loaded, the no-hitter and shutout in jeopardy.

Vander Meer got Ernie Koy to ground to third, forcing pinch runner Goodwin Rosen at home plate. That brought Brooklyn's player-manager, Leo Durocher, to bat. "I hit the ball as good as I could hit it, a line drive," Durocher recalled, "which Harry Craft, their fine center fielder, caught right off his shoetops."

Somehow, against all odds, Vander Meer had done the seemingly impossible—one of the few baseball records that may someday be tied, but will probably never be broken.

The next day, local newspapers proclaimed the young lefty the "Biggest Star in the Baseball World." But Vander Meer didn't see the headlines. He was away from the glare of the spotlight, fishing in New Jersey.

THE FIRST NIGHT GAME to be held at Ebbets Field became host to another baseball first—Vander Meer's second consecutive no-hitter.

TEAMMATES help escort Vander Meer off the field after he completed his second consecutive no-hitter.

THE LUCKIEST MAN

*July 4, 1939 was Lou Gehrig Day at Yankee Stadium. 61,808 fans packed Yankee Stadium to
pay tribute to The Iron Horse, who became the first baseball player to have his uniform number four retired. In a
moving speech, Gehrig told the fans that: "Today...I consider myself...the luckiest man on the face of the earth."
On May 2nd, at Detroit, Gehrig had asked manager Joe McCarthy to remove him from the lineup, thus ending his
magnificent streak of 2,130 consecutive games played. Shortly thereafter, he was examined at the Mayo Clinic
and was diagnosed with Amyotrophic Lateral Sclerosis, known today as "Lou Gehrig's Disease." Gehrig was
elected to the Baseball Hall of Fame by special vote in December, 1939.*

UP FROM THE MEAN STREETS

Very few American heroes live up to their reputations. Lou Gehrig was one who did. A gentle, modest man, he inspired fierce loyalty and affection among everyone who knew him. He was, in the words of teammate Sam Jones, "the kind of boy if you had a son he's the kind of person you'd like your son to be."

Gehrig grew up in the tenements of New York City's Upper East Side, a neighborhood made up of "bewildering convolutions of narrow streets, twisting elevated railways, tall tenements, saloons,

LOU GEHRIG SPENT 17 YEARS, his entire career, in a Yankee uniform. His career ended on May 2, 1939, when he retired due to the effects of Amyotrophic Lateral Sclerosis, now called "Lou Gehrig's Disease."

pushcart merchants and an ever-flowing stream of humanity," in sportswriter Harry Brundige's words. It was a place where "gangsters, gunmen and gamblers lolled in the entrances of saloons, pool halls and wine rooms."

As a child, Gehrig escaped the neighborhood as much as possible—swimming in the Hudson River and (above all) playing baseball in Central Park. Though he usually played catcher, he was already developing into a strong hitter, and helped lead a schoolboy team to a Central Park championship.

Still, when he began to attend college at Columbia University in the fall of 1921, his goal was to play college sports while concentrating on developing his skills for a career as an engineer. In 1923, though, both of his parents became sick, and when the New York Yankees offered him a bonus to sign with the team, he accepted. "That bonus bought a lot of food, paid a lot of house rent and doctor bills," Gehrig said. "It certainly was a godsend."

A godsend for the Yankees as well.

THE IRON HORSE

Lou Gehrig's career with the Yankees is one of the most familiar in all of baseball history. After a couple of brief trials with the team, he arrived to stay in 1925, when he was 21 years old. Still, he spent most of the first couple of months on the bench, until the fateful day of June 2.

A FIXTURE ON FIRST BASE for the Yankees, Gehrig recorded a remarkable 19,510 put-outs throughout his career, ranking ninth for first basemen in history of the Major Leagues. Perhaps more impressive were the 2,130 consecutive games he played, a record that stood until Cal Ripken, Jr. broke it in 1995.

As the famous story goes, Yankee first baseman Wally Pipp had a headache that day. Manager Miller Huggins suggested that Pipp take the day off "and let this big, awkward kid see what he can do." All the big, awkward kid—Lou Gehrig—did was play in the next 2,130 games, until his retirement on May 2 1939. Wally Pipp didn't see much more action in 1925—but it was hard for even him to complain, once he saw how magnificent a ballplayer the kid was.

In his 17-year career, Lou Gehrig hit .340, with 493 home runs and 1,995 runs batted in, the third most of all time. He hit 49 home runs twice, and 47 and 46 in other seasons, and led the league with mind-boggling RBI totals: 184, 175, 174, 165. He hit over .350 six times, with an astonishing high of .379. He was named American League Most Valuable Player four times.

Perhaps most importantly, he helped lead the Yankees to six World Championships. How dominant were Lou Gehrig's Yankees? In

their six World Series, they won 24 games to their opponents' three.

GONE TOO SOON

During the second half of the 1938 season, the 35-year-old Gehrig at last seemed to be slowing down. He finished the year with a batting average of .295, the first time he'd hit below .300 since 1925. His home run and RBI totals were down as well. Nor was his fielding up to its usual standards. Could it be that the day-in, day-out grind of playing every single game was beginning to get to him?

Or could it be something far worse? As spring training began in 1939, it was obvious that Gehrig seemed stiff and sluggish at bat and in the field. The change from just two seasons earlier was startling and sad to everyone who knew and liked Lou.

Eight games into the 1939 season, Gehrig had managed just four singles in 28 at bats, for a miserable .143 batting average. He would miss pitches he once would have slammed, and he even fell in the field while chasing ground balls. Finally on May 2—after 2,130 consecutive games, a record that stood until Cal Ripken broke it in 1995—Gehrig asked out of the Yankee lineup.

At first, he maintained a brave face with reporters. "I believe I will be back in the lineup

"HE'S THE KIND OF PERSON YOU'D LIKE YOUR SON TO BE."

WITH A LIFETIME BATTING AVERAGE of .340, including six seasons over .350, Gehrig's bat was legendary. He totaled an impressive 1,995 RBIs throughout his career, a total bettered only by Hank Aaron at 2,297 and Babe Ruth at 2,213.

Lou Gehrig— Lifetime Stats

Games Played	2,164
At Bats	8,001
Runs	1,888
Hits	2,721
Doubles	534
Triples	163
Home Runs	493
RBI	1,995
Batting Average	.340
Stolen Bases	102

in three weeks," he told reporters. But inside, he must have known something was seriously wrong. He entered the Mayo Clinic for tests, and found out that the news couldn't have been worse: He had amyotrophic lateral sclerosis (ALS), which is nearly always fatal and which today is best known as "Lou Gehrig's Disease."

Lou Gehrig died on June 2, 1941, just short of his 38th birthday. But before he died, he got the chance to learn how much the people of New York—and baseball fans everywhere— loved, respected, and admired him. July 4, 1939, was Lou Gehrig Day at Yankee Stadium. The stands were filled, and even Gehrig's old teammate Babe Ruth, with whom Gehrig had not always gotten along, was there. With the courage, grace, and modesty that characterized his life, Gehrig stepped to the microphone and uttered some of the most famous words ever spoken: "Today," he said, "I consider myself the luckiest man on the face of the earth."

GEHRIG on July 4, 1939— Lou Gehrig Day—when the Yankees retired his number.

OVER 61,000 PEOPLE CROWDED Yankee Stadium on Lou Gehrig Day to honor the legendary player. Clearly emotional, Gehrig thanked his teammates and fans, saying he was the "luckiest man on the face of the earth." He died a short two years later, just shy of his 38th birthday.

COOPERSTOWN

On June 12, 1939, the Hall of Fame was dedicated. Festive ceremonies highlighted by marching bands, ball games, and parades were held in Cooperstown all summer long, crowned by the Dedication of the National Baseball Museum and Hall of Fame, along with the first Induction Ceremony. As baseball had shut down for two days to allow full participation in the historic events, everyone who was anyone in baseball was there, including all 11 of the living baseball immortals elected to the Hall of Fame up to that point.

CHOOSING THE BEST

INDUCTED INTO THE HALL OF FAME in its inaugural year, Ty Cobb missed the official photo session (above).

Beginning in the early 1930s, many thought it was time to establish a monument to the greatest players in the game's history. Stephen C. Clark, a Cooperstown resident and philanthropist, sought the support of Major League Baseball to establish a National Baseball Museum and Hall of Fame in Cooperstown, New York, the legendary birthplace of baseball. Clark found an enthusiastic ally in Ford Frick, then President of the National

THE FIRST YEAR HALL OF FAME inductees. Seated left to right are: Eddie Collins, Babe Ruth, Connie Mack, Cy Young. Standing left to right are: Honus Wagner, Grover Cleveland Alexander, Tris Speaker, Napoleon Lajoie, George Sisler, and Walter Johnson. Ty Cobb arrived late and missed the photo session.

League. Together, the two men worked to turn their dreams into reality. Sportswriters from major publications would choose who warranted admission to the Hall. A building to house memorabilia and plaques celebrating the greatest players in the game's history was also planned.

The first voting for the Hall of Fame took place in 1936. Imagine the many superb players the voters had to choose from! Babe Ruth, Ty Cobb, Christy Mathewson, Walter Johnson, Honus Wagner, Nap Lajoie, Eddie Collins, Willie Keeler, Frank Baker, Cap Anson, and many other immortals were eligible. So were many of the finest managers of all time, along with the executives who had helped build major league baseball into the dominant sport it had become.

Five players were named in the first Hall of Fame vote. Ty Cobb was the leading vote-getter, closely followed by Babe Ruth, Honus Wagner, Christy Mathewson, and Walter Johnson.

But then as now, some voters just couldn't see their way to voting for even these baseball immortals. Of the 226 voters participating, four left Cobb off the ballot, 11 ignored Ruth and Wagner, 21 decided that Mathewson wasn't up to snuff, and 37 disqualified Johnson.

Beginning with that 1936 vote, election of new players to the Hall of Fame became a regular event. At the same time, the building that would house the museum was being built, with an opening date set for 1939.

Cooperstown was the site of General Abner Doubleday's legendary invention of the game of baseball in 1839, and 1939 would

mark the centennial year of the moment when he laid out the first baseball diamond on a corn pasture that is now the site of Doubleday Field.

Today, even Cooperstown residents concede that Doubleday may not have invented baseball. (He might not even have been aware that it existed.) But no one can deny that the town makes a beautiful setting for the Hall, a snapshot of small-town America that perfectly represents the values of the game.

Perhaps then-National League president John Heydler put it best. A former umpire, Heydler had worked an exhibition game on Doubleday Field in the 1920s, and had come away enamored of the town as a possible site for the Hall. "What sold me on Cooperstown and its people," he said, "was the town's boundless enthusiasm."

ONE BIG PARTY

The Hall of Fame was dedicated on June 12, 1939. But in truth the entire summer of 1939 was like one big party for both baseball and

A HUGE CROWD gathered in front of the new Hall of Fame and Museum for dedication ceremonies on June 12, 1939.

BASEBALL SHUT DOWN FOR TWO DAYS during the ceremonies, so many of baseball's bright lights took part in the celebrations. Detroit Tiger Hank Greenberg, who played in the special all-star exhibition game following the dedication, signs autographs and talks to young fans.

BABE RUTH was used as a pinch hitter in the all-star game managed by Honus Wagner and Eddie Collins. Always a crowd-pleaser, Ruth took a huge swing, which thrilled the audience, but the pop-up was caught by catcher Arndt Jorgens.

the town. Festive ceremonies featuring marching bands, ballgames, and parades were held in the town all summer long.

Nothing matched the excitement of June 12 itself, however. The day began with the dedication ceremonies themselves. All 11 of the living baseball immortals elected to the Hall of Fame up to that point were there: Babe Ruth, Honus Wagner, Ty Cobb, Walter Johnson, Eddie Collins, Connie Mack, Cy Young, Grover Cleveland Alexander, Tris Speaker, Nap Lajoie, and George Sisler.

The ceremony was followed by field events. The main attraction was a game between two major league all-star teams, chosen just for this occasion and managed by Hall of Famers Honus Wagner and Eddie Collins. (Baseball had shut down for two days to allow the celebration at Cooperstown to take place.) The players included a collection of people who would one day join Wagner and Collins in the Hall: Joe Medwick, Charlie Gehringer, Dizzy Dean, Hank Greenberg, Mel Ott, and others.

The most exciting moment occurred when Babe Ruth, four years after his retirement, went to bat as a pinch hitter for

Wagner's team. Pitcher Syl Johnson laid the ball in there, and the Babe took a mighty swing, but merely popped the ball into the air. The fans yelled, "Drop it! Drop it!" but catcher Arndt Jorgens grabbed the ball, and Ruth was out.

The day would also end at Doubleday Field, with a game of "town ball," an early

ancestor of baseball. *The Sporting News's* Fred Lieb reported that the players "appeared in long sailor pants, heavy boots and the odd flat derbies worn by our great-grandpappies." This spectacle was followed by a game between two soldier teams, dressed like the Knickerbockers and the Excelsiors of the 1850s, two of the earliest true baseball teams.

In his speech at the morning's ceremony, Babe Ruth captured both the honor of the day and the endless flow of baseball history. "You know, for me, this is just like an anniversary myself, because 25 years ago yesterday I pitched my first baseball game in Boston," he said. "I'm surely glad and it's a pleasure for me to come up here and be picked also in the Hall of Fame."

THE CROWD IN COOPERSTOWN on the road leading to Doubleday Field, the site for several exhibition games during opening ceremonies (below). A parade down Main Street in Cooperstown to celebrate the opening of the Hall of Fame (overleaf).

THE SUMMER OF '41

Joltin' Joe DiMaggio hit safely in 56 consecutive games, surpassing Wee Willie Keeler's all-time record of 44 straight, set in 1897. From May 15th to July 16th, The Yankee Clipper notched at least one hit in each game. On May 25th, Ted Williams' batting average climbed above .400 for the first time. At the All-Star break, he was at .405. On September 27th, the next-to-last day of the season, Williams was at .401, and Boston manager Joe Cronin suggested he take a couple of days off to ensure a .400 finish. Williams preferred to play, and went 1-for-4, lowering his average to .3995. On the final day of the sea-son, The Splendid Splinter went 6-for-8, to raise his average to .406. No one has surpassed the .400 mark since.

A Break from Real Life

In the summer of '41, the front pages of America's newspapers were consumed by the growing war in Europe. The sports pages, however, were dominated by what may have been the most spectacular baseball season of all time.

What happened to make the 1941 season so special? A dispatch from that year's All-Star Game, held in Detroit, gives a sense of the exciting events that unfolded during the course of that season. "Into the ninth All-Star game," wrote J. G. Taylor

"I WANT TO TELL YOU SOMETHING. I WOULD NEVER HAVE STOOD THAT PRESSURE AGAIN."

A PAIR OF WORLD-CLASS HITTERS, the Red Sox' Ted Williams, The Splendid Splinter, and Joe DiMaggio, The Yankee Clipper, completed pivotal records during the summer of 1941 that would help define the future of baseball.

Spink in *The Sporting News,* "the American League sent three men of the hour in baseball—Joe DiMaggio, who had hit in 48 straight games and whom the National League pitchers were determined to stop; Bobby Feller, who has won 16 games and whom the hitters of the old circuit were most eager to batter; and Theodore Samuel Williams, who was hitting over .400 and whom the hurlers of Ford Frick's organization were all set to baffle."

To be following three such sensational ongoing performances—the Indians' Feller aiming for 30 victories (he'd finish with 25), the Yankees' DiMaggio already having set a major league consecutive-game hitting streak record, and the Red Sox' Williams gunning to be the first player to hit over .400 since 1930—was unprecedented. Of the three, Williams was

the one who shone brightest in that All-Star Game, hitting a two-out, three-run home run in the ninth inning to give the American League a 7–5 victory. It was, Williams always said, "the most thrilling hit of my life."

Then it was back to the games that counted, as fans eagerly waited to see how long DiMaggio's streak would last and if Williams, the Splendid Splinter, could actually hit .400.

THE STREAK

As Joe DiMaggio got a hit, or more than one, in every game he played from May 15th onward, no one watching could claim to be very surprised. After all, just eight years earlier (while playing for the minor league San Francisco Seals) he'd hit safely in 61 consecutive games. Still, it was different doing it in the Majors.

ON JULY 16, 1941, DiMaggio hit safely in his 56th consecutive game, ending a streak that broke the back of Wee Willie Keeler's record 44 consecutive games.

JOE DIMAGGIO spent his entire career with the Yankees and batted over .300 in all but two of the 13 years he played for the Bronx Bombers.

For one thing, the pressure was far more intense. By the time his streak had reached 20 games, the press had begun to take notice.

DiMaggio, eternally cool and calm, didn't appear to be bothered by the increasing pressure as he moved past 40, and then 50, games. Yankee pitcher Lefty Gomez said in Maury Allen's *Where Have You Gone, Joe DiMaggio* that "Joe was probably the least excited guy in America over the streak." Or, as teammate Red Ruffing said, "He'd come into the clubhouse every day, sit down, get a cup of coffee from Pete, read the paper for a while, get dressed, go out, and get a base hit or two. It was something to see."

DiMaggio's streak finally came to an end at 56. But even in this game, on July 17 against the Cleveland Indians, he wasn't stopped easily. Twice he hit hard ground balls down the third base line—guaranteed doubles, except that they weren't. Both times, Indians' third baseman Ken Keltner made dazzling stops and threw DiMaggio out. One other time DiMaggio walked, and his last time up he hit another hard grounder, into a double play. That was it.

In later years, the ever-modest DiMaggio let on how much the grind of the streak had gotten to him, regardless of how little he'd shown it at the time. Speaking with Hall of Fame director Ken Smith in 1963, he pointed out that, after the game in Cleveland, he went on to hit in 16 more straight games. Then, laughing, he added, "I want to tell you something. I would never have stood that pressure again."

THE SPLINTER'S SEASON

If anyone could be expected to hit .400, it was Ted Williams, perhaps the best pure hitter baseball has ever known. In 1941 he was just 22 years old, and entering his third big-league season, but he'd already proven what he could do: In his first two seasons, he'd hit .327 and .344, with a combined total of 54 home runs and 258 RBI.

Longest Hitting Streaks—40 Games Plus			
Player	Team	Year	Number of Games
Joe DiMaggio	New York (A)	1941	56
Willie Keeler	Baltimore (N)	1897	44
Pete Rose	Cincinnati (N)	1978	44
Bill Dahlen	Chicago (N)	1894	42
George Sisler	St. Louis (A)	1925	41
Ty Cobb	Detroit (A)	1911	40

Williams kept his batting average above .400 from May 25 onward. On September 27, the next-to-last day of the season, his average stood at .401. Since his team was out of the pennant race, Red Sox manager Joe Cronin suggested that Williams take the final games off, to protect his average. "I told Cronin I didn't want that," Williams wrote in his autobiography, *My Turn at Bat.* "If I couldn't hit .400 all the way, I didn't deserve it."

Williams went only 1–4, dropping his average to .3995. Even this would be rounded off to .400—as long as he didn't play the Sox' final two games in a season-ending double-header in Philadelphia. But again he chose to play.

That final day in Philadelphia was cold and rainy. As Williams went to the plate for the first time, the umpire, Bill McGowan, took time to dust off the plate. As he did, he muttered to Williams, "To hit .406 a batter has got to be loose. He has got to be loose."

As Williams added, "I guess I couldn't have been much looser." Just barely reaching .400 wasn't for him—he went 6–8 in the double-header, including a home run and a double that was hit so hard it broke a loudspeaker horn in right field. His season average finished at a triumphant .406.

Ted Williams once said of DiMaggio: "I believe there isn't a record in the books that will be harder to break than Joe's fifty-six games." But both DiMaggio's streak and Williams' splendid .406 average have survived for the same number of seasons: 58 and counting.

LONG AND LANKY, Ted Williams' form at bat encouraged his nickname The Splendid Splinter (left). Williams put the power of his bat to work for the Boston Red Sox for his entire career, which spanned 19 years from 1939 to 1960 (above).

ONE THAT GOT AWAY

The 1941 World Series. New York Yankees vs. Brooklyn Dodgers. Game Four at Brooklyn. Yanks hold a 2-1 edge in the Series. Top of the ninth inning, Dodgers lead 4-3. Two men out. Bases empty. Relief pitcher Hugh Casey is poised to even up the Series if he can retire one last batter, Tommy Henrich. Two strikes. The Brooklyn crowd is humming, ready to celebrate. Strike Three! But wait—the ball glances off catcher Mickey Owen's glove and Henrich scrambles to first. The Yankees rally for 4 runs and win the game. The Yankees finished off the Dodgers the next day, and Mickey Owen became a part of World Series history.

THE BOMBERS VS. THE BUMS

If the Yankees were a predictable A.L. pennant winner in 1941, their N.L. counterpart was a legitimate surprise. The Brooklyn Dodgers were perennial, lovable losers, dubbed "Dem Bums" by their faithful fans. Under a parade of managers in the 1930s (including Casey Stengel), the Dodgers had lost, and lost, and lost some more.

Then, as the decade came to an end, the Dodgers named crafty and aggressive Leo Durocher their manager. And suddenly they began to win. In 1939 they finished third, in 1940 they finished second, and in 1941 they won 100 games and nipped St. Louis for the pennant. They were led by brilliant performances by Dolph Camilli (34 home runs and 120 RBI), 22-year-old Pete Reiser (at .343, he was the youngest batting champion ever), and pitchers Kirby Higbe and Whit Wyatt, who both won 22 games.

Still, the newly powerful Dodgers were up against the mighty Yankees. Most pundits gave the Bums just one game in the Series . . . if that.

CLOSER THAN EXPECTED

Those who had expected the Yankees to roll over the Dodgers were surprised. Each game was tightly contested, its outcome in doubt until the final out. Still, the battle-hardened Yankees simply knew how to win most of the big ones under the glare of the World Series spotlight. It was the Dodgers who kept making mistakes.

In Game One, for example, the Yankees (behind pitcher Red Ruffing) held a 3–1 lead when the Dodgers mounted a seventh-inning rally. They scored one run, and might have scored more, but rookie Pee Wee Reese was thrown out trying to advance from second to third on a foul fly. Final score: 3–2.

Brooklyn bounced back with a 3–2 victory behind Whit Wyatt in Game Two. But bad luck struck the Dodgers again in Game Three. Yankee starter Marius Russo and the Dodgers' Freddie Fitzsimmons matched zeroes into the seventh inning. Russo was at bat when he hit a sharp liner up the middle. The ball struck Fitzsimmons in the leg, forcing him from the game. The Yankees had managed just four hits off of Fitzsimmons, but they found reliever Hugh Casey easier to hit, scoring two runs off of him and holding on for a 2–1 victory and 2–1 Series lead.

Thus far, the Dodgers had played hard, and had held the vaunted Yankee offense nearly punchless. There was reason for them to believe that they were still very much in the Series . . . all they needed to do was win Game Four in Brooklyn.

BROOKLYN CATCHER MICKEY OWEN during the 1941 World Series that pitted the up and coming Dodgers against the Yankee threat from across town.

For most of Game Four, the Dodgers played the Yankees even. Pete Reiser hit a two-run home run for the home club, and after five innings the Bums led the Bronx Bombers, 4-3.

There the score stayed, for inning after inning. Hugh Casey, Game Three's loser, entered this contest in the fifth inning and shut the Yankees out . . . all the way until there were two outs in the ninth inning, and two strikes on Tommy Henrich, the Yankees' hitter.

DISASTER

At this moment, Dodgers catcher Mickey Owen called for a curveball. "Casey had two curveballs, one that broke big and broke good," Owen said years later, "and then had a hard, quick curve that looked like a slider." In this game, Owen went on to explain, Casey had relied on the sharp curve that looked like a slider.

Inexplicably, when Owen called for another curve with two strikes on Henrich, Casey chose to throw the big, sweeping curve. "I never dreamed he'd roll off that big one," Owen said. "Henrich missed it by more than I

did . . . It hit the heel of my glove and rolled toward the dugout." Henrich had swung and missed for strike three, but on a strike-three wild pitch or passed ball the batter is allowed to run to first base if first base is open. And that's what Henrich did. Instead of the game being over, the Yankees were still alive.

It doesn't pay to give a great team a second chance. As the Dodgers and their fans watched helplessly, Joe DiMaggio singled, Charlie Keller doubled, Bill Dickey walked, and Joe Gordon doubled. Suddenly the score was 7–4, Yankees, and that's how it ended.

The Dodgers bowed meekly, 3–1, in Game Five, to lose the Series. The heart had been taken out of them by the ninth-inning debacle the day before.

The press was scathing. *The Sporting News*, for example, didn't mince words: The headline read: "Owen Enters List of Classic 'Goats'."

In later years, Owen was able to gain perspective on his painful experience, saying "I knew I always tried as hard as I could and I vowed I'd never miss another and I never did."

OWEN SCRAMBLES for a strike-three wild pitch that would have earned the final out for Brooklyn and one more game in their World Series quest.

99

THE WAR AND POSTWAR PERIOD

Baseball often mirrored society, and it did so again during and after World War II. Much as the war left vacancies in industrial plants as it drew men into the army, it left vacancies on baseball teams. Many industries turned to women to fill vacant positions, and in 1943 ball club owner Philip K. Wrigley started a women's baseball league to take the place of the Major Leagues should the war force them to stop play. Officially called the All-American Girls Professional Baseball League (AAGPBL), it offered games to war-weary audiences and, after Wrigley sold it in 1944, continued in existence until 1954, when declining attendance took its toll.

In playing for Wrigley's league, women showed that they could work outside the home without society falling apart, much as their work in industry had proved this same point. Such social change presaged other changes that came in the late 1940s and 1950s. During those years, Americans found their daily lives altered by television, the building of suburbs, an intensifying cold war with the Soviet Union, and, perhaps most far-reaching in its impact, the civil rights movement.

When the United States entered World War II in December 1941, questions arose as to whether the Major Leagues should play ball the next year. President Roosevelt responded by urging them to go ahead with the season. He said war production would mean more people working longer hours who would need the diversion baseball could provide.

Roosevelt's prediction about work came true quickly, partly through his own action. Soon after Pearl Harbor, he established the War Production Board to lead industries in converting their

A 1942 POSTER urged women to keep American industry going while the nation's men fought World War II.

factories from civilian to military production. The economy shifted so rapidly—from cars to tanks, from shirts to mosquito netting—that one government official declared: "It was not so much industrial conversion as industrial revolution, with months and years condensed into days." Depression-era hardship ended. Between 1940 and 1945, America's gross national product jumped from $100 billion to over $200 billion, and wages and salaries from $50 billion to $120 billion.

Patriotism added extra motivation to the materialist drive. When the *Saturday Evening Post* displayed Norman Rockwell's drawing *Rosie the Riveter,* it stated that even women were sacrificing by working in factories to help America win the war. Baseball joined the patriotic fervor. Ballparks displayed signs urging people to buy war bonds, and before games teams held bond rallies, complete with marching bands to rouse support.

Although Roosevelt urged the Major Leagues to continue, he granted no special exemptions. As a result, the military draft cut deeply into team rosters. By the spring of 1945 about 60 percent of those players listed on big league rosters four years earlier were in the service.

The war hit baseball in other ways, too. Restrictions on fuel forced teams to hold spring training near their home cities; during the regular season they reduced their road trips; and wartime travel rules forced the cancellation of the 1945 All-Star game. But the loss of players hurt most. The level of play declined substantially as teams resorted to hiring players long past their athletic prime, or inexperienced ones, such as 15-year-old Joe Nuxhall (who, several years later, appeared in two All-Star games).

Organized baseball could have turned to the Negro Leagues for help, but the racial segregation of the day forbade them. When Brooklyn Dodger manager Leo Durocher said he had seen "a million good colored players" and would have them on his team were it not for the game's unofficial "color line," baseball commissioner Kenesaw Mountain Landis silenced him. Yet it was more than the owners and the commissioner who showed racist tendencies; players, sportswriters, and many others exhibited the trait—it permeated the game much as it permeated society.

To African Americans and many whites, it seemed hypocritical and morally wrong to be fighting a war against a racist dictatorship in Germany while racism oppressed millions in the United States. In both the North and South housing was segregated, as were public schools; so too was the Army when it went into battle for democracy. Throughout the South segregationist laws, called "Jim Crow" laws, maintained white supremacy, and to enforce them white southerners barred most blacks from voting.

In that environment, black activists intensified their fight for civil rights. James Farmer, a leader in the Congress of Racial Equality, expressed his group's goals as: "Not to make housing in ghettos more tolerable, but to destroy residential segregation; not to make Jim Crow facilities the equal of others, but to abolish Jim Crow; not to make racial discrimination more bearable, but to wipe it out."

Slowly—critics said too slowly—segregation weakened in the late 1940s and 1950s. In 1946, President Harry Truman created a Committee on Civil Rights to investigate abuses; it advocated reforms such as anti-lynching legislation and an end to segregated housing. Two years later, Truman ordered the integration of the armed forces. (The Army, however, was not completely desegregated until just after the Korean War.)

When Branch Rickey, general manager of the Brooklyn Dodgers, responded to the civil rights movement by deciding to integrate the Major Leagues, more than altruism guided him. Black players would bolster the Dodger organization and attract the increasing black urban population to ballparks.

But Rickey considered it a matter of principle, too. Thus in August 1945 he met with Jackie Robinson, then playing for a Negro league team, the Kansas City Monarchs, and asked him to break the color barrier that had been established before the turn of the century. Rickey liked what he saw in Robinson: a teetotaler, articulate, and experienced in race relations from his days as an All-American athlete at the predominantly white University of California at Los Angeles. "A Negro who would be his race's best foot forward," as *Time* magazine said. And a

In 1941, THE U.S. BEGAN DRAFTING MEN into military service. Here, a group of Army draftees receive instructions in St. Paul, Minnesota.

talented, tough, dogged player. "This guy didn't just come to play," Leo Durocher said. "He come to beat ya."

Rickey warned Robinson he would face severe taunting and worse, which he did. In 1947, in his inaugural year with the Dodgers, some of his teammates, at least early in the season, refused to sit next to him, while opposing players hurled racial epithets and baseballs at him and while sliding, dug their spikes into his legs. Off the field he suffered indignity when in some cities Jim Crow laws prohibited him from eating at restaurants with his teammates or staying in the same hotels with them. Yet he batted nearly .300, led the National League with 29 stolen bases, and was named National League Rookie of the Year. *Time* said, " . . . He is not only jackrabbit fast, but about one thought and two steps ahead of every base-runner in the business."

Although some African Americans disliked integration for destroying Negro league baseball, most applauded it, and they hailed Robinson as a hero, turning out in large numbers to watch him play. One report estimated that, on April 15, 1947, over half of the 26,000 fans that came to Ebbets Field for the Dodgers' cold, rainy home opener were black.

Other blacks entered the big leagues: Larry Doby and Satchel Paige played with Cleveland; Monte Irvin and Willie Mays with the New York Giants; Ernie Banks with the Chicago Cubs. By 1954, however, four all-white teams still remained.

That same year, the Supreme Court issued its momentous decision in *Brown v. Board of Education* that declared separate educational facilities inherently unequal and thus unconstitutional. Despite the resistance of the Deep South to the *Brown* decision, one legal scholar said, "It makes the beachhead. But the breakthrough, if it is to be significant, is broadened by forces from behind which take advantage of the opening to go the rest of the way." So too were Jackie Robinson and other early black players beachheads behind which rising waters would erode racial injustice.

When conflict over civil rights broke, Americans distant from the scene watched the events through a new device, television. In 1947, sales of TV sets stood at 7,000. Just three years later sales reached seven million. The phenomenal growth continued so that by the middle Fifties, TVs graced 66 percent of all homes.

Advertisers used the medium to create consumer demand—and companies needed little coaxing after lipstick maker Hazel Bishop's annual sales went from $50,000 a year before TV commercials to $4.5 million after. Most TV shows reinforced prevalent social values—including faith in family and its rigid social structures. Through its title alone, the hit comedy *Father Knows Best* advised who should govern the household.

As a clean "All-American sport," baseball fit the profile for TV shows, and enormous money could be made by connecting it to the medium's advertising. Clearly, baseball owners could benefit by charging TV networks to carry games, as they charged the radio networks, and by receiving a promotional boost through baseball's greater exposure. But the owners hesitated; they worried that TV might do more damage than help to baseball. They had a point.

TV SHOWS SUCH AS "FATHER KNOWS BEST" reinforced traditional values in the 1950s. Jane Wyatt and Robert Young played the parents.

In 1947, TV carried the World Series for the first time, and within four years baseball had struck it rich, taking in millions of dollars by selling radio and television rights. Nevertheless, the medium hurt attendance at big league games. After it topped 20 million in 1948, the turnstile count dropped to about 17 million in 1950 and about 15 million in 1952. Although attendance increased to 17.5 million in 1958, the rebound fell far short of the euphoric late Forties. As it turned out, Americans in large numbers opted to watch baseball on the tube rather than attend the games. Or they watched other team sports, for TV brought football, basketball, and hockey into living rooms. As the seasons grew longer for these sports, they overlapped with baseball (and one another) to produce more competition for viewers and sponsors.

The Minor Leagues took an even harder hit. After the war, they had rebounded to 59 leagues in 1949 and attracted a record 40 million fans; however, only 33 leagues were in operation in 1953 and 28 in 1957. Writing in *Our Game,* Charles C. Alexander concludes that "small-city professional baseball—a basic part of American life for eighty years—largely disappeared."

Other developments joined TV to worsen the attendance problem. Overall, the economy prospered. Median family income rose 30 percent during the Fifties and gross national product climbed 37 percent. Americans had more autos, telephones, electric lights, bathtubs, and supermarkets per capita than any other nation. At the same time, average hours worked per week fell to under 41. Presumably, such prosperity and leisure time would encourage people to spend money at baseball parks, yet baseball's share of the recreational dollar dropped as the 1950s began. Middle-class consumers instead spent money on their new suburban homes, on swing sets for their kids, on barbecue grills for their weekend cookouts.

Once home from work, fathers preferred to tend to their suburban homesteads rather than head back to the city for a game of baseball—or they preferred to see their children play little league or softball. A baby boom swept America then— more people were born from 1947 to 1953 than in the previous 30 years, and in 1954 births topped four million for the first time—so moms and dads stayed close to home. Besides, crime-ridden neighborhoods often surrounded many big league parks, and even with improvements, such as a scoreboard at Crosley Field in Cincinnati that flashed batting averages, the facilities were old and in many cases shabby.

As white families moved to the suburbs—laws and unofficial practices barred blacks from most suburban developments—their relocation represented only part of a massive population shift after World War II. In another move, large numbers of people from the northeast headed west for California. Thus beneath a surface conservatism, beneath traditional ideas about family and country, an uprooted population challenged the very notion of stability.

More than families moved from city to city and region to region in search of better opportunities: Big league baseball clubs did so too—thus shattering long-standing attachments to their home towns. The Boston Braves broke their ties in 1953, when they moved to Milwaukee and a brand new ball park. In his *Concise History of Major League Baseball*, writer Leonard Koppett calls the move "the crossroads event of twentieth-century baseball," for it showed that a change in location for a team lagging in attendance could work wonders—the Braves drew 1.8 million fans in 1953, the highest single-season mark for any team in National League history until that time. They achieved success on the field as well, winning two pennants and a World Series between 1953 and 1958. Koppett concludes: "The effect on baseball was much like the effect of the California Gold Rush on America: it changed the map forever."

The St. Louis Browns followed next, moving to Baltimore at the end of the 1953 season and renaming themselves the Orioles. Before the 1955 season began, the Philadelphia Athletics moved to Kansas City. Then came a monumental shift when New York City lost not one but two of its three teams.

Walter O'Malley, owner of the Brooklyn Dodgers, led the exodus. By 1955, the year his team won its first World Series, he wanted to leave Ebbets Field, which he considered too small and outdated. O'Malley tried to get the city to contribute to the cost of a new stadium, but after the government bureaucracy hesitated, he announced in 1957 that the Dodgers would move the following year to Los Angeles.

Not wanting his team to be the only big league club in California, he convinced the Giants to move as well. They played in New York's aging Polo Grounds and suffered from declining attendance, so they agreed and announced their new home would be San Francisco. Technology made these two moves possible—in 1957 the first Boeing 707 passenger jet went into service, making it easy for the Dodgers and Giants to connect with other teams. Like many families, they followed the moving van to California—the land of opportunity.

Almost since their inception the big leagues encouraged fans to equate baseball with Americanism. This became more marked after World War II when the cold war began with the Soviet Union. As Americans battled what they considered evil communism, they believed their own culture exemplified

ONE OF THE FIRST MIDDLE-CLASS SUBURBAN HOUSING DEVELOPMENTS was Levittown, New York. The houses were affordable and similar developments soon followed.

good, and with baseball central to that culture it was seen as an expression of such goodness and a bulwark against foreign assault. That the Soviets also recognized baseball's important role was evident when their Communist League, a political organization, attacked it as a brutal sport in which owners enslaved players; of course, attack the sport, and you attack a core American value. Eddie Stanky, who played second base in the Majors before becoming a manager, reacted to the condemnation by calling baseball "the big game of a free people."

The cold war involved fear, too. Fear that a nuclear war would annihilate everything, and fear that communists within the United States would undermine the country. Fear resulted in a Red Scare in which some communists and many more non-communists, people who had criticized the government or just didn't conform, found themselves fired from their jobs or ostracized from society. Even remote, unintentional references to communism became dangerous; thus the Cincinnati *Reds* baseball team insisted they be called the "Redlegs."

Exciting stars graced baseball in the 1950s: Jackie Robinson, Roy Campanella, Yogi Berra, Henry Aaron, Lew Burdette, Whitey Ford, Mickey Mantle, Willie Mays, Frank Robinson, Pee Wee Reese, and Duke Snider, to name a few. As in years past, the hitters hit, the fielders fielded, the managers managed—amid manicured grass, hot-dog hawkers, and eager kids seeking autographs. Thus despite new styles, new rules, and new records, baseball retained the features that earned it fan loyalty. But with the color barrier broken, with television broadcasting more and more games, with teams relocating, baseball had changed with society, and the changes, in the supposedly placid Fifties, portended a historic upheaval in the decade to come.

ONLY FIFTEEN

World War II saw many of baseball's best players serving in the military. Teams were forced to stock up with talent from the ranks of the 4Fs, the old, and the young. On June 10, 1944, Joe Nuxhall became the youngest player ever to appear in a big league ball game, at the age of 15 years and 10 months. Already behind 13-0, the Reds gave Nuxhall a shot. After he gave up five runs in two-thirds of an inning, the Reds ended the experiment and sent him to the minors. Eight years later, he returned to the Majors, where he fashioned a 16-year career, with a .536 winning percentage, and two All-Star selections. He then spent 30 years in the broadcast booth for the Reds.

THE SEARCH

The years during World War II were strange ones for organized baseball. Many of the game's greatest stars—including Hank Greenberg, Bob Feller, and Joe DiMaggio—were serving in the military in Europe or the Pacific. They were joined by dozens of less well-known players who were also absent from baseball for a season—or even for the duration of the war.

In fact, so many of the game's players served in the military between 1942 and 1945 that many baseball teams had trouble filling their rosters. As a result, they were forced to search far and wide, not only in the minor leagues, but even among players who would never have gotten a glance if not for the war. Quantity, not quality, was what teams were looking for during those years.

Probably the most famous wartime recruit to major league baseball was Pete Gray, who played outfield for the St. Louis Browns in 1945. He hit only .218 in 234 at bats—but this wasn't so bad, given that Pete Gray had only one arm.

Not surprisingly, Pete Gray didn't play for the Browns in 1946, when the war was over and the real major league players were back from overseas. In fact, fewer than a third of the regular players in 1945 still had jobs waiting for them the following year. Most went back to the minors, where they'd always belonged.

In 1944, the Cincinnati Reds found themselves with a typical problem: They were short of pitching. But the solution they decided on was one that would have taken place only during the bizarre wartime years.

The Reds decided to sign a left-handed pitcher named Joe Nuxhall and let him pitch in a major league game. What was amazing about this was that Joe Nuxhall was 15 years old at the time.

THE YOUNGEST EVER

"Actually, I tried out with the Reds in 1943 when I was 14 years old and an eighth-grader," Joe Nuxhall reminisced in a 1977 interview in *Baseball Quarterly.* "I told the Reds I'd like to finish the ninth grade . . . I did and then signed in February 1944."

"I TOLD THE REDS I'D LIKE TO FINISH THE NINTH GRADE."

YOUNG JOE NUXHALL who, at age 15, signed with the Cincinnati Reds.

Nuxhall wasn't a typical high school student in 1944. He stood 6 feet 3 inches and weighed 195 pounds. "I could throw hard," he said. "But, other than that, I didn't have much going for me—no curve, no change-up, no other pitch except a fastball."

Normally, a 15-year-old prospect would have been destined for the minor leagues, when he wasn't in school. Even this possibility was awe-inspiring for the teenage Nuxhall. "It scares you when you think that as a 15-year-old, you'll have to pitch to guys as old as your father."

Due to the wartime player scarcity, however, the Reds let Nuxhall suit up for home games. Still, he expected that he would do nothing but watch the games from the dugout. His first professional experience was sure to come in the minors, he thought.

Wrong. On June 10, the Reds were being blown out by Stan Musial's St. Louis Cardinals. The score was 13–0 when Nuxhall heard Cincinnati manager Bill McKechnie shout, "Joe!" He was sure the manager was calling someone else, until McKechnie caught his eye and told him to go warm up.

Nuxhall entered the game to start the ninth inning, the youngest player to appear in a major league game in modern times. At first, it seemed as if he might actually have a successful

NUXHALL returned to the Reds eight years after his disastrous debut, when he was 23. He would spend a total of 16 years in the big leagues, a career that would include two All-Star pitching spots.

debut, as he sandwiched two outs around a walk. He needed only one out and the game would be over.

Unfortunately, as he said later, "that's when I realized exactly where I was." The butterflies that had been occupying his stomach spread to his pitching arm, and he walked the next batter. Up to the plate stepped Stan Musial, one of the greatest hitters of all time.

Musial slammed Nuxhall's first pitch for a single, driving in a run. The rattled teenager then walked the next three men he faced, forcing in two runs. The batter after that, Emil Verban, singled, driving in two more. When Manager McKechnie took pity on the teenager and removed him from the game, Nuxhall's pitching line looked like this: two-thirds of an inning pitched, five runs allowed. Since these were the only two-thirds of an inning that Nuxhall pitched with the Reds that year, his season's earned run average was 67.50. It was a sour end to a great story.

SECOND CHANCE

Luckily for Nuxhall, his major league career didn't end with that disastrous performance against the Cardinals. He returned to the Reds in 1952, a remarkable eight years later. After all this time, he was still only 23 years old!

Nuxhall's second stint in the Major Leagues was a lot longer and much more successful than his first. He stuck around for 16 years, almost all with the Reds, and won a total of 135 games. In his best seasons with Cincinnati, he went 17–12 (1955) and 15–8 (1963). Although he never had the chance to pitch in a World Series, he did make the All-Star team twice. He would go on to spend the next 30 years as a well-liked broadcaster with the Reds.

AT OVER SIX FEET TALL and close to 200 pounds, Nuxhall stood out against his fellow high school students when he signed with the Reds.

TIGER, TIGER, BURNING BRIGHT

When Hank Greenberg returned to the Detroit Tigers midway through the 1945 season, he had given
more than four full seasons to the defense of freedom in World War II. Greenberg served in the Far East theater with
a B-29 unit, but he dropped quite a bomb of his own on September 30th, the final day of the 1945 season. His grand
slam in the ninth inning clinched the American League pennant for the Tigers, who would go on to beat the Cubs
in a seven-game World Series, in which Greenberg batted .304 with two more home runs.

THE MISSING YEARS

In the days following December 7, 1941, the day that the Japanese attacked Pearl Harbor, countless thousands of Americans enlisted in the military. The United States was going to war, and it was only right and just that all able-bodied Americans do their part.

Baseball players weren't exempt from the call. And that too was only right. In doing their duty, though, many ballplayers lost four years out of their careers, a huge and irreplaceable chunk of time. Even the greatest star shines for only 15 or so years—and for most players, their time in the majors is far shorter. Bob Feller, Ted Williams, Joe DiMaggio, Hank Greenberg and many others could never get back the time they spent overseas.

Cecil Travis provides a case in point of the war's impact on a career. Travis was perhaps the Washington Senators' biggest hitting star in the 1930s, hitting over .300 eight times in nine years. He had his biggest season of all in 1941: .359, with a league-leading 218 hits. He was 28 years old.

He enlisted in the military in 1942, and he didn't return to baseball until the end of the 1945 season. He never regained what four lost seasons had taken from him—and he also returned with a foot injury sustained in the Battle of the Bulge. In 1946, his first full season back, he hit only .252. In 1947, his

average slipped to .216, and he was out of baseball for good. And thus a potential Hall of Famer is nearly forgotten today—it was the price he had to pay for helping protect our nation's freedom.

Hank Greenberg's story has a slightly happier ending. Partly this is because he had already attained Hall of Fame numbers by 1942, when he went off to fight in World War II. But mostly Greenberg's is a happier story because he, unlike Travis, had the opportunity to shine one more time after the war was over and he was back in baseball.

GREENBERG THE HERO

Hank Greenberg didn't have to enlist in the Air Force after Pearl Harbor. He'd already fulfilled his military duty, a duty that took him away from baseball for most of the 1941 season. Like Travis, Greenberg's first tour of duty had followed perhaps his finest year. In 1940, Greenberg had hit .340, with a league-leading 50 doubles, 41 home runs, and 150 runs batted in.

Greenberg was discharged from the service in December 1941, just a few days before Pearl Harbor. As soon as he heard the news of the Japanese attack on the U.S. base in Hawaii, he turned around and re-enlisted. He was already 30 years old, and he knew that he might never get back to baseball.

"I WAS QUITE SATISFIED JUST TO BE ALIVE."

AS DID OTHER BALL PLAYERS, Hank Greenberg served in the military during World War II.

Greenberg was stationed at an Air Force base in India. One day, a bomber crashed on take-off from the base, and as Greenberg and others ran toward it, its gas tanks and a bomb blew up, hurling Greenberg into a ditch. "That was an occasion, I can assure you, when I didn't wonder whether or not I'd be able to return to baseball. I was quite satisfied just to be alive," he recalled.

But, midway through the 1945 season, Greenberg did have the chance to return to the diamond. And he made his return a glorious experience.

THE CONQUERING HERO

Hank Greenberg made his first postwar appearance with the Tigers on July 1, 1945. A massive crowd of more than 55,000 fans flooded Detroit's Tiger Stadium to welcome the war hero home. And Greenberg didn't disappoint, slugging a home run to help the Tigers win the game. "I was playing from memory," Greenberg recalled in Lawrence Ritter's *The Glory of Their Times*. "I'd hardly had a bat in my hands since I'd left in 1941, and after I hit that home run they gave me an unbelievable standing ovation."

An even bigger thrill took place on September 30, the last day of the season. The Tigers were engaged in an excruciatingly tight pennant race with the Washington Senators, and needed to win this game to capture the flag.

Going into the ninth inning, the Tigers trailed, 3–2. They managed to load the bases with two outs, and guess who strode to the plate against Senator pitcher Nelson Potter? Hank Greenberg. On Potter's second pitch, Greenberg unleashed a mighty swing and sent the ball rocketing into the left field stands. That one swing sewed up the pennant for the Tigers, who went on to win, 6–3.

"Never was a title won in more dramatic fashion," proclaimed the *New York Times* the next day. Greenberg put it eloquently to Lawrence Ritter: "[W]hat was going through my mind as I was rounding the bases is that only a few months before, I was in India, wondering if the war would ever end, and now the war was actually over and not only that but I'd just hit a pennant-winning grand-slam home run. I wasn't sure whether I was awake or dreaming."

GREENBERG finished 10 seasons with an average above .300. He batted .340 in 1940, his all-time high, and finished his career with a lifetime average of .313.

SOON AFTER SERVING in World War II, Greenberg, at right, helped the Detroit Tigers' take the lead in the World Series against the Cubs. He congratulates manager Steve O'Neill, center, and pitcher Hal Newhouser, left.

LET'S PLAY TOO

Throughout the first half of the 20th century, an unwritten rule barred African-Americans from playing in professional baseball alongside white players. Jackie Robinson and visionary executive Branch Rickey changed all that on April 15, 1947, when Robinson played his first game for the Brooklyn Dodgers. Robinson endured harassment and threats during his drive to integrate baseball, and led the way for generations of African-American athletes to follow in baseball and other sports. He was named Rookie of the Year in 1947, and led the Dodgers to the World Series. Larry Doby followed in Jackie's path and became the first African-American in the American League on July 5, 1947, with the Cleveland Indians.

"I AM NOT AFRAID TO TRY."

THE DOOR SLAMS SHUT

Every baseball fan knows that, when Jackie Robinson stepped onto the field with the Brooklyn Dodgers in 1947, he became the first African American to play major league baseball in decades. What is less well known is that he was not the first to do so. The color barrier that prevented black ballplayers from playing until 1947 hadn't always existed. It crashed into place in the 1880s.

During the late 1800s, the division between "major" and "minor" league teams wasn't nearly as well defined as it is today. The National League was the biggest league, but such leagues as the International League and the American Association could make the claim of being nearly as important. And, throughout the 1880s, many of these teams included African-American players.

Of these, perhaps the most prominent was Moses Fleetwood Walker, who played with Toledo in the American Association in 1884 and Newark of the International League in 1887, but there were more than a dozen others. Wherever they played, Walker and other black players immediately ran into the blatant racism of white players, including their own teammates, many of whom didn't want an African American anywhere near the ballfield.

One of the ringleaders of the opposition was the future Hall of Fame player and manager Cap Anson, but he was far from alone. White players made it a goal to throw at African-American batters, to spike them, to threaten them both on the field and off. The fans were just as bad, and sometimes worse: When an African-American pitcher named Robert Higgins walked to the mound to start a game in Toronto, he heard a chorus of "Kill the nigger."

Jackie Robinson— First Season Stats, 1947

Games Played	151
At Bats	590
Runs	125
Hits	175
Doubles	31
Triples	5
Home Runs	12
RBI	48
Batting Average	.297
Stolen Bases	29*

* League leader

JACKIE ROBINSON, the first player to break the color barrier in the Major Leagues, made his National League debut on April 15, 1947, with the Brooklyn Dodgers.

By 1890 the constant harassment had translated into a "gentleman's agreement" among team owners to forego signing any more black ballplayers. Neither these owners nor the ones who operated teams during the decades to come ever admitted having an organized policy to exclude blacks. But the plain truth was that they had drawn a line that would not be crossed for nearly 60 years.

RICKEY AND ROBINSON

From time to time, a more open-minded owner or manager would quietly suggest signing the best African-American ballplayers from the Negro Leagues. Giants manager John McGraw, who lived by the motto "The main idea is to win," would have loved to increase his chances of winning by signing black ballplayers. But nothing ever came of his or others' desires—at least not until Brooklyn Dodgers' general manager Branch Rickey stepped forward in 1945.

As Jackie Robinson was told by Branch Rickey, "a baseball box score is a democratic thing. It doesn't tell how big you are, what church you attend, what color you are, or how your father voted in the last election. It just tells what kind of a baseball player you were on that particular day."

No philosophy could be simpler, and others in the nearly 60 years since African Americans were driven from the game must have felt the same way. But Branch Rickey was the first to act. With the support of an unsung hero, Baseball Commissioner A.B. "Happy" Chandler, Rickey decided to start scouting for the best possible black ballplayer to bring to the Dodgers.

The major league club owners, hearing of these plans, voted 15–1 against allowing African Americans to play. But Chandler gave Rickey the go-ahead. Asked why, Chandler said later, "I thought someday I'd have to meet my maker and He'd say, 'What did you do with those black boys?'"

After an intensive secret search, Rickey's ace scouts recommended Jackie Robinson. Robinson wasn't the best or most famous player then starring in the Negro Leagues, but he had the strength of character that Rickey

Branch Rickey was the first major league general manager to hire a black ballplayer. Rickey's visionary strategy broke the color barrier and opened the door for other African Americans to play in the big leagues.

Brooklyn Dodgers general manager Branch Rickey, right, and Jackie Robinson, as Robinson signs his contract for the 1948 season, his second year in the Major Leagues.

thought would be essential to survival as the first black in the Majors.

Robinson had starred in several sports at UCLA, and had battled against racism while he was there. "I told him he would have to curb that aggressiveness, even though he would be the target of all sorts of vilification," Rickey said later. "I predicted in disgusting detail the name-calling he would have to take and warned him that he would have to turn the other cheek, to take it in silence."

After three hours of such talk, Rickey asked Robinson: "Well? Do you still want to go through with it?"

JACKIE ROBINSON with Brooklyn Dodger teammates during his first year in the Majors. From left to right: Spider Jorgensen, Pee Wee Reese, Eddie Stanky, and Robinson.

Robinson's answer: "Yes. I am not afraid to try."

THE PIONEER

From the moment he was signed by the Dodgers, Jackie Robinson faced treatment as hurtful and scathing as anything Branch Rickey could have predicted. The press was scornful: Jimmy Powers in the *New York Daily News* said, "We don't believe Jackie Robinson . . . will ever play in the big leagues. We question Branch Rickey's pompous statements that he is another Abraham Lincoln and that he has a heart as big as a watermelon."

1st Black Player on Each Team

Players Name	Date of Entry	Team Name
Jackie Robinson	April 15, 1947	Brooklyn (N)
Larry Doby	July 5, 1947	Cleveland (A)
Henry Thompson	July 17, 1947	St. Louis (A)
Henry Thompson	July 8, 1949	New York (N)
Sam Jethroe	April 18, 1950	Boston (N)
Minnie Minoso	May 1, 1951	Chicago (A)
Bob Trice	September 13, 1953	Philadelphia (A)
Ernie Banks	September 17, 1953	Chicago (N)
Curt Roberts	April 13, 1954	Pittsburgh (N)
Tom Alston	April 13, 1954	St. Louis (N)
Nino Escalera	April 17, 1954	Cincinnati (N)
Carlos Paula	September 6, 1954	Washington (A)
Elston Howard	April 14, 1955	New York (A)
John Kennedy	April 22, 1957	Philadelphia (N)
Ossie Virgil	June 6, 1958	Detroit (A)
Pumpsie Green	July 21, 1959	Boston (A)

Of course, Rickey had never said any such thing.

After a season with the Dodgers' minor league affiliate in Montreal (where he was treated well), Jackie Robinson was called up to the Dodgers in 1947. Before the season even started, some of Robinson's Dodger teammates rebelled against having to play alongside a black ballplayer, circulating a secret petition.

But when manager Leo Durocher heard about the petition, he called a team meeting to put an end to any rebellion. "I'm the manager of this ball club, and I'm interested in one thing. Winning," he said. "This fellow is a real great ballplayer. He's going to win pennants for us."

Then Durocher hit them where they lived. "From everything I hear," he said, "he's only the first. Only the first, boys! There's many more coming right behind him and they have the talent and they're gonna come to play. These fellows are hungry . . . Unless you fellows look out and wake up, they're going to run you right out of the ballpark."

The rebellion withered. While some of his teammates could never abide Robinson's presence, they were soon traded. Other players, especially star shortstop Pee Wee Reese, became his friend and defended him when he was not allowed to defend himself.

Facing bitter racism throughout the season—though also drawing huge crowds most everywhere he played—Robinson showed extraordinary strength of character. For his rookie season, he batted .297 and led the league with 29 stolen bases, helping lead the Dodgers to the National League pennant. At the end of the season, he was named the first Rookie of the Year by *The Sporting News*.

Robinson went on to compile a career that led him to the Hall of Fame. Perhaps even more importantly, by proving he could play in the Majors, and by turning the other cheek to the treatment he received, he opened the door for other African Americans. Later in 1947, Larry Doby was called up by the Cleveland Indians to become the first black player in the A.L., and he was soon followed by Satchel Paige, Roy Campanella, Don Newcombe, and others.

It took many years for every team to open its doors to African-American ballplayers. Without Jackie Robinson's brilliant play in the face of adversity, who knows how many more years would have passed before that injustice was righted?

RICKEY'S HIRING of Robinson encouraged other clubs to hire black ballplayers. Larry Doby became the first black player to sign with an American League team, the Cleveland Indians, on July 5, 1947.

MAD DASH

*The 1946 World Series pitted the St. Louis Cardinals against the Boston Red Sox. The two teams split
the first six games and faced a decisive seventh game on October 15 at St. Louis' Sportsman's Park. With the score
knotted at 3-3 going into the bottom of the eighth, Enos "Country" Slaughter led off with a single. Two outs later, Harry
Walker hit a shot to left center. Slaughter was off and running, rounding second, and then, against all odds, rounding
third. Shortstop Johnny Pesky's throw was a little late, and Slaughter slid home with the go-ahead run. In a tense ninth
inning, Boston's Rudy York and Bobby Doerr reached base to lead off the inning, before Cardinal pitching hero
Harry Brecheen put out the fire to give the Cardinals the championship.*

THE RED SOX' NEXT CHANCE

The Curse of the Bambino had done its work well. After Boston Red Sox owner Harry Frazee sold Babe Ruth to the Yankees after the 1919 season, the once-mighty Sox had not won a single American League pennant in 27 years.

In 1934, however, a Boston businessman named Tom Yawkey bought the Sox, and immediately began to spend what was necessary to build a winning team. In 1946 everything came together, as the Sox went 104–50 (one of the finest records of all time) and claimed the American League pennant.

The Red Sox' heroes that season were many. Ted Williams had a typical Ted Williams year: .342 with 38 home runs. Shortstop Johnny

St. Louis Cardinal's batter Harry Walker, whose hit brought baserunner Enos Slaughter around third and home to break a World Series tie against the Boston Red Sox.

Pesky hit .335. Rudy York and Bobby Doerr both drove in more than 100 runs. And pitchers Boo Ferriss (25 wins) and Tex Hughson (20) were having stellar seasons.

The Red Sox' opponents in the 1946 World Series were the St. Louis Cardinals, long a powerful team and the 1942 and 1944 World Champions. The Cardinals' team leader was Stan "the Man" Musial (who led the league in batting at .365), but in 1946 the team also got superb performances from Enos Slaughter (who led the league with 130 runs batted in) and pitcher Howie Pollett (with 21 wins).

EVENLY MATCHED

The first thing that happened was a stroke of horrible luck for the Red Sox. Before the Series began, the Sox played a three-game exhibition series against a team of A.L. stars. An errant pitch in the first of these games hit Ted Williams on the elbow; the elbow was sore and swollen throughout the Series. Williams hit only .200, with just five singles in 25 at bats.

Even with Williams' injury, the Series was expected to be a close one, and the first game was just what everyone expected: a tight, tense pitchers' duel. The Red Sox won, 3–2, on a 10th-inning home run by Rudy York.

The hero of Game Two was a slender Cardinals pitcher, "Harry the Cat Brecheen." Brecheen shut out the Sox on four hits, 3–0.

The seesaw Series continued, as the Sox took Game Three, 4–0, behind Boo Ferriss. Then the Cardinals came back to win Game Four, 12–3, on 20 hits. The Sox won Game Five, 6–3, but St. Louis won Game Six, 4–1, behind another dominant performance by Harry Brecheen.

So, after six games, the Series was knotted 3–3. The teams were as even as they'd been before the Series started, with one difference. Whoever won the next game would be champions of the world.

THE DASH

It seemed at first as if the Red Sox would break open Game Seven in the first inning. Their first two men up hit singles, and then Dom DiMaggio drove in a run with a long fly out. Up came Ted Williams, still struggling through his subpar Series.

This time Williams hit the ball hard, unleashing a long fly to left center. There was no way left fielder Harry Walker would reach the ball, and it seemed that Williams would have his first extra-base hit of the Series. But at the last second, center fielder Terry Moore came racing over and caught the ball on the fly. Williams was out, and a moment later the inning was over, with the Red Sox having scored only that one run.

The Cardinals tied the score in the second inning, then drove Sox starter Boo Ferriss from the game with two more runs in the fifth. Suddenly it seemed as if the game would go easily to St. Louis, in a disappointingly undramatic finale.

But the Red Sox had one more uprising left in them. In the eighth inning, the first two men got on, and Cardinal manager Eddie Dyer went to his ace—Harry Brecheen, working with just one day's rest.

Brecheen got two men out. But then Dom DiMaggio doubled, driving in two and tying the score. He also twisted his ankle on the play, and had to be replaced in centerfield by

Leon Culberson, a mediocre fielder with a weaker arm.

This, it turned out, would represent the last cruel twist of fate for the Red Sox. In the bottom of the eighth, Enos Slaughter led off with a single. With two outs, Harry Walker hit a line drive to center for a single. Culberson fielded it and threw in to second baseman Johnny Pesky. Everyone in the park assumed that Slaughter would stop at third base on the single.

But, in one of the most daring baserunning plays in World Series history, Slaughter never stopped running. In his "Mad Dash," he rounded third and headed straight for home. Pesky seemed to hesitate for a bare instant before pegging the ball to the plate—but his throw was fatally late. Slaughter scored easily with the run that put the Cardinals ahead to stay. Brecheen worked his way out of a ninth-inning jam for his third win of the Series . . . and again the Red Sox had come up empty.

The Curse of the Bambino lived on.

CARDINALS' ACE Harry Brecheen, pitching in his third World Series, retired Boston's last two batters, spoiling Boston's hope for the Series.

ENOS "COUNTRY" SLAUGHTER lands at home in one of the most aggressive baserunning feats in World Series history.

THE BABE'S LAST HURRAH

On June 13, 1948, the great Babe Ruth stood before his fans at Yankee Stadium for the last time. The occasion was the 25th anniversary of "The House That Ruth Built," and the official ceremony to retire his uniform number, three. The moment was immortalized in words by W.C. Heinz of the New York Sun: *"He walked out into the cauldron of sound he must know better than any other man." 50,000 fans cheered wildly for the Babe, and sang a round of "Auld Lang Syne." Two months later, the hero, who said "No one wants to live more than I do," passed away.*

WORTH REPEATING

Even decades later, the numbers Babe Ruth put into the record books are something to marvel at.

He began his major league career in 1914, a rawboned 19-year-old, fresh out of a Baltimore home for wayward boys and less than a year with two minor league teams, the Providence Grays and the Baltimore Orioles. Even in those early days he stunned observers with his hitting ability. "He is a whale with the willow," said Oriole owner Jack Dunn—a colorful way of saying that Ruth could hit the ball as far as anyone he'd ever seen.

Still, when the Boston Red Sox acquired Ruth from the Orioles in 1914, they saw him as a pitcher. And he was a great one: Pitching regularly from 1915 to 1919, Babe posted a record of 89–46. His 1.75 earned run average in 1916 led the league, and in 1917 he posted a 24–13 record with a 2.01 ERA. He was a major contributor to the Sox' world championships in 1916 and 1918.

But even in those early days, Ruth was a prodigious slugger.

By 1919 he was making the transition to full-time outfield play, in order to get his bat in the lineup more often. It was then, as he left pitching behind, that Ruth's true glory years began. His home run totals climbed to 29 in 1919, to a record-shattering 54 in 1920 (his first season with the New York Yankees), and to 59 in 1921. After that, he rarely hit fewer than 40 home runs a season, with a peak of 60 in 1927.

BABE RUTH SAYS HIS OFFICIAL GOODBYE to baseball on June 13, 1948. He had served the game well: playing for over two decades, pitching four seasons with an ERA under 2.50, and hitting over 50 home runs in four seasons.

When he retired in 1935, Ruth had posted the most breathtaking offensive numbers of all time: a lifetime .342 batting average and .690 slugging average (the highest of all time). His 714 home runs and 2,211 RBI stood as records until broken by Hank Aaron. He also helped lead the Yankees to seven World Series appearances and four championships.

But just as importantly, he gave the game his incomparable personality—the big smile, the love of food, the eagerness to clown and show off.

LOST SOUL

Babe Ruth always assumed that he would stay in baseball after he retired as a player. He thought he'd step right into a manager's job, able to share the knowledge he'd gained both on the mound and at the plate with young players.

But it was not to be. From the start, team owners decided that Ruth didn't have the discipline—or even the intelligence—to make it as a major league manager.

Even before Ruth retired, rumors floated about his being named to one managerial job after another. First he was going to the Cincinnati Reds, then to the Brooklyn Dodgers, then to the Philadelphia Athletics. In every case, the potential candidate was a mediocre team with little fan support, which might have seen the colorful Ruth as a sure publicity coup. Even so, all the rumors remained just rumors, and no one ever offered the Babe the job he craved.

Then, in 1946, he started feeling ill. His illness wasn't immediately diagnosed—and some believe he never knew what afflicted him—but from the moment he first started feeling under the weather, Babe Ruth was suffering from the cancer that would kill him.

ONE LAST MOMENT OF GLORY

As Ruth's condition worsened through 1947, the Yankees decided they had to do something to honor him. The choice was June 13, 1948, at Yankee Stadium, "The House That

Ruth Built," in a ceremony that also celebrated the 25th anniversary of the stadium's opening.

The Yankees gathered as many of their 1923 stars as they could, including Bob Shawkey (who pitched and won the first game ever played at Yankee Stadium, behind a home run by Babe Ruth), Bob Meusel, Wally Pipp, and Waite Hoyt.

Ruth wore his old Yankee uniform, Number three, as he made his slow way onto the field for the ceremony. "He walked out into the cauldron of sound he must know better than any other man," said the *New York Sun*'s W. C. Heinz.

When the cheering of the 50,000 fans died down, the Babe spoke briefly. "I am proud that I hit the first home run in this Stadium," he said over a microphone. "It is a marvelous privilege to come back here and to see 13 men of 1923 playing together again. It makes me proud."

And then he slowly walked back to the dugout. "As the Babe walked away from the mike, tears streamed down his face," wrote Dan Daniel of *The Sporting News*. His tears were shared by countless fans, who knew they were seeing Ruth in a Yankee uniform for the last time.

Babe Ruth died just two months later. Today, his monument stands at Yankee Stadium, among those of Lou Gehrig, Joe DiMaggio, and the other men who built the great Yankee teams of the past.

ON THE DAY the Yankees retired his number, the famous number three in pinstripes, Ruth was greeted by an ovation from 50,000 fans and former teammates from 25 years ago, when the new Yankee Stadium was officially opened.

OUT OF HIS PINSTRIPES, Ruth lived for 13 years after retiring from baseball in 1935. Illness began to trouble him in 1946 and he died two months after his day of honor at Yankee Stadium.

DON'T LOOK BACK

What might have been? Negro League pitching sensation Satchel Paige didn't get a chance to pitch in the Majors until 1948, when he was an estimated 42 years old. Signed by maverick Cleveland Indians owner Bill Veeck for the stretch drive, Paige was the object of immediate criticism. "To sign a hurler of Paige's age is to demean the standards of baseball," wrote one columnist. Paige pitched consecutive complete game shutouts against the White Sox on August 13th and 20th, both to record crowds. The Comiskey Park crowd was so large and boisterous that ticketless fans crushed one of the stadium gates and poured inside. In response to his critics, Paige said "I demeaned the league something considerable last year. Went 6-1."

THE GREAT SATCHEL PAIGE, signed into the Majors in his early forties, completed an enviable inaugural year with a 6-1 record.

WHAT MIGHT HAVE BEEN

Who knows what wonders Satchel Paige might have been able to perform on the major league diamond? Imagine the battles that Paige would have waged with Babe Ruth, Lou Gehrig, Jimmie Foxx, and other sluggers of the 1920s and '30s—if he'd only gotten to pitch against them in regular-season games, or even in the World Series. As it was, he got to face them only during their barnstorming tours, post-season ventures that pitted major leaguers against each other or Negro Leagues' all-star teams.

There was no major league star that Satchel Paige couldn't strike out, not even the Babe. He may have been the greatest pitcher of all time, a man with supreme baseball smarts coupled with outstanding control and great speed. Hall of Fame pitcher Dizzy Dean, who had pretty good stuff himself, said, "If Satch and I were pitching on the same team, we'd cinch the pennant by July 4 and go fishing until World Series time."

So why didn't Satchel Paige get to pitch alongside Dizzy Dean, or any other major leaguer, before 1947? For the usual reason: He was African American, and pitched his best ball before 1947, when Jackie Robinson broke through the color barrier and became the first black ballplayer to step onto a major league diamond in the 20th century.

Still, Paige was luckier than Josh Gibson, Judy Johnson, Smokey Joe Williams, Ray Dandridge, Pop Lloyd, and many other stars of the Negro Leagues who never had the opportunity to play even a single inning in the big leagues. Thanks to a man named Bill Veeck, he did finally get the call. In 1948, when he was at least 42 years old, Satchel Paige was signed to pitch for the Cleveland Indians.

THE PITCHER AND THE SHOWMAN

Among the careful, gray-suited businessmen who usually run baseball teams, Bill Veeck stood out like a cheerful salesman in a bright plaid jacket. Endlessly surprising, joyfully quotable, he brought life and excitement to the Cleveland Indians and other ballclubs beginning in the 1940s. Veeck was the inventor of many outrageous gimmicks designed to bring crowds to the ballpark. But no move Bill Veeck ever made garnered him more undeserved criticism than his decision to sign forty plus-year-old Satchel Paige to an Indians contract in 1948.

Veeck was cautious about signing Paige. First, he asked Indians all-star player-manager Lou Boudreau to take some practice swings against the aging pitcher. At the time, Boudreau was batting about .400 against the American League, but, as Veeck recounted in his book *Veeck—As in Wreck,* Boudreau couldn't do anything with Paige's deliveries. "Satch threw twenty pitches. Nineteen of them were strikes . . . . After a final pop fly, Lou dropped his bat, came over to us, and said, 'Don't let him get away, Will. We can use him.'"

The Indians in 1948 were in the midst of a tight pennant race, so Veeck believed that no one would question his signing of a pitcher with such a brilliant reputation as Paige had. He was wrong.

Leading the attack was *The Sporting News*'s publisher, J. G. Taylor Spink. "To sign a hurler at Paige's age is to demean the standards of baseball in the big circuits," he wrote in an editorial before Paige had pitched a single inning of major league baseball.

So, suddenly and unfairly, Satchel Paige—one of the greatest hurlers of all time—had to prove himself once again.

SATCHEL SHOWS 'EM

How did Paige do?

Just fine, as he would have been the first to predict. After getting his feet wet with a couple of successful relief appearances, he thrilled his fans by pitching consecutive complete game shutouts against the Chicago White Sox on August 13 and 20. Everywhere he went, the crowds were enormous—the August 13 game

SATCHEL PAIGE AND BILL VEECK, right, in 1948, when Veeck hired Paige to pitch for the Cleveland Indians, the first major league team Paige was to play for.

at Comiskey Park drew 51,000; the August 20 game at Cleveland drew 78,000.

With every strong appearance, Veeck sent a telegram to Taylor Spink at *The Sporting News*. It always read WINNING PITCHER: PAIGE. DEFINITELY IN LINE FOR *THE SPORTING NEWS* AWARD AS ROOKIE OF THE YEAR. Spink finally responded with an editorial that expressed grudging admiration for Paige, but added that his success showed how second-rate major league baseball hitters had become.

Paige finished the season 6–1, with a 2.48 ERA. (His comment: "I demeaned the league something considerable.") Since the Indians won the pennant by just a single game that year, Bill Veeck's signing of the aging star was shown to be an act of genius.

For Paige, his years in the Major Leagues (in 1952, when he was 46 years old, he went 12–10 with the St. Louis Browns) were a bittersweet end to a storied career. "They said I was the greatest pitcher they ever saw," he lamented late in his life. "I couldn't understand why they couldn't give me no justice."

But the ageless Paige lived long enough to see himself elected to the Hall of Fame in 1971 for his magnificent achievements in the Negro Leagues and his brief coda in the Majors. Standing before the crowd, he revealed another emotion, saying, "I am the proudest man in the place right today."

THE HALL OF FAME inducted Paige in 1971 in honor of his impressive achievements in both the Negro Leagues and the Majors. Pictured here is Paige with fellow inductees that year. From left to right, Chick Hafey, Paige, Harry Hooper, and Rube Marquard.

BASEBALL RETURNS TO THE COMMON

As early as 1820, baseball and other ball games were played on Boston Common. In October 1948, baseball returned. With the Boston Braves in the World Series for the first time since 1914, television manufacturers sought to capture fans' enthusiasm by setting up television sets on Boston Common, allowing everyone to see the broadcast of the Series games. While telecasts of baseball games on television became commonplace after World War II, the cost of television sets prevented many fans from watching in their own homes.

POSTWAR BOOM

Baseball's popularity exploded after World War II ended. As stars like Ted Williams, Joe DiMaggio, and Bob Feller returned to their teams in 1946 after years in the military, fans flooded the ballparks as well. Attendance in 1945 was 10.8 million, which was itself a record. But then, in 1946, attendance leapt to 18.5 million—a stunning gain of 71.1 percent in just one year.

Part of this was due to the return of the great players. After seasons in which fans had watched 15-year-old pitchers and one-armed outfielders pressed into duty, it was a relief to see baseball being played the way it was intended to be. But there were other factors at work, including a widespread acceptance of night baseball, which allowed far more people to go to games than ever before.

But perhaps the most important explanation was also the simplest: after the Depression of the 1930s and the war years, the postwar era was one of both peace and affluence. One of the ways in which people wanted to spend their free time and disposable income was by going to the ballpark.

Another entertainment source that was embraced with equal fervor by the postwar generation was television. While television had been around for years, in the late 1940s it finally began to attain a long-predicted popularity.

"THE MAJOR LEAGUES WILL HAVE TO BAR TELEVISION— OR SUFFER DIRE CONSEQUENCES!"

From the start, the television networks were insatiably hungry for new programming. And what better way to capture viewers' interest (and maybe get them to buy television sets for their own homes) than to televise baseball games?

A PERFECT MATCH?

At first, it seemed as if television and baseball would be an ideal marriage, benefiting each. The networks would get hours of programming, while the teams would get extra revenue (from fees paid by the networks) while also increasing their fan base. People who had never been to the ballpark might watch a

game on TV, get interested, and buy tickets for the next game.

Perhaps the peak of these early hopes came in October 1948. The National League's Boston Braves had won their first pennant since 1914, and were set to play the Cleveland Indians in a televised World Series. To commemorate the Braves' rare pennant, television manufacturers decided to set up rows of television sets on Boston Common. Baseball had been played on the Common as early as 1820, so it seemed appropriate that fans without sets in their homes could watch the Series in this historic setting.

FOR FANS WHO COULDN'T GET TICKETS and who didn't have TV sets at home, the 100 televisions installed at Boston Common offered them the opportunity to see their team in the World Series, a rare occurrence for the Braves.

The Braves lost the 1948 Series to the Indians, four games to two. But the marriage of TV and baseball was declared a success.

IT'S TELEVISION'S FAULT!

It didn't take long for baseball's love affair with television to turn sour, however. By 1950 club owners had noticed that attendance at games was falling rapidly. After peaking at 21 million in 1948, total attendance fell to 17.5 million just two years later, and then spiraled downward, all the way to 14.3 million in 1953. In just five years, baseball had lost almost a third of its attendance.

From the start, baseball owners accused television of "stealing" their fans. By 1950 (just two years after the triumphant televising of the World Series on the Boston Common), the Boston Braves decided to restrict television's access to their ballpark. The reason: The Braves' attendance for the 1950 season had fallen below one million, its lowest point in five years, and general manager Jack Quinn was sure that fans were watching the games on TV instead of journeying to the ballpark.

"Quinn did not say what the basis would be for permitting the TV cameras inside the park next year," reported *The Sporting News*,

Major League Attendance 10 Years Following Introduction of TV Broadcasting	
1948	20,920,842
1949	20,215,364
1950	17,462,976
1951	16,126,676
1952	14,633,044
1953	14,383,797
1954	15,935,883
1955	16,617,383
1956	16,543,250
1957	17,015,820

"but it seems evident that permission will be determined by the advance sale of tickets for a particular game." In other words: You'd be able to watch a game on TV only if enough tickets were sold.

At first the influential *Baseball Magazine* rejected such restrictions. In a 1950 editorial entitled "Games Must Be Televised," the magazine passionately argued for the televising of as many games as possible. "Why, for the benefit of invalids alone, especially those in the hospitals of the armed services, in the veterans hospitals, the games must be televised," it proclaimed.

But by 1952, in the face of increasingly dismal attendance reports, the magazine had changed its tune. Long-time baseball writer Dan Daniel argued that "TV Must Go—Or Baseball Will!" He didn't mince words. "The critic and the student on the sidelines is convinced by now that the Major Leagues will have to bar television—or suffer dire consequences!" he proclaimed.

The truth was that television wasn't to blame for baseball's problem in the 1950s. The real culprit was that teams were playing in aging, decrepit ballparks located in bad neighborhoods of cities that no longer had much interest in their teams. Beginning in 1953, teams began moving to new stadiums in better areas of cities that were excited to have them.

FANS PACKED BRAVES FIELD for the 1948 World Series against the Cleveland Indians, the first time since 1914 that the Braves made it to the Series.

The trend began when the Boston Braves moved to Milwaukee in 1953. Then the St. Louis Browns went to Baltimore in 1954 and the Philadelphia A's relocated to Kansas City in 1955. And then, in a joint move that still gives New York fans nightmares, the Giants and Dodgers picked up and headed to California. In addition, as the 1950s turned into the 1960s, several cities sought to keep their teams from moving by building them new ballparks.

As these changes took place, the chorus demanding the expulsion of television from the ballparks subsided. It was a close call, but the marriage of TV and baseball was once more a happy one.

THE 1948 SERIES gathered crowds in both Boston and Cleveland. Pictured here are the fans leaving Cleveland Municipal Stadium. The game hosted a crowd of over 86,000, the biggest attendance figure for any major league game to that date.

121

GEE WHIZ

*As the 1950 season opened, the Phillies faced a pennant drought which stretched all the way
back to 1915. The youthful team started slowly, but by mid-May had climbed to respectability. On July 25, they ascended
into first place for good, but would face a gut-wrenching see-saw pennant race with the Dodgers, Giants, Cardinals, and
Braves. By Labor Day the Phillies appeared to be firmly in command, but then their bats cooled and the pitching staff went
down one by one with injuries and freak accidents. Going into the season's final day,
the Whiz Kids led by one game against Brooklyn. Nineteen-game-winners Robin Roberts and Don Newcombe faced each
other at Ebbets field. The two teams played to a 1-1 tie after nine innings. In the top of the tenth,
Dick Sisler blasted a three run homer and the Phillies had finally won the pennant.*

NEW BLOOD

*The 1950 Philadelphia Phillies,
who won the National League pennant for the first time since 1915.
The "Whiz Kids," as they were
known, were stocked with young
overachievers, including Richie
Ashburn (back row, fifth from the
left) who, at 23, hit .303 for the season, and Del Ennis (seated, fourth
from left) who, at 25, slammed 31
home runs during the year.*

By 1950, baseball fans in both leagues must have been eager to see a new team or two win a pennant. By the late 1940s, the N.L.'s Brooklyn Dodgers and the A.L.'s New York Yankees were already perennial contenders and frequent pennant-winners. And when the Yankees and Dodgers didn't make it, they were usually replaced by other powerhouse teams, like Stan Musial's St. Louis Cardinals.

That's what made the story of the 1950 Philadelphia Phillies—the "Whiz Kids"—such an appealing one to fans nationwide. For decades, the Phillies had been a sad-sack team. They had bottomed out in 1945, going 46–108.

The rest of the '40s weren't much better, as the Phillies posted records like 69-85, 62–92, and 66–88. But suddenly, in 1949 things started looking up, as under the calm leadership of manager Eddie Sawyer, the team improved to 81–73. This was their best record since 1917.

Still, no one could have predicted that everything would come together for the Phillies in 1950.

TOO YOUNG TO SHAVE?

The 1950 Phillies were filled with eager, fresh-faced ballplayers who looked like teenagers. Center fielder Richie Ashburn, who hit .303 and fielded brilliantly, was 23. Del Ennis, who slugged 31 home runs, was 25. Pitcher Robin Roberts, who won 20 games, didn't turn 24 until near the end of the season, while Curt Simmons, who chipped in with 17 wins, was just 21. No wonder they were called the Whiz Kids.

Still, probably their most important addition was a grizzled veteran named Jim Konstanty. All of 33 years old, Konstanty pitched in a record-setting 74 games, winning 16, saving 22 more, and winning the N.L.'s Most Valuable Player award at the end of the season.

The Phillies took off at the beginning of the season like a house afire. At or near the top of the standings from the start, they moved into first place for good on July 25. But that didn't mean they ran away with the pennant flag. Boston, Brooklyn, New York, and St. Louis were all in contention throughout the season, taking turns at coming close and then falling back.

With nine games to go, the Phillies had a five-game lead. By a week later, with just one game remaining, the lead had shrunk to just a single game over the Dodgers. Now, on October 1, the two teams were set to play each other at Brooklyn's Ebbets Field. After such a wonderful, successful, surprising season, everything had come down to this single game.

ONE SWING OF THE BAT

The all-important game pitted Phillies' ace Robin Roberts against the Dodgers' brilliant Don Newcombe, who came into the game with 19 wins. Unsurprisingly, the game was a tight, tense pitchers' duel from the start. The Phillies' Dick Sisler scored the first run, but the Dodgers tied the game in the sixth inning on one of the freakier plays in baseball

history. Brooklyn's Pee Wee Reese hit a long fly ball that landed on a ledge between the scoreboard and the rightfield stands—and stayed there. No outfielder could reach it, so Reese circled the bases for a home run.

The game remained tied, 1–1, as the innings rolled on. Then Robin Roberts led off the 10th with a single. Eddie Waitkus followed with another single, and suddenly the Phillies had the go-ahead run in scoring position.

With one out, Dick Sisler stepped to the plate to face the tiring Newcombe. Quickly the pitcher got two strikes on him—and, as Sisler knew but Newcombe didn't—it wouldn't have been hard for Newcombe to get strike three. "I was hiding a sprained wrist and I couldn't get my bat around on an inside pitch," Sisler recalled later. "If he'd ever given me the mustard and fired in a fastball, I was dead."

But Newcombe elected to try a breaking pitch instead, and Sisler hit it hard. "I knew I'd hit the ball pretty good but I didn't think I'd hit it hard enough to carry all the way," he said. "When I turned at first, I saw it land in the seats for a three-run homer."

The Phillies went on to win, 4–1, for their first pennant since 1915.

BELEAGUERED with a sprained wrist, the Phillies' Dick Sisler launched a three-run home run to give the Phillies their 4-1 win and their pennant crown against the Brooklyn Dodgers.

JUBILATION SWEPT THE TEAM and congratulations flooded Sisler, number eight, following his game- and pennant-winning home run in the top of the 10th against the Dodgers.

VEECK'S MINI-MASTERPIECE

Bill Veeck owned the Cleveland Indians, St. Louis Browns, and the Chicago White Sox twice. He brought Larry Doby and Satchel Paige to the big leagues. He planted the ivy at Wrigley Field. He let the fans manage a game in St. Louis, by holding up "YES" or "NO" placards at key moments. (The fans won the game.) He had relievers pop out of birthday cakes. But most of all, Veeck reminded baseball that the game was supposed to be fun. He is best remembered for sending Eddie Gaedel to bat on August 19, 1951. You see, the 26-year old Gaedel was only 3 feet, 7 inches tall. As he strode to the plate, wearing the number 1/8 on his back, the fans went wild. By crouching at the plate, Gaedel reduced his strike zone to about an inch and a half, and drew a walk on four pitches from pitcher Bob Cain. He was immediately lifted for a pinch runner, and is still in the record books with a 1.000 on-base percentage. Though Gaedel signed a contract and was paid, he was disallowed from ever again appearing in a game.

A LIFELONG DREAM

I n 1951, in a moment of madness, I became owner and operator of a collection of old rags and tags known to baseball historians as the St. Louis Browns."

These were the words of Bill Veeck, Jr., describing why he chose to buy one of the worst teams of all time, the St. Louis Browns. Over the course of three decades, he owned the Cleveland Indians and the Chicago White Sox twice. But at their worst, those teams were never as bad as the Browns.

The Browns somehow managed to lose 100 games—or close to it—every year, quite a feat when teams played only 154 games in a season. In 1951, for example, they went 52–102, with a team batting average of .247 and earned run average of 5.18—both statistics were the worst in the Major Leagues. They had no power, no speed, no hope.

But Bill Veeck, a famous showman, always relished a challenge. He was an eternally creative and cheerful publicity hound, and perhaps the most quotable man in baseball history. He was at his best in his efforts to bring fans to the ballpark to watch his teams.

For example, he bucked public opinion and the scathing response of the press to bring the Negro Leagues' pitching great Satchel Paige to the Major Leagues at age 42—a move that both brought out enormous crowds and helped the Indians capture the 1948 American League pennant.

Some of Veeck's other stunts were entirely for show. He had relief pitchers jump out of enormous birthday cakes. He planted the ivy that still adorns the walls of Wrigley Field in Chicago. He handed out placards reading YES and NO to fans entering the ballpark, and then allowed the fans to vote on strategy as the game went on. (The fans won the game.)

But nothing Bill Veeck ever did for publicity's sake matched the uproar he created when he sent a 3 feet 7 inches-tall man named Eddie Gaedel up to bat for the Browns in 1951.

THE BIG MOMENT

Veeck decided to unveil Eddie Gaedel during an August 19, 1951, double-header with the

BILL VEECK, as much a savvy PR man as he was manager, was known for the inventive tricks he used to fill ballparks.

IN ONE OF HIS FINEST MOMENTS, Veeck left the managing up to the fans in a stunt that allowed the crowd to vote on game strategy.

Detroit Tigers, a mediocre team not destined to bring fans into the Browns' ballpark. Gaedel's appearance was to be the centerpiece of a celebration of both the American League's 50th birthday and the birthday of St. Louis sponsor Falstaff Brewery.

But first Veeck had to convince Gaedel that the stunt wouldn't humiliate him. He did so with a stream of words that would have done P. T. Barnum proud. "I said, 'Eddie, you'll be the only midget in the history of the game. You'll be appearing before thousands of

people. Your name will go into the record books for all time. You'll be famous, Eddie,' I said, 'you'll be immortal.'"

Gaedel, bowled over by Veeck's palaver, agreed. And Veeck knew he'd made the right decision when he asked Gaedel to get into his batting crouch. Gaedel's strike zone was about an inch and a half high.

Veeck kept his big gimmick a secret, but the fans knew something was brewing. Brought out as well by a variety of free gifts associated with the Falstaff birthday party

VEECK CONVINCED THE 3 FOOT, 7 INCH EDDIE GAEDEL that batting in the Major Leagues would not humiliate him. At bat, when he confounded pitcher Bobby Cain, the spectators roared their support.

As soon as he was announced as a pinch hitter, the crowd went wild. The Tigers pitcher and catcher huddled at the mound to discuss strategy, and when the catcher returned to the plate, he got down on his knees to receive the pitch.

Pitcher Bobby Cain tried to get his first two pitches over the plate, but all he succeeded in doing was nearly braining Gaedel. "By the third pitch, Cain was laughing so hard that he could barely throw," Veeck said. "Ball three and ball four came floating up about three feet over Eddie's head." Gaedel trotted down to first base in front of the cheering fans, and was immediately lifted for a pinch runner. He then took his time leaving the field, pausing after every step to doff his cap, bow, or wave his arms.

Before the next game, Gaedel was forbidden by American League President Will Harridge from ever appearing in a game again. But he'd had his moment in the sun—and Bill Veeck had produced the stunt that forevermore would be associated with his name.

GAEDEL IN THE DUGOUT alongside St. Louis Browns' teammates Matt Batts, left, and Jim McDonald. Gaedel's debut was his last game, since the American League barred Veeck from using Gaedel after his first appearance.

(including a slice of cake and a can of beer), more than 18,000 fans showed up. For the Browns, this was a veritable flood of humanity.

Between games of the double-header, Veeck introduced jugglers, trampoline acts, and a band featuring Satchel Paige on drums. But the big show was to come in the second game.

In the bottom of the first inning, Eddie Gaedel came striding out of the dugout, waving three little bats. On his back was the number 1/8.

"THEY'RE GOING CRAZY!"

"The Giants win the pennant! The Giants win the pennant! The Giants win the pennant! They're going crazy! I don't believe it. I do not believe it." Radio broadcaster Russ Hodges was as excited as everyone else in the Polo Grounds as the Giants defeated the Dodgers in Game Three of a special playoff made necessary because the clubs finished the 1951 season tied. Bobby Thomson homered off Ralph Branca with two men on and the Giants trailing 4-2 in the bottom of the ninth. The dramatic home run immediately became known as "The Shot Heard 'Round the World."

A SEASON TURNED UPSIDE-DOWN

During spring training, 1951, the conventional wisdom said that the Giants and the Dodgers would contend for the National League pennant. It wasn't a stretch to predict this: In 1950, the Dodgers had finished second and the Giants third, both close at the heels of the miracle Philadelphia Phillies "Whiz Kids," who had come out of nowhere to win the pennant—yet who remained unproven.

When the season started, it looked like the predictions were right. The Phillies played disappointingly mediocre ball, and the Dodgers won game after game. But the big surprise was the Giants. After winning their first game of the season, they plummeted into a shocking 11-game losing streak. By August 12, they were 13½ games behind the Dodgers, a hopelessly large deficit.

Or was it? The Giants' manager was fiery Leo Durocher, a master at driving his teams to exceed even their own expectations. Suddenly the Giants began to win, and win again, and win some more. They won an astounding 37 of their last 44 games—and, in fact, actually pulled ahead of the stunned Dodgers going into Brooklyn's last game of the season. Only a tense

BOBBY THOMSON, whose ninth-inning homer became "The Shot Heard 'Round the World," clinched the pennant for the Giants.

extra-inning win against the Phillies allowed the Dodgers to tie the Giants at the end, with identical 96–58 records.

As if the season hadn't been strange and stressful enough, now the two teams would have to play a best-two-out-of-three series to determine who would face the New York Yankees in the World Series.

EVERY MOMENT COUNTS

Just five years earlier, in 1946, the Dodgers had faced off against the St. Louis Cardinals in just such a playoff—and had lost it. When they dropped the first game to the Giants, 3–1, despite having the home field, it seemed as if history would soon repeat itself.

So now the Dodgers were down, one game to none, with the next game and the one after that (if necessary) both to be played at the Giants' ballpark, the Polo Grounds. Surprising everyone, the Dodgers exploded for a 10–0 win behind rookie pitcher Clem Labine, with Jackie Robinson, Gil Hodges, Andy Pafko, and Rube Walker all hitting home runs.

Given the exciting and exhausting ups and downs of the season up to this point, it seemed only fair that the pennant rest on a single game. As the fans filed into the Polo Grounds on October 3 for that ultimate game, the only question that remained was: What on earth could these two teams do to match the tension that had led up to this point?

THE SHOT

Game Three of the play-off saw two crafty pitchers take the mound. The Dodgers' Don Newcombe had already won 20 games during the 1951 season, while the Giants' Sal Maglie (who ended the season with 23 wins) was famed for his ability to beat the Dodgers.

Both pitchers pitched well. The game was tied, 1–1, until the eighth inning, when the Dodgers broke through for three runs and a 4–1 lead.

Going into the last of the ninth inning, the score was still 4–1. It seemed that the Giants' valiant effort to climb out of the hole created by their early-season failures was destined to fall just a few runs short.

Giants manager Leo Durocher did what he could to rally the troops. "I'm proud of every one of you," he told his team. "It's not over yet. Let's go out there and give them all we got, and let's leave this ball field, win or lose, with our heads in the air."

Newcombe held the lead until there was one out in the ninth inning, but it was clear that he was out of gas. With two men on, Whitey Lockman doubled to drive in a run, bringing the score to 4–2 and putting runners on second and third. Just one more hit, one little single, would tie the game.

With Giants' slugger Bobby Thomson coming to the plate, Dodgers' manager Charlie Dressen knew it was time to go to the bullpen. His choice was Ralph Branca—despite the fact that Branca had already lost to the Giants five times that season, and

had just given up a home run to Thomson two games earlier.

With the Giant fans roaring, Branca got one strike on Thomson. On his next pitch, he tried another fastball, and Thomson climbed all over it, hitting a wicked line drive that hurtled to the left field wall. Durocher and everyone else in the park thought the ball was a sure double, but suddenly the ball cleared the wall and disappeared into the seats. Bobby Thomson had hit a three-run home run to give the Giants a 5–4 victory and the National League pennant.

Giants radio broadcaster Russ Hodges was handling play-by-play for the national broadcast of the game. When Thomson's blast (forever after known as "The Shot Heard 'Round the World") cleared the fence, Hodges let his true feelings be known. "The Giants win the pennant! The Giants win the pennant! The Giants win the pennant!" he shouted to the four corners of the Earth. "They're going crazy! I don't believe it! I do not believe it."

TEAMMATES MOB BOBBY THOMSON after he slammed the home run that won the 1951 National League pennant race against the Dodgers. The Giants' jubilation was understandable. By mid-August, they had dug themselves into a massive 13½ game hole behind the Dodgers. Their turn-around was astounding.

A MANTLESQUE SHOT

It is said that a truly long home run could leave any park except Yellowstone. The one Mantle hit on April 17, 1953, could well have been close to leaving even that venue. A tremendous hitter with power from both sides of the plate, Mantle crushed a ball out of Washington's Griffith Stadium, an estimated 565 feet. Still early in his career, Mantle's homer at Griffith Stadium would be the longest in his career, one that spanned 18 years. In two of those seasons, he would hit over 50 home runs, including another shot, in 1955, over the 500-foot mark.

BIG BOPPERS

Fans know it when they see a home run hit by a true slugger. They appreciate a prodigious blast far more than they do the wind-blown fly that lands five rows beyond the outfielder's reach.

In the 1920s, an era that specialized in the long ball, lots of players hit home runs. But there was only one Babe Ruth. Only he, on a regular basis, hit balls that sounded like a rifle shot as they left the bat, that soared outward on parabolic arcs that had to be seen to be believed, that broke windows across the street from the ballparks.

Today's Babe Ruth, of course, is Mark McGwire. Other players hit mammoth shots from time to time, but no one else has the ability to crush the ball seemingly every time he steps to the plate.

MICKEY MANTLE'S PROWESS at bat was well-recognized, even as a younger player. In 1953, when his reputation was still on the rise, he slammed a 565-foot home run in Griffith Stadium, the longest shot he ever hit.

In the 1950s, the hitter who slammed the most monstrous home runs of all was a switch-hitter named Mickey Mantle. And he never hit them higher or farther than he did on April 17, 1953, against the Washington Senators.

THE SHOT

As a rising star in 1953, 21-year-old Mickey Mantle still had something to prove. From spring training onward, he seemed to be hitting the ball harder than he ever had before. In one exhibition against the Pittsburgh Pirates, he blasted a ball over the roof at Pittsburgh's Forbes Field. "It was estimated that Mantle's wallop traveled at least 400 feet to attain the height necessary to clear the barrier and was still rising as it left the park," reported *The Sporting News*. Only two other players had ever hit the ball over the roof at Forbes Field: a Pirate named Ted Beard and a man named Babe Ruth.

The most remarkable of all of Mantle's round-trippers in 1953 may have been the blast he hit on April 17. It was the fifth inning of that early-season game, and the Senators had lefty Chuck Stobbs on the mound. Stobbs got one strike on Mickey, who was batting right-handed, and then tried to bust a fastball past him.

Bad idea. Mantle swung, and the ball seemed to leap off his bat and accelerate as it soared higher and higher into the sky. As the crowd gasped, the ball crashed against a beer sign in left field—a sign located 60 feet off the ground and 500 feet from home plate.

But this home run ball wasn't finished traveling. It ricocheted off the sign and out of sight.

The minute he saw the ball leave the stadium, Yankee public relations man Red Patterson set out to find it. He searched on Fifth Street, which bordered the outfield wall, with no luck, but then followed the sound of excited children's voices to a yard several houses up the street. The ball had been hit so hard that it had flown entirely over Fifth Street and rolled into the yard. The best measurement put the distance the ball traveled at 565 feet.

Patterson ransomed the ball from the boy who found it for $5.00 and a pair of autographed balls. Both Mantle's bat and the ball were immediately requested by the Hall of Fame. They were exhibited first at Yankee Stadium, and then went to the Hall.

Bill Dickey, a Hall of Fame catcher for the Yankees who played with Babe Ruth, Lou Gehrig, and Joe DiMaggio, was stunned by the grandeur of Mantle's blast. "I saw Babe and Lou hit balls out of parks all over the country," Dickey said. "Frankly, I never thought I'd see their like again, but now I've changed my mind. For sheer power, Mickey ranks with the best of them."

KEEP ON DOING WHAT YOU DO

Mickey Mantle was just getting started in 1953. By 1956, the year he led the American League in batting average, home runs, and runs batted in, he seemed to be hitting another gargantuan blast every other day. Right at the beginning of the season, for example, he hit two balls that cleared the center field fence in Washington, D.C., ending up in a grove of trees that lay just beyond the stands.

By this point, the 24-year-old Mantle—who would end his career with 536 mostly awesome home runs—had caught the attention of even the great Ted Williams. "My guess

Player	Year	Distance	Park
Highlights in Baseball's Longest Home Runs*			
Babe Ruth	1926	626 ft.	Detroit, Navin Field
Harry Heilmann	1926	660 ft.	Detroit, Navin Field
Josh Gibson	1934	580 ft.	New York, Yankee Stadium (Negro League)
Jimmie Foxx	1936	620 ft.	Chicago, Comiskey Park
Ted Williams	1946	502 ft.	Boston, Fenway Park
Mickey Mantle	1953	565 ft.	Washington (DC), Griffith Stadium
Mickey Mantle	1955	550 ft.	Chicago, Comiskey Park
Frank Robinson	1966	541 ft.	Baltimore, Memorial Stadium
Harmon Killebrew	1967	522 ft.	Minneapolis, Metropolitan Stadium
Reggie Jackson	1969	600 ft.	Detroit, Tiger Stadium
Dave Kingman	1976	550 ft.	Chicago, Wrigley Field
Willie Stargell	1978	535 ft.	Montreal, Olympic Stadium
Jose Canseco	1990	600 ft.	Toronto, SkyDome
Mark McGwire	1998	545 ft.	St. Louis, Busch Stadium
Sammy Sosa	1998	500 ft.	Chicago, Wrigley Field

*No official record of long home runs exists and all distances are estimates.

is that he's now heading definitely for his peak," Williams said in 1956. And then, laughing, he added, "Don't worry about Mantle. In another fifteen or twenty years you'll be voting for him for the Hall of Fame."

Williams knew hitting and hitters both. Mickey Mantle was elected to the Hall 18 years later, in 1974.

GRIFFITH STADIUM in Washington, D.C., home of the Washington Senators and site of Mantle's crushing home run that traveled some 565 feet, ricocheted off a beer sign on the left field wall, and disappeared into the streets outside of the park.

OFFENSIVE EXPLOSION

On June 16-18, 1953, the Boston Red Sox hosted the Detroit Tigers for a three-game series. Detroit won the first game 5-3, but the Red Sox exploded in the second and third, winning 17-1 and 23-3. In the last game of the series, Boston took a 5-3 lead into the seventh inning when they scored 17 runs. Outfielder Gene Stephens' three hits and catcher Sammy White's three runs in the inning were both 20th-century records. In the three-game series, the Tigers were outscored 43-9.

CYCLES

If one takes a broad view of baseball's past, it's easy to see that hitters' eras and those dominated by pitching have taken turns during the game's history. In the 19th century, when the game was in its infancy, fielders wore no gloves, fields were bumpy and unkempt, even the ball was misshapen. This resulted in hundreds of errors and scores that would be more at home on the football field.

By early in this century, though, the pendulum had swung. This was the "dead ball" era, and though stars like Honus Wagner and Ty Cobb racked up high batting averages, in general runs were hard to come by and home runs almost nonexistent.

In 1920, the dead ball era came to an end with a stunning crash. Led by Babe Ruth, the hitters took over, slamming home runs in great abundance. This hitting frenzy, now remembered fondly as the "lively ball" era, lasted until World War II, but it probably peaked in 1930, when the entire National League as a whole batted .303.

After World War II, the pitchers started to reclaim the game. Sluggers like Ted Williams, Mickey Mantle, Willie Mays, and Hank Aaron hit their share of home runs, but team batting averages fell far from the peaks they'd reached in the 1930s.

THE 1953 BOSTON RED SOX, whose hitting and scoring extravaganza against the Detroit Tigers in June made baseball history.

Still, on any given day, a team could erupt for an earth-shaking offensive explosion. And that's exactly what the Boston Red Sox did on June 18, 1953, when they scored 17 runs in a single inning.

A PRETTY GOOD DAY

Actually, the Red Sox' offensive heroics began on June 17, when they pounded the Detroit Tigers 17–1. At first, the June 18 game seemed like a return to normality, as the score stood just 5–3, Boston, in the seventh inning.

Then the floodgates opened. Here's how the Sox' seventh inning proceeded: Single, single, single (two runs scoring), strike out, double, walk, single (two runs scoring), home run (three runs scoring), single, walk, double (two runs scoring), walk, single (one run scoring), fly out, single (one run scoring), walk, walk (one run scoring), single (two runs scoring), single (one run scoring), single (one run scoring), single (one run scoring), walk, fly out.

The final tally: 17 runs on 14 hits (including 11 singles!) and six walks. Gene Stephens, who entered the game batting .210, set a major league record by getting three hits in that one inning. Meanwhile, catcher Sammy White also got on base three times and scored a record three runs.

Oh yes, the Sox won the game, 23–3, meaning that Boston had outscored Detroit 40–4 in the two games. Rarely has a team been happier to leave an opponent's ballpark than the Tigers were when they limped away from Fenway Park after this thrashing.

HOME-RUN DERBY

While the Red Sox explosion came during a comparatively quiet offensive era, it would not have seemed so out of place in the late 1990s. Today baseball is in the midst of the greatest hitting era in its history, and games in which a team scores more than 20 runs are, if not common, at least a semi-regular occurrence.

Still, on September 4, 1999, the Cincinnati Reds did something that no National League team had ever done before: They hit nine home runs in a single game against the Philadelphia Phillies en route to a 22–3 victory.

The glory was spread around by the Reds, until then considered just an average-hitting team. Catcher Ed Taubensee slammed two round-trippers, while Brian Johnson, Pokey Reese, Greg Vaughn, Jeffrey Hammonds, Dmitri Young, Aaron Boone, and Mark Lewis chipped in with one each. Lewis' homer, a three-run shot in the eighth inning, broke the previous N.L. record of eight, shared by several teams.

The day after their nine-homer onslaught, the Reds went back to work. Still playing the shellshocked Phillies, Greg Vaughn hit another home run, Jeffrey Hammonds chipped in with two, Taubensee slammed his third in two days, and Dmitri Young also hit one. Amazingly, the Reds had added five home runs to their previous day's total of nine, for a major league record 14 home runs in two games.

GENE STEPHENS, another leader of Boston's June 1953 offensive explosion against Detroit, recorded three hits in one inning, a major league record that still stands.

CATCHER SAMMY WHITE scored a record three runs in one inning in the last game of a June series against the Detroit Tigers.

THE CATCH

With Game One of the 1954 World Series tied 2-2 in the top of the eighth inning, nobody out, and runners on first and second, Vic Wertz smashed a 462-foot drive to deepest right-center field. The fleet-footed Willie Mays turned his back on the ball and caught it over his shoulder in what many consider the greatest defensive play in World Series history. Mays caught, whirled, and threw the ball to second all in one motion, before collapsing to the grass. His strike to second base prevented Cleveland from scoring. The Giants went on to the win the game and the World Series.

A SIGNATURE PLAY

Seldom is a man's career as well defined by a single play—a single defensive play, no less—as was the career of the great Willie Mays.

Yes, many have hit signature home runs, or hurled no-hitters, or stolen enough bases to mark a milestone. But for Willie Mays, perhaps the most complete player the game has ever known, it was appropriate that a defensive play would become his signature moment. For "The Say Hey Kid," the defense was as legendary as the offense.

Mays had arrived in the big leagues in 1951, putting on a New York Giants uniform and playing for fiery manager Leo Durocher. He had been highly touted, for he had

WILLIE MAYS, at age 23, the year after Leo Durocher signed him to play with the New York Giants. Said Durocher of Mays, he was "the best looking kid I've seen in 25 years of baseball."

begun the season at Minneapolis in the American Association, and after more than a month of play, was only four hits short of a .500 batting average! It was an unheard of level, and put enormous pressure on him to succeed in baseball-crazed New York.

He started slowly, but Durocher's patience and reassurance kept him going until he found his stride and became a major contributor to one of the great comebacks of all time—the "Miracle at Coogan's Bluff," which culminated with a Bobby Thomson homer in the final game of the '51 playoff. Willie hit 20 home runs for that team, and played in a World Series in his rookie year.

TWO SEASONS, TWO PENNANTS

When he went off to military service in 1952 and 1953, Brooklyn won. When he came back in 1954, it was the Giants who won. Coincidence? Those who came to worship Willie would argue that it wasn't.

Willie would capture the league's MVP award that year, winning the batting title at .345, belting 41 home runs, and beginning a streak of 12 consecutive years in which he would surpass 100 runs scored. He had perfected his "basket catch," in which he would take routine fly balls at his waist. If they weren't quite so routine, he'd find a way to make the play anyway, often losing his cap in the process. He was a showman, and he was also a superstar as the word was just finding its way into the nation's sports vocabulary.

Still, the Giants were the underdogs in the '54 World Series. Although they had won 97 games, the American League champions—the Cleveland Indians—had set a league record with 111 wins, snapping the Yankees' streak of five straight flags. So good was the Indians pitching staff that the immortal Bob Feller was their fifth starter. No one had to explain why they were favorites—they were one of the best teams of all time.

Game One was played at the Polo Grounds on September 29, 1954. The Polo Grounds was a horseshoe-shaped ball field where center field went back 483 feet. Willie needed all of his great speed to cover that territory, but few were as good as he was at going back on a ball.

The Indians scored two in the first when Vic Wertz belted a triple, driving in both runs. The Giants got even in the third, when Hank Thompson singled home the tying run. And there the score still stood, 2–2, into the eighth, when Larry Doby led off for the Indians with a walk, and Al Rosen sent him to second with a base hit. The Indians were in position to win Game One, as expected, and perhaps use it as a jumping off point to dominate the entire Series.

That brought up Wertz, now 3-for-3 on the day, and Durocher brought in Don Liddle to pitch.

AS HARD AS I EVER HIT ANYTHING

Liddle's first pitch was to Wertz' liking. He hit it "as hard as I ever hit anything," he said, and sent it soaring to center.

At once, Mays was off for the ball. Did he just sense where it would be coming down? Was he somehow watching its flight with eyes behind his head?

With his number 24 facing the infield, racing at full speed nearly 450 feet from home plate, Mays stuck out his glove in front of his left shoulder, and caught the ball! The Giants

fans roared, but the play wasn't over yet. In a flash, he turned and fired a perfect strike to his second baseman, Davey Williams. For Wertz, it was not even a sacrifice fly. It was an "8" on the scorecard, a fly out to center. A fly out that was one for the ages.

The Giants would win that game in the 10th inning on Dusty Rhodes' pinch homer, and would win the next three to score a stunning sweep of Cleveland. Those who followed the Series would forever claim that Willie's catch had simply broken the Indians' backs, and they never recovered.

He would always be the kind of player who could change the course of a game either at bat, on the bases, or in the field.

BEFORE SIX A.M., over 200 fans lined up to gain entrance to the Polo Grounds to see the New York Giants, and Mays—The Say Hey Kid— against the Cleveland Indians in the 1954 World Series.

MAYS EARNED EVEN MORE ADULATION than ever following his Herculean catch in Game One of the 1954 World Series.
Mays robbed Cleveland's Vic Wertz of a 462-foot blast to center field in the top of the eighth inning.

TOPPING HIS EXTRAORDINARY CATCH, Mays fired the ball to the second baseman with perfect aim, not only robbing Wertz of a three-run home run, but cheating him of a sacrifice fly.

BUMS NO MORE!

The Brooklyn Dodgers lost the World Series in 1916 to the Red Sox, and in 1920 to the Indians.
Then they lost the Series to their cross-town rivals the New York Yankees in 1941, 1947, 1949, 1952 and again in 1953.
In 1955, the two teams matched up again. In the crucial Game Seven at Yankee Stadium, The Dodgers held
a 2-0 lead in the sixth inning. With none out and runners on first and second, Yogi Berra sliced what looked like an
extra base hit down the left field line, but newly inserted left fielder Sandy Amoros miraculously appeared
and gloved the ball, relaying it to first for a double play. Without this great catch, the game would have been tied, with
Berra on second and nobody out. The Dodgers Johnny Podres held on to pitch a complete game and lift
the borough of Brooklyn to baseball's pinnacle for the first and only time.

A LONG, FUTILE ROAD

IN FOR THE LONG HAUL. Five Dodger fans in high spirits, despite having spent two days waiting to buy tickets to the 1955 World Series. They are, left to right, John Barr, George Schneider, Edward Connelly, DonMartin (standing) and Jack Martin.

As long as the Brooklyn Dodgers were the most consistently mediocre team in the National League, they didn't have to concern themselves with the mighty Yankees up in the Bronx. But it was still annoying to watch a succession of superstars, ranging from Babe Ruth to Lou Gehrig to Joe DiMaggio, lead the Yankees to a seemingly endless series of world championships in the 1920s and '30s, while the Dodgers struggled to reach .500.

In the late 1930s, though, the Dodgers (long known as Dem Bums by faithful Brooklyn fans) woke up under the leadership of manager Leo Durocher and began to win. They won the 1941 National League pennant, but then lost the

World Series to the Yankees. In 1947, led by Jackie Robinson, they won another pennant—and proceeded to lose to the Yankees in the World Series. In 1949 the Dodgers won the pennant again, and lost to the Yankees. In 1952 they won the pennant, and lost to the Yankees again. In 1953 they repeated as pennant winners, and lost to the Yankees. Again.

In 1955 the Dodgers dominated the National League, winning yet another pennant. Guess who their opponent in the World Series was? Right: the Yankees.

TRY, TRY AGAIN

The Dodgers had a typically strong team in 1955. Jackie Robinson was well past his prime at age 36, but Brooklyn had other heroes to rely on. Center fielder Duke Snider slugged 42 home runs and led the league with 136 RBI, while first baseman Gil Hodges followed with 27 round-trippers. On the mound, the team was led by Don Newcombe, who had a 20–5 season.

Of course, the Yankees weren't any slouches in 1955 either. They'd been stunned in 1954, when they won 103 games and still finished behind Cleveland in the A.L. In 1955, they wanted revenge on anyone who stood in their way. And they were well-equipped for revenge, with such superstars as Mickey Mantle (37 home runs), Yogi Berra (27 home runs), and pitcher Whitey Ford (18 wins).

The Series started out as many had predicted. Neither Ford nor Newcombe had his best stuff, but it was the Yankees who knew how to win. Final score: 6–5. Game Two was more of the same, a complete-game performance by the Yankees' Tommy Byrne for a 4–2 win and a 2–0 Series lead.

Refusing to panic, Dodgers manager Walt Alston chose to let Johnny Podres, who was turning 23 that day, start Game Three. At first this seemed like the sort of hunch that so often comes back to haunt a manager, as Podres had finished just 9–10 during an injury-plagued year. But this time the choice panned

out. Despite giving up a home run to Mantle, Podres pitched nine innings in an easy 8–3 win for the Dodgers.

Brooklyn knotted the Series with another easy win in Game Four, and then, stunningly, won Game Five as well, 5–3, to go up 3–2 in the Series. The last two games were to be played in Yankee Stadium, but still the Dodgers were poised to finally win their first championship.

The question was: Could they actually do it?

SANDY AND JOHNNY

Things didn't look good after Game Six—the Yankees cruised, 5–1, behind nine smooth innings by Whitey Ford. It seemed fore-ordained that the Yankees would win the next game and take home yet another set of championship rings.

Game Seven matched two unlikely potential heroes: the Yankees' Tommy Byrne versus the Dodgers' Johnny Podres. For a man who'd had such a spotty regular season, Podres was remarkably confident before Game Seven. Seeing Dodgers' shortstop Pee Wee Reese

CLEM LABINE, Brooklyn's relief pitcher, is congratulated by catcher Roy Campanella (left) and first baseman Gil Hodges (right) at the end of Game Five, Oct. 2, 1955.

hanging his head after the Game Six loss, Podres clapped his teammate on the shoulder. "Don't worry, Pee Wee," he said. "I'll shut 'em out tomorrow."

Podres and Byrne began the game as if they intended to throw joint shutouts. Then, in the fourth inning, the Dodgers scored on a double by Roy Campanella and a single by Gil Hodges. They added another run in the sixth, on a Hodges sacrifice fly.

In the bottom of the sixth, it seemed as if Podres would give back both those runs and more. With two men on and nobody out, Yogi Berra hit a fly ball down the left field line. Berra usually hit the ball to right, so Dodgers left fielder Sandy Amoros (who had just entered the game) was playing toward center. He had a long run to catch the ball—such a long run, in

SANDY AMOROS snares a shot to left field off of Yankee slugger Yogi Berra, preserving Brooklyn's lead in the final game of the World Series.

fact, that it seemed inevitable that the ball would fall in for a hit, and both runs would score.

All Johnny Podres could do was watch the ball descend as Amoros ran desperately toward it. "I'll tell you," he said later, "that's a helpless feeling, standing on the mound at a moment like that."

But Amoros never gave up. At the last possible moment, just as he was about to crash into the fence, he put out his glove and snared the ball. In an instant he straightened and threw it back into the infield, where a relay throw caught runner Gil McDougald off first base for a double play. Podres got the next out, and the threat was over.

That was the last good chance the Yankees had. Podres gave up just one hit in the last three innings, retiring the side in order in the ninth to give the Dodgers their long-awaited first World Series victory.

DODGER FAN ROSE AREÑA proudly displays the headline proclaiming her team as world champs.

WITH MUCH TO CELEBRATE, Dodgers' owner Walter O'Malley hugs manager Walter Alston in the locker room after their first World Series victory. Their triumph was sweeter than could be expected since they defeated their ever-present cross-town rivals, the Yankees.

TRIPLE CROWN

Baseball's Triple Crown, leading the league in batting average, home runs, and RBI, is a rare feat, only accomplished 14 times in the 20th Century. In 1956, Yankee centerfielder Mickey Mantle had his best year for the Series champions. He batted .353, hit 52 home runs, and drove in 130 runs. Despite hitting over .300 for most of his career, this was his only batting title. Mantle also led the league in home runs three other years and RBI five other years. Who is the last player to take the Triple Crown? Boston's Carl Yastrzemski in 1967.

THE PHENOM

Few ballplayers have ever arrived in the Major Leagues more highly hyped than Mickey Mantle. Yankee fans had grown accustomed to an endless string of all-time great ballplayers leading their teams. Babe Ruth had dominated the headlines in the 1920s. Then, Lou Gehrig was there to carry the team. Before the tragic end to Gehrig's career, a young outfielder named Joe DiMaggio arrived from San Francisco to capture Yankee fans' hearts.

In 1951, DiMaggio was near the end of the line. It was time for a new hero to take the stage, and fans anointed a 19-year-old boy out of Commerce, Oklahoma.

The pressure on the unworldly Mantle was intense. He'd hit a passel of home runs during spring training, and fans expected him to continue that torrid pace. It was too much to expect. "I think the biggest crowd I ever played for was like 500 people," he told interviewer Roy Firestone, "and I go to Yankee Stadium for the first time, and there's 68,000 people there and they're playing the Red Sox, and I lost my confidence."

It is no surprise that Mantle had trouble adjusting to those 68,000 people staring at him. What bothered him the most, though, was how quickly they turned on him. "What did begin to pierce my hide," he recalled, "was the virulence that was tossed at me from the nearby stands."

Mantle began to strike out again and again. Finally, he was sent to the minors, and seriously considered quitting baseball. Only a harsh but timely intervention by his father kept him from going home. Instead, he gradually got his batting stroke back, and soon returned to the Yankees for good.

THE BIG YEAR

Mantle was a good, productive ballplayer during his early years with the Yankees, but not quite a superstar. As he put it in his autobiography, *The Mick,* "Before 1956 I was doing pretty well, but I sure wasn't Babe

ALREADY A FAVORITE with fans in 1954, four short years into his career with the Yankees, a relaxed and confident Mantle holds an autographed ball for a fan.

MANTLE's powerful swing launched 52 home runs in 1956, the year he won the Triple Crown. All told, he hit over 40 home runs in four of the 18 seasons he played in the Majors.

Triple Crown Hitters
20th Century

Player	Team	Year	Home Runs	RBI	Batting Average
Nap Lajoie	Philadelphia	1901	14	122*	.422
Ty Cobb	Detroit	1909	9	115*	.377
Heinie Zimmerman	Chicago	1912	14	98*	.372
Rogers Hornsby	St. Louis	1922	42	152	.401
Rogers Hornsby	St. Louis	1925	39	143	.403
Jimmie Foxx	Philadelphia	1933	48	163	.356
Chuck Klein	Philadelphia	1933	28	120	.368
Lou Gehrig	New York	1934	49	165	.363
Joe Medwick	St. Louis	1937	31	154	.374
Ted Williams	Boston	1942	36	137	.356
Ted Williams	Boston	1947	32	114	.343
Mickey Mantle	New York	1956	52	130	.353
Frank Robinson	Baltimore	1966	49	127	.316
Carl Yastrzemski	Boston	1967	44	121	.326

*The RBI was not officially adopted until 1920.

Ruth, Joe DiMaggio, and Lou Gehrig all rolled into one." He'd hit over .300 three times, but never higher than .311. His high in home runs was 37 in 1955, not exactly a Ruthian total. And he'd surpassed 100 RBI just once.

In 1956, though, Mantle broke through. "That season I started to do the things they thought I would do," was how he put it.

Did he ever. Mantle hit .353, slammed 52 home runs, and drove in 130 runs. Each of these three totals led the American League, which meant that Mantle had won the coveted Triple Crown, one of the rarest feats in baseball.

Mickey Mantle was thrilled to have won the Triple Crown, and also to be named the league's Most Valuable Player. Still, as he said in *The Mick,* "I don't mind saying the biggest kick was beating out Ted Williams for the batting championship." According to Mantle, Williams was asked what he thought about the Mick's feat. His reply: "If I could run like that [bleep], I'd hit about .400 every year."

POST-SEASON RECORDS

Mantle's Triple Crown year was, on balance, his finest season. But he had plenty more great seasons to come. In 1957 he batted .365, his career high. In 1961, he slammed 54 home runs, second only to Roger Maris's 61. And even in 1964, after injuries had robbed him of much of his skill, he managed to hit .303 with 35 home runs, 111 RBI, and a .591 slugging average.

But his most spectacular numbers were ones that didn't count in his regular season totals. Mantle played in an astonishing 12 World Series, of which the Yankees won seven. He set Series records that no other player has yet approached: 18 home runs, 42 runs scored, and 40 RBI.

Mickey Mantle was elected to the Hall of Fame in 1974, in his first year of eligibility.

MANTLE's PLEASURE is apparent after signing his 1956 contract with the Yankees. Yankee executives were clearly pleased that year as well. Mantle won the Triple Crown, leading the American League with 52 homers, 130 RBI, and a .353 batting average.

ABSOLUTE ZERO

Game Five of the 1956 World Series at Yankee Stadium featured a matchup of Sal Maglie for the Brooklyn Dodgers and Don Larsen for the Yankees. Larsen had a 30-40 lifetime record, while Maglie was nearing the end of a strong career. Neither pitcher allowed anyone to reach base until Mickey Mantle drilled a homer off Maglie with two out in the fourth. Larsen, however, continued to throw goose eggs at the Dodgers. The final out was a strikeout of Dale Mitchell, a .312 career hitter who had only struck out 119 times in 11 years. Larsen required only 97 pitches to dispose of the Dodgers. In all of baseball history, there have been only 16 perfect games, with only Larsen's coming in post-season play.

THE BAD BOY

By the time pitcher Don Larsen came to the Major Leagues, with the St. Louis Browns in 1953, he already had the reputation of a player who enjoyed a good time as much as he did a well-pitched game. In his first two seasons, the result was not very many well-pitched games, and a cumulative record of 10–33.

Larsen was traded to the Yankees prior to the 1955 season. He went 9–2 his first season in New York, leading Yankee manager Casey Stengel to predict better days ahead. But Larsen was inconsistent for the Yankees again in 1956, going 11–5 while appearing both as a starter and a reliever. The 1956 Yankees, led by super-

YANKEES' DON LARSEN throwing a pitch in the ninth inning of Game Five of the 1956 World Series. The scoreboard tells it all: Larsen was closing a no-run, no-hit game, the first and only perfect game in World Series history.

stars Mickey Mantle, Yogi Berra, and Whitey Ford, were an easy team to win with: They went 97–57, capturing the A.L. pennant easily.

In the last four games he started during the regular season, Larsen was impressive, pitching a three-hitter and three four-hitters. This earned him a prominent place in the World Series against the Brooklyn Dodgers.

THE ARCH-RIVALS

In 1956, the Yankees and Dodgers were set to meet in the World Series for the sixth time in 10 seasons. And, while the Yankees had won the first four of their meetings, in 1955 the Dodgers had finally captured their first championship.

The 1956 Series started as if the Dodgers were determined to begin a dynasty of their own. They knocked Whitey Ford out of the box in the third inning on a three-run home run by Gil Hodges, on their way to an easy 6–3 win.

The Yankees jumped out to a 6–0 lead in Game Two, but their starter—Don Larsen—couldn't hold the lead. The Dodgers scored six times in the bottom of the second, and went on to beat up seven Yankee pitchers in a 13–8 rout.

If the Yankees were going to avoid being blown out in this Series, they needed a win, and badly. Luckily, they had Whitey Ford pitching for them in Game Three. Ford had pitched poorly in the opening game, but in general he was the most reliable and calm of their great pitchers. He responded with a complete-game, 5–3 victory. Then the Yankees knotted the Series, two games apiece, the next day, behind pitcher Tom Sturdivant.

The fifth game would be the tensest, most crucial of all. Whoever won it would be just a game away from a World Championship. And Casey Stengel decided to hand the ball to Larsen to pitch the all-important game.

PERFECTION

At first glance, the game looked like a mismatch. Larsen, who'd been knocked out of Game Two, would face the Dodgers' Sal Maglie. Though nearing the end of his career, Maglie had gone 13–5 that year. Perhaps more importantly, he was a rock-solid veteran pitcher with previous World Series experience.

For the first three innings, neither pitcher allowed a hit. Now Larsen was in complete command. "He was a master of control that day," marveled home plate umpire Babe Pinelli later. "[H]e was making them hit his pitch."

Mickey Mantle slammed a home run in the fourth for the Yankees' first hit off Maglie, and then followed that with a terrific lunging catch to rob Gil Hodges of an extra-base hit in the fifth. The Yanks then added another run in the sixth—their last run of the game, but one more than they would need.

From early on, the ballplayers and the crowd of more than 64,000 fans sensed that they might be watching a historic game. The tension built, inning by inning, as Larsen mowed down the Brooklyn line-up without allowing a hit, or even a man to reach base.

In the ninth inning, it seemed as if everyone in the park was holding their breath. "Yankee Stadium," said anouncer Vin Scully, broadcasting the game on television, "is shivering in its concrete foundation right now."

Carl Furillo led off for the Dodgers in the ninth. After fouling off several pitches, he hit a long fly ball to right field, caught by Hank Bauer. Then Roy Campanella grounded out.

YANKEE CATCHER YOGI BERRA jumping up and down in a bear hug, congratulating Don Larsen, who just finished pitching the first perfect World Series game.

Larsen, and the Yanks, had one out to go. The Dodgers' next batter was pinch hitter Dale Mitchell, a lifetime .312 hitter who had struck out only 119 times in an 11-year career. Mitchell took a ball. Then Larsen got two strikes on him. On the next pitch, Mitchell fouled the ball into the left field stands.

Finally, on the last pitch of the game, Larsen put a low fastball on the outside part of the plate. Mitchell checked his swing, but umpire Pinelli threw up his right arm: Strike three! Don Larsen had pitched the first perfect game in World Series history.

Afterward, Larsen revealed how much the tension had gotten to him. "I was so weak in the knees out there in the ninth inning, I thought I was going to faint," he said.

The Dodgers, showing their resilience, came back to win a thrilling Game Six, 1–0 in 10 innings. But the Yankees weren't to be denied. They clubbed Brooklyn 9–0 in the seventh game, winning yet another World Championship.

"I WAS SO WEAK IN THE KNEES . . . I THOUGHT I WAS GOING TO FAINT."

LARSEN, with relief and satisfaction clearly written on his face, relaxes after he completed nine perfect innings in Game Five of the 1956 World Series.

STAY TEAM STAY

In the 1950s, five major league teams moved to take advantage of postwar population shifts
which created major untapped markets for the Major Leagues. The first to move were the Boston Braves,
who departed for Milwaukee in 1953. In 1954, the St. Louis Browns moved to Baltimore. 1955 saw the Philadelphia A's
move to Kansas City. But the earth shaking moves happened after the 1957 season, as New York, the capital of baseball,
lost two of its three teams. The Dodgers left for Los Angeles and the Giants for San Francisco. Despite the protests of
a core of loyal fans, the teams felt forced to move in the face of declining attendance at their inner city ballparks.
The moves proved to be an attendance bonanza, and inaugurated baseball's coast-to-coast era.

BASEBALL MOVES WEST

Stability was the watchword for Americans through much of the first half of the 20th Century. For a remarkable stretch of 12 years (1933–45), Franklin D. Roosevelt was the president. Furthermore, it seemed that Joe Louis was always the heavyweight champion, and Irving Berlin was always turning out hit music. The national pastime, too, was remarkably stable. The Major Leagues saw no franchise shifts, and no expansion, between 1903 and 1953. The game was played in the nation's northeast quadrant, from Boston to St. Louis, from Chicago to Washington.

In fact, five cities accounted for 11 of the 16 big league teams—New York, St. Louis, Boston, Chicago, and Philadelphia. Five others—Washington, Detroit, Cleveland, Pittsburgh, and Cincinnati—completed the roll call. Calling base-

In 1957, a year of tumultuous change for New York baseball, the Giants pack it up and move to the West Coast.

ball the "national pastime," was, truth be told, a stretch.

But as the nation enjoyed postwar prosperity in the early '50s, not everyone was realizing the gains. The Boston Braves, struggling to draw fans, finally conceded and moved to Milwaukee in 1953, breaking a 50-year hold on franchise movement. A year later, the St. Louis Browns went to Baltimore to become the Orioles, and in 1955, the Philadelphia Athletics moved to Kansas City. Three years, and three moves, brought the big leagues to three new markets without leaving any abandoned. Instead of 10 cities representing major league baseball, 13 now did. None crossed the central time zone or went into the south, but the pattern had been set for movement.

It would catch many by surprise that the next whisperings of change would come from New York.

TWO GLAMOUR FRANCHISES

Here were two of the most glorious franchises of the game's history. In the first three decades of the century, the New York Giants were baseball's glamour team, led by John McGraw, and featuring such stalwarts as Christy Mathewson, Carl Hubbell, Bill Terry, and Mel Ott. They were the favorites of New York's Broadway crowd and were themselves a model of stability. You could count their 20th-century managers—among them John McGraw, Bill Terry, Mel Ott, Leo Durocher, and Bill Rigney—on two hands.

The Brooklyn Dodgers did not have that early glamour. They were often more humorous than successful, with characters like Wilbert Robinson, Casey Stengel, Babe Herman, and Dazzy Vance. But by the 1940s they had matured into one of the greatest teams ever assembled—the Boys of Summer, as author Roger Kahn later called them. With Duke Snider, Pee Wee Reese, Jackie Robinson, Roy Campanella, Gil Hodges, Don Newcombe, and Carl Furillo, they would win pennants in 1947, 1949, 1952, 1953, 1955, and 1956. The

thought of them moving, with all that success, was hard to imagine.

But Walter O'Malley, the Dodgers owner, was an astute businessman. He knew that little Ebbets Field had outgrown its usefulness, and was not very "fan friendly." He knew that even with winning teams, his attendance would decline there. And he knew that jet travel

THE FANS PLEADING at the Polo Grounds couldn't convince the Giants' executives to keep them in town.

FANS IN BROOKLYN matched the fervor of the Giants' supporters, their crosstown rivals. In the end, of course, they lost their campaign due to the demands of geography, demographics, and economics.

THE MOVE of the Dodgers and the Giants took center stage in New York during much of 1957. This picture shows the press crowding around (left to right) Dodgers' president Walter O'Malley, New York Mayor Robert F. Wagner, and Giants' owner Horace Stoneham following a meeting in early June on the proposed move.

EBBETS FIELD was abandoned when the Dodgers left. It was demolished three years later, in 1960. The same wrecking ball used in Brooklyn took down the Polo Grounds four years later.

would make a West Coast team possible. He wanted to be the one to get there first.

Los Angeles was ripe for major league baseball. Its population was soaring, what with faster planes, interstate highways, and the advent of air conditioning. The city had been

big time in the entertainment business for decades, and O'Malley knew baseball was another form of entertainment. Plus, the place was loaded with ex-New Yorkers.

TWO TEAMS MUST MOVE

But O'Malley didn't want to go alone. He wanted to keep his rivalry with the Giants alive, and he wanted the Giants' owner, Horace Stoneham, to go to San Francisco, so that 11 of each other's road games each season would be conveniently West Coast-based. It also made sense that a team traveling west could play two different teams there.

Stoneham's situation was similar to O'Malley's in that his ballpark—the Polo Grounds—was getting old. While his team had won in 1951 and 1954, it was on the decline and had become the number three team in New York, behind both the Yankees and the Dodgers.

Secret talks began to be held with public officials in Los Angeles and San Francisco as the 1957 season proceeded. Efforts, which some considered either half-hearted by New York City officials, or lacking in substance by the teams, were made to keep them from fleeing. Many thought they would simply never abandon the nation's most populous city. Dodger fans, especially, were considered among the most loyal in the nation.

But by September of 1957, all the hurdles had been cleared, and the moves had become formalities. Fans in New York knew they were attending their teams' final games at both Ebbets Field and the Polo Grounds.

On April 15, 1958, teams with LA and SF on their caps met at Seals Stadium in San Francisco to officially put major league baseball in the Pacific time zone. The Giants won 8–0, but more importantly, big league baseball was now a coast-to-coast affair, truly, as never before, the national pastime.

YOUNG FANS, Bob Martin (left) and Gary Holland, celebrate the August 4th news about the Giants' move to San Francisco.

THE FORMER NEW YORK GIANTS get a hero's welcome upon their arrival in San Francisco.

PARADISE LOST

On May 26, 1959, a cold and sometimes rainy evening, the Milwaukee Braves hosted the Pittsburgh Pirates. The Braves, pennant winners in 1957 and 1958, featured a powerful lineup including Hank Aaron, Eddie Mathews, and Joe Adcock. The Pirates sent Harvey Haddix to the mound against Lew Burdette. Both pitchers pitched shutout baseball for 12 innings, with the Pirates Haddix also tossing a perfect game. Despite collecting 12 hits, his Pirate teammates couldn't score a run for him. In the 13th, he lost the perfect game on a throwing error by Don Hoak. After intentionally walking Aaron, it all came crashing down for Haddix, who was tagged for a three run homer by Joe Adcock. Haddix' performance, one of the best in baseball history, counted as nothing more than a loss.

Lewis Burdette, Milwaukee Braves pitcher, who faced the Pirates' Harvey Haddix in a grueling pitching duel that lasted 12 innings.

THE KITTEN

One of the wonders of baseball is that, on any given day, you can witness something you've never seen before. On May 26, 1959, the Milwaukee Braves' fans got to see a pitcher throw 12 consecutive perfect innings—and go on to lose the game.

What made the event even more surprising was that the pitcher who took the heartbreaking loss in that game wasn't future Braves Hall of Famer Warren Spahn. It wasn't the Braves' perennial 20-game winner, Lew Burdette. It wasn't a Brave at all. It was a Pittsburgh Pirates' left-hander named Harvey Haddix (affectionately known as "The Kitten"), a 33-year-old journeyman and one of the last pitchers you'd expect to attain such perfection.

Like many pitchers who are not possessed of blinding speed, Haddix had trouble convincing a major league team that he had the stuff to pitch in the big leagues. He bounced around the minors for several seasons, finally showing his stuff with Columbus in the American Association, when he pitched 10 hitless innings in one game. This got him a contract with the St. Louis Cardinals in late 1952.

At first, it seemed as if Haddix might be a big winner in the Majors. In 1953, his first full season with the Cardinals, he went 20–9, and pitched one game in which he didn't allow a hit until the ninth inning. He

followed up this fine season with one that was almost as good, 18–13.

After that, though, Haddix' skills and win totals started to diminish. He bounced from St. Louis to Philadelphia to Cincinnati and finally to Pittsburgh in 1959. And although he was a regular starter with the Pirates in 1958, he'd managed only eight wins that year, and it seemed that his major league career was coming to an end.

EVERYTHING WAS WORKING

It was a stormy, windy night in Milwaukee, with thunder rumbling in the distance, as

HARVEY HADDIX in the middle of his near-perfect 13-inning game.

Haddix faced off against the Braves' Lew Burdette. Burdette had won 20 games in 1958, and was on his way to a league-leading 21 victories in 1959, so it looked like the game might be a mismatch.

But it didn't turn out that way. The Pirates got men on base in nearly every inning, but couldn't manage to plate any of them. Outfielder Bob Skinner had a particularly frustrating day. "Once I was on third and Bob Skinner hit one down the line that looked like a homer, but drifted foul by three or four inches," Haddix recalled a few years later. "Another time, Skinner hit one out, but the wind blew it back in."

Meanwhile, Haddix had to face a powerful Braves lineup that included sluggers Hank Aaron (who would hit .355 with 39 home runs that year), Eddie Mathews (46 home runs), and Joe Adcock (25 round-trippers). But, as he found out early in the game, he had the best stuff of his life.

"The Braves didn't really come close to a hit until the end," Haddix recalled. "I was pretty sharp, and there weren't even any close ones to speak of." The Braves kept hitting lazy outfield flies, and any that were hit harder were beaten down by the stiff wind blowing in from the outfield. When they weren't getting the ball in the air, they were hitting easy grounders to Pirates' third baseman Don Hoak.

In the ninth inning, Haddix struck out Andy Pafko, got Johnny Logan on an outfield fly, and fanned Lew Burdette. He'd pitched a perfect game, retired all 27 men he'd faced in the nine innings he'd pitched. When Burdette whiffed, it should have been one of the happiest moments of Haddix' life.

There was just one problem: The game wasn't over. Despite getting hit after hit against Burdette, the Pirates hadn't managed to score. The game remained tied, 0–0, with extra innings ahead.

HEARTBREAK

Haddix was getting tired—"more tired than nervous," was how he put it—but he wasn't coming out of the game. In the 10th, he retired the side in order once again, getting Eddie Mathews on a fly and Hank Aaron on a grounder. In the 11th, he retired all three he faced once more. And then he did it again in the twelfth.

Harvey Haddix had now faced 36 men, and gotten them all out. It was one of the greatest performances in the history of baseball— yet the game was still tied, 0–0, as Haddix plodded out to the mound to pitch the 13th.

The first man up for the Braves was Felix Mantilla, who was hitting only .215. Haddix got two quick strikes on him, and then threw what he thought was strike three, but it was called a ball. Mantilla then hit a grounder to Don Hoak, a sure out—except that Hoak threw badly to first. The Braves had their first baserunner of the game on the error.

Eddie Mathews laid down a sacrifice bunt, moving Mantilla to second base. The Pirates decided to walk Aaron intentionally, bringing up Joe Adcock with men on first and second.

By this time Haddix was exhausted, but he was in the game to win or lose. "I was trying to keep it low," he lamented, "and he hit the second pitch just over the fence in right-center. The wind had died down by then." It was, he added, "the only mistake I made."

Adcock's blow was a three-run home run, but Adcock passed Aaron on the basepaths. After much wrangling among the umpires (and then by the league office), Adcock's drive was reduced to a double, and the final score went into the books at 1–0. Still, it was enough to beat Haddix, perhaps the unluckiest pitcher of all time.

MILWAUKEE'S JOE ADCOCK whose 13th-inning home run broke the back of Haddix' almost perfect game.

A CRESTFALLEN HADDIX following the perfect game that slipped through his fingers.

OUT WITH A BANG

42-year-old slugger Ted Williams donned the Red Sox uniform for the last time in 1960. He had a good season, hitting .316 with 29 home runs in 113 games. But as the long season wound down, he decided to retire at Boston's last home game, rather than going to New York for the season's final two games. In a pregame ceremony on September 28, the Red Sox retired Williams' number nine, and he spoke briefly, thanking the "greatest fans in America." Williams walked his first time up, and then hit towering drives that were caught at the wall the next two times. In the eighth, he approached the plate for what would almost certainly be his last at-bat. Williams hit Jack Fisher's third pitch deep into the right-center field bullpen and circled the bases to a tremendous ovation.

THE SPLINTER ARRIVES

From the moment he joined the Boston Red Sox as a 20-year-old rookie in 1939, Ted Williams knew he was something special. While most other rookies are overwhelmed to find themselves among major league stars they had idolized as kids, Williams was sure from the start that he belonged in the bigs.

He proved this during the first game he ever played in the Majors, under the most awe-inspiring conditions possible: against the Yankees at Yankee Stadium. Williams sat in the dugout watching the Yankees take batting practice—Joe DiMaggio, Tommy Henrich, Bill Dickey and other all-time stars—and he wasn't thinking, What am I doing here. He was thinking, I can't wait to play against these guys.

The Yankee pitcher was future Hall of Famer Red Ruffing, who struck Williams out the first time on a high fastball. One of Williams' teammates teased him, provoking Williams to reply: "This is ONE guy I KNOW I'm going to hit, and if he puts it in the same place again I'm riding it out of here."

He didn't, quite. But the second time Ruffing tried to get

TED WILLIAMS, *whose 19-year career with Boston ended with a .344 lifetime batting average, sixth highest in the Major Leagues.*

a high fastball past him, Williams whacked it for a double—the first major league hit for perhaps the greatest hitter in the history of baseball.

ONE HIGHLIGHT AFTER ANOTHER

Williams, soon nicknamed the Splendid Splinter, had one of the greatest rookie seasons ever in 1939. He hit .327, with 44 doubles, 11 triples, 31 home runs, and a league-leading 145 runs batted in. "I can't imagine anyone having a better, happier first year in the big leagues," he said in *My Turn At Bat,* his autobiography.

And he was just getting started. In 1941, when he was just 23 years old, he hit .406—the first person to break the nearly mythical .400 barrier since 1930. No one has done it since.

Hitting seemed to come so easily to him from the start, but Williams always said it wasn't so. "Choose any of the noted hitters, and none of them hit any more balls, swung a bat in practice any more times than Theodore Samuel Williams," he pointed out.

After another spectacular season in 1942 (.356 with 36 home runs), Williams joined the military during World War II. Like many other stars, he lost three full seasons out of the peak of his career to the war. He came back in 1946 to post a .342 batting average for the year. Then, in 1951, he went off to fight in the Korean War, missing parts of another two seasons.

When Ted Williams retired in 1960, he had posted stunning career totals: a .344 career average, 521 home runs, 1,839 RBI. But imagine what those numbers would have been if he hadn't lost those five seasons to the military! He almost certainly would have been the first to challenge Babe Ruth's 714 career home runs. He could have reached 2,500 RBI, the most of all time.

Even without those missing totals, his numbers warranted election to the Hall of Fame on the first ballot.

TED'S FINAL BOW

Although he hit .316 for the season, the 42-year-old Williams knew that 1960 was to be his last hurrah. For many all-time-great players, their final season is an opportunity to take a farewell tour around the Majors, basking in praise and applause before they hang up their spikes.

It was a little different for Williams. He'd always had a complicated, often contentious, relationship with both the media and Red Sox fans. Hot-headed and outspoken, he made more than his share of enemies, especially among certain members of the Boston press. In a 1955 interview with *Sports Illustrated,* he admitted his part in these battles. "When somebody says nice things about me, it goes in one ear and out the other," he said, "but I remember the criticism longest. I hate criticism—and the sportswriters who write the way they feel instead of what they've actually seen."

Near the end of the 1960 season, Williams decided to play his last game in Boston's Fenway Park, skipping the final two games in New York. The Red Sox set up a ceremony for the last game at Fenway, on September 28. In a pregame ceremony to retire his number, Williams spoke briefly. "If I were asked where I would like to have played, I would have to

TED WILLIAMS CROSSES THE PLATE for the final time, after ending his career with a home run at Fenway Park. Congratulating him is the next batter, Red Sox catcher Jim Pagliaroni.

say Boston," he said, and went on to thank "the greatest fans in America."

Williams walked his first time up. His next two appearances at the plate, he hit long fly balls. Both would have been home runs on other days, but both were kept in the park by heavy, late summer air and a stiff breeze blowing toward home plate.

Williams came to the plate again in the eighth inning. "This was surely going to be my last time at bat in baseball," he recalled. "Twenty-two years coming down to one time at bat."

As the fans yelled and cheered, imploring Ted to hit one out, he took a ball and then swung and missed at a fastball from pitcher Jack Fisher. On the third pitch, Fisher tried another fastball, and Williams crushed it. The ball fought its way through the wind and into the right-center field stands. In his last at bat of all, Ted Williams had slugged a home run.

Manager Pinky Higgins sent Williams out to left field for a final curtain call in the ninth, and then sent a substitute in to replace him. As Red Sox fans cheered and cheered, the Splendid Splinter left the field for the last time.

WILLIAMS WAS A NERVOUS GUEST of honor at a ceremony held in his honor before leaving for the Korean War. Two interruptions in his major league career—during World War II and the Korean War—took Williams out of play at the peak of his career.

THE DREAM

Every child in America dreams of it. Bottom of the ninth, seventh game of the World Series. And you're at the plate. In the dream, you hit a home run and your team wins the World Series. You round third base at a wild gallop, and you're mobbed at the plate by teammates. On October 13, 1960, Pittsburgh Pirates second baseman Bill Mazeroski stepped up to the plate at Forbes Field, with the Pirates and the Yankees tied 9-9, and did just that. It had been a tremendous, see-saw battle until Mazeroski silenced the mighty Yankees, who had outscored the Pirates 55-27 in the Series.

END OF A DYNASTY?

In 1960, the Yankees faced challenges they hadn't confronted in decades. The 1959 season had been a disaster, with the team finishing only 79–75, their worst record since 1925. Mickey Mantle, Yogi Berra, Whitey Ford, and other long-time stars all had indifferent seasons, and the farm system didn't seem to be producing the next generation of superstars, as it had always done before.

Worse, the whispers had grown louder and louder throughout 1959 that Casey Stengel was too old to be an effective manager. He had been 58 years old when he took over the Yankees' reins in 1949, but in his first 10 years as manager, the Yankees took home nine American League pennants.

Stengel turned 69 in 1960, and was beginning to show his age. He'd even been seen dozing on the bench during games. His time was clearly drawing to an end, and the Yankees made plans to replace him with the far younger Ralph Houk.

But in what turned out to be his final season with the team, old Casey surprised everyone by piloting the team to a 97-57 record and the pennant. Their opponents in the 1960 World Series were the Pittsburgh Pirates, who hadn't been in a World Series since 1927.

The Pirates had a strong line-up headed by future Hall of Famer Roberto Clemente and 20-game winner Vern Law. But compared to the Yankees, the Pirates seemed pitifully undermanned. The general consensus was that the Yankees would win the Series easily.

NEVER A DULL MOMENT

In the seven games of the 1960 World Series, the Yankees scored 55 runs, almost eight per game. They had an amazing 91 hits—13 a game, including 10 home runs. They won games by scores like 16–3, 12–0, and 10–0.

As a team, they hit .338, and plenty of their stars did even better. Catcher Elston Howard hit .462, Mantle managed .400, and light-hitting second baseman Bobby Richardson hit .367. Richardson drove in 12 runs, while Mantle drove in 11—two of the highest single-Series totals ever.

On the other hand, the Pirates hit only .256 for the seven games. They had far fewer hits, doubles, triples, and home runs than the Yankees did. Bobby Richardson had almost as many RBI as any three of their hitters. Their team earned run average for the Series was an eye-popping 7.11, compared to a strong 3.54 for the Yankees.

How on earth did this mismatch of a Series ever go seven games?

The Pirates won Game One, 6–4, behind second baseman Bill Mazeroski's home run and strong pitching by Vern Law. In Game Two, the Yankees jumped on six Pirate pitchers for 19 hits and 16 runs in an easy 16–3 win. Mickey Mantle had a career year in that one game, hitting three-run and two-run homers to lead the onslaught.

PITTSBURGH'S BILL MAZEROSKI, whose home run in the bottom of the ninth inning in Game Seven defeated the Yankees and won the 1960 World Series.

Game Three was no better. Whitey Ford pitched a four-hit shutout while the Yankees scored six runs in the first inning on their way to a 10–0 win. Mantle hit yet another home run, while Bobby Richardson drove in six runs—still a World Series single-game record.

It would have been entirely forgivable if the Pirates had chosen to roll over and cry uncle at this point. But they didn't. Instead, amazingly, they rose to capture the next two games, both tense, well pitched affairs, 3–2 and 5–2.

Now it was the Yankees who were on the ropes. But their hitters couldn't be kept down for long. In Game Six, Whitey Ford pitched another shutout, and though Mickey Mantle didn't hit any more home runs, the team scored 12 runs for a big win.

Now Pittsburgh's Forbes Field was to be host of Game Seven. Was it going to be another well-pitched game, or a slugfest?

MAZEROSKI'S MOMENT

In a word: slugfest.

But this time the Pirates were in on the fun. They scored two runs in the first on a home run by Rocky Nelson, then added two more in the second.

But the Yankees weren't through, pushing across one run in the fifth inning and then piling on four more in the sixth. The big blow here was a three-run home run by Yogi Berra. Two more runs in the eighth gave the Yankees a 7–4 lead—but this game wasn't over yet.

In their half of the eighth, the Pirates benefited from one of the most famous bad hops in baseball history. With a runner on first, Bill Virdon hit a hard grounder to Tony Kubek, the Yankee shortstop. It should have been a double play, but at the last second the ball took a wicked hop and struck Kubek in the throat. Both runners were safe and Kubek had to leave the game.

This bad break opened the floodgates. Two runs had already scored when Hal Smith slammed a home run, giving the Pirates a 9–7 lead.

This game was far from over. The Yankees scored twice in the top of the ninth and now the game was tied, 9–9.

After that, the end came quickly. Bill Mazeroski, long known as a brilliant fielder but mediocre hitter, was up first in the bottom of the ninth. On the second pitch by Ralph Terry, Mazeroski slammed the ball high, and deep, and over the left field fence. Just like that, the game was over, and the Pirates had won their first World Series in 35 years.

MAZEROSKI coming home after he slammed a home run over the left field wall to end the game and win the Series for the Pirates.

PIRATES FANS in downtown Pittsburgh celebrating a long-awaited World Series win.

EXPANSION

The Amazin' Mets. The Miracle Mets. What else could the New York team be called after going from cellar-dweller to 1969 World Series champion? Writing in his *Concise History of Major League Baseball,* Leonard Koppett calls the Mets' triumph over the Baltimore Orioles "truly one of the great upsets . . . in sports history." This great turnaround capped a historic change in the big leagues— the beginning of divisional play.

The change came amid social turmoil unsurpassed by any other period in 20th-century America. In the 1960s and early 1970s, as a Baby Boomer generation engaged in protest and infused America with tremendous energy, baseball found itself caught in the upheaval while it worked mightily to make the game more appealing for the supercharged times. That changes such as divisional play worked, that baseball remained relevant and exciting, could be found in the improved turnstile counts— average attendance for major league clubs increased from 1.15 million in 1968 to 1.25 million in 1973.

THE WOODSTOCK MUSIC FESTIVAL of 1969 has come to symbolize the 1960s counterculture. Here, a couple rests as the crowds begin to leave the festival.

By the mid-1960s "another long hot summer" meant more than baseball's glory season. It meant violence; it meant riots and flames sweeping through black ghettos . . . Watts and Chicago in 1965, Detroit in 1967. Every year of the Sixties brought more upheaval across a spectrum so wide America seemed to be falling apart. Black Power. Brown Power. Anti-war protests. Hippies. Women's liberation.

A baby boom and an economic boom combined in the 1960s to exert enormous pressure on society. The Baby Boom began in 1946 with an all-time U.S. record 3.4 million births— one every nine seconds! The Boom, led by urban and suburban middle-class parents, continued through 1964. America's economy also flourished. Per capita income jumped from $2,157 in 1960 to $3,050 in 1970, a 41 percent increase (in

terms of constant 1958 dollars). Over the same period, per capita gross national product went from $2,699 to $3,555.

As much as Baby Boomers enjoyed America's prosperity, they criticized society for its shortcomings. Foremost among their criticisms was racism. Jackie Robinson's 1947 breaking of the color barrier in the Major Leagues had only begun to address the divide between whites and blacks in America. To eradicate injustice, Martin Luther King, Jr., stressed nonviolent protests.

When four black college students staged a sit-in at a segregated lunch counter in Greensboro, North Carolina, in 1960, they showed that young people no longer had to accept the injustices handed down by their elders, or wait for their elders to take action. Thousands of college students, white and black, worked in the South in the mid-1960s to register African-American voters. Youthful protest took yet another turn in 1965, the first year of American ground combat in Vietnam. An anti-war rally in Washington, D.C., signaled that more than a few people opposed the conflict.

As the civil rights movement and Vietnam War exposed injustice, the Baby Boomers formed a countercultural movement that challenged a wide span of middle-class values and practices. For example, many young men wore long hair to declare their liberation from parental rules; musicians infused rock music with social consciousness; hippies founded communes dedicated to peace, love, and psychedelic drugs. To mainstream Americans such behavior meant moral collapse, and some found in baseball a refuge, a bastion of traditional values, where Old Glory fluttered in summer breezes, a patriotic symbol to counter the protesters.

By the late 1960s, young political protesters grew more radical in demanding change; some even called for a violent revolution. Radicalism overtook the civil rights movement as some African Americans proclaimed "Black Power," a more strident, no-compromise approach against racism.

Suddenly, the gradualist approach to civil rights as represented by baseball's integration, seemed lacking. Black and Hispanic ballplayers were numerous. In 1965, for example, 48 players from the Caribbean were on the rosters of major league teams; eight were in the All-Star game. Yet some activists pointed out that not one African American managed a ball club.

Adding to the social upheaval, three assassinations shook America: that of President John Kennedy in 1963, and within a few weeks of each other in 1968, those of Martin Luther King, Jr., and Senator Robert Kennedy. King's assassination led to riots in many cities and forced Major League Baseball to postpone the start of its season. No such consensus to suspend games occurred with Robert Kennedy's assassination, and as a result disputes broke out among players over whether they should take the field during and soon after the senator's funeral. The Houston Astros team revolted against management and refused to play, until the club owner threatened economic reprisals.

Such turmoil and a faster-paced world encouraged organized baseball to change. So, too, did the looming competition from the Continental League, being formed by Branch Rickey, who as general manager had brought Jackie Robinson into the Dodger organization. Rickey planned to place teams in New York City, Atlanta, Houston, Dallas, Denver, Minneapolis-St. Paul, Buffalo, and Toronto. He said he wanted to take advantage of the shift in population to the West.

The A.L. and N.L. club owners criticized Rickey for betraying organized baseball and then proceeded to expand their leagues by two teams each in order to counteract Rickey's plans (his league never got off the ground), and to extend the season from 154 games to 162. The A.L. expanded in 1961 into California with the Angels and into Minnesota with the Twins—actually the Washington Senators, who moved to Minnesota, while a new Senators club was organized. The N.L. expanded into Houston in 1962 with the Colt .45s and into New York City with the Mets, who partially filled the gap left by the departure four years earlier of the Dodgers to Los Angeles and the Giants to San Francisco. At the outset, these expansion teams, especially the Mets, consisted largely of aging veterans and young players of limited ability. In 1962, the Mets won only 40 games and committed more errors than any major league team in 24 years: 204. Their manager, Casey Stengel, said, "I've been in this game a hundred years, but I see new ways to lose I never knew existed before." New Yorkers fell in love with the hapless team,

AMERICA LOST *President John F. Kennedy in 1963, and both Martin Luther King, Jr. and Senator Robert F. Kennedy in 1968. Here King gives his "I Have a Dream" speech in August 1963.*

and the club drew almost one million fans to the deteriorating Polo Grounds during their inaugural season.

With expansion came new stadiums, mainly in the National League. In 1970, the N.L. had new parks for 11 of its 12 teams while the American League had new parks for three of its 12. New construction included the Chavez Ravine ballpark for the Dodgers in Los Angeles and ballparks in Baltimore, Kansas City, Minneapolis-St. Paul, San Francisco, and Washington. The Harris County Domed Stadium in Houston, called the Astrodome, cost $31.6 million to build. It became the first indoor baseball stadium. The weather was always fine inside, but the lack of direct sunlight caused the grass to die and forced the installation of a new product, a green, plastic, artificial grass quickly christened "Astroturf." Some criticized the stadium as sterile; sports writer Roger Angell called it "a giant living-room" that "so drearily resembles" the one the fan just left. The Astrodome, however, pointed the way to other domed stadiums and yet more expensive structures.

With more teams, both leagues split into divisions in 1969, creating a League Championship Series to go with the World Series. They each had West and East divisions, with six teams per division. Thus in addition to the pennant races, fan interest could be maintained with the contests for divisional titles. In 1969, the N.L. West race involved five teams down to the wire—all of the teams were within two games of the lead with only three weeks left to play.

Along with expansion, several teams changed locations. In 1966, the Milwaukee Braves moved to Atlanta, and in 1968 the Kansas City A's moved to Oakland. In 1970, the Seattle club, formed just the year before in the decade's second round of expansion, moved to Milwaukee to become the Brewers; and two years later, the Senators left Washington for Dallas-Fort Worth where they became the Texas Rangers.

In 1964, baseball showed its attachment to corporate money, too, when the Columbia Broadcasting System bought the New York Yankees for $11.2 million, in that day a substantial sum. This was the first time a corporation owned and operated a major league club. (CBS sold the Yankees in 1973 to a group of investors led by George Steinbrenner.) The purchase was testimony as well to the important role of television in the sport.

During the 1960s and early 1970s, players generated ever more excitement with their individual accomplishments. Roberto Clemente of the Pittsburgh Pirates achieved batting averages of .357, .352, .345, and .339; Hank Aaron of the Milwaukee and Atlanta Braves chased Babe Ruth's career home run record; and Sandy Koufax of the Los Angeles Dodgers pitched his way to an incredible record in 1963: 25–5 with a 1.88 ERA. Right-hander Bob Gibson of the St. Louis Cardinals shut down the Boston Red Sox in the 1967 World Series with a dominating pitching performance. Yet the Red Sox had their own star player in outfielder Carl Yastrzemski who excited Red Sox fans that same year when he hit .326 with 44 home runs and 121 runs batted in—the major league leader in all three categories, thus winning baseball's coveted Triple Crown.

Despite this excitement, some Baby Boomers claimed baseball was too slow, the games too long: batters stepping from the batter's box, conferences at the pitcher's mound, long warm-ups for relief pitchers. The *Sporting News* referred to this Baby Boomer complaint when it said sarcastically, "If your kicks are psychedelic, if Bonnie and Clyde are your heroes, then baseball and Willie Mays and Mickey Mantle will be dull."

MARVIN MILLER, the executive director of the Major League Baseball Players Association, announced in March 1972 that the association had voted to strike.

In keeping with the times, organized baseball adopted the countercultural attachment to bright colors and rebellious fashion. The Pittsburgh Pirates uniform combined solid colors with stripes (and according to historian David Q. Voigt, a "sexy, skin-tight cut"). While winning three World Series titles from 1972 to 1974, the Oakland Swingin' A's wore flashy green and gold uniforms complemented by white shoes and a bedraggled look created when the players sported mustaches, beards, and long hair.

On a more serious matter, much as college students, blacks, women, and others confronted the societal status quo, big league baseball players organized to expand their rights and improve their economic position. They had founded the Major League Baseball Players Association (MLBPA) in 1954 and through it fought to protect their pensions and increase their minimum salaries. By the mid-1960s, the players had concluded that they needed to strengthen the MLBPA and make it a true union.

The Sporting News said "ball players . . . win recognition as individuals," and warned that making them into union members would turn teams into "faceless organizations." Nevertheless, Marvin Miller, executive director of the MLBPA and a talented labor organizer, convinced the players that Major League Baseball was lucrative enough to fund a bigger pension and provide higher salaries, and that through unity they could gain a voice in a business run by the owners. According to historian Ron Briley, "With authority and tradition being openly confronted on the streets and campuses of America . . . the time seemed right for players to assert their position under a more aggressive leader such as Miller."

The players won some pension and salary gains in the late Sixties. They even convinced the Topps Chewing Gum Company to pay royalties of several million dollars for the baseball cards they sold, a big improvement over the one-time fee of $125 Topps usually paid to each player whose photo and signature it used. August "Gussie" Busch, owner of the St. Louis Cardinals, confronted the players at spring training in 1969. After linking their protests to the general upheaval in society, and condemning both, he told them they had a pension plan most American workers would envy.

Miller and the MLBPA pushed forward, and in 1972 the players demanded that the owners increase their contribution to the pension fund and improve the existing medical plan. When the owners refused—"Let them strike," declared Gussie Busch—the players voted 663–10 to start the first general walkout in baseball's modern era and, according to *The Sporting News*, bring "the darkest day in sports history." The strike forced spring training to end early and delayed the start of the regular season. The players went back to work in mid-April after reaching a new agreement with the owners that improved the pension fund, raised minimum salaries, and established the right to salary arbitration.

Despite these gains, Miller and the MLBPA were unable to obtain changes in the reserve clause, which in effect kept each ballplayer tied to his club unless the club decided to trade him. The issue came to a head away from the bargaining table in a case involving center fielder Curt Flood, an African-American player who identified with the civil rights movement and may have been motivated by it to fight what he considered to be an injustice that transcended economics.

The Cardinals had decided in October 1969 to trade Flood, a 12-year veteran, to Philadelphia, but he wanted to negotiate with other clubs. He told the baseball commissioner: "I do not feel I am a piece of property to be bought and sold irrespective of my wishes." He subsequently sued to get the reserve clause overturned. (The MLBPA paid his legal fees.) "Win or lose," recalled Flood in his book *The Way It Is,* "the baseball industry would never be the same. I would leave my mark." Flood lost. In 1973, one year after the players' strike, the Supreme Court ruled 5–3 against him.

Among all the issues that shook America in the 1960s, few tore more severely at the social fabric than Vietnam. As disagreements over the war pitted Americans against one another, baseball club owners generally supported the U.S. military presence as a patriotic duty. Many, probably most, players agreed. Several willingly made trips to Vietnam to boost morale among the troops. Ernie Banks said he was proud of the soldiers, and he criticized young people back home who did nothing but complain. But some players felt differently.

The tempest spilled over to the 1969 World Series—the same Series in which the New York Mets defeated the Baltimore Orioles four games to one. On October 15, antiwar protesters distributed leaflets at New York's Shea Stadium in which Mets pitcher Tom Seaver was quoted as opposing the war. Although Seaver distanced himself from the pamphlets because, he claimed, he had been misquoted, he had previously expressed his opposition to America's military role in Vietnam. Under the headline "Tom Seaver Says U.S. Should Leave Vietnam," the *New York Times* reported his remarks, made the day before the Series began. "I think it's perfectly ridiculous what we're doing about the Vietnam situation. It's absurd! When the Series is over, I'm going to have a talk with [Massachusetts Senator] Ted Kennedy,

THE U.S.'S INVOLVEMENT *in the Vietnam War divided baseball players, just as it divided U.S. society. An ammunition dump under attack in November 1967 is shown above.*

convey some of my ideas to him and then take an ad in the paper. I feel very strongly about this."

During the Series, New York mayor John Lindsay ordered all flags on city buildings flown at half-mast to protest the war. The city buildings included Shea Stadium. When a color guard of wounded Vietnam War veterans threatened to boycott a pregame flag ceremony, it appeared as if the World Series would be overshadowed by the ruckus. As controversy raged, about 500 war supporters jeered Lindsay on the steps of city hall, and police drove their patrol cars in the daytime with headlights on to declare their opposition to the mayor's antiwar stance. The crisis eased when baseball commissioner Bowie Kuhn stepped in and talked with Lindsay on the phone. The result: The flag at Shea was flown full-staff.

By and large baseball's traditional conservatism made it inhospitable to antiwar activism. But in the Sixties, hardly any institution escaped the pressure for change, the cries for equity, the demands that the old and the traditional reshape themselves, including baseball. When characteristics long-embedded in the sport met the challenges emanating from the counterculture, baseball too donned a new look.

61 REVISITED

In the summer of 1961, two outstanding Yankee sluggers dueled for the league's home run crown, spurring each other on to greater and greater heights. Mickey Mantle would finish the season early with 54 homers, his personal best. Roger Maris, under the glare of media attention, continued. On October 1, Maris blasted number 61, toppling Babe Ruth's long-standing record of 60. A seemingly unbreakable record had fallen.

THE M & M BOYS

Roger Maris, in his first season with the Yankees, won the 1960 American League MVP award, edging out teammate Mickey Mantle by three votes. Maris led the Yankees to the pennant by socking 39 homers, his personal best, and driving in a league-leading 112 runs. With numbers like that and teammates like Mantle, Yogi Berra, Tony Kubek, Bobby Richardson, and Moose Skowron, Yankee fans had high hopes for 1961.

But Maris got off to a slow start, not hitting his first homer until the Yankees' 11th game. Yankee management suggested that the slugger visit an eye doctor, which he did, receiving a clean bill of health.

Maris caught fire soon enough, however, and pulled even with Mantle for the team—and league—lead in home runs. Throughout the summer, the two sluggers—dubbed the M&M boys by the press—would spur each other on, trading the homer lead frequently. By mid-season, the press and fans were beginning to wonder if Babe Ruth's record of

ALTHOUGH THEY SPENT most of the season trading home runs in pursuit of Babe Ruth's record, Maris and Mantle remained good friends. They provided each other with the encouragement needed to overcome the pressure to set a new record.

IN RESPONSE TO ALLEGATIONS THAT BASEBALLS WERE "LIVELIER," MANTLE REMARKED, "MAYBE THE PLAYERS NOW ARE LIVELIER."

60 home runs, set in 1927, might not be in jeopardy.

On July 1, Maris led Mantle 28–27. Both hitters were on a pace to demolish the record. On July 18, Commissioner Ford Frick announced that, in order to break the record, a player would need to hit his 61st home run before the 155th game of the season. As this was the first expansion year in major league history, the schedule had grown from 154 to 162 games. Frick suggested that, if either player broke the record after the 154th game, a "distinctive mark," such as an asterisk, would need to be placed alongside his name in the record books. A week later, Maris responded by smashing four homers in a double-header against the White Sox.

Speculation about the record was joined by a lively debate about whether the baseball itself was "juiced." Investigations were conducted by the *New York Times* and the testing labs at M.I.T., with inconclusive results. Hall of Fame pitcher Dizzy Dean

ON OCTOBER 1, 1961 Maris became the new single season home run champion, breaking a record many claimed would never be touched.

pronounced the ball livelier: "Hold it in your hand and you can feel its heart beating." Mantle remarked dryly, "Maybe the players now are livelier."

MARIS FEELS THE HEAT

By September 1st, Maris led Mantle by 51–48, and both players remained well ahead of Ruth's 1927 pace. The heat was on, and the

MARIS LINED A PITCH OFF Boston's Tracy Stallard to become the new single-season home run champion in 1961, capping off a grueling season in which the media followed his every move. The new record would stand for 37 years.

Yankees were in another pennant race. The media descended on the Yankees. The quiet, almost sullen Maris tired of answering the same questions, and the stress began to show everywhere but on the field. Clumps of his hair fell out, and at one point, he even broke down in tears before manager Ralph Houk, asking "Why don't they leave me alone?" But he kept hitting home runs.

In mid-September, Mantle fell ill with the flu. He played his last game on September 26th, finishing with 54 homers, his personal record. Meanwhile, Maris had failed to break Ruth's record in the 154th game of the season, hitting his 59th that day as the Yankees clinched the pennant. To read the news accounts, the chase was over. Maris admitted to a mixture of disappointment and relief, but also said that as far as he was concerned, a season was a season, regardless of the number of games. On September 26th, he blasted his 60th homer against Baltimore's Jack Fisher, with Claire Ruth, the Babe's widow, in attendance.

Exhausted, Maris then took a day off. On the final day of the season, October 1, the Yankees hosted Boston. In the fourth inning, with the score knotted at 0–0, Maris lined a pitch from Tracy Stallard 15 rows deep into the right field seats, where 19-year-old Sal Durante of Brooklyn caught it. The 23,154 fans in attendance (less than half the capacity of Yankee Stadium, perhaps because of the asterisk pronouncement or the fact that the Yankees had already clinched the pennant) gave Roger Maris a standing ovation and he took a couple of curtain calls. The Yankees went on to beat Cincinnati four games to one in the World Series, with Maris chipping in a homer in Game Three. His record would stand for 37 years, longer even than the Babe's record had stood.

ONLY 23,154 FANS were in attendance at Yankee Stadium for the final game of the year. Most were hoping to see Maris hit his 61st home run. When he did, it was 19-year-old Sal Durante who earned a place in baseball folklore by catching the ball in the right field seats.

Single-Season Home Run Records

Year	Player	# of Homers	Team	# of Games in Season
1876	George Hall	5	Philadelphia (N)	154
1879	Charley Jones	9	Boston (N)	154
1883	Harry Stovey	14	Philadephia (N)	154
1884	Ned Williamson	27	Chicago (N)	154
1919	Babe Ruth	29	Boston (A)	154
1920	Babe Ruth	54	New York (A)	154
1921	Babe Ruth	59	New York (A)	154
1927	Babe Ruth	60	New York (A)	154
1961	Roger Maris	61	New York (A)	162
1998	Mark McGwire	70	St. Louis (N)	162

CLASS OF '62

Jackie Robinson, the first African American in the Major Leagues, in 1962 became the first African American to be inducted into the Baseball Hall of Fame. He was elected in his first year of eligibility. In his acceptance speech, Robinson thanked Dodger executive Branch Rickey, his mother, his wife Rachel, and "the people throughout this country who were so wonderful during those trying days." Joining Robinson on the dais were fireballing pitcher Bob Feller, longtime manager Bill McKechnie, and outfielder Edd Roush.

THE PIONEER

I n 1947, Jackie Robinson became the first African-American ballplayer to play major league baseball in 60 years. That October, he was the first African American ever to play in the World Series. After the season, he became the first recipient of the new Rookie of the Year award. And in 1962, he became the first African-American ballplayer ever to be inducted into baseball's Hall of Fame. From beginning to end, Robinson was a pioneer.

AT THE HALL OF FAME induction ceremonies in 1962, Robinson posed with his wife Rachel and Branch Rickey, the Dodger executive who selected him as the player to break the color barrier in the Major Leagues.

That he succeeded in the face of racial prejudice and hatred that would have destroyed a weaker man is testimony to Jackie Robinson's enormous strength, sturdiness of character, and firmness of purpose. He never forgot, as columnist Wendell Smith put it, "that he was representing 14 million people who were pulling for him day in and day out"—the African-American fans who saw him as opening doors for them as well.

His success began in his very first game in 1946, when he was playing with the Montreal Royals, a Dodgers farm team. He was by far the best player in the minors that year. Yet, even though the fans in Montreal were by and large supportive, by the end of the year Robinson had come perilously close to suffering a complete mental and physical collapse. "Robinson's condition last year was not the result of playing baseball every day," wrote columnist Wendell Smith. "The difficulty came in remaining poised at all times . . . ignoring the bench jockeys and insulting racial epithets hurled by prejudiced fans from the stands."

But, as Smith added, Robinson "came through like a champion."

TOWER OF STRENGTH

Whatever prejudice Jackie Robinson had faced with the

Royals was multiplied infinitely when he joined the Dodgers. Writers for newspapers and magazines sneered at his ability, suggesting that Branch Rickey had brought him to the Majors just as a publicity stunt. Some, though not all, of Robinson's own teammates resisted playing alongside him. Players on opposing teams used every vile insult they could to try to distract him.

Not every opposing player acted this way, though. In his 1948 autobiography, *Jackie Robinson: My Own Story,* Robinson described a play in which he collided at first base with Hank Greenberg, then finishing his career with the Pittsburgh Pirates. Greenberg asked if Robinson was okay, and then went on to say, "Listen, don't pay any attention to these guys who are trying to make it hard for you. Stick in there. You're doing fine."

Greenberg, a Jew, had faced abundant prejudice himself during his Hall of Fame career.

"Those words of encouragement helped me tremendously," Robinson recalled. "That man had class, Hank Greenberg did."

When the long, difficult 1947 season had come to an end, Jackie Robinson had posted superb numbers, including a .297 batting average and a league-leading 29 stolen bases.

The Dodgers went to the World Series in 1947. Though the team lost to the Yankees, Robinson had several important hits, and two more stolen bases. He called his appearance in that Series "one of the most important moments in my life."

For his overall performance in 1947, Jackie Robinson was awarded the first Rookie of the Year award—an award that is now named after him.

ROAD TO GLORY

Jackie Robinson was 27 before he made it to the Major Leagues, already at his peak as a player. As a result, he played for only 10 years with the Dodgers—though he would have had a far longer major league career if he'd been allowed to play earlier than 1947.

Still, even in his truncated career, he had several superb seasons. The finest was 1949, when he led the league with a .342 batting average, 37 stolen bases, and had 16 home runs and 124 runs batted in. He played in six World Series, including 1955, when the Dodgers finally overcame the rival Yankees and won their first World Championship.

In 1962, Jackie Robinson was elected to the Hall of Fame, along with pitcher Bob Feller, long-time manager Bill McKechnie, and outfielder Edd Roush. Robinson thanked his wife Rachel—who had been a pillar of strength and support during his career—as well as his mother, Branch Rickey, and "the people throughout this country who were so wonderful during those trying days."

"I've been riding on Cloud Nine since the election, and I don't think I'll ever come down," he added. "Today, everything is complete."

IN HIS ACCEPTANCE SPEECH, Robinson thanked his wife, his mother, Branch Rickey, and "the people throughout this country who were so wonderful during those trying days."

ROBINSON is flanked by family members at the Hall of Fame induction in 1962.

STOLEN MOMENTS

Maury Wills of the Los Angeles Dodgers stole 104 bases in 1962, shattering Ty Cobb's record of 96.
While Wills' new record would later be eclipsed by Lou Brock and Brock's record bested by Rickey Henderson,
the real importance of Wills' achievement was that he almost single-handedly brought speed back into baseball
as an important offensive factor. For much of the 20th century prior to Wills, baseball teams had been
content to let sluggers drive runs home with extra base hits. Wills brought back the fast-paced, hit-and-run
baseball that had been forgotten shortly after Babe Ruth invented the power game.

ONE BASE AT A TIME

The late 1940s and 1950s are remembered today as a "golden age" of baseball. People have fond memories of Joe DiMaggio gliding across centerfield to catch a long fly ball, Jackie Robinson electrifying the crowd by stealing home, Mickey Mantle blasting a long home run, Willie Mays running the bases with joyful abandon.

Those were exciting times for baseball—especially if you rooted for one of the New York teams. In fairness, however, it's important to remember that baseball then, especially in the 1950s, was a far less varied and strategic game than it is today.

The 1950s was the era of the three-run home run. Every team had its big slugger, its Gus Triandos or Rocky Colavito or Ralph Kiner or Gus Zernial or Hank Sauer. With line-ups anchored by these slow-footed power hitters, teams developed a method of play that relied on a hit, a walk, and a three-run home run. The stolen base, once so central to the game, became rare—used only occasionally to surprise and cross up the opposition.

During the first seven years of the 1950s, no team stole 100 bases. In 1958, the Dodgers led the National League with 73 steals (about as many as the league-leading individual player gets today), while other teams logged in with such stunningly low totals as 26, 30, and 39.

With its hint of illegality, of larceny, the stolen base had always been one of the more exciting plays on the diamond. As the 1950s came to an end, however, it seemed like a play that had been relegated to history's dustbin, a relic of the olden days.

MAURY WILLS stole an incredible 104 bases in 1962, bringing the element of speed back into baseball (top). Wills would land safely at the bag in his 81st steal of the 1962 season, on his way to breaking Ty Cobb's record (bottom). Wills stole bases with sheer determination: "I don't think I might steal a base," he said, "I know I can."

Single Season Stolen Bases— 100 and Over, 20th Century		
Player	Year	Stolen Bases
Rickey Henderson	1982	130
Lou Brock	1974	118
Vince Coleman	1985	110
Vince Coleman	1987	109
Rickey Henderson	1983	108
Vince Coleman	1986	107
Maury Wills	1962	104
Rickey Henderson	1980	100

Until a man named Maury Wills came along and changed the future of baseball.

RUNNING AT WILL

Largely because he weighed just 150 pounds and couldn't slug the ball, Maury Wills spent most of nine years in the minors before getting his shot with the Dodgers. As soon as he made it to the bigs, though, he began to leave his imprint on the game. "When I broke in with the Dodgers, I knew I couldn't hit the ball as far as Frank Howard nor could I hit it as often as Hank Aaron," he explained. "So I had to try something else."

Beginning in 1960, when he stole 50 bases, Wills saw speed as a weapon designed not only to gain an extra base, but also to disrupt the opposition. Dancing off of first base, telling the world that he could steal whenever he wanted, he forced pitcher after pitcher to lose concentration.

But his 1960 season was just a warm-up to 1962. Just a season after Roger Maris broke Babe Ruth's hallowed home run mark, Wills set his sights on another record long considered out of reach: Ty Cobb's total of 96 stolen bases, set in 1915. To steal more than 96 bases, you've got to be ready to steal every time you get on base. "I don't think I might steal a base," he said. "I know I can."

As the season went on, Wills piled up one stolen base after another. He reached 75 stolen bases by early September, the press began to

take notice, and he became the object of intense scrutiny. At the same time, the pounding of all that running, all those slides, began to catch up with him. He suffered an ankle injury and even a strained hamstring, but he didn't stop.

Wills passed Ty Cobb in the 156th game of the season, and reached 100 by the end of the regular season. But the Dodgers finished tied with the Giants for first place, and the two teams played a three-game playoff to determine who would play the New York Yankees in the Series. Wills took advantage of the three extra games to steal four more bases—ending the season with an astonishing 104. Amazingly, he was thrown out only 13 times.

The Dodgers lost the pennant in 1962, but Maury Wills' legs carried him to the Most Valuable Player award. Perhaps more importantly, he showed teams in both leagues how potent a weapon the stolen base could be.

LOU BROCK slides to safety, racking up steal number 105. With this steal, Brock surpassed Maury Wills' record on his way to 118 stolen bases in 1974. Umpire John McSherry made the call.

RICKEY HENDERSON, the "Man of Steal," broke Lou Brock's record of 118 stolen bases in a season in 1982, finishing the year with 130. Here, Henderson slides into his 130th steal. He still holds the record.

JUST AN INCH HIGHER

Giants fans will never forget it. With the 1962 World Series tied at three games apiece, the Yankees took a tense, 1-0 lead into the bottom of the ninth at San Francisco. The Giants' Matty Alou led off with a bunt single. After two strikeouts, Willie Mays doubled to right, Alou holding at third. With Giants fans smelling a championship, Willie McCovey ripped a screaming line drive to right, or so it seemed, except that Yankee second baseman Bobby Richardson leaped and snared the ball, making the Yanks champs.

SAME OLD SAME OLD

Even a change of cities didn't make any difference. Never have a trio of teams dominated the American and National Leagues the way the Yankees, Dodgers, and Giants did from the late 1940s through the mid-1960s. Between 1947 and 1964, the Yankees captured 15 A.L. pennant flags. During the same 18-season span, the Dodgers made it to the World Series eight times (plus again in 1965 and 1966), while the Giants won three N.L. pennants. It didn't even seem to matter when the Dodgers and Giants moved to Los Angeles and San Francisco, respectively, in 1958—they all just kept winning.

The 1962 season was full of diversions. The Los Angeles Angels and Minnesota Twins played their first seasons. Fans got to enjoy splendid years from Willie Mays, Hank Aaron, Harmon Killebrew, and other sluggers. The Dodgers' Maury Wills stole 104 bases, revolutionizing baseball by reintroducing speed to the game.

Still, as the season came to an end, no fan was surprised to see the Yankees cruise to another pennant—or to see the Giants and Dodgers fight it out to the last day of a three-game playoff to see who would meet the Yankees in the World Series.

THE PENNANT THAT NOBODY WANTED

That's what they called the bizarre 1962 pennant race in the National League. Taking advantage of the weak teams at the bottom of the league, both the Dodgers and Giants piled up win after win as the season went on. Until the very end, it seemed that the Dodgers would win easily; they led by four games with only eight to go.

But then, suddenly, the Dodgers began to lose, game after game. They even lost two games to the new Colt 45s (later the Astros). Meanwhile, the Giants were winning, drawing ever closer as the season wound down.

BOBBY RICHARDSON, Yankee hero. The Giants had a chance to win the 1962 World Series in Game Seven, with two men on and a Willie McCovey hit that looked like it was headed through the infield. But Yankee second baseman Bobby Richardson reached up and caught the ball, ending the inning and the series with the Yankees victorious.

On the last day of the season, the Dodgers had a one-game lead. All they had to do was win their finale against the St. Louis Cardinals—but they couldn't do it, losing 1–0. Then the Giants went out and won a 2–1 thriller against Houston, and the regular season had ended with two teams sporting identical 101–61 records. A three-game playoff loomed to determine who would be the pennant-winner.

The Dodgers, shell-shocked, didn't have enough gas left in their tank, and the Giants won the tightly contested playoff and the right to face the Yankees.

What Might Have Been

Both the Yankees and the Giants had won during the regular season on the strength of their batting, not their pitching. Both teams had led their leagues in hitting and had been close to the top in home runs. A wild slugfest of a Series was expected.

But then, as *Sports Illustrated* put it, "Somebody took the rabbit out of the ball and put spaghetti in the bats." After six tight, well-pitched games, the teams were tied, three games apiece, and the Series was set to go to Game Seven.

Game Seven matched the Giants' Jack Sanford (who'd gone 24–7 during the season) against Ralph Terry (23–12), and it was clear from the start that both pitchers were at the top of their game.

The Yankees managed to plate a run in the fifth, and as the innings rolled by it looked as though the Giants might not even mount a threat in return. Going into the ninth, they'd managed only two hits.

Leading off the bottom of the ninth, pinch hitter Matty Alou bunted for a base hit. Terry struck out the next two hitters, but then Willie Mays slammed a ball down the right field line. At first it looked as if it would bounce past right fielder Roger Maris all the way to the wall, with Alou scoring from first. But Maris cut the ball off in the corner, and Giants' third base coach Whitey Lockman held Alou at third. "If it had

been me," Mays wrote in his autobiography, *Say Hey,* "I would have tried to score."

Instead, the Giants had runners on second and third, two men out. Onlookers thought that Terry would walk the dangerous Willie McCovey to face Orlando Cepeda, but the Yankee pitcher chose to pitch to McCovey.

On the first pitch, McCovey drove a long fly ball to right—just foul. Two pitches later, he slammed a liner toward right field. If it got through the infield, two runs would score and the Giants would win the World Series.

But the ball never made it to the outfield. Yankee second baseman Bobby Richardson plucked the sinking liner out of the air—he didn't have to move a step to reach it—and just like that, the Series was over, and the Yankees had added yet another notch to their championship belt.

RALPH TERRY, the Yankees' winning pitcher in Game Seven of the 1962 World Series, celebrates with his ecstatic teammates after the last out. Terry and the Yankees shut out the Giants with the final score of 1-0.

WILLIE McCOVEY came to the plate in the bottom of the ninth with two Giants on base. On the third pitch, he hit a line drive toward right field that would have won the game—but Richardson caught the ball.

ANY WAY YOU GO

The New York Mets didn't give their fans much to cheer about in 1963. But on June 23 at the Polo Grounds, fans saw two things they definitely had never seen before. Outfielder Jimmy Piersall hit his 100th home run and proceeded to do the improbable. Drawing upon his remarks when he signed with the Mets, "I will do anything to keep spectators entertained," Piersall proceeded to run the bases backward. And while that gave the Mets fans something to talk about, they swept the Phillies in that day's doubleheader, another improbable event for the expansion Mets. Citing his .194 average with the Mets and not this stunt, Piersall was released later that season.

THE OLD PROFESSOR

Few individuals in baseball's long and colorful history have had a more eventful, satisfying, or colorful career than Casey Stengel did during his more than half a century in the game. He started out as a smart but modestly talented outfielder with the Brooklyn Dodgers in 1912 and went on to play for 14 years for five teams. His final career batting average was .284, not bad, but nothing to get excited over. He did play impressively in three World Series, hitting .393.

Regardless of his lack of star quality, the press took extra notice of Stengel—and Stengel, seemingly born with a nose for publicity, ate it up. He didn't even mind when *Baseball Magazine* described him as having "awesome ears of about the same size, shape and constituency of rib lamb chops." Any publicity was good publicity.

After Stengel retired as a player, he had the chance to prove that he could be a different sort of manager. At first, though, his hands were tied by the fact that he was put in charge of very weak teams: first, the Dodgers before they got good, and later the Boston Braves. During those years (1934–36, 1938–43), he posted just one plus-.500 season. After he was fired by the Braves in 1943, it seemed that he would join the long line of ex-players who washed out as managers.

VETERAN MANAGER CASEY STENGEL came to the expansion New York Mets in their first year, 1962. For Stengel, a publicity hound himself, Jimmy Piersall's attention-getting antics were too much.

AFTER HITTING HIS 100TH HOME RUN, the always unpredictable Jimmy Piersall treated Mets fans to a backward run around the bases.

But Stengel was the exception, because he got a third chance. He was named to replace Bucky Harris as manager of the always-dangerous New York Yankees in 1949, a move that provoked scorn from fans and the media. The scorn didn't last too long, though: The Yankees won the World Series the first five years that Casey was manager.

Stengel's legend grew during his years as Yankee manager. But after the 1960 season, he was let go, largely because the Yankees considered him too old at age 70.

Now, it seemed that it was time for the Old Professor to ride into the sunset. He'd had a magnificent career, and now it was time for him to move into a garrulous, quotable retirement.

Not quite. When the National League expanded in 1962, one of the new teams was the New York Mets. And the new team's first manager was an old man named Casey Stengel.

AMAZING

The baseball writer Fred Lieb, who'd been covering the game since 1911, described the 1962 Mets as a "collection of overage veterans, humpty dumpties, misfits, and alleged ballplayers." The Mets finished 40–120 their first season. They hit .240 as a team and their pitching had a 5.04 earned run average, both by far the worst in the league. "Sometimes when I go back in my mind to our play of 1962," Stengel said later, "I just wonder how we ever got to win forty games."

Stengel also said, famously, "Can't anybody here play this game?" Though the answer was no, Mets fans simply didn't care. Apparently, hundreds of thousands of fans in New York had been waiting impatiently for a new team in the National League. In 1963, when they went 51–111, the Mets drew nearly as many fans as the Yankees. And the Mets would outdraw the Yankees from 1964 to 1975.

Why did the fans flock to the ballpark to watch such a pathetic team? It certainly wasn't in the hope of seeing good baseball being played. No, the Mets were lovable because they were so bad—because their eager, ineffective play provided such grand entertainment value.

And, during his brief stay with the Mets, few provided more entertainment than Jimmy Piersall.

WRONG-WAY PIERSALL

Jimmy Piersall had been in the Major Leagues since 1950, making headlines as much for his antics as for his play on the field. Early in the decade, his erratic behavior led to a diagnosis and treatment of what now

would be called bipolar disorder (manic depression), a battle later memorialized in the movie *Fear Strikes Out*.

Although Piersall's behavior after treatment was far less bizarre, he remained an unpredictable presence both on and off the field. When the Mets obtained him from the Washington Senators in 1963, he said, "I will do anything to keep the spectators entertained." No one knew what that meant but Piersall himself.

Soon after he arrived, Piersall witnessed the Mets' Duke Snider (near the end of his career) slug his 400th career home run. Piersall was dismayed by how little notice that feat received in the local papers. "I decided that when I got my 100th, there would be some attention paid," he said later.

He wasn't kidding. On June 23 at the Polo Grounds, he hit home run number 100. As Mets fans watched in astonishment, Piersall proceeded to run the bases backward. (That is, he went to each base in the right order, but did it running backward, looking over his shoulder).

Piersall's stunt gained front-page coverage in the New York papers, as he'd hoped. But it didn't thrill Mets manager Casey Stengel. "There's room for only one clown on this team," he growled—and he was that clown.

Jimmy Piersall was released by the Mets soon afterward.

DISAPPOINTED by the lack of press his teammate Duke Snider's 400th home run received, Jimmy Piersall vowed to make his 100th home run something to remember.

WHILE WITH THE WASHINGTON SENATORS in a June 1963 game against the Detroit Tigers, Piersall, not content to take a lead off first base, made fun of opposing pitcher Don Mossi. Tiger first baseman Norm Cash and umpire Bill McKinley looked on.

STAN THE MAN

On the final day of his 22-year career with the Cardinals, Stan Musial collected two more hits to move to 3,630 for his career. The "Stan Musial Day" crowd in St. Louis expressed thunderous admiration for a great hitter and a 20-time All-Star. In 1969, Musial was inducted into the Hall of Fame in his first year of eligibility.

Stan Musial— Lifetime Stats

Games Played	3,026
At Bats	10,972
Runs	1,949
Hits	3,630
Doubles	725
Triples	177
Home Runs	475
RBI	1,951
Batting Average	.331
Stolen Bases	78

THE ROOKIE

Some rookies take a while to hit their stride. Stan Musial wasn't one of them. He made a big splash as soon as he was called up to the Cardinals at the tail end of the 1941 season. In his first game, he hit a double and single and drove in two runs. He added another hit the next day, then had his first "perfect day," 3-for-3, the day after that.

Then, on just his fifth day with the Cardinals, Musial had what he called "one of the finest days I'd ever have in the Majors." Musial began a double-header against the Chicago Cubs with a double. Then he added a single, another double, and another single. He capped off the game by running aggressively to score from second base on a little infield hit.

The phenomenal rookie wasn't done yet—after all, there was the second game of the double-header to be played. "I dived to my right for one low line drive and charged for another, turning a double-somersault," he recalled in his autobiography, *Stan Musial: "The Man's" Own Story.* "I bunted safely toward third base and singled to center to make it a memorable six-hit day of all-around delight."

Stan Musial finished his first stint in the Majors with a .426 batting average in 47 at bats. Fans nationwide knew they'd seen the arrival of a new superstar.

MR. CONSISTENCY

Year in and year out, Stan Musial put up spectacular numbers. When he hit "only" .312 in 1947, that was considered an off-year for him—because it was surrounded by years in which he hit .357, .347, .365, .376, .338, .346, and .355. He never hit as many as 40 home runs in a season, but posted totals of 39, 36, 35, 33, 32, and 30. He drove in more than 100 runs 10 times, and scored 100 runs 11 times.

The fans in St. Louis adored him from the start, of course. He was a modest, likable, hard-working man who could also field brilliantly and hit like Lou Gehrig.

Early in his career, his spectacular hitting helped lead the Cardinals to four National

ON SEPTEMBER 29, 1963, "Stan Musial Day" in St. Louis, Musial got a hit in the last at-bat of his career.

League pennants in five years. The first took place in 1942, when Musial was still just a 21-year-old rookie, and pitted the Cardinals against the dreaded Yankees, led by Joe DiMaggio, Phil Rizzuto, Red Ruffing, and other stars.

The Cardinals, with Musial just getting started and few other stars, seemed over-matched against the Yankees—especially after New York rolled to an easy Game One victory. But then, shockingly, the Cardinals won four straight, sending the Yankees to their worst World Series loss since 1922.

The Cardinals were back in the Series in 1943 (losing to the Yankees) and in 1944, when they beat the St. Louis Browns. Musial was away from baseball due to stint with the Navy in 1945, but he and the Cardinals came back to nipp the Dodgers in a playoff to win yet another National League pennant in 1946, and then went on to beat the favored Boston Red Sox for their third World Championship in four years.

For Stan Musial it must have seemed as if the winning would go on forever. But it wasn't to be. Musial would play for 17 more seasons after 1946, and never make it into another World Series.

AFTER 22 YEARS OF SERVICE with the St. Louis Cardinals, Musial had earned affection and respect not just from home-town fans, but also from opposing players and opposing teams' fans.

THE MAN SAYS GOODBYE

Stan Musial had a great year in 1962, hitting .330 with 19 home runs. As the season came to an end, some suggested that Musial hang up his spikes. But the Man wasn't having any of it. "I was having too much fun hitting to want to quit," he wrote later.

So he went back to play in 1963. Although he hit just .255 in this, his final season, he never regretted his decision. The Cardinals finished 93–69, in second place. Even more importantly, he wrote in his autobiography, "I had the satisfaction of reaching that point where, without anyone else having to tell me, I realized my liabilities were about to outweigh my assets as a ballplayer." `In other words, he went out on his own terms.

Musial's last trip around the league turned into a kind of farewell tour, with fans and

opposing players getting the chance to show their affection and respect. "[T]he fans and ball-clubs treated me wonderfully, with a warmth and hospitality that stopped just short of the foul lines," he recalled.

On the final day of his 22-year career, Musial played before the adoring home crowd in St. Louis. It was "Stan Musial Day," and the Man came through with two more hits. He also came through in his closing speech, saying, "Baseball has taught me the opportunity that America offers to any young men who want to get to the top in anything."

Stan Musial retired with 3,630 hits (fourth most of all time), 475 home runs, 1,951 RBI, and a lifetime .331 batting average. He was inducted into the Hall of Fame in 1969, his first year of eligibility.

MUSIAL was inducted to the Hall of Fame in 1969.

BUNNING'S MASTERPIECE

On Father's Day, June 21, 1964, Jim Bunning of the Phillies, himself the father of a large family, pitched a perfect game. The Phils beat the hometown Mets, 6–0, as Bunning also drove in two runs. Bunning would spend 17 years in the Majors before retiring at the end of the 1971 season. After his baseball career, Bunning went on to become a United States representative from Kentucky in 1986 and a senator in 1998.

LONG TIME COMING

When the Philadelphia Phillies' Jim Bunning pitched a perfect game against the New York Mets on Father's Day, June 21, 1964, he became the first pitcher to accomplish that feat since Don Larsen pitched his World Series perfecto against Brooklyn in 1956. Bunning also set another, even more remarkable mark: He was the first National League pitcher to throw a perfect game in 84 years.

Way back in 1880, both John Lee Richmond (of Worcester) and John Montgomery Ward (of Providence) pitched perfect games. But in the modern era—generally defined as post-1900—every perfect game had been pitched in the American League. Even such National League superstars as Christy Mathewson, Three-Finger Brown, Carl Hubbell, and Warren Spahn never managed to retire 27 out of 27 men.

Jim Bunning wasn't the most likely candidate to pitch a perfect game in 1964—after all, the Los Angeles Dodgers had a pair of aces named Sandy Koufax and Don Drysdale—but he was a fine pitcher. Before coming to the Phillies in 1964, he'd won 118 games with the Detroit Tigers during nine years with the team, including pitching a no-hitter against the Red Sox in 1958.

NO RUNS, NO HITS, NO ERRORS

The Mets had moved from the aged Polo Grounds to brand-new Shea Stadium in 1964, but their new digs didn't make them any better as a team. They'd improved from 40–120 in 1962 (their first year) to 51–111 in 1963—and though they were destined to win a club-record 53 games in 1964, they were still one of the weakest-hitting teams in the

IN THE FIRST GAME of a double-header against the New York Mets on June 21, 1964, Philadelphia Phillies' pitcher Jim Bunning was in fine form. So good, in fact, that Bunning went on to pitch the seventh perfect game in major league history that day.

league, batting just .246 for the season.

The Mets did have a pair of legitimate .300 hitters, though (Ron Hunt and Joe Christopher), and third baseman Charlie Smith was on his way to 20 home runs for the season. This was not a team of automatic outs.

The Mets seemed that way on

JIM BUNNING *is about to retire the 27th batter of his perfect game, Mets pinch hitter John Stephenson.*

this day, though. One by one, such hitters as Jim Hickman, Eddie Kranepool, Christopher, and Hunt would stride to the plate, and one by one they would walk back to the dugout after being retired on weak grounders, easy pop flies, or strikeouts.

In nearly every no-hitter, there is a great fielding play that prevents a hit. In this game, the play was made by Phillies' second baseman Tony Taylor in the fifth inning. The Mets' Jesse Gonder smashed a low line drive toward right field. Taylor dived for it, and almost caught it in the air, but his impact with the ground jarred the ball loose. With his back to first base, he grabbed the ball, turned on his knees, and fired to first, getting Gonder by two steps.

"When he did that, I knew I had something special going," said Bunning.

SILENCE ISN'T GOLDEN

There is a long-time baseball superstition that says no one—not players, nor fans, nor announcers—should mention when a pitcher has a no-hitter going. The theory is that, once the possible feat has been mentioned, the pitcher is jinxed. He will lose his bid for the no-hitter.

Jim Bunning was one pitcher who didn't believe in jinxes. "Yes, I talked about it," he said after the game. "That way you're not so disappointed if you don't get it."

Therefore, from the middle innings on, he was chattering away about the possibility that he'd throw a perfect game.

Catcher Gus Triandos was amazed by how talkative Bunning was. "He was jabbering like a magpie," Triandos said after the game. "Then he's out there with two hitters to go and he calls me out and says I should tell him a joke or something, just to give him a breather."

Bunning may have needed a breather in the ninth, but it sure didn't seem that way to the Mets. Charlie Smith hit a foul pop-up that was caught by third baseman Cookie Rojas. George Altman struck out. Then John Stephenson fanned as well, giving Bunning 10 strikeouts, a 6–0 win, and the first perfect game in the National League in 84 years.

BUNNING READS the newspaper account of his accomplishment with six of his children looking on. Shown from left to right are Jimmy (9), Barbara (11), Cathy (7), Joanie, standing behind her dad (9), Mark, on dad's lap (2), and Billy (6).

THE BROTHERS ALOU

In September of 1963, the San Francisco Giants brought outfielder Jesus Alou up from Tacoma to join his big brothers Felipe and Matty. In a September 15th game against the Pirates at Forbes Field, Jesus entered the game as a defensive replacement and went to right field. Matty also came in as a substitute and took over left field. Felipe, who had started the game in right field, moved over to center field. For the first time in history, three brothers comprised a team's outfield in a major league game. The Alous remain the only three-brother set on one team in the history of the Major Leagues.

SAN FRANCISCO GIANTS Jesus, Matty, and Felipe Alou (left to right) pose for a picture before a September 10, 1963 game against the New York Mets. The Alou brothers made history when Jesus was brought up from the minors that year—it was the first time three brothers had played on the same major league team at the same time.

LATIN BALLPLAYERS ARRIVE

During the long decades when African-American ballplayers were barred from playing in the Major Leagues, a prohibition against men from Latin America was never as strongly enforced. As early as 1911, the Cincinnati Reds had Rafael Almeida at third base and Armando Marsans in the outfield, both of whom were from Cuba. Another Cuban, Dolf Luque, had a more successful career. A hero in his hometown, Havana, Luque pitched for 20 years in the National League, winning 194 games. In 1923, his best season, he went 27–8 for the Reds, with a league-leading 1.94 earned run average.

Despite such performances, Latin ballplayers were few and far between before 1947. That was the year

Jackie Robinson shattered the color barrier, opening the door wide to nonwhite ballplayers. By the mid-1950s, Latin stars in the Major Leagues included Minnie Minoso (from Havana), Roberto Clemente (from Puerto Rico), and Bobby Avila (from Mexico).

The face of baseball had changed forever. Beginning in the 1960s, it was to change even further.

GIFTS FROM AN ISLAND

In early 1963, *Sports Illustrated* published a long feature article entitled,

"Invasion from Santo Domingo," which described the trend in awestruck terms. "More than 50 baseball players from the Dominican Republic will be playing in the major and minor leagues in the U.S. this summer," the article began, "which makes the island one of the world's major per capita producers of baseball talent."

The magazine reserved its greatest praise for a trio of brothers, who it thought had the best chance to become superstars in the big leagues. Their names were Felipe, Matty, and Jesus Alou.

BROTHERS

All three Alou brothers had fine major league careers. The oldest and first to make the Majors was current Montreal Expo manager Felipe, who debuted with the Giants in 1958. His best year came with the Atlanta Braves in 1966, when he hit .327 with 31 home runs and a league-leading 218 hits and 122 runs. He finished his career with 2,101 hits and a .286 batting average.

Matty Alou followed Felipe to the Giants in 1960. Like his older brother, Matty had perhaps his finest season in 1966, when he played with the Pittsburgh Pirates. That season, he led the league with a .342 batting average. He never had as much power as

Felipe, but stole more bases and, on balance, hit for a higher average, ending his career with a .307 lifetime average.

When Felipe and Matty were both with the Giants in 1960 and 1961, their brother Jesus was still in school, planning for his own major league career. He got that chance in 1963, when—like both his brothers—he joined the San Francisco Giants. Playing for four different teams during his career, he ended up with a .280 lifetime average—the third of three good-hitting brothers.

In 1963, while they were all with the Giants, Felipe, Matty, and Jesus made two particularly indelible impressions on fans nationwide. The first moment took place in a September 10, 1963, game against the Mets at New York's Polo Grounds. Jesus, just up from the minors, entered the game as a pinch hitter, striking out against the Mets' Carlton Willey. Matty and Felipe were up next, and Willey retired them too, completing an All-Alou 1–2–3 inning.

Then just five days later, in a game against the Pittsburgh Pirates, the Alous made major league history. As the Giants took the field late in that game, manager Alvin Dark inserted Jesus in right field. Felipe, giving regular Willie Mays a break, was in center. And Matty was stationed in left. There was a brother at all three outfield positions.

In an interview after his career was over, Jesus shrugged off that unusual moment. "It was no big deal; we didn't telephone home or anything," he said. "After all, we played together all the time in winter ball back in the Caribbean."

Still, in the history of major league baseball, the Alou brothers remain the only three-brother set to play side by side on the same team.

A NATIVE OF THE DOMINICAN REPUBLIC, Felipe Alou, now the manager of the Montreal Expos, came to the New York Giants in 1958. Alou was the second Dominican player in the Majors behind Ozzie Virgil, and became the first Dominican-born manager in major league history in 1992.

FELIPE'S YOUNGER BROTHER Matty Alou came to the Giants in 1960, two years after Felipe.

JESUS ALOU was the last of the three brothers to join the Giants in 1963.

UNDER THE BIG TOP

On April 12, 1965, major league baseball entered the indoor era with the first regular season game at Houston's brand new Astrodome. Within a week, it became necessary to paint the exterior of the translucent roof, as the glare of the sun through the roof was blinding the outfielders. The paint in turn caused the Astrodome's indoor natural grass to die, which led to the introduction of artificial turf.

GOING WHERE THE FANS WERE

Beginning in the early 1950s, baseball went through a horrific slump in attendance. In just half a dozen years, the ballparks saw a 30 percent drop in the number of fans coming to the games, and there were many who thought the downward spiral would continue until the Major Leagues themselves were driven out of business.

Frightened team owners and the media tried to figure out who to blame for the collapse in attendance. Since the networks had just begun televising games widely, TV was considered a prime culprit. Why would people pay their way into the ballpark if they could watch the game for free on TV?

But the truth was more complicated. Almost every team in both leagues was playing in a ballpark built 30 or 40 years earlier—and these ballparks were definitely the worse for wear. Even more importantly, many of the parks were located in neighborhoods that had gone downhill. Fans who had the money to attend the games suddenly found themselves unwilling to venture into those neighborhoods, especially at night.

In response to these factors, one team after another began to relocate to cities where the fan base was larger and the stadiums were newer and better situated. In some cases, the teams moved into old ballparks that had been vacant for a while. But often they moved into

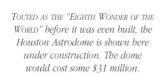

TOUTED AS THE "EIGHTH WONDER OF THE WORLD" before it was even built, the Houston Astrodome is shown here under construction. The dome would cost some $31 million.

spanking new stadiums—ones that had been built to lure them into greener pastures.

Thus, when the St. Louis Browns moved to Baltimore, they knew that their new home would be shiny Memorial Stadium, a far cry from dingy old Sportsman's Park in St. Louis. The same was true for the Boston Braves, who in 1953 moved into Milwaukee's County Stadium, the second to be built with public money.

As the 1950s ended and the 1960s began, more and more new stadiums rose all across the country. San Francisco opened Candlestick Park in 1960, Los Angeles followed with Dodger Stadium in 1962, Minneapolis-St.Paul had Metropolitan Stadium, the new home of the Minnesota Twins, in 1961, and New York saw the arrival of Shea Stadium to house the Mets in 1964.

All of these ballparks were far shinier and more up-to-date than the old ballparks they replaced. But none was as ambitious as Houston's Astrodome, proclaimed even before it was completed as the "Eighth Wonder of the World."

BOON OR BOONDOGGLE?

The Houston Astros began play as the Colt 45s in 1962 as one of the National League's two expansion teams (the Mets were the other). For their first three seasons, the team played at Colt Stadium. During this time, fans became reacquainted with the fact that in mid-summer, Houston can be blisteringly hot, swelteringly humid, and populated by squadrons of mosquitoes.

Judge Roy Hofheinz, one of the city's wealthiest businessmen, knew all these things after a lifetime in Houston. He dreamed of building the world's first domed baseball stadium—and then made his dream become a reality. By 1965, the enormous, $31 million dome had risen on 10 acres of Texas flatland outside the city.

Hofheinz named it the Houston Astrodome, and the team dumped its previous name and became the Astros. Hofheinz eagerly talked about the dome's plush offices, carpeted in deep gold and furnished with velvet chairs, its huge $2 million scoreboard, and the weather station on the roof to feed data to computers, which in turn would keep the temperature inside at a perfect 72 degrees.

Oh, and one other thing: At first, the Houston Astrodome boasted a field made of real grass. As *Sports Illustrated* put it in an article published just days before the first exhibition game was to be played, "the stadium roof is made of 4,596 Lucite skylights that enable the

THE HOUSTON BASEBALL CLUB'S new stadium was named the Astrodome, so the team changed its name from the Colt 45s to the Astros. The first of its kind, the domed stadium made for an impressive aerial view.

three and a half acres of Bermuda grass on the diamond to grow healthily indoors."

Well, not exactly. All was not right with the Astrodome.

FIXING THE EIGHTH WONDER

There was just one problem with those skylights: They were translucent. In fact, they seemed to magnify the sunlight outside, creating a fierce and blinding glare. Outfielders would watch a ball leave the hitters' bat and ascend into the glare, and then they would run for their lives, hoping that the descending ball wouldn't hit them.

Within a week, workers had to cover every skylight with nontranslucent paint. This helped the players actually play baseball, but it meant death for the Bermuda grass. Deprived of sunlight, the grass turned brown, and had to be dug up and carted away.

The replacement: Astroturf, otherwise known as plastic grass, the first artificial turf installed at any big-league stadium.

In its article about the soon-to-open Astrodome, *Sports Illustrated* wondered if the new dome would "make obsolete all other stadiums in the world." That didn't happen, although the durable and low-maintenance artificial turf was installed at several ballparks built in the 1960s and '70s. Almost from the start, though, players complained about playing on the unnatural surface, and fans missed the sight of real grass.

Today, artificial turf seems to be a thing of the past. All of the many new ballparks that have opened in recent years boast of real grass—and even some of the parks originally equipped with artificial turf have replaced it with grass.

Interestingly, the Astrodome's more lasting legacy may be the domed stadium. The new ballparks in Arizona, Seattle, and elsewhere all have roofs. But there's a big difference between them and the Astrodome: The roofs are all retractable, so that the real grass on the field can thrive.

THE FIRST GAME played in the Houston Astrodome was an exhibition contest between the Astros and the visiting New York Yankees. On this night, April 9, 1965, President Lyndon Johnson was in attendance.

FASTEST OF THEM ALL?

Sandy Koufax posted impressive numbers in 1966, leading the league in ERA for the fifth consecutive year, on his way to his third Cy Young Award. Hardly a time to retire. But that is just what Koufax did. Suffering from a 1964 arm injury and arthritis, Koufax pitched with great pain. Despite his success, Koufax retired from the game at age 30, at the peak of his career. Five years later, Koufax became the youngest man enshrined into the Baseball Hall of Fame.

SANDY KOUFAX struggled in his first six years in the Major Leagues, posting high ERAs and too many walks. He settled into his winning style by the 1961 season.

THE WILD ONE

Sandy Koufax could always throw hard. "When I was a little kid I was aware that any time I got into a snowball fight I could retreat back to where I could pepper the other kids and they couldn't come close to reaching me," he wrote in *Koufax,* his 1966 autobiography. "Very useful."

When he moved on from snowballs to baseballs, joining the Brooklyn Dodgers as a rookie in 1955, he impressed onlookers and opposing batters with his blinding fastball and sharp curve.

Unfortunately, the young left-hander also showed them that he had little idea where his pitches were going, walking 28 men in just 41 innings. Today, the legend of Sandy Koufax' greatness looms so large that it's easy to forget that, for many years, he was considered a great prospect who might never develop. In 1956, his second season, he went 2–4 with a 4.91 earned run average. He followed that up with seasons of 5–4, 11–11, 8–6, and 8–13— not the stuff that legends are made of. His ERA never dipped below 3.88, and every year he walked five or six men per nine innings, an unacceptable number.

As the 1961 season began, Koufax was still only 25 years old, but time was running out for him to harness his ability. Frustrated, he almost quit the game entirely.

Instead, he learned how to pitch. "It wasn't a question of throwing the ball up slower," he wrote of his new approach. "I was trying to throw the ball as fast as, or maybe even faster than ever, but I was trying to go about it without pressing. I was still throwing hard, in other words. I was just taking the grunt out of it."

This decision turned out to be the magic bullet for his career. From then on, he was one of the most dominating pitchers baseball has ever known.

THE ACE

How good was Sandy Koufax between 1961 and 1966? "Trying to hit him," said Hall of Fame slugger Willie Stargell, "was like trying to drink coffee with a fork." Added sportswriter Jim Murray, creating a fantasy baseball team, "With the Babe Ruth Yankees, Sandy Koufax would probably have been the first undefeated pitcher in history."

In 1961, his first big year, Koufax went 18–13, with a 3.52 ERA. These were not yet

KOUFAX RECEIVES A WHIRLPOOL TREATMENT for a sore pitching arm in April 1964. That year, despite an elbow injury, he won 19 games and led the league with a 1.74 ERA.

Hall of Fame numbers, but Koufax was already giving a hint of what was to come: 15 complete games, a league-leading 269 strikeouts in 255⅔ innings, and only 96 walks. By taking the "grunt" out of his fastball, he'd finally mastered his wildness.

Battling a finger injury, Koufax went 14–7 in 1962, leading the league with a 2.54 ERA. He also threw his first no-hitter, against the Mets. But this was just a warm-up for 1963, when he threw 20 complete games, including 11 shutouts. He pitched 311 innings, striking out an astounding 306 men and walking only 58. He finished the season with

Multiple No-Hit Pitchers

Pitcher	# of No-Hitters
Nolan Ryan	7
Sandy Koufax	4
Larry Corcoran	3
Bob Feller	3
Jim Maloney	3
Cy Young	3
Addie Joss	2
Adonis Terry	2
Al Atkisson	2
Allie Reynolds	2
Bill Stoneman	2
Bob Forsch	2
Carl Erskine	2
Christy Mathewson	2
Don Wilson	2
Frank Smith	2
Dutch Leonard	2
Jim Bunning	2
Jim Galvin	2
Johnny Vander Meer	2
Ken Holtzman	2
Steve Busby	2
Ted Breitenstein	2
Tom L. Hughes	2
Virgil Trucks	2
Warren Spahn	2

KOUFAX ANNOUNCED HIS RETIREMENT on November 18, 1966, at age 30. He had been diagnosed with arthritis in the elbow of his pitching arm, and doctors said he could permanently injure the arm if he continued to pitch. At left is Koufax' attorney, Bill Hayes.

not carry the Dodgers to a championship, pitching well but losing Game Two in his only appearance against the Orioles.

Shockingly, that Game Two loss was Sandy Koufax's last appearance in a professional baseball game. Soon after the Series ended, he announced his retirement. He was only 30 years old.

THE PRICE OF PERFECTION

"Pitching, as any pitcher can tell you, is an unnatural act," Koufax wrote in his autobiog-

a sterling 1.88 ERA, pitched another no-hitter, and finished 25–5. He was the overwhelming choice for the Cy Young Award.

Koufax battled an elbow injury in 1964, but still won 19 games, led the league in ERA, and pitched yet another no-hitter. He bounced back in 1965, going 26–8, leading the league again in ERA (2.04), striking out a then-record 382 men, throwing eight shutouts, and pitching his fourth no-hitter in four years—this one a perfect game. He won the Cy Young Award again.

Koufax's 1965 season was one of the most towering years that a major league pitcher has ever had. But he may have matched it in 1966, when he pitched to a 27–9 record and led the league for the fifth straight year with a 1.73 ERA, his best ever. For the third time in four years, he was voted the Cy Young Award.

During this unparalleled streak of brilliance, Koufax also got to show his stuff in three World Series. And he was just as spectacular there. In the Dodgers' four-game sweep of the Yankees in 1963, he won two games and struck out 23 men in 18 innings. In 1965, he lost Game Two against the Minnesota Twins, but then came back to pitch two consecutive shutouts, including a three-hitter in the pivotal Game Seven. Only in 1966 did he raphy. "When you perform this unnatural act every fourth day, your arm is going to rebel."

Beginning in 1962, Koufax' arm began to rebel. His worst fears came true in 1966, when he was diagnosed with worsening arthritis in his pitching elbow. Doctors told him that, if he continued to pitch, he might damage his arm permanently. "There are a lot more things in life I want to do," he said at the end. "I don't want to do them as a sore-armed person."

With the same grace and modesty that he exhibited during his career, Sandy Koufax bowed out in a poignant press conference. Memorializing his departure, *Sports Illustrated* wrote, "Not all of us can choose our endings, as it were; Koufax chose a good one. We're going to miss him out there, but he'll miss it more. Oh, what an artist he was!"

Sandy Koufax was elected to the Hall of Fame in 1972, when he was still just 36 years old. He remains the youngest man ever to be enshrined in the Hall.

As Koufax sits on the dais with four other 1972 Hall of Fame inductees, his relative youth is obvious. From left to right are Yogi Berra, Lefty Gomez, Koufax, Buck Leonard, and Early Wynn. At 36, Koufax was then and remains the youngest man ever to enter the Hall.

SLAMS

Only two National League hitters have ever hit two grand slams in one game—and they did it more than 30 years apart. Atlanta Braves pitcher Tony Cloninger achieved this feat on July 3, 1966. Cloninger drove in nine of Atlanta's runs in its 17–3 defeat of the San Francisco Giants at Candlestick Park. Then in April 1999, Fernando Tatis, third baseman for the St. Louis Cardinals, hit two grand slams in the same inning, helping the Cards to a 12-5 victory over the Dodgers. Just a few weeks later, in the A.L., Boston Red Sox shortstop Nomar Garciaparra hit two grand slams in a game against the Seattle Mariners.

TEAM OF SLUGGERS

When the Milwaukee Braves moved to Atlanta for the 1966 season, they brought with them one of the most powerful teams in baseball history. Led by Hank Aaron, the Braves always seemed to have three or four players who hit more than 30 home runs—compared to other teams, which might have one. This power surge hit its peak in 1973, when three Braves (Davey Johnson, Darrell Evans, and Hank Aaron) hit more than 40 home runs.

EARNING HIS KEEP, Atlanta Braves pitcher Tony Cloninger not only pitched his team to a 13–7 victory over the San Francisco Giants on July 3, 1966, but batted in nine of the runs himself by hitting two grand slams in a single game.

But the Braves were no slouches in 1966, their first year in Atlanta. Hank Aaron slugged 44 home runs, while Joe Torre walloped 36, Felipe Alou slugged 31, and Mack Jones smacked 23.

None of the team's burly sluggers, however, had a bigger day at the plate in 1966 than a man named Tony Cloninger, who happened to be a pitcher.

TONY THE THREAT

From 1964 through 1966, Tony Cloninger was one of the Braves' best pitchers, winning 19, 24, and 14 games. Before 1966, he hit like a pitcher as well, getting five hits in 37 at bats in 1963 and hitting .162 in 1965. One of his hits in 1965 was a home run, however, providing a preview of things to come.

The burly Cloninger, who stood 6 feet 2 inches and played at 210 pounds, always had tremendous belief in his ability as a hitter. "I used to hit 'em out consistently in batting practice," he said after his career ended. "I knew if I got good wood on the ball, I could hit home runs."

But even the self-confident Cloninger could never have predicted what would happen on July 3, 1966. The Braves were playing against the Giants in San Francisco, and the two teams' lineups included future Hall of Famers Hank Aaron, Willie Mays and Willie McCovey, and future batting champions Rico Carty and Joe Torre. But it was Cloninger's day. As Torre said ruefully after the game, "I hit a three-run home run in the first inning and nobody paid attention to it."

The Braves put the game out of reach in the first inning, scoring seven runs. After Torre's three-run blow, the team loaded the bases again, bringing Cloninger to the plate. On reliever Bob Priddy's 3–2 pitch, he swung and connected. "I was just trying to get a hit up the middle," Cloninger said. "I knew I hit the ball well, but I was running hard because No. 24 [Willie Mays] was playing center field."

But even the great Mays couldn't reach this one. It went over the fence for a grand slam.

Flash forward three innings. The Braves' lead had stretched to 9–0 when Cloninger stepped to the plate with the bases loaded once again. This time he was facing Ray Sadecki, and this time he hit the ball to right field, but the result was the same: Cloninger had hit *another* grand slam.

Cloninger wasn't yet done for the day. He added another hit and another run batted in, ending the day with three hits in five at bats and nine RBI. And he also tossed a complete-game seven-hitter in the Braves' 17–3 victory. Not a bad day's work, all in all.

Until recently, Tony Cloninger was the only player in the National League ever to hit two grand slam home runs in a single game (through 1999, nine men had accomplished the goal in the American League). In 1999, though, St. Louis Cardinal third baseman Fernando Tatis stepped forward and became the second N.L. player to do it. He also managed to outdo every player who had ever hit two slams in a game before him.

FERNANDO'S FEAT

Fernando Tatis was a rising star as the 1999 season began, a 24-year-old player of great potential. Prior to 1999, however, he had a major league total of 19 home runs, so he was not the most likely player to hit two slams in one game.

In fact, Tatis had never hit a grand slam in 2,424 at bats as a professional player

(minor and Major Leagues) going into the April 23 game against the Dodgers. But all that was about to change as he came to bat in the third inning with the bases full. He got a good swing against Dodgers pitcher Chan Ho Park and watched the ball soar over the wall.

The Cardinals kept hitting in the inning, and soon it was Tatis's turn at the plate again. Amazingly, the bases were loaded once more, and Park was still pitching. Even more amazingly, Tatis swung and connected, and again the ball flew out of the park. He'd not only hit two grand slams in one game—he'd also hit them in one inning.

But Tatis was not alone in crashing the record books in 1999. Little more than two weeks after his big day, Boston's Nomar Garciaparra hit two grand-slam home runs in a single game—though not in one inning. The same season saw Ken Griffey, Jr., hit slams in two consecutive games, and the New York Mets' Robin Ventura became the first ever to hit a grand slam in both games of a double-header.

Someday, maybe soon, some player will hit three grand slams in one game. Who knows? Maybe star pitcher Greg Maddux will be the one to do it.

Fernando Tatis, the St. Louis Cardinals' third baseman. In an April 23, 1999 game against the Dodgers, Tatis not only hit two grand slams, he hit them both in one inning. It was the first (and second) time Tatis had ever hit a grand slam as a professional ballplayer.

THE YEAR OF THE PITCHER

Known as the "Year of the Pitcher," the 1968 season featured many tremendous pitching performances.
The Giants' Juan Marichal logged 26 wins, and the Cardinals' Bob Gibson set a modern National League mark with
a 1.12 ERA. Possibly the finest accomplishment that season was Tiger pitcher Denny McLain's 31 victories. McLain
is the sole major league pitcher to log 30 wins since Dizzy Dean won 30 in 1934. Despite the 31 wins, McLain
did not lead the American League in ERA; that honor went to Cleveland's Luis Tiant.

IN 1968, A YEAR OF STELLAR PITCHING performances, Tiger pitcher Denny McLain stood taller than the rest with 31 wins. He was the first pitcher in either league to win 30 games since 1934.

HURLERS RULE

Every once in a while, the balance of power shifts in baseball, favoring either pitchers or hitters. The 1920s and 1930s were perhaps the most famous of all hitters' eras—led by Babe Ruth and Lou Gehrig, sluggers who slammed all but the best pitchers into oblivion. The culmination of that era came in 1930, when the entire National League—including pitchers, scrubs, rookies, and middle-infielders— hit .303.

If the '20s and '30s favored the hitters, the 1960s were their mirror image: a time when pitchers dominated the game to an almost absurd degree. The trend had begun as the Braves, Dodgers, Giants, and other teams left their rickety old ballparks in the 1950s and early '60s for spacious new homes. In every case, these were moves from cozy hitters' parks to stadiums that strongly favored pitchers.

In addition, a variety of other factors contributed to pitchers' dominance as the 1960s progressed, including the restoration of a larger strike zone in 1963, an increase in the number of night games (with their poor visibility), the ever-increasing size of fielders' gloves, and higher and higher pitcher's mounds. By 1965, neither league could hit even .250, and a league-leading batting average might be as low as .320.

But the worst was yet to come for hittters. Never in baseball's long and varied history have pitchers dominated the way they did in 1968, the season that writer Roger Angell dubbed "The Year of the Infield Pop-up."

AN EXERCISE IN FUTILITY

How much did pitchers dominate in 1968? They threw 339 shutouts during the season (as opposed to a total of 93 shutouts in the two leagues in 1930). An amazing 82 games ended with scores of 1–0. The American League had just one hitter who managed to hit over .300 (Carl Yastrzemski at a measly .301), and the league as a whole hit a stunningly low .230.

Individual pitchers put up numbers unlike any ever seen before. The Dodgers' Don Drysdale threw six consecutive shutouts at one point— yet still managed to go only 14–12, with a 2.15 earned run average that wasn't even in the National League's top five. Jerry Koosman had a better ERA (2.08), though it was his rookie year. So did the Giants' Bobby Bolin (1.99), and he won only ten games.

Meanwhile, in the American League, giving up just two earned runs per nine innings didn't even get you into the top five. League-leader Luis Tiant had a 1.60 ERA, while number five Tommy John gave up 1.98 runs per game. Where today an ERA of 3.00 would make you one of the best pitchers on your team, in 1968 you would have been below average: The pitching staffs of 13 entire teams had lower ERAs than 3.00.

Clearly, the pitchers' command in 1968 was spread far and wide. Even in a season of such a wealth of eye-opening pitching statistics, however, two men stood out.

One was the St. Louis Cardinals' Bob Gibson, long considered one of the finest pitchers in the National League. But no one could have predicted what he'd do in 1968. In what must rank as one of the most extraordinary seasons ever for a pitcher, Gibson went 22–9 with a mind-boggling 1.12 earned run average. Imagine: Over the course of 34 starts covering 304 innings, Gibson gave up just a bit more than one run per game. His season also included 28 complete games (more than most entire teams these days), 13 shutouts, and 268 strikeouts.

Gibson's 1968 year might be the finest ever by a starting pitcher. It's a testament to that odd, unbalanced season that he was overshadowed by a young pitcher on the Detroit Tigers. In 1968, the Tigers' Denny McLain won 31 games, becoming the first pitcher to win 30 games in a season since Dizzy Dean accomplished it in 1934.

Denny started 41 games and completed 28 of them, pitching a stunning 336 innings (about 100 more than most starting pitchers do today) with a 1.96 ERA. From the beginning of the season through the end, he piled up win after win, ending the season with a record of 31–6. No one has had 30 wins since.

Unsurprisingly, McLain and Gibson's transcendent performances led the Tigers and Cardinals to the World Series. They also convinced baseball's powers-that-be to take action to restore baseball's balance.

FOR THE HITTERS

The rules changes that followed the 1968 season were simple. The pitcher's mound was lowered from 15 inches to 10 inches, making it harder for pitchers to break off big curveballs and reducing a fastball's movement. In addition, the strike zone was reduced to the size it had been prior to 1963. And, quite possibly, the ball was juiced—although, as always, baseball officials refused to acknowledge any change in the contents or manufacturing techniques of the ball.

Hitters breathed a big sigh of relief. Runs scored leapt upward by about 43 percent in each league in 1969, while home-run totals climbed by 56 percent. Pete Rose, Roberto Clemente, and Cleon Jones all hit .340 or better in the N.L., while in the A.L. five men reached the 40-home-run plateau (compared to just one in the entire Major Leagues in 1968). The hitters were back to stay.

Dizzy Dean had been the last pitcher to log 30 wins in a season in 1934, until McLain matched the feat in 1968. Dean also led the league in strikeouts four times. He was inducted in the Hall of Fame in 1953 (top). The Tigers' Denny McLain helped take his club to the 1968 World Series against the St. Louis Cardinals. The Tigers prevailed in Game Seven (bottom).

CLASH OF THE TITANS

Any list of World Series standouts would have to include Cardinals' pitcher Bob Gibson. In three World Series with the Cardinals, Gibson started nine games, completed eight, won seven, and compiled an ERA of 1.89. Gibson recorded 92 strikeouts, including 17 to shut out the Detroit Tigers in Game One of the 1968 World Series. As dominating as Gibson was during the 1968 Series, the hotter pitcher was Detroit's Mickey Lolich, who won three games, including Game Seven against Gibson, to lead the Tigers to the championship.

THE BEST PREVAIL

Every team had good pitching in 1968, the Year of the Pitcher. The Chicago White Sox' Tommy John, for example, ended the season with a spectacular 1.98 earned run average—for a team that went 67–95. In the National League, the Pittsburgh Pirates had two starting pitchers with superb ERAs—Bob Veale at 2.05 and Steve Blass at 2.12—but the Pirates finished below .500 as well.

The teams that won the pennants that year had great pitching too, of course. The St. Louis Cardinals finished first in the National League, led by such pitchers as Nelson Briles (19–11), Steve Carlton (13–11), and Ray Washburn (14–8). Meanwhile, the American League pennant was captured by the Detroit Tigers, whose successful starters included Mickey Lolich (17–9) and Earl Wilson (13–12).

But Mickey Lolich and Nelson Briles were no better than the aces on other teams in that year dominated by pitching. What carried the Cardinals and Tigers to their respective pennants was the presence of two pitchers having among the best seasons in baseball history: Bob Gibson and Denny McLain.

OPPOSITES ATTRACT

By 1968, Bob Gibson was already well known as one of the best—and most intimidating—pitchers in the game. Fiercely competitive, Gibson possessed one of the fastest fastballs in the game. And he wasn't afraid to use it to make a hitter hit the dirt. Gibson might hurl a ball under a batter's chin, but he rarely hit anyone with a pitch.

Gibson parlayed his aggressiveness, his blinding fastball and devastating curve, into a series of great seasons beginning in 1962. But nothing matched his 1968 performance, in which he went 22–9 with an almost unbelievable league-leading 1.12 earned run average.

ONE OF THE FIERCEST COMPETITORS baseball has ever seen, Bob Gibson dominated batters with his fastball and slider. Gibson won two Cy Young Awards and the 1968 National League MVP, and was inducted into the Hall of Fame in 1981. In the 1968 season, Gibson went 22-9, had a 1.12 ERA, pitched 13 shutouts, and posted 268 strikeouts.

In 1968, Bob Gibson started 34 games and finished 28 of them. In the other six games, he was lifted for a pinch hitter, which meant that he was never driven from the mound by the opposing team. During one stretch of 92 innings, he gave up a total of two runs. Overall, he pitched 13 shutouts. "As I recall, he didn't make one bad pitch over the plate that year," said teammate Lou Brock.

Denny McLain did even better that year. McLain (31–6) became the first pitcher in either league to win 30 games since Dizzy Dean in 1934. Even in a year filled with great pitching performances, Denny McLain's stood as one of the most towering accomplishments of all time.

As the regular season came to an end, it seemed only appropriate that the dour and forbidding Bob Gibson would be facing the burly and talkative Denny McLain in a highly anticipated World Series.

MICKEY'S TIME

No baseball fan was surprised to hear that a pitcher won three games in the 1968 World Series. What was surprising was that the pitcher's name was neither Gibson nor McLain.

The two men faced each other in Game One. Gibson pitched a masterpiece, striking out a record 17 Tigers in an easy 4–0 Cardinal win. "It was," McLain said later, "the single greatest pitching performance I have ever seen."

Game Two was won by the Tigers, 8–1, behind Mickey Lolich. Lolich had been Detroit's second-best pitcher all year, so no one was surprised to see him pitch well in the Series. Nor were fans surprised to see the Cardinals' offense spring to life in Game Three, an easy 7–3 victory highlighted by three-run home runs by Tim McCarver and Orlando Cepeda.

Game Four featured the second confrontation between Gibson and McLain, and again Gibson prevailed, 10–1. The Cardinal ace had now won seven consecutive complete-game World Series games, stretching over three Series. St. Louis held a 3–1 Series

AFTER PITCHING IN THE SHADOW of stellar teammate Denny McLain all season, Mickey Lolich won three World Series games for the Tigers in 1968, including Game Seven, making the Tigers world champs.

advantage—and with Gibson guaranteed another start if the Series went seven games, it seemed unlikely that Detroit could recover.

But the Tigers weren't buried yet. Mickey Lolich quieted the Cardinals' bats in Game Five, winning 5–3. And then McLain, pitching on just two days rest, finally got a Series win, a complete-game 13–1 victory.

So, like all classic World Series, this one came down to a seventh game. This game pitted Gibson against Lolich—both had already won twice.

The game was scoreless through six innings. Fans began to wonder if perhaps neither team would ever cross the plate. Perhaps the game would go on forever at 0–0. That would be a fitting ending to the Year of the Pitcher.

Then, in the top of the seventh, with two men on, Cardinal centerfielder Curt Flood misjudged a line drive hit by Jim Northrup. The ball went for a two-run triple, and the Tigers were on their way to a 4–1 victory and a Series win. Mickey Lolich had his third victory in the seven games, and Detroit had finally beaten Bob Gibson.

DEFYING GRAVITY ON THE MOUND, Bob Gibson delivers a strike to the Detroit Tigers' Norm Cash in the ninth inning of Game One of the 1968 World Series (overleaf). Cash became Gibson's 16th strikeout victim of the game, helping Gibson set a new record of 17 strikeouts in a World Series game.

A YANKEE'S DAY

One of the greatest tributes to an athlete is a day in their honor. As Yankee greats Babe Ruth, Lou Gehrig, and Joe DiMaggio left the game, the Yankees held celebrations for these fabled ballplayers. On June 8, 1969, the Yankees held such a day for the great Mickey Mantle. Mantle ended his 18-year career with 536 home runs, 1,509 RBIs, a .298 batting average, 12 World Series appearances, and seven World Championships.

GREAT EXPECTATIONS

Today Mickey Mantle is remembered as a Yankee through-and-through, as the best player on the greatest team of all time, as a slugger who always played his best in the big games, and as a brave man who battled his final illness with grace and dignity.

In truth, though, it took Yankee fans a long time to warm up to Mantle during his early years with the team. His arrival was perhaps the most highly touted call-up of any player in the 1950s, and from the start fans' expectations of him were enormous and unreasonable.

In his 1985 autobiography, *The Mick*, Mantle remembered those painful early days. "The New York fans were led to believe some kind of Superman had arrived on the scene," he wrote. "He was going to hit ball after ball over the center field bleachers, clear into the Harlem River. He was another Ruth, another DiMaggio, maybe better than both. But I was neither. I had enough trouble trying to be Mickey Mantle."

MANTLE STRUGGLED to meet the fans' high expectations of him in his first years with the Yankees, and actually dreaded going to the ballpark to face them.

AT CITY HALL, Mickey Mantle is presented with an official proclamation that September 18, 1965, will be Mickey Mantle Day.

A baseball crowd can be noisily abusive to players it feels have disappointed, and Mantle bore the brunt of New Yorkers' high expectations. Every year, he'd put up solid numbers—27 home runs, 102 runs batted in, a .306 batting average. But the fans could never forget that Mantle was supposed to be the next Ruth, the next DiMaggio, and he never had a year like they had. "I actually dreaded the idea of going to the ballpark," Mantle recalled.

Then came 1956, when Mantle finally lived up to and surpassed the fans' great expectations.

GREAT SEASONS

In 1956, Mickey Mantle led the league in every major offensive category. He hit .353, slammed 52 home runs, and drove in 130 runs, a performance that garnered him the Triple Crown award at the end of the year. He was also given the American League Most Valuable Player award and was named Player of the Year by *The Sporting News*. He then went on to hit three home runs during the Yankees' seven-game World Series victory over the Brooklyn Dodgers. (Though to be honest, Don Larsen's perfect game in that Series earned more notice than Mantle's round-trippers.)

After his spectacular 1956 season, Mantle seemed to play at a higher level. He posted averages of .365, .321, and .317, hit as many as 54 home runs, and had seasons with 128 and 111 RBI. He also battled constant injuries, earning the fans' respect and affection by playing hurt. Between his arrival as a raw teenage rookie in 1951 and his final game 18 seasons later, Mickey Mantle had ascended to the pantheon of true Yankee stars.

A DAY FOR THE MICK

The 1968 season would be Mantle's last. He was only 36, but a career's worth of leg and other injuries had left his body battered and diminished his reflexes. He hit his final home run—number 536 in his career—on September 20 of that season. "A week later at Fenway Park, I came up in the first inning, made an out, and returned to the bench," he recalled in *The Mick*. "I knew that I had reached the end of the line."

MANTLE WAS HONORED *by fans and teammates alike on "Mickey Mantle Day" at Yankee Stadium, held on September 18, 1965.*

Teams with Multiple World Series Wins

Team (League)	Number of Wins
New York Yankees (A)	25
St. Louis Cardinals (N)	9
New York Giants (N)	5
Philadelphia Athletics (A)	5
Boston Red Sox (A)	5
Pittsburgh Pirates (N)	5
Los Angeles Dodgers (N)	5
Cincinnati Reds (N)	5
Detroit Tigers (A)	4
Oakland Athletics (A)	4
Baltimore Orioles (A)	3
Chicago White Sox (A)	2
Chicago Cubs (N)	2
Cleveland Indians (A)	2
Minnesota Twins (A)	2
New York Mets (N)	2
Toronto Blue Jays (A)	2

It was a terrific career: 536 home runs (eighth most of all time), 1,509 RBI, 1,677 runs scored, and a .298 batting average. To these totals he added 18 home runs in World Series play, a record. Those were Hall of Fame numbers, and Mantle was elected on the first ballot in 1974.

Long before that occasion, however, the Yankees retired Mickey Mantle's number in a ceremony at Yankee Stadium—placing his number seven beside Babe Ruth's number three, Lou Gehrig's number four, and Joe DiMaggio's number five. On June 8, 1969, before more than

60,000 cheering fans, he was presented with a plaque by DiMaggio and with a uniform by Whitey Ford. Then he stepped forward and spoke to the adoring fans.

"I just want to say that playing 18 years in Yankee Stadium for you folks is the best thing that could ever happen to a ballplayer. Now having my number join three, four,

AFTER MANTLE PLAYED HIS LAST SEASON in 1968, the Yankees retired his number, number seven, in a June 8, 1969 ceremony. Mantle spoke to the more than 60,000 fans in attendance, telling them how much he had enjoyed playing for them over the course of 18 years.

and five kind of tops everything," he said, then added, "I often wondered how a man who knew he was dying could get up here and say he's the luckiest man in the world. Now I know how Lou Gehrig felt."

Afterward, he told reporters, "I wish something like this could happen to everyone in America just one time."

MIRACLE METS OF '69

To underdog fans, the 1969 Mets have no equal. Mired at the bottom of the second division for the first seven years of their existence, the "Miracle" Mets came alive that year with a mixture of young arms (Tom Seaver, Jerry Koosman, Gary Gentry, and Nolan Ryan) and veteran hitters (Tommie Agee, Donn Clendenon, and Cleon Jones). After overcoming the Cubs, defeating the Braves in the playoffs, and spotting the Orioles a one game lead in the World Series, the Mets took four straight to defeat the highly favored Baltimore team. Amazing!

In the Mets' World Series matchup with the Baltimore Orioles in 1969, Tommie Agee made a diving catch in the seventh inning of Game Three that saved the game for the Mets and gave them the momentum to keep on winning.

LOVABLE LOSERS

Understanding the miracle of 1969 – the year the Mets won the World Championship – requires understanding the team's history. For this was not just any team, winning it all against great odds.

The Mets were, in fact, notorious losers from their very beginning. They lost the first nine games of their first season, 1962, and, with Casey Stengel's encouragement, became somewhat of a national joke. He mixed clowning with the task of managing this expansion franchise, and turned them into such lovable losers, that any standup comedian on the *Ed Sullivan Show* was likely to throw in a Mets joke. They remain, unlike any other expansion team in any sport, the team that fans immediately identified with as *lovable* losers. From a business standpoint, it worked. The Mets were the darlings of New York.

Suffice it to say, it was not uncommon to think that the Mets would win a World Series when men walked on the moon.

In 1962, they won only 40 out of 160 games, the worst showing of the century. As the years went on and Stengel retired, their standing barely improved. Last, last, last, last, ninth, last, and ninth were all they had to show for their first seven seasons.

But things were beginning to happen in 1968. Gil Hodges, an excellent manager, and one-time Brooklyn Dodger hero, came over to run the team. Young players were emerging— particularly a pitching staff with Tom Seaver, Jerry Koosman, and reliever Tug McGraw. There was even a future star by the name of Nolan Ryan. They were still ninth, but only eight games out of the first division. Students of the game could see something stirring. So could emerging players like Jerry Grote, Bud Harrelson, Cleon Jones, Ron Swoboda, and Tommie Agee.

Naturally, the experts still expected a ninth or tenth place finish in '69. This was not a team of big stars. They were young kids, just learning to play together, and a few journeyman veterans, without pennant race experience. One player, Ed Kranepool, went back to the first season and knew all there was to know about losing.

LEARNING HOW TO WIN

But a funny thing happened to this Mets team. They began to learn how to win. They began to see small miracles in each week. The laughter was ending.

In August, they won five straight by scores of 2–0, 2–1, 3–2, 3–2, and 1–0. The old

METS THIRD BASEMAN Ed Charles takes to the air while pitcher Jerry Koosman leaps into the arms of catcher Jerry Grote after the Mets won their fourth straight game with the Baltimore Orioles to take the 1969 World Series.

Mets would have lost them all. In fact, starting on August 16, the team won 34 out of 44 games and the pitchers had an incredible 2.03 earned run average. This impressive burst came just after—well, just after men first walked on the moon!

Amazingly, the '69 Mets would bat .360 over the full season when there were two outs

THE METS, long regarded as a hopeless team, surprised fans and critics alike by taking the 1969 season all the way. Team members ran to safety as fans flooded the field on October 16, 1969.

and men in scoring position. That statistic is one of the highest figures ever compiled in that situation. And during the 34–10 streak, Seaver, Koosman, and the veteran Don Cardwell went 19–1 with a 0.99 ERA.

The Cubs were the team to beat—Leo Durocher was managing one of the best Cubs teams in history. But the Mets rose to the occasion and beat the Cubs head-to-head, and on September 10, moved into first place. It was the first miracle of the season. They had never been in first after the first week of the season. The fans could not believe what was happening. But Hodges believed, and now the players did as well.

Fourteen days later, the Mets clinched the National League East, beating Steve Carlton and the St. Louis Cardinals to wrap it up. New York was delirious, but many felt they had gone as far as they had a right to expect.

But the team kept rolling! They finished the season with 100 victories, and then swept the Braves in the first National League Championship Series ever played, beating the likes of Hank Aaron, Orlando Cepeda, Felipe Alou and Rico Carty. Ryan, just starting out on his Hall of Fame career, won the deciding game in New York, and again the fans went crazy.

Bring on the Orioles!

Now came the World Series. A Series against the great Baltimore Orioles, led by Frank and

IN THE LOCKER ROOM, Ed Kranepool (right) poured champagne on teammate Tug McGraw after the Mets defeated Baltimore in the fifth game of the World Series to become world champs.

Brooks Robinson, Boog Powell, Paul Blair, and a great pitching staff of Jim Palmer, Dave McNally, and Mike Cuellar.

No problem! After Cuellar won the opener 4–1, the Mets didn't sulk.

"We saw in that loss," said Seaver, "that we could play ball with this club. We knew we were not outmatched."

And so the Miracle Mets continued their magic—winning four straight, with Koosman pitching the deciding fifth game. Remarkable catches by Agee and Swoboda in the outfield made it seem as though a higher force was watching over them. It was, as Mets fans liked to say, a miracle.

"Whatever came in later years," said Seaver, "for me, for Nolan, for Tug, for Jerry, for any of us – we will always be '69 Mets."

OFFICE WORKERS spontaneously began throwing paper out their windows in celebration of the Mets' victory, carpeting the city's streets.

THE BLEACHERS EMPTIED as jubilant fans poured onto the field at Shea Stadium following the Mets' five-game series against the Orioles in 1969 (opposite page).

TOM TERRIFIC

Many baseball fans thought that the Miracle Mets of 1969 were a "flash in the pan." Tom Seaver's pitching performance early in the season on April 22, 1970, let the baseball world know that the Mets were for real. Seaver tossed a two-hitter and struck out 19 batters, tying a National League record set the year before by Steve Carlton. Seaver improved as the game progressed, striking out the last 10 men he faced. However, the Mets fell short of reaching the postseason, finishing six games behind the Pittsburgh Pirates.

PURE COMPETENCE

From the moment Tom Seaver came to the New York Mets in 1967, it was clear that he wasn't willing to be a part of the traveling circus that the Mets had been since their arrival in 1962. From 1962 to 1966, they'd compiled a cumulative record of 260–547 (by far the worst in the league), finishing last, last, last, last, and next-to-last.

These sorry teams had been composed of over-the-hill stars like Gil Hodges, Yogi Berra, and Frank Thomas (the Thomas of the 1950s and '60s, not the White Sox slugger) and a stunning lack of anything resembling a true young star.

Until Tom Seaver came along. Standing on the mound, glowering in at home plate, moving hitters back with a blazing fastball and devastating curve, he made a statement from his first pitch.

That statement was: I'm here to win, not to lose gracefully.

In 1967, Seaver's first season, the team finished 61–101, and fell back into last place once again. But Seaver finished 16–13, with 18 complete games and a 2.76 earned run average. For this superb performance he was given the Rookie of the Year award.

And despite the team's seeming step backward, the Mets management had finally become serious about building a winning team. Along with Seaver, by 1968 they had added such other good young players as Bud Harrelson, Jerry Grote, Tommy Agee, Cleon Jones, and Jerry Koosman. Perhaps most importantly, they also added Gil Hodges as their manager—and he proved to be exactly the stern, steady leader the young team needed.

TOM SEAVER made a splash when he joined the Mets in 1967, winning the Rookie of the Year award by pitching 18 complete games and posting a 2.76 ERA.

In 1969, as everyone knows, the New York Mets, led by Tom Seaver's spectacular 25–7 record, swept to the National League Eastern Division championship, then the pennant, and finally to victory in the World Series.

ONE GREAT DAY

Tom Seaver received the Cy Young Award for his superb 1969 performance. Still just 24 years old, he'd struck out 208 men in 273 innings, one of the higher totals in the league. He began 1970 as if he intended to pitch even better, as if he wanted to strike out every man he faced.

On April 22, he almost did. He was presented with his Cy Young plaque before the game began, and then went out to start earning another. Facing the San Diego Padres, Seaver gave up Al Ferrara's solo home run in the second inning, but other than that, hitters found it well nigh impossible to even make contact with his pitches. "He was like a machine out there, whomp, whomp, whomp," said first baseman Ed Kranepool after the game.

One by one, the Padres went down on strikes, interspersed with an occasional weak grounder or fly ball. After striking out two in the first, he fanned one in the second, then two in each of the third, fourth, and fifth. He then fanned the last man in the sixth and struck out the side in the seventh.

As Seaver went to bat in the seventh inning, Mets pitching coach Rube Walker glanced at the crowd and said to manager Gil Hodges, "I'll bet those people don't know how many strikeouts Tom has already."

"Eleven?" Hodges guessed.

"No, he has 13," said Walker.

"You're kidding!" Hodges exclaimed, as surprised as any fan.

In the eighth inning, Seaver struck out the first batter. Then he whiffed Ramon Webster, tying the Mets' team strikeout record of 15. (The record had been set just four days earlier, by a young pitcher named Nolan Ryan.) Four pitches to the next hitter, Ivan Murrell, and Seaver had the strikeout record all to himself.

Going into the ninth, the Mets had a 2–1 lead. No one seriously thought that the Padres would come back to beat Seaver. Now the question was: How many strikeouts would Seaver get?

Van Kelly swung and missed at three straight pitches to become strikeout victim number 17. Cito Gaston swung and missed, swung and missed again, and then left the bat on his shoulder for a called strike three.

The Padres' last batter was Al Ferrara, who'd hit the home run off Seaver in the second inning. Ferrara swung at the first pitch, took a ball, and then swung twice more. Both times he hit nothing but air, and the game was over.

Tom Seaver set or tied several major league records that day. His 19 strikeouts tied the mark set the year before by Steve Carlton (in a game that Carlton somehow lost to the Mets), and his 10 strikeouts in a row set a new record.

Seaver was on his way to a season in which he would fan a league-leading 283 men in just 291 innings. By now he was not only a great pitcher, but a strikeout artist as well.

SEAVER WORKS ON A NO-HITTER in a July 10, 1969 game against the Chicago Cubs at Shea Stadium. The no-hitter was spoiled in the ninth inning, but Seaver still shut out the Cubs, with the Mets winning, 4-0.

SEAVER POSES with his third Cy Young award, received in 1975. He also won in 1969 and 1973.

EXHIBITION GAME?

In the 1970 All-Star Game, Pete Rose scored the winning run in the 10th inning by barreling over Cleveland Indians catcher Ray Fosse. Rose played the All-Star game like any other game, with full intensity and desire to win. Fosse injured his shoulder on the play and, after that injury, never performed at the level that was expected of this promising catcher.

THE YEARLY BATTLE

"I PLAY TO WIN"

Every so often, people complain that the players don't seem to be trying hard enough in the All-Star Game. They're lackadaisical, say the accusers. They're treating it like it's just for fun.

Undoubtedly many players see the three-day All-Star break as a chance to relax and socialize with players on other teams and in the other league. But a remarkable amount of the time, the game is played with utter seriousness. Baseball players are intensely competitive, and those who are good enough to get named to an All-Star team seem to live and breathe competition.

If there was any doubt that both leagues were playing to win, then the 1970 All-Star Game must have proven it. This was the game in which Pete Rose risked life and limb—and that of catcher Ray Fosse—to score the winning run.

AN AGGRESSIVE BASERUNNER and fierce competitor, Cincinnati Reds star Pete Rose scored from second base in the 12th inning of the 1970 All-Star Game to give the N.L. a 5-4 victory over the A.L.

BOTTOM OF THE TWELFTH

Like the ones that immediately preceded it, the 1970 All-Star Game (played in Cincinnati) featured an array of the finest pitchers of all time: Jim Palmer, Tom Seaver, Bob Gibson, and Gaylord Perry. For the first six innings, the American League clung to a bare 1–0 lead.

In the next two innings, the American League broke through with three more runs, while the N.L. could manage just one. Going into the bottom of the ninth, the A.L.—which had lost the last seven All-Star Games—held a 4–1 lead, with Catfish Hunter pitching. But Hunter and the pitchers who followed him couldn't hold the lead, as the N.L., powered by big hits from San Francisco Giants Dick Dietz and Willie McCovey, came back to tie the score.

The game remained tied, 4–4, until the bottom of the 12th. With two out, Pete Rose singled, and then moved to second on Billy Grabarkewitz' single. The next batter, Jim Hickman, hit a single to center.

WHILE TRYING TO BEAT the throw to home plate, Rose collided violently with Cleveland Indians catcher Ray Fosse, then a rookie with a promising future.

As Pete Rose rounded third base, he knew he was going to try to score the winning run. And if catcher Ray Fosse was in his way—well, Rose would just have to run over him.

COLLISION AT HOME PLATE

As the A.L.'s center fielder, Amos Otis, fielded Hickman's single and threw home, Ray Fosse positioned himself at the plate. In a later interview, the catcher remembered thinking, "I know there might be a collision but I'm gonna stand right in this spot until the ball gets here."

Waiting for the ball, Fosse glanced at Rose as the runner barreled toward him. At first, it looked as if Rose would try to slide—which, as it turned out, would have allowed him to score the winning run. At the last moment, though, he put his head down and ran straight into Fosse. Said Rose later: "I play to win."

The collision made the crowd wince. Fosse had never had the ball in his glove; as it flew past, Rose landed on home plate. The game was over, and the National League had won, 5–4.

The aftereffects of the game lasted far longer, though. Rose missed a week of play with assorted bruises. At first, Fosse didn't miss any playing time, though he couldn't lift his left arm above his shoulder. Not until the following spring were his injuries diagnosed correctly, as doctors found that he had both separated and fractured his left shoulder.

These injuries left a clear and serious mark on Fosse's career. In 1970, he was a 23-year-old rookie of infinite promise. At the All-Star break, he'd already slugged 16 home runs, and many were predicting that he would become baseball's next great catcher. But, struggling with his undiagnosed injuries, he hit only two home runs during the rest of the '70 season—and never hit more than 12 in an entire season after that. Although he was a contributor to two World Championships with the Oakland A's in the early '70s,

Two views of the collision at home plate that ended the 1970 All-Star Game. As Fosse stood waiting for the throw from center field, Rose came straight for him, knocking him to the ground. Both players were sore immediately after the incident, but while Rose's injuries healed quickly, the shoulder injury Fosse sustained was serious, and his career was forever altered.

by 1979 his career was over . . . a career forever marred by an injury sustained during an exhibition game.

In interviews, Fosse has always been rueful about his fate, expressing no regrets about the course of his career. "If it happened 100 times again, 99 I would probably do it," he said of standing in Rose's path. "Maybe the 100th time I'd be smart enough to get out of the way."

THE "HOOVER" ADMINISTRATION

Brooks "Hoover" Robinson is considered one of the best, if not the best, defensive third baseman who ever played the game. After all, his nickname stems from his ability to "vacuum" up all balls hit his way. For sixteen straight years (1960-1975), Robinson won the A.L. Gold Glove Award. Robinson showcased his talents during the 1970 World Series, batting .429 while routinely robbing Cincinnati's batters of hits down the third base line.

"THAT GUY CAN FIELD A BALL WITH A PAIR OF PLIERS."

THE REAL DEAL

Lindsay Deal's entire major league career consisted of four games with the Brooklyn Dodgers in 1939, during which he came to bat seven times and got zero hits. Lifetime batting average: .000. To the Baltimore Orioles, however, Deal was a Hall of Famer. That's because he was a great judge of baseball talent, and took the time to write Orioles' management a letter in early 1955. "I am writing you in regard to a kid named Brooks Robinson," Deal reported. "I think he measures up to having a good chance in major league baseball. I think he is a natural third baseman although he has been playing both second and third."

Then Deal went on to nail the personality that Brooks Robinson would exhibit throughout his storied career. "Brooks has a lot of power, baseball savvy and is always cool when the chips are down," he wrote. "I thought you might be interested in him."

Deal was right—the Orioles were interested. Interested enough to sign Robinson as soon as he graduated from high school. Robinson actually made his first appearance with the Orioles late in the 1955 season, when he was still just 18 years old, only a few months after Lindsay Deal first alerted Baltimore to the presence of the talented youngster. He wouldn't leave the team until his retirement, 23 years later.

THE HUMAN VACUUM CLEANER

For the first few years of his career, Robinson struggled with the bat in limited playing time with the Orioles. Beginning in 1960, though, when he was still just 23 years old, he began to hit his stride. He hit .294 that season, with 14 home runs and 88 runs batted in. Even more importantly, he made only 12 errors all season long, and began showing the spectacular instincts and brilliant glovework

ON THE RECOMMENDATION OF TALENT SCOUT LINDSAY DEAL, the Baltimore Orioles signed Brooks Robinson right out of high school.

had an important home run in the first game, for the Series he batted just .214.

The Orioles were back in the World Series in 1969. But this was the year of the Miracle Mets, who manhandled Baltimore in five games. Brooks had a terrible series at the plate, getting just one hit in 19 at bats.

that made him famous far outside the confines of Baltimore.

In 1959 Boston Red Sox 3rd baseman Frank Malzone won the American League's Gold Glove, which is given for the best fielder at each position. In 1960, Brooks Robinson won the Gold Glove for his play at third. He then went on to win the award the next 15 years in a row. No one else received it until 1976.

Along with his consistently brilliant fielding, Robinson continued to develop as a hitter. He had six seasons with more than 20 home runs, two years with more than 100 RBI, and two .300-plus seasons. By the time his career ended, he'd racked up 2,848 hits—not bad for a player known primarily for his glove.

In the mid-1960s, the Orioles became a great team. Along with Brooks, they were led by Frank Robinson, Boog Powell, and a trio of superb pitchers: Jim Palmer, Dave McNally, and Mike Cuellar. Their team defense was so great overall that it left other teams grumbling in disbelief. As Detroit manager Mayo Smith commented, "Hitting a ball through the Baltimore infield is like trying to throw a hamburger through a brick wall."

In 1966 the Orioles went to the World Series, and proceeded to dominate the Los Angeles Dodgers as no one has ever dominated before. After winning Game One, 5–2, the Orioles pitchers went on to shut out the Dodgers in the next three games, for a numbing four-game sweep. Although Brooks

After winning 109 games in 1969, yet coming up empty in the Series, the Orioles went right back and won 108 games in 1970. Again they marched into the Series, this time against the Cincinnati Reds. This time, they knew that if they came up short, they would forever be branded a team that couldn't get it done in the clutch.

Luckily for them, Brooks Robinson wouldn't let that happen.

THE BROOKS SHOW

Both at bat and in the field, Brooks Robinson put his stamp on a World Series like few other players ever have. "When all other details of the Orioles' conquest are faded or gone, Robbie's contributions will live undimmed," is how *The Sporting News* put it.

A quick glance shows that the Orioles won two laughers and two tight games en route to a five-game Series victory over the Reds, despite the presence on the Cincinnati team of Pete

ROBINSON WAS EXCEPTIONAL in the Orioles' 1970 World Series against the Cincinnatti Reds, on the field and at the plate. In the fifth inning of Game Three, he dove to snare a line drive by Johnny Bench.

Most Consecutive Golden Gloves—Top 5

Player (League)	Position	Number of Years	Years
Brooks Robinson (A)	3rd base	16	1960-75
Ozzie Smith (A)	Shortstop	13	1980-92
Keith Hernandez (N)	1st base	11	1978-88
Ryne Sandberg (N)	2nd base	9	1983-91
Mike Schmidt (N)	3rd base	9	1976-84

Rose, Johnny Bench, Tony Perez, and other great players. A closer look, though, shows that Brooks' efforts contributed to every victory.

In Game One, he hit the game-winning home run, giving the Orioles a 4–3 win. His remarkable backhanded grab of Lee May's ground smash, followed by a perfect, long throw to first to nail the runner, stopped a possible Reds' rally.

He was equally prominent in Game Two, driving in the tying run with a single and scoring the deciding run during a five-run rally. In the field, he robbed poor Lee May again, turning May's potential game-breaking hit into a double play. Then, in Game Three, he hit two doubles and drove in two runs—and stole a hit from Johnny Bench with a diving grab of a line drive—as the Orioles cruised to an easy 9–3 win.

In Game Four, the Reds got smart. Although Brooks went 4-for-4 with a home run, he only had one easy chance in the field. The Reds hit the ball away from him, and won the game, 6–5.

Then came Game Five. Brooks hit a single, to end the Series with a .429 batting average. In the field, he dove across the foul line to stab Johnny Bench's liner in the ninth inning, and followed that up by throwing out Pat Corrales for the final out of the Orioles' five-game Series victory.

After the Series was over, all the dejected Reds could do was marvel. "That guy can field a ball with a pair of pliers," said Pete Rose. Added Robinson, "I never had five games in a row like I had in that particular World Series."

DENIED. Once again, Robinson leaps to stop a Johnny Bench hit—this time in the ninth inning of Game Five of the 1970 World Series. The Orioles defeated the Reds in five games.

RIGHTFULLY ENSHRINED

By 1971, two major league players who also played in the Negro Leagues, Jackie Robinson and Roy Campanella, were enshrined in the Baseball Hall of Fame. That year, pitching great Satchel Paige was bestowed the honor of being the first player elected to the Hall of Fame for his performance in the Negro Leagues. Fellow greats Josh Gibson and Buck Leonard joined him in 1972. Including inductees Willie Wells in 1977, and Smokey Joe Williams in 1999, a total of 23 Negro League veterans have been enshrined in Cooperstown.

DENIED TOO LONG

Oh, what players they were! Cool Papa Bell, the man who was so fast, it was said that he could turn out the light and jump in bed before the room got dark.

Josh Gibson, a Paul Bunyan among sluggers. "If Josh Gibson had been in the big leagues in his prime," said Hall of Famer Judy Johnson, "Babe Ruth and Hank Aaron would still be chasing him for the home run record."

"THE BEST PITCHER

I EVER SEEN…

IT'S OLD SATCHEL

PAIGE"

In 1971, Leroy Robert "Satchel" Paige became the first man to be enshrined in the Hall of Fame for his performance in the Negro Leagues. Paige told the Hall of Fame induction audience, "I'm the proudest man in the place right today."

Buck Leonard, who had such a quick swing that (in the words of pitcher Dave Barnhill) "you could put a fastball in a shotgun and you couldn't shoot it past him."

And so many more: Buck O'Neil, Oscar Charleston, Willie Wells, Ray Dandridge, Martin Dihigo, Judy Johnson . . . brilliant ballplayers who were forever denied the opportunity to demonstrate their talents on the major league stage, for one absurd reason.

Because they weren't white.

Receiving a brotherhood award from Howard University in 1971, all-time great Hall of Famer Ted Williams cut to the heart of the matter, as always. He said:

> As I look back on my career—and it was wonderful to me, and I'm thankful that I was given the chance to play baseball; it's about the only thing I could do—and I've thought many a time, what would have happened to me if I hadn't had a chance to play baseball? A chill goes up my back when I think I might have been denied this if I had been black.

That's what these men—these great ballplayers—had to face throughout their lives. In 1947, those who were still alive watched Jackie Robinson break the color barrier that had existed for decades, and knew that they had been born too soon. That it was only mindless prejudice that had prevented them from playing where they rightfully belonged.

As a further insult, until 1971 they were also denied entry into the Hall of Fame, which was limited to major league players. That year, finally, baseball began to right its wrongs and acknowledge the greatness of those who hadn't been allowed to play in the Majors.

HONORED AT LAST

By 1971, two African-American ballplayers had been elected to the Hall of Fame: Jackie Robinson and Roy Campanella. Both of these men had played in the Negro Leagues, but both had been elected primarily for their brilliance in the Majors after the color line finally came down.

In 1971, Satchel Paige joined them. Paige had pitched well in the Major Leagues at the tail end of his career—including helping the Cleveland Indians win the 1948 pennant—but he was the first man elected to the Hall of Fame due to his performance in the Negro Leagues.

JOSH GIBSON, "the Babe Ruth of the Negro Leagues," was a formidable slugger, hitting well over .300 for the Homestead Grays and the Pittsburgh Crawfords. He died at the age of 35 in 1947, just a few months before Jackie Robinson became the first black man to play in the Major Leagues. He was enshrined in the Hall of Fame in 1972.

How superb was Satchel Paige in his prime? "I know who's the best pitcher I ever seen and it's old Satchel Paige," said Dizzy Dean, a Hall of Fame pitcher himself. "My fastball looks like a change of pace alongside that little pistol bullet old Satchel shoots up to the plate."

Paige had been upset and disappointed when Jackie Robinson was chosen to be the man who broke the color barrier. But when he was elected to the Hall of Fame in 1971, old Satchel said, "I'm the proudest man in the place right today and I know my wife is, my sister and my sister-in-law, and everybody."

WRONGS RIGHTED

A year after Satchel Paige made it into the Hall, voters elected two other players who never got a chance to play in the Majors. They were Josh Gibson and Buck Leonard, two of the greatest hitters ever to wield a bat.

Josh Gibson died at age 35 on January 20, 1947, less than three months before Jackie Robinson first walked onto the field as a regular season member of the Dodgers. By then, though, Gibson's exploits with the Homestead Grays and Pittsburgh Crawfords were already legend among those who watched him play in the Negro Leagues.

Writing in 1939, on the eve of an exhibition game between Negro league and white stars at Yankee Stadium, *New York Daily News* columnist Jimmy Powers said, "I have seen personally at least ten colored ball players I know are big leaguers, but who are barred from play. . . . I am positive that if Josh Gibson was white, he'd be a major league star."

Powers went on to describe two consecutive doubleheaders, during which Gibson hit five home runs, a triple, two doubles, and a single. "Imagine the headlines such a slugging streak would merit if Gibson wore the uniform, say, of our Brooklyn Dodgers," Powers said.

One year, when the Grays played three or four games a week, at most, in Griffith Stadium in Washington, Gibson is reported to have hit more home runs than every player on the Washington Senators hit, combined, during the entire season. Said Hall of Fame pitcher Carl Hubbell: "I know he'd tear plenty of fences down in the Majors."

Sadly, Gibson never got the chance. Nor did first baseman Buck Leonard, long Gibson's teammate on the Homestead Grays, and second only to Josh in his ability to terrify opposing pitchers. "Buck Leonard was the equal of any first baseman who ever lived," said Hall of Famer Monte Irvin, who played against him in the Negro Leagues and later starred with the New York Giants. "If he'd gotten a chance to play in the Major Leagues, they might have called Lou Gehrig the white Buck Leonard."

But Leonard was 39 in 1947, and was considered too old for the Majors.

Unlike Josh Gibson, Leonard lived long enough to see his career celebrated with a place in the Hall of Fame. In his speech upon induction, he called his election, "the greatest moment of my life."

The enshrinements of Satchel Paige, Josh Gibson, and Buck Leonard have been followed by the election to the Hall of other superb ballplayers who played most or all of their careers in the Negro Leagues, including James "Cool Papa" Bell (1974), Judy Johnson (1975), Oscar Charleston (1976), Martin Dihigo (1977), John Henry Lloyd (1977), Ray Dandridge (1987), Leon Day (1995), Bill Foster (1996), Willie Wells (1997), Bullet Rogan (1998), and Smokey Joe Williams (1999).

FIRST BASEMAN BUCK LEONARD was compared with Lou Gehrig, just as his Homestead Grays teammate Josh Gibson was compared with Babe Ruth. Leonard was consistently among the league leaders in home runs and batting average.

BY THE TIME THE DOOR TO THE MAJOR LEAGUES WAS OPENED TO him in 1947, Leonard was 39 and considered too old.
But he lived to see himself selected to join an even more elite club—the Baseball Hall of Fame–in 1972.

THE FOUR ACES

Orioles Manager Earl Weaver had a stellar starting rotation in 1971. Four pitchers, Dave McNally,
Mike Cuellar, Pat Dobson, and Jim Palmer, each won 20 games (going a combined 81-31) leading Baltimore to
a 101-win season. This marked the first time since the 1920 White Sox that a team had four pitchers logging 20 wins.
Incidentally, McNally was the Orioles hottest pitcher in the World Series that year, winning two. However,
the other pitchers combined for only one victory and Pittsburgh took the Series in seven games.

NOT SINCE 1920

"I STILL THINK
WE'RE THE BEST
DAMN TEAM IN
BASEBALL"

During many seasons, there might be four pitchers to win 20 games in an entire league. In 1971, the Baltimore Orioles could claim four 20-game winners all by themselves. Not since 1920 had one team featured four pitchers who crossed that magic threshold—the Chicago White Sox. Two of those 20-game winners (Lefty Williams and Eddie Cicotte) were among the eight players banished for life by Commissioner Kennesaw Mountain Landis for throwing the 1919 World Series.

The four Oriole pitchers—Dave McNally (21–5), Pat Dobson (20–8), Jim Palmer (20–9), and Mike Cuellar (20–9)—never threw anything but baseballs. Palmer was a future Hall of Famer who

THE ORIOLES' FOUR 20-GAME WINNERS in 1971, left to right: Mike Cuellar, Pat Dobson, Dave McNally, and Jim Palmer.

would pitch 268 career victories. Early on, it seemed as if Palmer might never get to fulfill his promise. He suffered from arm miseries that restricted him to nine appearances in 1967 and forced him to miss the entire 1968 season.

But Palmer came back to go 16–4 in 1969, and then 20–10 in 1970, two more seasons that saw the Orioles go to the World Series. That began a streak—amounting to eight years out of nine—that he would win at least 20 games.

Dave McNally's career numbers—184 wins and 119 defeats—left him shy of the

Hall of Fame. But for a four-year period (1968–71) he may have been the Orioles' best pitcher, gaining 87 wins against just 31 losses. He was also a workhorse, starting 41 games one season, 40 another, and completing as many as 18 games in a season.

Mike Cuellar ended up with almost identical career numbers to McNally: 185–130. His stretch of great years spanned 1969–74, during which he won 125 games and lost just 63, winning more than 20 games four times.

Pat Dobson, the final member of the Orioles powerhouse of 1971, had his best season that year. In compiling his 20–8 record, he threw 18 complete games and four shutouts. It must have been demoralizing to have already lost games to Palmer, McNally, and Cuellar, and then find Pat Dobson glaring at you from the mound in the fourth game of a series.

THREE IN A ROW

In both 1969 and 1970, the Orioles had won the A.L. East and had then gone on to meet the Western Division champion Minnesota Twins in the playoffs. Both seasons, the Orioles brushed off the Twins on their way to the World Series, winning the best-of-five playoffs three games to none. In 1971, the Twins were replaced by the Oakland A's as Western Division champs, but the result was the same. The Orioles won three games in a row and earned a ticket to the World Series for the third straight season.

Orioles manager Earl Weaver was ebullient before the Series started. "I've got the best damn ballclub in the universe," he told the press. "I've got *too* good a ballclub. It just keeps on winning."

The Orioles' opponent in the World Series was the Pittsburgh Pirates. The Pirates had some good pitchers, including Steve Blass (15–8) and Dock Ellis (19–9), but no one thought that their pitchers could match up with Baltimore's aces. What made Pittsburgh a scary opponent were such fearsome hitters as

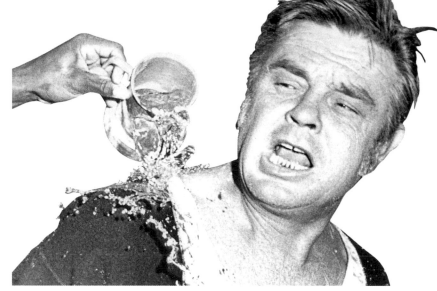

Willie Stargell (48 home runs) and Roberto Clemente (.341).

Still, the Orioles had their four aces, along with such superb hitters as Frank Robinson and Boog Powell. The general consensus was that the Orioles would win the Series easily.

THE BIG COMEBACK

For the first two games of the Series, it seemed that the predictions would come true. Dave McNally pitched beautifully, and the Orioles won Game One, 5–3. In Game Two, the Orioles' hitters ran roughshod over six Pirates' pitchers in an 11–3 win for Jim Palmer.

So far, it was shaping up to be a dull, predictable World Series.

But then, suddenly, the Series' momentum turned. The Pirates won Game Three, 5–1, behind a brilliant performance by Steve Blass. They won Game Four, 4–3, as rookie pitcher Bruce Kison pitched one-hit relief for 6⅓ innings. They won Game Five, 4-0, as Nelson Briles shut out the Orioles on just two hits.

The Orioles came back to pull out Game Six, 3-2, in 10 innings. But in Game Seven, the Pirates' Steve Blass was at the top of his game again, holding Baltimore to just one run on four hits. The Pirates managed just six hits of their own, but cashed two of them in for runs (including a home run by Roberto Clemente) and held on for a 2–1 win and a thrilling World Series victory.

THE ORIOLES' MANAGER, Earl Weaver, had confidence to spare going into the 1971 A.L. pennant race. He is pictured here in the celebration following the Orioles' capture of the A.L. Eastern Division title.

TAKEN TOO SOON

At the end of the 1972 season, Pittsburgh Pirates outfielder Roberto Clemente doubled to record his 3,000th hit. Three months later, on New Year's Eve, Clemente died in a plane crash while attempting to deliver food and medical supplies to Nicaragua after an earthquake devastated the country. The Hall of Fame election rules were modified for Clemente and he was enshrined in 1973. The award given out annually by Major League Baseball to the player who best contributes to his community was named in Clemente's honor.

MOST UNDERRATED

Roberto Clemente came to the Major Leagues with the Pittsburgh Pirates in 1955, and soon distinguished himself as a strong hitter and a brilliant outfielder.

Or, rather, he distinguished himself among those who noticed—and that was remarkably few. Despite his superb play in right field and consistent batting averages above .300, Clemente labored for years in the shadow of better known superstars. Pittsburgh was a small market, and players with the names of Willie Mays, Mickey Mantle, and Duke Snider patrolled the outfield in New York, garnering most of the available publicity.

Clemente himself gave another reason for being slighted: racism. He believed that fans were prejudiced against Latin players, preferring to root for either white or African-American stars.

Looking at press coverage of Clemente throughout his career, it's hard to argue with his conclusions. For

> "HE COULD FIELD A BALL IN NEW YORK AND THROW OUT A GUY IN PENNSYLVANIA"

ROBERTO CLEMENTE began to get noticed during the 1960 season. He would take the Gold Glove award every year from 1961 to 1972 and win the National League MVP in 1966.

years, he was characterized as an injury prone, hot-headed, unpredictable player who appeared to be feigning his aches and pains. He was born and raised in Puerto Rico, and during his early seasons, his speech was often transcribed in pidgin English. So was the speech of other Latin stars, including Luis Aparicio and Juan Marichal. As a result, they appeared uneducated, even stupid.

In truth, Roberto Clemente was an intensely proud, fiercely competitive, and intelligent man. In 1964, explaining to *The Sporting News* why Latin stars so often went through difficult transitions to major league play, he came across as thoughtful and sensitive as well. "We lead different lives in America," he said. "The language barrier is great at first and we have trouble ordering food in restaurants. Even segregation baffles us."

If given time, though, the Latin players could make the adjustment, he went on. "Once we're at peace with the world, we can do the job in baseball," he pointed out. "The people who have never experienced these problems don't know what it's like."

Roberto Clemente was living proof that what he said was true.

A GREAT CAREER

Roberto Clemente truly hit his stride beginning with the 1960 season. He hit .314, with 16 home runs and 94 runs batted in. More importantly, he hit .310 in the World Series against the Yankees—but the Pirate who got most of the publicity in that Series was Bill Mazeroski, whose home run in the bottom of the ninth inning of Game Seven gave the Pirates an improbable 10–9 victory.

Clemente took his play to an entirely new level in 1961, leading the league with a .351 batting average. He accumulated 201 hits, 30 doubles, 10 triples, 23 home runs, and 89 RBI.

It was a tremendous season by anyone's standards, and he followed it with a string of them: batting averages of .357, .352, .345, .341, and .339, more than 200 hits three more times, and a high of 29 home runs in 1966. He posted these numbers while facing pitchers like Sandy Koufax, Don Drysdale, Tom Seaver, Juan Marichal, and others, at a time when pitching dominated the game.

At the same time, he seemed to be rewriting the rulebook when it came to how right field should be played. Leaping and diving, he seemed to catch balls that would have gotten past any other player. And his throwing arm! He could throw the ball on a line from the deepest corner all the way to the plate on the fly, drawing gasps from the crowd. Said Dodger announcer Vin Scully: "He could field a ball in New York and throw out a guy in Pennsylvania."

Before runners stopped trying to take the extra base on him, he once threw out 27 men on the basepaths in a single season. Between 1961 and 1972, Roberto Clemente won the Gold Glove every year.

Still, despite these extraordinary accomplishments, Roberto Clemente labored in relative obscurity. That is, he did so until the 1971 World Series, when he shone as few ever had before him.

ROBERTO'S TIME

He'd had a remarkable year during the 1971 regular season, battling through injuries to hit .341. But in the World Series, people finally started to notice how great a ballplayer he'd

ROBERTO CLEMENTE'S FAMILY stands with his Hall of Fame plaque at the 1973 induction ceremonies, not long after Clemente's death in a plane crash on December 31, 1972. From left to right are his wife Vera, their three sons, and mother Luisa.

been. After hitting .414, with a crucial home run in Game Seven, he was named the World Series Most Valuable Player.

The next season, 1972, was another good one for Clemente. Age was catching up with him, but he still managed to hit .312. On the fourth to the last day of the season, he hit a double to become only the 11th player ever to reach 3,000 hits. That solid-gold total included 440 doubles, 166 triples, 240 home runs, and 1,305 runs batted in—the hitting numbers of a world-class ballplayer.

Clemente had every intention of coming back to play again in 1973, but it was not to be. On December 31, 1972, he took off from San Juan, Puerto Rico, on a cargo plane loaded with relief supplies for victims of a massive earthquake in Nicaragua. The plane crashed soon after take-off, and Clemente and all others aboard perished.

In honor of this brilliant ballplayer and intelligent, complex, and caring man, the Hall of Fame waived its usual five-year waiting period and the Baseball writers' Association of America voted Roberto Clemente into the Hall in 1973, just a few months after his death.

CLEMENTE joined one of baseball's most elite clubs on September 30, 1972, when he got his 3,000th hit (overleaf).

SIT THIS ONE OUT

Yankees Manager Ralph Houk had the opportunity in 1973 to use Ron Blomberg in the lineup despite injuries that curtailed his defensive play at first base. As part of an effort to increase offensive production and, ultimately, fan interest, the American League rules were changed to create the designated hitter in 1973. On April 6, 1973, Blomberg was penciled in as the DH for the New York Yankees and, with the bases loaded against Boston Pitcher Luis Tiant, drew a run-scoring walk. That trip to the plate was the first ever by a DH, earning Blomberg's bat a trip to Cooperstown, and changing the way baseball is played in the American League.

RED SOX PITCHER LUIS TIANT faced the first designated hitter in baseball history.

"DESIGNATED WALKER WOULD BE MORE LIKE IT"

SHAKY TEAMS

Over the years, there have always been differences between the American and National leagues, times when one or the other league dominated competitions between the two. In the 1920s, 1930s, and 1950s, for example, the Yankees were so powerful that the American League won a majority of the World Series. The 1960s saw the other side of the coin: From 1960 through 1970, the National League won 13 out of 14 All-Star Games. (From 1959 to 1962, two All-Star Games were played each season.)

But beginning in the late 1960s, there was another difference between the two leagues: The N.L. was consistently far more successful financially than the A.L.

There were several reasons for this. First, the A.L. had several franchises located in cities that simply didn't support their teams. Some of these teams were also owned by people or corporations that didn't have enough money to run a successful franchise.

THE WEAK SISTER

Another, even bigger problem, was the fact that in the 1960s the A.L. became a far weaker league offensively than the N.L. The Yankee dynasty came to an end in 1964, and the team soon degenerated to become one of the weakest in the league. Unfortunately, no other team took up the slack.

In 1968 (the "Year of the Pitcher"), for example, the N.L. batted only .243. But this was far better than the A.L., which managed only a paltry .230 league batting average. The once-mighty Yankees managed to hit only .214, and close ahead of them in futility were the Washington Senators (.224), California Angels (.227), and Chicago White Sox (.228). The Baltimore Orioles managed to win 91 games that year while batting only .225!

Not surprisingly, by 1973 the A.L.'s unstable franchises and persistent offensive weaknesses led many to consider it inferior to the N.L. Some reporters even began to refer to the A.L. as if it were on its way to becoming a minor

IN RON BLOMBERG's historic first at bat as a designated hitter, he drew a walk.

league, not worthy of comparison with the more successful N.L.

In response to these disturbing trends, the American League decided it had to do something. What it chose to do was to rewrite the rulebook more drastically than had ever been done in the history of major league baseball.

THE DESIGNATED HITTER ARRIVES

Since the earliest days of professional baseball, the rules have always been the same: Nine men in the field, and everyone takes a turn at bat. In 1973, the American League decided to invent the designated hitter (DH), who would hit in place of the pitcher but who would otherwise never set foot on the field. The National League declined to follow suit.

The first designated hitter came to bat on April 6, 1973, in a game between the Yankees and Red Sox at Fenway Park. Yankee manager Ralph Houk chose Ron Blomberg as his pioneer, the first DH of all. Previously, Blomberg had played right field and first base for the Yankees, but injuries had reduced his mobility. It was DH or nothing for the part-time player.

Blomberg came to bat for the first time in the first inning. He was facing the Sox' Luis Tiant with the bases loaded and two men out. Blomberg waited as Tiant threw four bad pitches, then trotted to first on the base on balls, forcing home a run. ("Designated walker would be more like it," griped a reporter.)

The Yankees eventually won the game, 15–5, but this was no thanks to Blomberg or the Sox' DH, Orlando Cepeda. Blomberg went 1–3, with that lone run batted in, while Cepeda didn't manage a single hit in six at bats. The occasion was historic enough that Blomberg's bat went off to the Hall of Fame after the game had ended.

The purpose of the designated hitter was to boost offense, and in that it succeeded. After trailing the National League in most offensive categories for years, the A.L. outhit its rival, .259 to .254, in 1973, while also hitting more home runs and scoring more runs. The substitution of relatively productive hitters for pitchers—who rarely get hits—was the reason.

American League attendance went up substantially in the years following the introduction of the DH. Then, as now, fans loved to see offense, and the DH allowed the A.L. to feature higher-scoring ballgames.

Today, more than a quarter-century after its arrival, the designated hitter remains controversial. Opponents feel that it robs the game of strategy, especially the manager's decision-making on whether to pinch hit for a pitcher in a close game. Proponents feel that the excitement the extra hitter brings to the game is worth any loss of strategy.

Others, however, just can't stand the fact that the two leagues operate under different rules. (The DH is used in the World Series only during the American League representative's home games.) As Hall of Famer Catfish Hunter said on the twentieth anniversary of the DH: "I think the only thing that should be changed in baseball today is the designated hitter rule. Either have it in both leagues or don't have it."

YANKEES MANAGER RALPH HOUK was the first manager to insert a player as a designated hitter, in an April 6, 1973, game against the Boston Red Sox at Fenway Park.

THE RED SOX' Orlando Cepeda went in as that team's first DH in the same game, and had a dissapointing day, going 0 for 6.

First Designated Hitters

American League, 1973

Team	Player
Baltimore	Terry Crowley
Boston	Orlando Cepeda
California	Tom McCraw
Chicago	Mike Andrews
Cleveland	John Ellis
Detroit	Gates Brown
Kansas City	Ed Kirkpatrick
Milwaukee	Ollie Brown
Minnesota	Tony Oliva
New York	Ron Blomberg
Oakland	Bill North
Texas	Rico Carty

NOLAN'S NO-NOS

Nolan Ryan holds a number of records that may never be surpassed. The one that may stand the longest is his seven no-hitters, three better that Sandy Koufax's previous record. In 1973, at the age of 26, Ryan tossed two no-hitters for the Angels, both on the road, and exactly two months apart. Remarkably, his final two no-hitters were thrown at age 43 (in 1990) and 44 (in 1991) for the Texas Rangers. At the age when many major league pitchers are working as coaches, one might say that Ryan was teaching by example.

GREEN PEA

Nolan Ryan was something special from the start. From the moment scouts first began to take notice of him as a teenager, they saw him as a pitcher with great potential. "Big League prospect all the way," reported his manager at the New York Mets' Greenville farm team in June 1966. "When he stays overhanded with fast[ball] and curve he is at his best. Good attitude toward the game."

"BIG LEAGUE
PROSPECT ALL
THE WAY"

AFTER BRINGING HIM TO THE BIG LEAGUES in 1966, the Mets traded Nolan Ryan to the California Angels in 1971, a move they would soon regret. Ryan put up impressive numbers in his first year with the Angels—he completed 20 of 39 starts, and had a 2.28 ERA—but this was just the beginning.

The report, sent when Ryan was just 19 years old, was right on in all respects. It got him a late-season call-up with the Mets, who didn't have so many good pitchers on the major league team that they could afford to leave their top prospects on the farm too long.

Nolan Ryan was terrible during his brief appearance with the big club in 1966. He started one game and relieved in one, but pitched a total of just three innings, giving up five hits, three walks, and five runs, for an earned run average of 15.00.

But take a glance at another statistic, and it's easy to see why the scouts were so high on the young Ryan. In those three dismal innings, he struck out six men—two an inning. Even then, he could blow the ball by you.

After spending a couple of years back in the minors, Nolan Ryan pitched with the Mets for four more seasons, with only middling results. Although he always struck out a high percentage of the batters he faced, he was also always struggling with his control, giving him mediocre earned run averages and records like 6–9 and 7–11.

After Ryan posted a disappointing 10–14 record in 1971, the Mets decided that he would never live up to his potential, and shipped him to the California Angels for aging infielder Jim Fregosi. In their wildest dreams, they could never have predicted that their failed prospect would pitch 22 more years in

In a May 15, 1973 game against the Kansas City Royals, Ryan pitched the first no-hitter of his career. There would be six more.

In 1981, RYAN'S ASTRO teammates held him aloft in celebration of no-hitter #5. With this game, Ryan bested Sandy Koufax' four no-hitter record (top).

In 1990, at age 43, Ryan pitched his sixth no-hitter, with the Texas Rangers. After shutting out the Oakland A's, Ryan was congratulated by Ranger catcher John Russell.

the Majors, and become the greatest strikeout pitcher of all time.

THE DOMINATOR

During his first year with the Angels, Nolan Ryan put to rest any idea that he couldn't make it in the Majors. He started 39 games, completing 20 of them, and went 19–16 with a 2.28 ERA. He pitched 284 innings while giving up only 166 hits, a spectacular ratio (anything less than one hit per inning is considered good), and led the league in both walks (157) and strikeouts (329, still one of the ten-highest modern totals of all time).

Even more eye-opening numbers were to come. During his eight seasons with the Angels, Ryan both won and lost an enormous number of games, posting such records as 21–16, 22–16, 17–18, and 16–14. He walked as many as 204 men in a season, while also toting up amazing strikeout numbers: His 383 strikeouts in 1973 remains the modern all-time record, but he also posted totals of 367, 341, 329, and 327.

In 1973, the year he struck out 383 batters while winning 21 games, Ryan also recorded his first no-hitter . . . and then his second. In the first, on May 15, he no-hit the powerful Kansas City Royals. Just two months later, he did the same to the Detroit Tigers, this time adding 17 strikeouts. "I had the best curveball I've ever had," he said later about this game.

Remarkably, Ryan almost pitched *another* no-hitter in the start after his brilliant performance against the Tigers. He pitched seven hitless innings against the Orioles, only to see his chance ruined on a bloop single by weak-hitting Mark Belanger.

In all, Ryan pitched 12 one-hitters in addition to the seven no-hitters in his career. "[W]hen I think how close I came to no-hitters in all those one-hitters," he wrote near the end of his career, "it makes me wonder where the no-hit record might be but for one bad pitch or one bad break."

Amid all those one-hitters, Ryan added no-hitters in 1974, 1975 (to tie Sandy Koufax's record of four no-no's), and in 1981, after he moved to the Houston Astros. Then, in the seasons that followed, he continued to pitch well, but without posting any no-hitters. It seemed that he and his fans would have to settle for just a record-setting five no-hitters for his career.

But Nolan Ryan had two more surprises up his sleeve.

VETERAN FLAMETHROWER

In 1989, when he was 42 years old, Nolan Ryan moved on to pitch for the Texas Rangers. People wondered how much he could possibly have left.

Plenty, as it turned out. On June 11, 1990, when he was 43, he faced the defending A.L.-champion Oakland A's and shut them out, 5–0. He struck out 14 men, issued two walks, and gave up no hits, becoming the oldest pitcher ever to hurl a no-hitter.

Then, on May 1, 1991, Ryan chose to pitch on short rest against a potent Toronto Blue Jays team on Fan Appreciation Night in Texas. On this night, when he was already 44 years old, Ryan had some of the best stuff of his career. This time he struck out 16 while walking only two, and again giving up no hits. The final out was a strikeout of Roberto Alomar, who was born in 1968, two years after Ryan first pitched in the Major Leagues.

Nolan Ryan's career finally came to an end in 1993. The numbers that led to his first-ballot election to the Hall of Fame included 324 wins, 5,714 strike-outs (by far the most of all time), and, of course, those seven no-hitters, a record that is likely to stand for a very long time.

NOT DONE YET. On May 1, 1991, at age 44, Ryan completed his seventh no-hitter by striking out 23-year-old Toronto Blue Jay Roberto Alomar.

SAY HEY

After playing 22 years, Willie Mays retired, leaving behind a legacy that few will match.
Mays posted great numbers including 660 home runs, 12 straight Gold Glove Awards, and 22 consecutive
All-Star Game appearances. Mays departure was more significant than just the numbers. He was the last
link to a different era in baseball, the days of Willie, Mickey, and the Duke.

"HE COULD HELP
A CLUB JUST BY
RIDING ON THE
BUS WITH IT."

*JANIS PAIGE, THE ACTRESS AND SINGER who
recorded "Say Hey," a song about
Willie Mays, in 1954, hands Mays the
record. In 1954 Paige was best known
for starring in the Tony-award winning Broadway musical, "The Pajama
Game," which opened that year.*

IRREPRESSIBLE

Starting with his first appearance with the New York Giants in 1951, Willie Mays burst across the baseball scene like a comet. He talked fast, ran faster, made unbelievable catches in the field, threw strikes from the outfield fence to home plate on the fly, and hit the ball nine miles. He was the definition of a phenom.

He was also the most cheerful, charming, and likeable man you could ever hope to meet. He brightened the Giants clubhouse with his irrepressible high spirits. In the words of one opposing manager, "Mays is the only ball player I ever saw

A YOUNG WILLIE MAYS with Giants teammates Don Mueller (center) and Dusty Rhodes (right).

who could help a club just by riding on the bus with it."

Mays was just 20 when the Giants called him up in 1951. He wasn't supposed to be with the big club that year. He was supposed to spend one more season with the Minneapolis Millers, a Giants' minor league affiliate, before joining the big club.

He had begun the season by hitting .477 in 35 games with the Millers, and was understandably a huge fan favorite. When the Giants called him up, the howls of outrage were so loud in Minneapolis that Giants' owner Horace Stoneham had to take out advertisements in Minnesota newspapers explaining why he'd stolen Willie away.

In his 121 games with the Giants in 1951, Mays showed hints of what he could do, hitting .274, with 20 home runs and 68 RBI. It was here that he also picked up his nickname, the "Say-Hey Kid": Since he didn't know the names of many of his teammates, he'd simply yell "Say, hey!" when he wanted to catch their attention.

From the start, Mays also made some spectacular catches in centerfield. After one such play, in which Mays caught a fly ball while sprinting full-tilt toward the outfield wall, he then spun around and threw a runner out at the plate.

When someone said that Mays had made a remarkable play, Giants' manager Leo Durocher said, "What was so remarkable about that? He does it every day! Every day!"

Only a few weeks after Mays arrived with the Giants, Durocher made a bold pronouncement. He said, "I wouldn't trade Willie for DiMaggio, Williams, Musial, or anybody else you can name."

A LEGEND AT HIS PEAK

In 1954 Willie Mays took the baseball world by storm. He led the league with a .345 batting average, rapped out 33 doubles and 13 triples, slugged 41 home runs, scored 119 and drove in 110 runs, and continued to play defense at a higher level than anyone else.

The Giants went to the World Series in 1954, facing the powerful Cleveland Indians. Mays' over-the-shoulder catch of a tremendous clout by the Indians' Vic Wertz is considered by many to be the greatest catch in the history of baseball.

Mays was at his peak from the 1950s through the mid-1960s. Who can tell what his best year was? Perhaps 1955, when he hit .319 with 51 home runs and 40 stolen bases. Or 1957, when his average rose to .333 and he led the league with 20 triples. Or 1958, when he hit .347. Or maybe it was 1962, when he drove in 141 runs, or 1965, when he hit a career-high 52 home runs.

Of course, even as he was posting these all-time hitting totals, he continued to play with unparalleled brilliance in the field—a brilliance that would earn him a dozen Gold Glove awards.

LAST HURRAH

By 1970, when he was nearing 40, Mays' skills had begun to erode. Midway through the 1972 season, the Giants traded him to the Mets. Many thought Willie should retire, but the great Mays had one more showcase to perform in before hanging up his spikes—and where better to perform than back in New York?

In 1973, the Mets shocked baseball fans by winning the National League East with a late-season rush. Mays had played sparingly during the season, batting only .211 and hitting just six home runs. But he had important hits in both the playoffs (where the Mets beat the favored Cincinnati Reds) and the World Series, which the Mets lost in seven games to the Oakland A's.

After the Series ended, Mays retired. On his farewell day at the Mets' Shea Stadium, he gestured toward the Mets' dugout and said, "I look at the kids over here, and the way they're playing and the way they are fighting for themselves, tells me one thing: 'Willie, say goodbye to America.'"

Mays said goodbye with 660 career home runs (third most of all time), 3,283 hits, 1,903 RBI, and a passel of the greatest fielding plays of all time. Five years later, he said hello to the Hall of Fame.

WILLIE MAYS had his last major league at-bat on October 16, 1973, playing for the New York Mets in a World Series game against the Oakland A's.

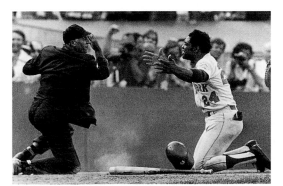

EVEN AFTER PLAYING FOR 22 YEARS, Mays' passion for winning remained obvious as he argued a call with umpire Augie Donatelli during the 1973 World Series.

715

Henry Louis Aaron is the first name that appears when all major league players who ever played the game are listed alphabetically. Appropriately, Aaron is the all-time leader in home runs and RBI and in the top three in four other categories. He became baseball's home run champion on April 8, 1974, smashing home run number 715 off Al Downing to break Ruth's long-standing record. Aaron returned to Milwaukee for the last two years of his career and finished with 755 home runs.

"714, 715, I'VE

FORGOTTEN THEM

ALREADY"

CAREER HOME RUN leader, Henry Louis Aaron.

THE UNBREAKABLE RECORD

During baseball's long history, a whole slew of records have been declared unbreakable. Ty Cobb's base-hit record, Babe Ruth's 60 home runs in a season, Lou Gehrig's consecutive-game streak—all these were thought to be far out of reach . . . until someone broke them. Baseball history teaches us that, sooner or later, someone is eventually going to come along who can outdo the previous record-holder.

For decades, the one career record that was considered unassailable was Babe Ruth's mark of 714 home runs. After all, if Willie Mays (660 career homers), Mickey Mantle (536), and Ted Williams (521) couldn't do it, who could? Mays simply didn't hit enough home runs late in his career, Mantle was laid low by injuries, and Williams lost several years to military service. How likely was it that any other slugger could avoid these pitfalls—and others—to accumulate Ruthian home run totals?

Early on in his career, it sure didn't look like Hank Aaron would be the one. During the first 11 years of his career (1954–64) with the Milwaukee (later Atlanta) Braves, he led the league in round-trippers exactly twice. His season high during that time was 45, a healthy total, but not anything to stir up the ghost of Babe Ruth. After all, during the first 11 years of *his* career (beginning in 1918, when he largely made the transition from pitcher to outfielder), Ruth could boast seasons in which he slammed 54, 59, 60, and 54 home runs.

But what Hank Aaron lacked in single-season fireworks (he never hit as many as 50 home runs in a season), he made up in longevity. No power hitter has ever hit so many home runs for so many seasons. Aaron slugged 44 homers in 1957, when he was 23 years old, and he slugged 40 home runs in 1973, when he was 39. In the 15 seasons in between, he hit 30, 39, 40, 34, 45, 44, 24, 32, 44, 39, 29, 44, 38, 47, and 34. All in all, it was a stunning string of consistent home run seasons. As Aaron's teammate Joe Adcock, no timid hitter himself, said: "Trying to sneak a pitch past Hank Aaron is like trying to sneak the sunrise past a rooster."

Beginning in the early 1970s, the media and the public began to realize that here was a player with a legitimate shot at breaking Babe Ruth's hallowed record.

And the toughest days of Aaron's career were just beginning.

PRESSURE

When Babe Ruth was piling up his amazing home run totals, he was competing with no one but himself. Almost immediately, his totals were far beyond what anyone could dream of hitting. (In 1920, when Babe hit 54 home runs, no other *team* hit as many). And it seemed to be clear early on that neither Mays nor Mantle nor any of the other contenders were going to approach Ruth's record.

When Aaron hit his 649th home run in June 1972, passing Mays and leaving only Ruth ahead of him, he suddenly became a news story. From that moment on, the pressure he faced from the media was intense—far greater than anything Babe Ruth had to face, in the days before television.

Aaron handled the onslaught with grace and modesty. "Even if I'm lucky enough to hit 715 home runs," he said, "Babe Ruth will still be regarded as the greatest home run hitter

who ever lived." At another point he said, poignantly, "I don't want them to forget Ruth. I just want them to remember me!"

Aaron also never let the intense media attention distract from his high level of play. He hit 34 home runs in 1972, and then 40 in 1973, leaving him at 713, just one shy of the Babe's record.

By this time, though, the intense focus on his chase had worn him out. "I used to love to come to the ballpark. Now I hate it," he said. "Writers, tape recorders, microphones, cameras, questions and more questions. Roger Maris lost his hair the season he hit sixty-one. I still have all my hair, but when it's over, I'm

AARON'S RELIEF at the temporary end to his pursuit of Babe Ruth's lifetime home run record is written on his face at a press conference following the end of the 1973 season. He ended the year just one home run short of tying Ruth's record. The following season, he quickly set out to breaking it.

TYING RUTH'S RECORD, Aaron connects on April 4, 1974—with his first swing of the season.

going home to Mobile and fish for a long time."

Even more painful than the relentless attention of the media was the barrage of hate-filled, racist letters (including many death threats) that Aaron began to receive as people began to realize that he would break the record. "I hope you hit 713 and get a heart attack on the field," said one, and others were even more disgusting.

All the letters did was strengthen Aaron's resolve, however. As the 1974 season began, he was just one home run short of the Babe. Breaking the record was just a matter of time.

THE MOMENT

With the efficiency that characterized his entire career, Aaron wasted no time matching the Babe's 714. On April 4, 1974, he hit one out with his first swing of the season, off of Cincinnati pitcher Jack Billingham.

Four days later, before 53,775 people in Atlanta and about 35 million television viewers, Aaron walked in the second inning. In the fourth, he took another ball from Los Angeles pitcher Al Downing, then reached down and whacked a low pitch over the left field fence. Afterward, Aaron had only fragmented memories of the moments following his historic swing. "I was in my own little world at the time," he said. "It was like I was running in a bubble."

Blessedly free of the media onslaught and hate mail after setting the record, Aaron kept on going until he reached 755 home runs.

Lifetime Home Runs Over 500

Player	Number of Home Runs
Hank Aaron	755
Babe Ruth	714
Willie Mays	660
Frank Robinson	586
Harmon Killebrew	573
Reggie Jackson	563
Mike Schmidt	548
Mickey Mantle	536
Jimmie Foxx	534
Mark McGwire	522
Willie McCovey	521
Ted Williams	521
Ernie Banks	512
Eddie Mathews	512
Mel Ott	511
Eddie Murray	504

("714, 715, I've forgotten them already," he said upon hitting number 716.)

When Aaron retired, some said that his record would never be broken. Of course, that was before a couple of ballplayers named Mark McGwire and Ken Griffey, Jr., had hit even a single home run.

THE LAST AT BAT of a major league giant. Aaron taps his 3,771st hit.

AARON HITS HIS HISTORIC 715TH home run on April 8, 1974, just four days following his homer that tied Ruth's record.

TODAY'S GAME

Thirty teams, several new; many more players than 20, or even 10 years ago; players moving from team to team. Today Major League Baseball runs on a different engine than years earlier. Reflecting societal developments from the 1970s through the 1990s, it has been reshaped by labor strife and made wealthier by television contracts while attracting fans through players' spectacular feats—those of Ken Griffey, Jr., Cal Ripken, Mark McGwire, and Sammy Sosa, to name a few.

Many people believe that the 1960s counterculture and its upheavals ended with the decade's demise in 1970. On the contrary, although certain parts of the counterculture lost their energy, others gained momentum in the 1970s. As one example, activists who had formed the National Organization for Women in 1966, fought in the 1970s to obtain equal rights under the law and gain entry into mainstream leadership positions, such as executive roles in corporations. In another example, the American Indian

COORS FIELD IN DENVER, Colorado, the Colorado Rockies' new stadium. Part of the newest wave of expansion, the Rockies played their first season in 1993.

Movement used radical tactics to protect and advance Native American rights. A protest at Wounded Knee, South Dakota in 1973 led to a violent showdown between about 200 Indians and federal forces.

Such challenges to the status quo also surfaced in the Major Leagues. Journalist Leonard Koppett claims that from 1973 to 1976, "the entire structure of baseball [changed] more than it had in the preceding 90 years." The reason: The reserve clause, which had meant that once a player signed with a team he stayed there the rest of his career unless the club decided otherwise, was ended.

During the 1976 season, pitchers Andy Messersmith of the Los Angeles Dodgers and Dave McNally of the Baltimore Orioles played without contracts so they could go to arbitration

and claim that, with no binding commitment, the reserve clause no longer applied to them. Arbitrator Peter Seitz indeed ruled in the players' favor, thus allowing them to sell their services to any club that wanted them.

A new collective bargaining agreement that followed Seitz' ruling permitted ballplayers to become "free agents" and offer their services to the highest bidder after six years in the big leagues. This change brought the acrimony already present in the relationship between owners and players to a higher level. As a result, labor issues would intensify over the next two decades and lead to several work stoppages—even the cancellation of a World Series.

At the end of the 1976 season, 58 players became free agents, and their demands, plus arbitration awards granted to other players, pushed average salaries up substantially. Of course, with players moving more frequently from one club to another, continuity within baseball suffered, clubs found it more difficult to hold teams together for any lengthy period, and fans found their teams less stable, less familiar. Despite concerns to the contrary, though, free agency created more equity among teams and made pennant races more competitive.

While labor developments changed baseball, so too did action on the field. This came in part from the American League adopting the designated hitter rule that boosted scoring. Greater change came, however, from the nail-biting 1975 World Series. The Cincinnati Reds, or "Big Red Machine," as they were called, entered the Series with an impressive record: They had won the National League West division by 20 games over the Dodgers. The players who produced this triumph and the team's subsequent pennant victory included outfielders Ken Griffey, Cesar Geronimo, and George Foster; catcher Johnny Bench; first baseman Tony Perez; second baseman Joe Morgan—MVP of the league with a .327 batting average and 67 stolen bases—shortstop Dave Concepcion; and third baseman Pete Rose.

They faced the Boston Red Sox, a team with its own notable players: outfielders Dwight Evans, Fred Lynn, and Jim Rice (the latter two were rookies); catcher Carlton Fisk; pitchers Luis Tiant and Bill Lee; and the aging but still formidable team leader, Carl Yastrzemski.

Boston easily won the first game at Fenway Park, but Cincinnati rallied from behind to win the second, 3–2. The excitement from that game built a larger TV audience for Game Three, and the teams delivered, providing yet more suspense as the Reds won at Cincinnati, 6–5 in 10 innings. Boston won Game Four by an equally close score of 5–4. Game Five was won by Cincinnati, meaning Boston had to win Game Six to stay alive. Would this be another cliffhanger? Yes . . . the Red Sox rallied from a 6–3 deficit in the eighth inning to tie the game, and then Fisk hit a home run in the 12th for the victory. With such action and with the entire Series on the line, Game Seven attracted 75 million television viewers, the largest for any sports event ever. Boston built a 3–0 lead, only to have the Reds score two runs in the sixth, another in the seventh, and then the winning run driven in by Morgan in the ninth. Cincinnati thus won its first World Series in more than 30 years.

The 1975 World Series revived major league baseball as a spectator sport. Attendance surged from 1.25 million per club in 1973 to 1.76 million in 1977 and 1.93 million in 1980. At the same time, baseball's contract for national TV coverage climbed in value from $18 million in 1973 to $41.57 million in 1980, reflecting better ratings and higher advertising revenues.

Yet while baseball was prospering in the 1970s, America was going through hard times. With the economy already shaken by large government deficits, in 1973 the Organization of Petroleum Exporting Countries, whose many Arab-member nations objected to American policy in the Middle East, embargoed oil shipments to the United States. The embargo, and then price hikes on oil shipments that resumed in 1974, fueled inflation. America's economy went into a tailspin. Prices for heating oil and gasoline rose 33 percent, and by the late 1970s the price of crude oil was nearly seven times higher than it had been in the late 1960s. Unemployment shot up too. Factory after factory reduced its work force or shut its doors. United States Steel closed 14 plants in eight states, which cost 13,000 jobs; Chrysler closed 13 plants, which cost 31,000 jobs . . . and so on.

Battered by the economy and disillusioned by the counterculture and its assault on traditional values, Americans in large numbers sought conservative solutions to the nation's problems.

THE ENERGY CRISIS of the 1970s unleashed inflation in the U.S. economy. Since then, the economy has gone through many cycles, but the late 1990s have brought steady growth.

They pushed social reform aside to pursue business development and stability. After a continued slump in the early 1980s, the economy picked up, stimulated by President Ronald Reagan's program of selective tax cuts. In 1984, the GNP rose seven percent, surpassing every yearly increase since 1951.

To critics, selfish material pursuit created social problems. While the economy rebounded, more homeless people appeared on city streets—among them some 500,000 children—and the gap between the wealthy and the rest of society widened. During the decade, income for the bottom fifth of families decreased 13 percent while for the top fifth it increased 27 percent. Yet prosperity grabbed headlines, and high living led *Newsweek* magazine to label 1984 the "Year of the Yuppies." The word stood for young, upwardly mobile, urban professionals—Baby Boomers who pursued the good life.

Major league baseball reveled in the decade's general prosperity. Attendance climbed from 44.6 million in 1982 to 53 million in 1988, and revenues from national TV continued their climb from the 1970s, reaching $197 million by 1988.

Then in 1989 scandal rocked the sport when an investigation undertaken for Commissioner Bart Giamatti indicated that

Pete Rose, then manager of the Cincinnati Reds, who likely was destined for the Hall of Fame with his career record 4,256 base hits, had bet on baseball games. Rose denied the charge, but eventually signed an agreement with Giamatti that, while citing no specific findings as to whether or not Rose bet on baseball, led to him being banned from baseball for life and, as a result, removed from consideration for the Hall of Fame.

Baseball entered the 1990s a lucrative business enriched by an increasingly commercialized society that bought T-shirts, caps, jackets, and other items emblazoned with team logos—all licensed by Major League Baseball—and by ever-bigger national television contracts. According to historian David Q. Voigt, "Television transformed the game into entertainment and the ballplayers into celebrity-entertainers." TV influenced the location of expansion teams and encouraged more night games (particularly in the post-season). Revenues from television contracts reached $377 million in 1993.

Amid this financial growth however, labor problems again reared their head. After the owners adopted a negotiating strategy aimed at rolling back salaries and eliminating or reducing salary arbitration, the players retaliated by striking in August 1994. They believed the owners would want a settlement by Labor Day to keep the pennant races going and the playoffs and World Series alive, but the owners held firm and in September canceled the remainder of the season and with it the World Series. After the National Labor Relations Board dealt the owners a blow by declaring they had failed to bargain in good faith, and the terms of a pre-strike agreement took effect, the ballplayers returned in early April of 1995 to a revised spring training schedule and a shortened regular season.

TELEVISION CONTRACTS represent a lucrative revenue stream for Major League Baseball. In 1995, patrons watched a playoff game at Michael Jordan's Restaurant in Chicago, Illinois.

Observers wondered if the strike would ruin major league baseball. Would the fans return to the game? What would happen to attendance and TV ratings?

Baseball provided evidence in the remaining years of the 1990s to support both pessimists and optimists. *Business Week* found that although sales of baseball merchandise picked up in 1996, the first full post-strike season, they remained behind those in 1993. In addition, television ratings for Saturday afternoon games, broadcast nationally, trailed those of three years earlier. The magazine reported, too, that baseball had lost much of its African-American audience to basketball and other sports. The *Journal of Business Strategy* confirmed most of these findings and added lagging attendance to the list.

Baseball's problems seemed so great that in October 1999 San Diego Padres president Larry Lucchino declared: "The game of baseball is alive and well, but the business of baseball is in fairly desperate straits." Commissioner Bud Selig went so far as to appoint a blue-ribbon task force to study the sport's economic problems and report back in the year 2000. There was even talk of eliminating two or more weak franchises. Critics of that alternative, however, insisted it would do nothing to address an even greater problem: the widening gap between wealthy franchises and poorer ones. The New York Yankees, for example, reported revenues triple those of the Pittsburgh Pirates, an income that allowed them to obtain more higher-priced, and presumably higher-quality, ballplayers than other teams.

Yet there was much encouraging news. Both the American and National Leagues reorganized into three divisions in 1994 and provided for a wild card team to enter post-season play. This move allowed more teams to enter the playoffs and thus generated greater fan interest. The Florida Marlins and Colorado Rockies had been added to the National League in 1993, and after the strike their achievements attracted widespread notice. The Marlins won the World Series in 1997, an incredible feat for a fourth-year expansion team. The Rockies packed their stadium game after game as they made serious runs for their division title. The same *Business Week* magazine that offered pessimistic reports waxed ecstatic in September 1995 when it reported the Rockies "have sold out 38 consecutive home games." Well known teams also got into the act. The Cleveland Indians, for one, showed that a bottom dweller could win the American League pennant, as they did in 1995 and again in 1997.

Amid these developments, Major League Baseball signed a new five-year television contract in 1995 with NBC, Fox, ESPN, and Liberty Sports that promised to bring in about $1.7 billion, or between $11 million and $12 million per team per year. The contract combined non-cable broadcasts with cable as Liberty agreed to carry three games per week over its FX network and ESPN agreed to carry Wednesday and Sunday night games, along with several first-round playoff games. NBC, ESPN, and Fox all reported ratings increases in 1998. (Fox said ratings for its Saturday afternoon games were up 15 percent over the previous year.) Ed Goren, executive producer of Fox Sports, proclaimed: "I don't think there is any question . . . this has been a breakthrough year for baseball."

The more lucrative TV deal and the increased attendance resulted in part from a surging economy, which, late in 1996, entered its 26th consecutive quarter of growth, the second-longest stretch in peacetime. Though economic indicators sagged early in 1998, by July they had rebounded, and in August the economy grew for the 88th month in a row. Low interest rates, stable financial markets, and low inflation—under 2 percent—all encouraged the boom. Federal Reserve Board chairman Alan Greenspan declared: "The current economic performance, with its combination of strong growth and low inflation, is as impressive as any I have witnessed in my near half-century of daily observation of the American economy."

Big companies merged and grew more influential, and Major League Baseball followed the trend when it added more corporate owners to its ranks. Time Warner acquired the Atlanta Braves, Disney bought a controlling interest in the Anaheim Angels, and Rupert Murdoch purchased the Los Angeles Dodgers from the O'Malleys, ending what newspapers called "the last family ownership" among the clubs. During these developments, baseball expanded again in 1998, when the Tampa Bay Devil Rays joined the American League and the Arizona Diamondbacks joined the National League.

By far the best news for big league baseball came from the playing fields, the main source of the sport's appeal since its inception more than a century earlier. In 1995, Cal Ripken broke Lou Gehrig's record of 2,130 consecutive games played. The following year, Eddie Murray of the Baltimore Orioles became only the 15th player to hit 500 home runs.

Then in 1998 a home run race between Mark McGwire, first baseman for the St. Louis Cardinals, and Sammy Sosa, right fielder for the Chicago Cubs, showed that baseball could still produce heroes for its fans. On September 8, McGwire broke Roger Maris' single-season record of 61 home runs, and then went on to hit eight more, finishing with 70. Sosa broke the Maris record a few days after McGwire and finished the season with 66 home runs.

MAJOR LEAGUE BASEBALL has benefited from the recent success of the U.S. economy. Alan Greenspan, the Chairman of the Federal Reserve Board, has become a symbol of the economy's continued growth.

Four players hit more than 50 homers that year—a first. More than a dozen players hit more than 40. Seattle Mariners shortstop Alex Rodriguez became only the third player in history to combine more than 40 home runs with 40 stolen bases, with 42 in the first category and 46 in the second. Ken Griffey, Jr., center fielder for Seattle, hit 56 homers in 1998—more than anyone else in the American League—and by the end of the 1999 season had recorded 398 career homer runs, a feat that put him in line to break the career record held by Hank Aaron. That November, his fellow major league ballplayers voted him the "player of the decade."

Adding to the spectacular individual stories, the 1998 New York Yankees won an American League-record 114 games—the first team to play above .700 since the 1954 Cleveland Indians—on their way to a World Series title. That they had won the Series two years earlier and then repeated their October victory in 1999—for an all-time total of 25 World Series wins—raised the possibility that another Yankee dynasty was in the making. Others, however, labeled the Atlanta Braves the "team of the Nineties" for its participation in five of the decade's nine World Series.

Despite major league baseball's trials and tribulations, its strife and strikes, its ever-bigger television contracts and ever-larger leagues, valiant efforts by individual players and teams remain at its heart. Fans look to these players and teams for assurances that in the new millennium baseball will continue to bridge past and present—Babe Ruth and Roger Maris to Mark McGwire and Sammy Sosa—and provide ever greater moments that say "This is America's game. This is home."

ANOTHER DOOR OPENS

In 1947, Jackie Robinson became the first African-American to play in the Major Leagues in this century. In 1975, another Robinson, Frank, became the first African-American to manage a major league club when he was named the Indians' player-manager. He started brilliantly in 1975, hitting a home run in his first at-bat and leading the Indians to a 5-3 victory over the Yankees. Robinson opened the door for other African-American managers such as Don Baylor and Cito Gaston, manager of the back-to-back World Champion Toronto Blue Jays in 1992 and 1993.

MOST QUALIFIED

During his 21-year career, Frank Robinson showed again and again why he was one of the greatest hitters of all time. During his prime years, spent with the Cincinnati Reds and Baltimore Orioles, he hit more than 30 home runs 10 times (with a high of 49), drove in more than 100 runs six times, and consistently hit above .300. In 1966, he became only the 13th player ever to achieve the Triple Crown, leading the American League in home runs (49), RBI (122), and batting average (.316).

Most of all, though, Frank Robinson was a smart ballplayer. Articulate and intelligent, he was always a leader both on the field and in the clubhouse. Players respected him, and so did opposing managers. From early in his career, observers said Robinson was managerial material.

There was only one problem: Frank Robinson was African American,

FRANK ROBINSON, as player-manager for the Cleveland Indians.

and in the 1960s and '70s, when his possible managerial future was being discussed, there had never been an African-American manager in the Major Leagues.

Frank Robinson made it clear from early on that he was interested in managing. The question was whether the door would open for him.

PROOF POSITIVE

Frank Robinson did get an opportunity to manage in 1968, when he was just 33 years old. But he wasn't tabbed to manage the Reds or the Orioles or any other big league team. Robinson's first managerial stint was at the helm of the Santurce Crabbers in the Puerto Rican winter baseball league. Here he would gain invaluable experience while managing a team that included several major league ballplayers, including Jim Palmer, Robinson's Oriole teammate.'

By 1968, Robinson learned quickly how much he still had to learn as a manager. "My biggest problem the first year in Puerto Rico—which probably took me two or three years to work out fully—was in handling pitchers," he wrote in *Extra Innings*, his 1988 autobiography. "Elrod Hendricks, my Oriole teammate and my Santurce catcher, told me, 'Frank, I think you have hated pitchers for so long as a player that you have trouble relating to them as a manager.'"

Robinson's reaction to Hendrick's criticism: "He was right."

Regardless of any flaws he exhibited as a manager, Robinson clearly knew how to push the right buttons to motivate the Crabbers. At one point the team won 14 games in a row on its way to a runaway pennant victory.

The Crabbers had by far the strongest team in the league that winter. Robinson's achievement, in the words of *Sport Magazine*, was that "he didn't mishandle it. Like Mayo Smith and Red Schoendienst and Casey Stengel and Walter Alston, he won when he should have won."

For several seasons, Robinson played baseball in the summer and managed in Puerto Rico in the winter. Every year, he waited for the call to come, telling him he would become the first African-American manager of a major league team.

The call finally came in 1975, from Cleveland.

AT LAST

The Cleveland Indians finished three consecutive mediocre seasons with manager Ken Aspromonte. When Aspromonte was fired after the 1974 season, the Indians wasted no time in getting Frank Robinson to be their new manager—and a player as well.

In the press conference that followed the announcement, Robinson said, "If I had one wish I was sure would be granted, it would be that Jackie Robinson could be here, seated alongside me, today." But it could not be: Jackie Robinson had died in 1972, still bitter over how long it was taking baseball to name an African-American manager.

Commissioner Bowie Kuhn also attended the press conference. "Now that it had happened," he said, "I'm not going to get up and shout that this is something for baseball to be exceptionally proud of, because it is so long overdue."

After the furor of publicity died down, Frank Robinson settled down to try to improve

the Indians. On Opening Day in Cleveland, he showed not only that he had his team ready to play, but also that he wasn't done as a player. In the Indians' exciting 5–3 victory over the Yankees, Robinson stepped to the plate in the first inning and slugged a home run. "Wow, will miracles never cease?" he asked himself as he rounded third base.

Robinson's tenure with the Indians was productive but ultimately frustrating. He piloted the team to an above-.500 record in 1976—the first time they'd had more wins than losses in a season since 1968—but the team was never able to take the next step to excellence.

In a larger sense, though, Robinson was a huge success. By paving the way, he opened the door to other nonwhite managers. Recent years have seen, for example, Cito Gaston's Toronto Blue Jays win back-to-back World Championships, Dusty Baker pilot the San Francisco Giants to the playoffs, and Felipe Alou brilliantly manage the undermanned Montreal Expos.

Baseball still has a way to go before its managerial pool is as ethnically diverse as it should be. But the game owes Frank Robinson a great debt for proving to those who wouldn't believe it that nonwhite men have what it takes to manage major league baseball teams.

HEADLINES ANNOUNCED that Robinson would manage the Cleveland Indians, an impressive piece of news since he was the first African American to manage a major league team.

WITH THE DOOR OPENED by Robinson, other black managers followed in his footsteps. Cito Gaston was one of them; he shepherded the Toronto Blue Jays to two consecutive World Championships.

LUCKY 7

On June 21, 1970, Detroit shortstop Cesar Gutierrez became the first player of the modern era to record seven hits in seven at bats in the Tigers 12-inning victory over the Cleveland Indians. The only player to accomplish that feat in a nine-inning game was Pirates second baseman Rennie Stennett. He turned the trick on September 16, 1975 in the Pirates' 22-0 drubbing of the Cubs. Stennett recorded hits against four of the five Cub pitchers that day, including brothers Paul and Rick Reuschel. Stennett's record wasn't the only one set that day. The Cubs gave up the most runs ever in a shutout loss.

MOST UNLIKELY TO SUCCEED

W ho was the first ballplayer to have seven hits in seven at bats in a single major league game in the modern era?

It's easy to come up with a list of plausible candidates: Ty Cobb, Tony Gwynn, Rogers Hornsby, Ted Williams, Stan Musial, and Babe Ruth all leap to mind.

All these were likely candidates to go 7 for 7 in a game, but the truth is, none of them ever

"SOMETIMES YOU HAVE TO BE LUCKY"

did. No, the first hitter in the 20th century to get seven hits in a single game was Cesar Gutierrez.

Cesar who? Cesar Gutierrez, who played just 223 games in the Majors in his four-year career. Whose lifetime batting average was .235. Who got more than 72 at bats in a season just once.

In 1970, Gutierrez was playing shortstop with the Detroit Tigers. He'd hit .245 in a handful of games with the Tigers the year before, and had gone on to win the shortstop job in spring training of 1970. "Everybody wants to hit .300," he said realistically that spring, "but I think I help this club if I can finish with .260 or .265."

Unfortunately, although Gutierrez started the season hot, getting his batting average up to .299, he then went into a terrible slump. When his average had plummeted to .211, Tiger manager Mayo Smith benched him.

Gutierrez returned to the line-up in mid-June. On June 21, just a few days after his return to play, he started a game against the Cleveland Indians. "Watch me get two hits," he told teammate Willie Horton. Horton asked why he should stop at two—perhaps he could even get four hits.

Gutierrez got the four hits Horton was asking for, but he didn't stop there. He looped a single to center in the first inning, singled to left in the third, hit an infield single to shortstop in the fifth, doubled to left in the seventh, singled to right in the eighth, and

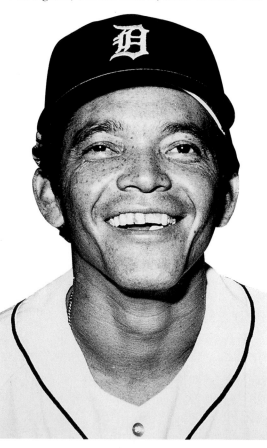

Cesar Gutierrez	
1970 Season Stats	
Games Played	135
At Bats	415
Runs	40
Hits	101
Doubles	11
Triples	6
Home Runs	0
RBI	22
Batting Average	.243
Stolen Bases	4

DETROIT TIGERS' CESAR GUTIERREZ delivered seven hits in seven at bats in a 12-inning game in 1970, setting a major league record.

beat out a grounder to shortstop in the 10th. This made him 6-for-6.

Then, in the 12th inning, he followed Mickey Stanley's tie-breaking home run with a grounder that went off the glove of Indians pitcher Phil Hennigan. The ball ricocheted to third baseman Graig Nettles, but his throw to first was too late to catch the hustling Gutierrez. That made him 7-for-7.

"Sometimes you have to be lucky," was Gutierrez' comment after the game. "Never in my life did I ever think of a record."

RENNIE'S DAY

Five years after Cesar Gutierrez' feat, another player went Gutierrez one better. This time, it was a hitter who might have been expected to have a big day: Rennie Stennett. By 1975 he had become an outstanding defensive second baseman for the Pittsburgh Pirates and a consistent .280 hitter.

In September 1975, the Pirates were engaged in a nip-and-tuck pennant race with the Philadelphia Phillies. Every game counted, including the game on September 16 against the Chicago Cubs.

It didn't take long, however, for the Pirates to realize that this game was going to go in their win column. They scored nine runs in the first inning (Cubs starter Rick Reuschel retired only one of the nine men he faced), and were on their way to an astounding 22–0 shellacking of the hapless Cubs.

In that nine-run first inning, Rennie Stennett came up twice, stroking first a double and then a single to right field. When he went to play second base in the bottom half of the inning, umpire Dutch Rennert told him he was on his way to a four-hit game.

Like Willie Horton talking to Cesar Gutierrez, Rennert barely knew the half of it. Stennett came up next in the third inning, and singled to center. Then, in the fifth inning, the Pirates scored six more runs, and *again* Stennett came up twice. Once again he took advantage, doubling to center and singling to right.

Rennie Stennett was now 5-for-5, and the game was still only in the fifth inning. At this point umpire Dutch Rennert pointed out that Stennett might have a six-hit game. "The umpire gave me the idea that I might do something big," Stennett said.

Again, though, Rennert was underestimating Rennie, who came up in the seventh inning and singled for his sixth hit of the game. The other Pirate batters kept the game going long enough that, amazingly, Stennett had yet another at bat, his seventh, in the eighth inning.

This time he slammed a drive to right. "I thought the ball was a hit, then it started to rise and I wasn't sure," he said. But on this day, he needn't have worried. The ball bounced in front of outfielder Champ Summers, and then bounced past him all the way to the wall.

Stennett wound up with a triple. He had become the first modern-era ballplayer ever to go 7-for-7 in a nine-inning game.

As he stood on third, Pirates manager Danny Murtaugh sent in a pinch runner for him. If ever a player deserved a breather, it was Rennie Stennett on September 16, 1975.

FIVE YEARS AFTER Gutierrez' feat, Rennie Stennett, of the Pittsburgh Pirates, went one better. He hit seven times in seven at bats, but did it in a regular nine-inning game.

Rennie Stennett
1975 Season Stats

Games Played	148
At Bats	616
Runs	89
Hits	176
Doubles	25
Triples	7
Home Runs	7
RBI	62
Batting Average	.286
Stolen Bases	5

FAIR, FAIR, FAIR, FAIR!

Any baseball fan will remember where they were in 1975 when Carlton Fisk's towering clout cleared Fenway's Green Monster, fair by the slimmest of margins. Even if you didn't see the game, the image of Fisk steering the ball into fair territory will endure forever. His homer forced a seventh game with the Reds that year. Alas for Red Sox fans (and Yankee fans the next year), Cincinnati's Big Red Machine was not to be derailed.

GOOD NEWS FOR BASEBALL

Boston Red Sox fan Eileen Fisher comes up lucky. After waiting all night at Fenway Park, equipped with sleeping bag, she gets tickets for the 1975 World Series against the Cincinnati Reds.

Maybe it was a matchup of two charter teams that produced the magic. For there was indeed magic to the 1975 World Series, played between the Cincinnati Reds and Boston Red Sox, both charter members of their respective leagues.

The Reds were baseball's "Big Red Machine," spurred by a powerful line-up featuring Johnny Bench, Pete Rose, Joe Morgan,

George Foster, and Tony Perez. The Red Sox, carrying the "Curse of the Bambino" since they had sold Babe Ruth to the Yankees in 1920, had a team led by Carl Yastrzemski, Carlton Fisk, Jim Rice, Fred Lynn, and Dwight Evans. (Since the Ruth trade, the Yankees had won 20 world championships, the Sox, none.)

Baseball needed a little magic in 1975. The sport had been criticized by the media for seven or eight years. The media liked to say that baseball wasn't "violent enough for our times," was "too slow," or even that it had been "replaced by football as the 'National Pastime.'"

And although the game's dedicated fans were its primary defenders, it was true that attendance had been flat, and many of the great retired stars of the '50s and '60s had not been replaced by worthy successors. The game's marketing efforts had improved, in some cases with resistance (night World Series games being a prime example). But new fans were hard to come by: The fan base was not growing.

Thus the '75 World Series would presumably be another Fall Classic fighting for attention, and the good news for baseball was that, indeed, attention it gained.

Both the Reds, managed by Sparky Anderson, and the Red Sox, managed by Darrell Johnson, had swept their League Championship Series. Both had three days off before the World Series and the opportunity to start their well-rested aces and let the Series evolve on an equal footing.

FIGHTING THE CURSE OF THE BAMBINO

The teams split the first two games at Fenway Park, and then the Reds captured two of three at Riverfront Stadium, taking the Series back to Boston for the sixth game. The Red Sox needed to win twice to break their World Championship jinx.

At this point, weather entered into the picture, causing three consecutive rainouts

A CENTERPIECE of the 1975 Boston team, catcher Carlton Fisk crushes a home run in the second game of the World Series. He would hit another, more critical homer that Series—at the end of Game Six.

following the travel day. It could be said that the attention span of the general public was being tested. Game Six would now come after a four-day layoff.

Those who waited it out would be rewarded with one of the greatest games ever played.

Luis Tiant was the Bosox starter, a matador on the pitching mound with his body-twisting, deceptive deliveries. He was quickly staked to a 3–0 lead on a first inning home run by Fred Lynn. Lynn would be named both MVP and Rookie of the Year for 1975, a remarkable feat. Some were already calling him the new "Joe DiMaggio."

But when Lynn hit the outfield wall running down a drive by Ken Griffey in the fifth, the Reds found the game tied, 3–3.

In the seventh, Foster's double led to a 5–3 Cincy lead, and then Cesar Geronimo homered in the eighth to put the Reds up 6–3,

"THIS IS SOME KIND OF GAME."

In the bottom of the 12th inning of Game Six, Carlton Fisk slammed a long shot to left field. If it stayed fair, Boston would win and go on to Game Seven. Fisk knew how close he was, as he waved and waved, urging the ball to stay in fair territory.

and leave them just six outs away from a World Championship.

But in the last of the eighth, Boston pinch hitter Bernie Carbo slugged a dramatic three-run homer to tie the game. The thrill of the moment was all over Bernie's face as he crossed the plate. He was a former Red, and this was the biggest single moment of his career. He had saved the Red Sox from defeat, at least for the moment.

MIDNIGHT PLAY

And so, at 6–6, the teams perservered through the ninth, the 10th and the 11th. No one was scoring, but the nation was discovering the thrill of baseball at its best. The tension was enormous—every inning was sudden death for the Sox. And for the Reds, well, as Rose said to Fisk when he batted late in the game, "This is some kind of game."

In the 11th, Morgan belted what looked like a home run, but Evans made a spectacular catch in front of the right field stands, and fired to first for a double play! On they would play.

And now, the clock moved past midnight. Throughout the country, people were making late night phone calls. "Turn on the game! Turn on the game!" Now it was the 12th. The Reds failed to score, and Fisk came to bat to face reliever Pat Darcy. On the clock, it said 12:33.

The first pitch was high for a ball. And then Fisk swung and sent one high into the night sky toward the left field foul pole. Fair or foul, fair or foul? Fisk did what he could, and like a bowler coaching a strike, he

moved his body and waved his arms to coax the ball fair. And then, with a plunk against metal, the ball hit the foul pole and settled back on the field.

Home run! Home run! The Red Sox won it 7–6, and Fisk, the native New Englander, rode triumphant around the bases.

Yes, the Reds would win the next day, and the "Curse of the Bambino" would continue. But people would talk about Game Six, and about the 1975 World Series, all winter long and for years to come.

A MASSIVE CROWD assembled midday in the Fountain Square area in Cincinnati, to honor the 1975 World Series victors.

OUTFIELD ASSIST

On April 25, 1976, Cubs outfielder Rick Monday became an American hero. During the fifth inning of the game between the Cubs and Dodgers, two people ran into shallow left field determined to burn an American flag. As players and fans stood in amazement, Monday ran toward the protesters. Their first match blew out in the wind, giving Monday a chance to grab the flag before they could light another one. He presented the flag to Dodger pitcher Doug Rau and returned to his position amid a standing ovation.

BASEBALL AND AMERICA

Major league baseball has always been an essential part of American life. Put in the same category as hot dogs and apple pie, it has been with us through good times and bad, through the Great Depression and two world wars. Baseball has always been there for us.

How essential is baseball? When America came under attack at Pearl Harbor and entered World War II, there were many voices that called for the game to be suspended for the duration of the war. It seemed a frivolous pursuit to continue while American men were dying overseas.

The owners of the major league teams declared themselves prepared to shut down, if that was what President Franklin Roosevelt desired. In early 1942, just a few weeks after the attack at Pearl Harbor, Judge Kenesaw Mountain Landis, the commissioner of baseball, communicated the owners' feelings in a letter to the president.

If, at this moment, President Roosevelt had requested that play be suspended, there would have been no baseball for four seasons. But the president chose another course. In one of the most famous announcements ever given about baseball, he responded in a letter to Judge Landis:

I honestly feel that it would be best for the country to keep baseball going. There will be fewer people unemployed and everybody will work longer hours and harder than ever before.

And that means that they ought to have a chance for recreation and for taking their minds off their work even more than before.

Baseball provides a recreation which does not last over two hours or two hours

RICK MONDAY, whose heroics on the field would earn him a place in baseball history, had a 19-year career in the Major Leagues. He played with the Cubs from 1972 to 1976.

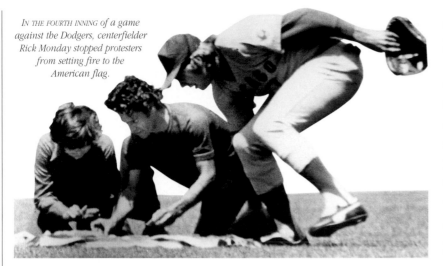

IN THE FOURTH INNING of a game against the Dodgers, centerfielder Rick Monday stopped protesters from setting fire to the American flag.

MONDAY'S HEROIC ACT was hailed by fans, teammates, and commentators alike. Below, he poses for cameras.

and a half, and which can be got for very little cost. . . .

Here is another way of looking at it—if 300 teams use 5,000 to 6,000 players, these players are a definite recreational asset to at least 20,000,000 of their fellow citizens— and that in my judgment is thoroughly worthwhile.

With every best wish,
Very sincerely yours,
Franklin D. Roosevelt

This response, known as the Green Light Letter, kept baseball going, while also reaffirming its place in American society. But, while the game kept on, many great and lesser players—including Ted Williams, Joe DiMaggio, Hank Greenberg, Bob Feller, and dozens of others—joined the military. When the Korean and Vietnamese conflicts followed, the game provided a continuing solace from the upheavals of the real world.

But it wasn't until 1976 that a ballplayer got to show his love for his country and its flag on the ballfield itself.

MONDAY'S MOMENT

The game took place on April 25 in Los Angeles' Dodger Stadium. The Dodgers were playing the Chicago Cubs, and the game proceeded uneventfully until the fourth inning. Then, suddenly, Cubs center fielder Rick Monday saw an adult and a child climb out of the stands into shallow leftfield.

"I saw these clowns come on the field, and I didn't know what they were doing," Monday said after the game. "I thought they were out there just to prance around."

But the two had something else in mind. As fans and players watched in amazement, they bent over the field and began to unroll an American flag. "They spread the flag out like a picnic blanket," said Monday. "I was just going to run them over until I saw them with the can of lighter fluid. I could see that they were going to try to burn it."

As they lit a match, Monday raced over from center field. "If you're going to burn the flag, don't do it in front of me," he said. "I've been to too many veterans' hospitals and seen too many broken bodies of guys trying to protect it."

The protesters' first match blew out in the wind. As they tried to light another one, Monday grabbed the flag away from them, took it into the infield, and handed it over to Dodger pitcher Doug Rau. The protesters were removed from the field, while the flag was taken into the dugout and to safety.

When Monday next came to bat, he received a standing ovation from Dodger fans. "They were cheering for the flag," he said.

MR. OCTOBER

Through the first five games of the 1977 World Series with the Dodgers, Yankee slugger Reggie Jackson was having a fine series. In Game Six, with the Yankees up three games to two, Jackson earned his nickname. Jackson homered on three consecutive pitches from three different pitchers, to put the game, and the Series, away. Jackson was the first player to hit three home runs in a World Series game since Babe Ruth turned the trick in 1926 and 1928. He was an easy choice for the Series MVP and the nickname, "Mr. October."

REGGIE'S EARLY YEARS

Was there ever a player who invited pressure as much as Reggie Jackson did? It is unlikely. He did it with the force of his personality. And few players have ever met high expectations better than he did.

Reggie was one of the big stars of the game beginning in the late '60s. Despite playing in the small market of Oakland, he made himself into one of baseball's best known players, helping the Athletics to five consecutive division titles and three consecutive World Championships, winning an MVP award, hitting a historic home run over the roof of Tiger Stadium in an All-Star Game, and even, early in his career, making a serious challenge to Roger Maris' single-season home run record, even though he fell short at the end. He was, after all was said and done, a guy you paid to see.

SLUGGER REGGIE JACKSON began his major league career with the Kansas City Royals and Oakland Athletics and quickly distinguished himself as a young hitter. He regularly hit over 30 home runs in a season and hit over 40 in 1969 and 1980.

He hit with power, he stole bases, and his strikeouts, while many, were part of the show.

In 1974, Reggie's Oakland teammate, Catfish Hunter, became baseball's first million-dollar free agent, taking advantage of a missed payment to be so declared by an arbitrator. Two years later, with a formal free agency structure in place and a market value having been established for a big star, Reggie was in the spotlight in the game's first class of free agents. He had spent the '76 season in Baltimore, did not sign, and now was able to sit back and await his dollars.

"If I ever played in New York," he said, "they'd name a candy bar after me."

It was a funny, smart, and prophetic comment made by a player who was positioning himself to take big dollars in the big market town of New York. Although Jackson had impressive offers from many teams, George Steinbrenner wanted Reggie, and Reggie wanted the Yankees. Not only did Reggie join the team in 1977, but also in that first season, a candy bar—the "Reggie" Bar—was indeed introduced in New York.

CONTROVERY ALL SEASON

For Reggie, however, that first season of a five-year contract was not a happy one. Before he even reported to spring training, he told a national magazine that he was the

EARNING HIS NICKNAME MR. OCTOBER, Yankee outfielder Reggie Jackson blasts his third home run in Game Six of the 1977 World Series against the Dodgers (right).

"straw that stirs the drink—[Thurman] Munson [the Yankees' popular team captain and 1976 MVP] can only stir it bad." This immediately set him on the outs with his new teammates.

He also failed to establish a good relationship with his fiery manager, Billy Martin, who didn't want him on the team and considered him to be "George's boy." When Reggie failed

TEAMMATES Thurman Munson (left) and Chris Chambliss (middle) congratulate Reggie Jackson on his third home run in Game Six of the 1977 World Series.

to hustle after a fly ball in Boston, Billy pulled him out of the game, and the two almost came to blows in the dugout on national television. He was in the manager's doghouse all season, and Martin embarrassed him again in the League Championship Series, benching him in the final game because of a brief batting slump.

A pinch hit by Reggie late in that game helped the Yankees win the pennant, and they found themselves facing their historic rivals, the Los Angeles Dodgers, in the World Series. For Reggie, it was a return to October Baseball—and he would soon earn the nickname of "Mr. October."

Reggie's slump continued in the first two games, with just one bloop single in Yankee Stadium. But he came alive in the middle games, homering in the fourth game and again in his last time up in the fifth. Now he was home in Yankee Stadium, the "House that Ruth Built," with the Yanks needing one victory for their first world championship in 15 years. The network cameras were rolling, and Reggie was up for the moment.

A NIGHT TO REMEMBER

Game Six, October 18, 1977. He walked his first time up, and then took Burt Hooton's fourth-inning pitch and homered to right, to put the Yankees on top, 4–3. The scoreboard urged the fans on, posting REG-GIE, REG-GIE, and the fans responded.

In the fifth, Elias Sosa was on the mound. First pitch to Jackson, and there it went, another two-run homer to right, deeper than the first one, and the Yankees now led, 7–3!

In the last of the eighth, Reggie came up again, facing knuckleballer Charlie Hough. And once again, there it went, soaring deep into center, deeper than the others! It was a three-home run game, a Yankee championship, and Reggie became the first man to ever hit five home runs in a World Series. He would be Mr. October forever after.

JACKSON WAVES HIS CAP to the fans at Yankee Stadium, acknowledging their ovation, as he returns to his outfield position following his third consecutive home run in Game Six. The Yankees victory in that game clinched the 1977 World Series against the Dodgers.

BUCKY'S BAT

*The defending champion New York Yankees were 8½ games out of first place on August 20, 1978.
Under manager Bob Lemon, the Yanks put on one of the best comebacks in history and by season's end were
tied with the Red Sox. In a one-game playoff Bucky Dent became an unlikely hero when he belted
a three-run home run to put the Yanks up for good. The ultimate irony for Red Sox fans is that Dent hit only
five homers all year. And this last homer of the season was the one that really counted.*

*BILLY MARTIN, manager of the
Yankees during the first part of the
1978 season, argues with home
plate umpire Jim McKean in
Oakland. The fiery manager didn't
last through July with the Yankees.*

TEAM TURMOIL

After years of mediocrity and a disappointing four-game loss to the Cincinnati Reds in the 1976 World Series, the 1977 Yankees had finally reached the pinnacle once again. Riding the hot bat of Reggie Jackson, they took a World Series championship over the Dodgers. It had been

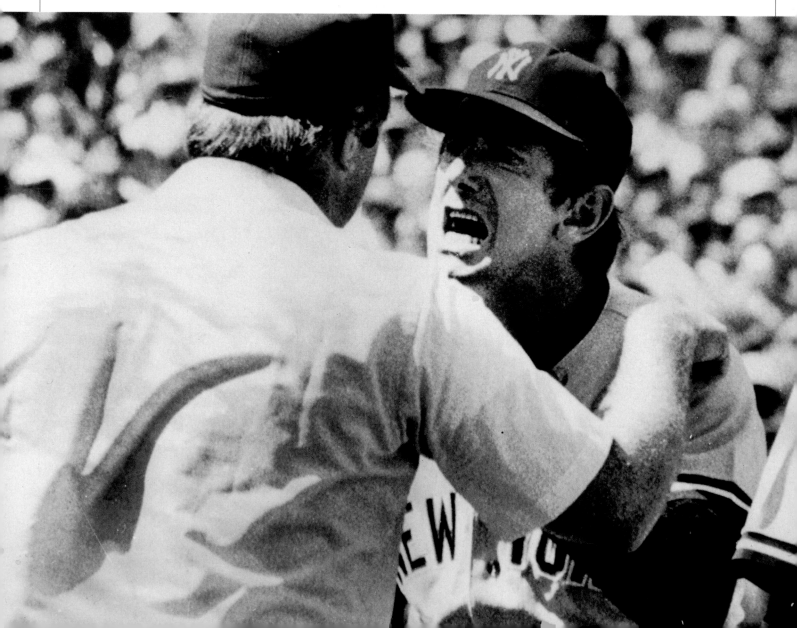

a tumultuous year for the Yankees—punctuated by a running battle between hotheaded manager Billy Martin and moody superstar Reggie Jackson—but when the season ended in a championship, both Martin and Jackson predicted even greater achievements ahead. "Next year is going to be super," Martin said. "We'll win it again next year."

MANAGEMENT DIFFICULTIES

Always intense and unpredictable, Martin began the 1978 season seeming as happy as he'd ever been. After all, he'd piloted his team to its first World Championship since 1962, and the 1978 team had improved itself by signing the overpowering relief pitcher Goose Gossage. Plus, he and Reggie Jackson had seemingly patched up the differences that had roiled the team and fascinated the public the year before.

But 1978 didn't turn out to be as easy as Martin hoped it would be. The team started slowly, and couldn't ever seem to get itself righted. Stars Thurman Munson and Willie Randolph got hurt, and so did staff ace Catfish Hunter and other pitchers. Reggie Jackson's eyes were bothering him—and as the season went on, so was Reggie's relationship with Billy Martin.

The team's low points came in mid-July. First Reggie Jackson was suspended by Martin for bunting against orders. Then, a week later, Martin made some insulting comments about Jackson and Yankee owner George Steinbrenner and resigned under pressure. At the lowest of low points, the Yankees trailed the Boston Red Sox by 14½ games, as the Sox—led by the brilliant hitting of Carl Yastrzemski, Jim Rice, and Fred Lynn—seemed to win every day.

The Yankees were out of it.

No, they weren't.

THE BOSTON MASSACRE

Under the calm, steady hand of new manager Bob Lemon, the Yankees began

CALM AND RELAXED, manager Bob Lemon ushers in the new 1979 Yankee season. Lemon led the New York team to a World Series victory the previous year, following the demise of former manager Billy Martin.

to win. At the same time, the Red Sox began to show some chinks in their armor. Their stars' bats cooled, and their pitching (thin to begin with) began to wilt in the midsummer heat. In one eight-day stretch, the Yankees gained six games on the Sox, part of a long, steady catchup to the leading team.

The Yankees had many heroes during their long comeback, but the man who carried the team on his back was pitcher Ron Guidry. Guidry hadn't gotten a real chance to pitch in the Majors until he was 26 years old—but after a strong 1977 season, he was phenomenal in 1978, going 25–3 with nine shutouts and a 1.74 earned run average.

Throughout August, Guidry and the Yankees climbed closer and closer to the Red Sox. Finally, in September, with the Sox' lead down to four games, the two teams played a pair of series on successive weekends. The first series, played in Boston, was forever after known as the Boston Massacre: The Yankees swept the four games, outscoring the Sox 42–9. When the Yankees went on to win two out of three games played between the two teams in

New York, they actually had a 2½-game lead over the Sox.

It's a testament to the Red Sox' resilience that they didn't just fold right there. Instead, they battled back, winning 12 of their last 14 games. On the final day of the season, the Yankees lost and the Sox won, leaving the two teams in a flat-footed tie.

This meant that, after the whole exhausting, thrilling season, the two teams had to play a one-game play off to see who would be crowned Eastern Division champions.

EVEN THOUGH PITCHING ACE RON GUIDRY wasn't in his best form the night the Yankees squared off against the Red Sox in a one-game divisional playoff, his performance throughout the season was remarkable. He went 25-3, with an ERA of 1.74.

BUCKY'S MOMENT

October 2, 1978.

The Yankees and Red Sox squared off on a sunny, crisp fall day before a packed house at Fenway Park in Boston. "Today is the biggest ballgame of my life," said Carl Yastrzemski before it began.

The Yankees sent Ron Guidry to pitch against Mike Torrez, and it was clear from the outset that Guidry didn't have his best stuff. In the second inning, Yaz slammed a home run, and in the sixth Jim Rice drove in a run with a single. The Yankees threatened, but could not score off of Torrez, so after six innings the score was 2–0, Red Sox.

But in the seventh inning, the Yankees put two men on against Torrez. The next batter was light-hitting Bucky Dent, and the count quickly went to 0–2. But the next pitch caught too much of the plate, and Dent sent a high drive toward Fenway's fabled left-field wall, the Green Monster. Carl Yastrzemski went back to the wall, but the ball was out of reach, landing in the netting above the Monster.

"As I rounded second and third and was trotting toward home, Fenway was dead silent," Dent said later. Suddenly, shockingly, the Yankees had a 3–2 lead, with only three innings to go.

The Yankees quickly added two runs (one of them on a home run by Reggie Jackson), but the Sox came back with two of their own in the eighth inning. Going into the ninth, the score stood at 5–4, Yankees.

The Sox put the tying run, Rick Burleson, on base with one out against Goose Gossage. The next batter, Jerry Remy, hit a wicked line drive to right field. The Yankees' Lou Piniella lost the ball in the sun, sticking his arms out and hoping the ball would bounce off of his body. Instead, it bounced right into his glove. Burleson, who had hesitated because he thought Piniella might catch the ball on the fly, had to stay at second, and Remy held at first.

Now Gossage had to face Jim Rice and Carl Yastrzemski. Rice hit a long fly ball that

fell into Piniella's glove just a few feet short of the stands. Burleson tagged up and moved to third.

With two outs, the tying run 90 feet from home, Yaz stepped to the plate. He took ball one, but on the next pitch he swung. The ball lofted up, in foul territory but playable. Yankee third baseman Graig Nettles gloved it for the final out.

Once again, the Yankees were headed to the World Series, and the Red Sox were headed home.

NOT KNOWN FOR HIS BAT, Bucky Dent surprised his teammates—and himself—when he slammed a three-run homer in the top of the seventh inning. The three runs gave the Yankees a lead that Boston just couldn't pull away from.

ALMOST .400

George Brett was one of the best all-around players of his generation. A career Kansas City Royal, he ended the 1980 season with a .390 batting average. Brett was batting .400 as late as September 19th, but injuries that limited him to 117 games took their toll. Still, Brett's batting average was the Major Leagues' highest since Ted Williams hit .406 in 1941. Three years before, another hitter came almost as close. Rod Carew hit .403 as late as June 26th, but finished the season with .388.

THE EVEREST OF STATISTICS

If you can hit .300 with some regularity, you're a good hitter. But if you can hit over .400—even once—you have to be a great hitter. No one ever lucked into a .400 average. In fact, every single player who hit .400 between 1900 and today is in the Hall of Fame, with just one exception. And that exception, Joe Jackson, would be in the Hall today if he hadn't allegedly helped throw the 1919 World Series with seven other members of the Chicago White Sox.

The height of the modern over-.400 frenzy took place in the 1920s and 1930s. This was the greatest hitters' era of all time, when an entire league might hit over .300 (as the National League did in 1930). George Sisler (twice), Rogers Hornsby (three times!), Ty Cobb, and Harry Heilmann all scaled the peak between 1920 and 1925. All these, and then, suddenly, no more. With the exception of Bill Terry's standout .401 average in 1930, plenty of hitters came close, but no one could reach .400.

That is, until Ted Williams came along. In 1941, Williams closed the season at

.406, the highest batting average since Hornsby's .424 in 1924.

Watching Ted Williams' feat, fans wondered if baseball was about to enter another golden age of .400 hitters. But it didn't happen. Williams came close to .400 again, batting .388 in 1957, but no one else did.

Not until 1977.

ONE SWEET SWING

The Minnesota Twins' Rod Carew was the perfect candidate to make a run at .400. From his third season (1969) up until his final two seasons, he consistently hit well over .300. Much as Tony Gwynn does today, Carew had an easy, economical swing that sent baseballs flying all over the park.

GEORGE BRETT THRILLED Kansas City fans for 21 years—his entire major league career. He finished 11 of those seasons with a batting average over .300 and ended his career with .305

Single-Season Batting Averages over .400—20th Century

Player	Year	Batting Average
Nap Lajoie	1901	.426
Rogers Hornsby	1924	.424
Ty Cobb	1911	.420
George Sisler	1922	.420
Ty Cobb	1912	.409
Joe Jackson	1911	.408
George Sisler	1920	.407
Ted Williams	1941	.406
Harry Heilmann	1923	.403
Rogers Hornsby	1925	.403
Rogers Hornsby	1922	.401
Ty Cobb	1922	.401
Bill Terry	1930	.401

ROD CAREW finished 15 of his 19 major league seasons with a batting average over .300. His career average was .328, with his lowest season dipping only to .273.

Carew himself knew exactly what he was capable of. "I get a kick out of watching a team defense me," he said in 1979. "A player moves two steps in one direction, and I hit it two steps the other way. It goes right by his glove. And I laugh."

Entering the 1977 season, though, even Carew couldn't have believed that he had any real chance of hitting .400. He was already past 30, a time when most ballplayers' skills start to fail, and his previous high had been .364 in 1974. (He did hit .366 in 1970, but played only 51 games that year.)

Yet Carew started 1977 as if he might hit .500. He was hitting .356 by the end of April, .388 by the middle of June, and .403 after a four-hit day on June 26.

But then the media took notice and descended on him. In *Carew,* his autobiography, he paints a chilling picture of what it feels like to be the focus of such intense attention. "People are calling my house so frequently that I have to change my number every two weeks," he wrote. "At times I couldn't even leave the clubhouse; the crush of people waiting for me was gigantic."

Unsurprisingly, Carew was bothered and distracted by the unrelenting media focus. His average dipped below .400 on July 11, later falling to a low of .374. Then the naturally brilliant hitter reasserted himself, ending the season at .388, matching Ted Williams' 1957 high.

GEORGE BRETT'S YEAR

By 1980, George Brett had already played six joyful, high-energy seasons with the Kansas City Royals. He'd proven himself to be a consistent .300 hitter—but, unlike Rod Carew, he never seemed likely to approach the .400 level. After all, his previous high (in 1976) had been .333, a fine average but not one to put any fear into the ghost of Rogers Hornsby.

Just as every one of Rod Carew's swings in 1977 seemed to produce a line drive base hit, in 1980 George Brett seemed to be playing at a different level. At first, .400 seemed like a ridiculous expectation, as Brett began the season injured. By the All-Star break he was batting just .337, on the way to his finest season but still no threat to the pantheon of hitting statistics.

After the All-Star break, though, Brett began hitting at the most torrid pace imaginable, despite continuing to battle assorted injuries. In little more than a month, he'd raised his average from .337 to .400, capping off his streak—as Carew had—with a four-hit game.

Then, in a duplication of what befell Carew three years earlier, Brett became the focus of magnified press scrutiny. Would he hit .400? Could he? Every day he had to contend with hordes of reporters and cameras, and the same questions were asked over and over. As late as September 19, he was still hitting over .400, but injuries and pressure finally took their toll. A stretch of three hits in 19 at-bats finally put .400 out of reach. He still finished at .390, by far the highest average of his Hall of Fame career.

Brett didn't blame the press for distracting him—he blamed himself for getting too wrapped up in the chase for .400. "I took the whole thing too seriously," he said later. "I just didn't enjoy myself very much during the last month, and I guess I play best when I enjoy myself."

BRETT PUSHED his batting average to over .401 during the 1980 season. However, he ended the season just shy of the magic number, at .390.

THE RISE
OF THE CLOSER

Along with relievers Sparky Lyle, Goose Gossage, and Bruce Sutter, Rollie Fingers helped change the way that teams use pitchers. With the expanded role of relievers in the 1970s, their importance to a team increased. While playing for Milwaukee in 1981, Rollie Fingers became the first reliever to win both the MVP and the Cy Young Award. Others to accomplish that feat were Detroit's Willie Hernandez in 1984 and Oakland's Dennis Eckersley in 1992.

THE WAY THINGS USED TO BE

Baseball teams have always needed to use relief pitchers. Early in the game's history, though, the relief pitcher was a last resort. Starters were expected to finish what they started, and were taken out mid-game only if they were injured or so ineffective that the manager simply had no other choice.

That philosophy allowed Cy Young to set one baseball record that almost surely will never be broken. During his career, Young started 815 games—and completed 749 of them. That's an average of more than 34 complete games a season for 22 years, compared to perhaps 10 complete games a year for even the best pitchers today.

Since relievers were called up only in case of irretrievable disaster, the role was perhaps the least respected on the team. No one wanted to be a reliever; everyone wanted to start.

Remarkably, the only pitchers who didn't mind coming in in relief were the staff pitching aces. When a starter was knocked out of the game with his team in the lead, the man who relieved him was often the team's best starter. This meant that, in addition to starting 40 games a season, Cy Young might be called to relieve two or three times in important spots. In 1896, for example, Young started 46 games, relieved in five, and led the league with three saves (though the statistic wasn't kept officially back then).

The first true relief ace was Fred "Firpo" Marberry, a superb pitcher for the Washington Senators. In the 1924 World Series, Marberry came in late to win a game, leading the *Washington Post* to declare, "World's Series heroes there have been without number, but Washington and the baseball world today acclaim one crowned in a fashion new and strange. Fred Marberry, six-foot Texan, won the second game of the 1924 post-season baseball classic on three pitched balls."

In doing so, Marberry stepped into the closer's role exactly as the team's best relief pitcher would do today. For many years, though, he remained a lonely pioneer.

THE NEW BREED

It wasn't until the 1950s that managers once again began to view relievers as important components of a winning team. Starters were no longer pitching 30 complete games a year, and it became obvious that populating the bullpen with has-beens and never-weres wasn't a good idea.

It took a while, though, for the new breed of relief pitcher to realize he wasn't being insulted by being asked to come out of the pen. For example, when the Yankees' Joe Page (a great reliever in the late 1940s) was first sent to the bullpen in 1947, he was bitterly disappointed, seeing it as punishment for poor pitching. "I didn't like the sound of being a

ROLLIE FINGERS STARTED his career with the Oakland A's and finished with the Milwaukee Brewers. He added spark and fire to any team's bullpen, and brought dominance to any pitching staff he was a part of.

FINGERS COULD BE RELIED ON for closing games, quickly and efficiently. He finished his career with 341 saves, the sixth all-time highest.

'relief pitcher,'" he said later. "Sounded like a first cousin to a second-stringer."

But when Page realized how often he could get into games, and how important he was to the Yankees' success—he helped lead them to a World Championship in 1947—he knew he'd found his niche. And this time, others followed suit.

TODAY'S STOPPER

The evolution of the closer didn't come to an end with the arrival of Joe Page, however. He and other closers of the 1950s and '60s—including Hoyt Wilhelm, the first pitcher to go to the Hall of Fame for his work as a relief pitcher—would often come into a game in the sixth or seventh inning and pitch the rest of the way.

Rollie Fingers, the Hall of Fame relief ace for the Oakland A's, San Diego Padres, and the Milwaukee Brewers in the 1970s and '80s was another workhorse, pitching as many as 134 innings in a season as a reliever. But he along with Bruce Sutter, Sparky Lyle, and Rich "Goose" Gossage, took the role of the closer to another level entirely. They made it the center of attention.

These were pitchers with personality. The Yankee Stadium organist played "Pomp and Circumstance" whenever Sparky Lyle strolled into a tight game, looking as if he didn't have a care in the world. Goose Gossage, on the other hand, looked dangerous— and batters facing his overpowering fastball certainly thought so too.

Rollie Fingers may have been the most colorful of all. With his free-spirited manner and manicured moustache, he cut a dashing figure on the mound. And, unlike many who came before him, there was no place he wanted to be but in the bullpen. "I just couldn't stand waiting every four days to pitch," he said. "You want to throw that ball right now."

When Fingers helped lead the A's to three consecutive World Championships (1972–74), and again when he won both the Cy Young and Most Valuable Player awards with Milwaukee in 1981, Rollie Fingers showed that good relief pitching was central to a team's success. Today, it's hard to imagine a successful team that doesn't have a dominant closer.

Top 10 Relievers
Most Lifetime Saves

Pitcher	Number of Saves
Lee Smith	478
John Franco	416
Dennis Eckersley	390
Jeff Reardon	367
Randy Myers	347
Rollie Fingers	341
Tom Henke	311
Rich Gossage	310
Bruce Sutter	300
Jeff Montgomery	304
Doug Jones	301

JOE PAGE often confronted similar odds as those he met when he entered this September 1949 game: bases loaded and only one out. He forced the first batter he faced to hit into a double play, retiring the side.

LEFTY

Not a particularly original name for a left-handed pitcher. But then again, this "Lefty" was one of the finest pitchers of his generation. Steve Carlton won the Cy Young Award a record-setting four times, besting Sandy Koufax's record three. In 1972 with the Phillies, possibly his most impressive season, Carlton won the pitching Triple Crown, leading the league in wins, ERA, and strikeouts. Most impressive was Carlton's win total. He was credited with 27 of the team's 59 wins that year.

YOUNG GUN

Most left-handed pitchers take far longer to develop than right-handers do. A righty like Dwight Gooden might sweep in and win 20 games while barely out of his teen years, but many lefties struggle with their control for years before solving the riddle and reaching their peak.

Sandy Koufax, perhaps the prime example, was in his seventh season before he attained the dominance that carried him into the Hall of Fame. Another, more recent, example is Ron Guidry, who was 26 before he started pitching well in the Majors.

UNUSUAL FOR LEFT-HANDED pitchers, Steve Carlton pitched well from the very beginning of his career. He was able to master his control early on.

But not Steve Carlton. Nicknamed "Lefty," Carlton was successful from the get-go, posting a 2.52 earned run average in limited work with the St. Louis Cardinals in 1965, when he was just 20 years old. He followed that debut with four straight good years, culminating in a 17–11 mark in 1969, when he also posted a dazzling 2.17 ERA and struck out 210 batters. Still just 24 years old, he had already ascended to the highest rank of pitchers in the National League.

His 1969 season was distinguished by what should have been one of the highlights of his career—but for one little problem. While he struck out 19 New York Mets in one game (then a major league record), he somehow managed to lose, 4–3, on a pair of two-run home runs by Ron Swoboda.

Carlton had gotten so far, so fast, largely because of his devastating slider, a fast breaking pitch that absolutely tied up batters. But then, in a pattern that would repeat itself in years to come, his slider deserted him in 1970—and his record plummeted to 10–19. "I was getting underneath the slider and releasing it improperly," he said later. "It gave me a sore arm before the year was over, so I decided to scrap it."

It's sobering to see how the command of just one pitch can affect a pitcher's success so markedly. Luckily for Carlton, his slider was back in 1971, and he blossomed to his best record yet: 20–9.

During his years with the Cardinals, Carlton had appeared in two World Series (in 1967 and '68). After the 1971 season, though, he got into a contract dispute with Cardinal management, and was unceremoniously shipped off to Philadelphia, home of one of the worst teams in the league.

Who could have guessed that he would have his finest season with that sorry team?

ONE AMAZING SEASON

In 1972, Steve Carlton won 27 games while losing just 10. He started 41 times and completed 30 games, a number more reminiscent of Cy Young than of modern-day pitchers. He threw eight shutouts and led the league in innings pitched (346), strikeouts (310), and ERA (1.97), thereby winning the Triple Crown.

By any standards, this is one of the greatest seasons any pitcher has had in the history of baseball. What makes it astounding—almost unbelievable—is that Carlton accomplished it while pitching for one of the worst teams of the past 50 years, a team that in 1972 won 59 games and lost 97.

Think about it. Steve Carlton's 27 victories made up 46 percent of his team's total wins for the year. Or look at it this way: Without Carlton, the Phillies went 32–87, a record worthy of the Mets during their woeful early seasons.

Usually, good pitchers on lousy teams struggle to win half their games, but somehow Carlton posted a record that a pitcher on a 100-win team would have been proud of. How did he do it?

Shortstop Larry Bowa, who played behind Carlton that year, gave an explanation in an interview. "When Lefty was on the mound, we always felt confident that we could win," Bowa said. "I guess we were trying to live up to his excellence."

TURNING THE PHILLIES AROUND

Fortunately for Steve Carlton, the Phillies improved from their dismal 1972 showing. They added a young third baseman named Mike Schmidt and other talented players, and by 1975 they were competing for the N.L.

East title. In 1976 they won 101 games and finished first in their division.

Carlton was a big part of the team's resurgence, of course. He won 20 games in 1976, and though the Phillies lost in the League Championship Series that year, everyone knew that the team would be competitive for years to come.

In fact, the Phillies won the National League East in both 1977 and 1978. Both times, however, they went no further, losing to the Dodgers in the play-offs. It began to seem as if Carlton and the Phillies might never be quite good enough.

Then came 1980, when Carlton was 35 years old. Carried by Schmidt's 48 home runs and Carlton's 24–9 record (which earned him the third of his four Cy Young Awards), the Phillies barely nipped the Montreal Expos to win the N.L. East yet again. This time, though, they managed to get past the Houston Astros in a tight N.L. Championship Series, with Carlton winning one game and pitching so well in another game that the Phillies eventually won in extra innings.

He was even better in the World Series against the Kansas City Royals. Starting two games, he won them both, striking out 17 men in 15 innings. When he won Game Six, 4–1, he had led the Phillies to their first-ever World Championship.

CARLTON HELPED LEAD the Philadelphia Phillies from their bleak 1972 season to the heights of their first World Series victory in 1980, a victory relished by the team in the photo above.

PRESIDENT EMERITUS WARREN GILES of the National league formally presents Steve Carlton with the Cy Young Award for the 1972 season with the Phillies. Carlton was responsible for nearly half of the team's wins that year, a year in which the Phillies ended up in last place.

RULE 1.10

As written, this rule prohibits using a sticky substance such as pine tar on a bat beyond 18 inches from the bottom. On July 24, 1983, Kansas City's George Brett learned this rule the hard way when, after hitting a two-run homer to give the Royals a lead over the Yankees in the ninth inning, he was called out because the pine tar on his bat exceeded the 18 inches. Brett was apparently using an illegal bat. A.L. President Lee MacPhail overruled his umpires, saying that Brett's bat did not violate the spirit of the rules, restored Brett's home run, and the last inning of the game was completed almost a month later, with the Royals winning.

GRIPPING THE BAT

As long as hitters have strode to the plate, carrying with them a bat made of sculpted ash wood, with the goal of whacking a baseball to the far reaches of a

A HUGE ARGUMENT between Kansas City Royal player George Brett and umpire Tim McClelland ensues over Brett's use of pine tar on his bat. McClelland invalidated Brett's two-run homer, which gave the Yankees a 4-3 win.

ballpark, they have tried just about anything to make their grip on the bat as firm as possible.

We've all seen batters lose hold of the bat. At the end of a vicious swing, the bat goes flying, sometimes almost cutting off the legs of the pitcher or an infielder, other times even reaching the stands near homeplate. It's not surprising—hitters have to swing as hard as they can, often with sweaty palms on hot summer days.

The preferred choice of grip-improvement is pine tar, a sticky substance made through (in the words of Merriam-Webster's dictionary) "destructive distillation of the wood of the pine tree." In other words, pine wood is boiled down until all that remains is sticky goop.

The dictionary goes on to say that the primary uses of pine tar are "in roofing and soaps and in the treatment of skin diseases." But Merriam-Webster forgot one more place to find pine tar: on the handles of baseball bats.

On July 24, 1983, this became the most famous use of all.

GEORGE BRETT'S MISTAKE

By 1983, the New York Yankees and Kansas City Royals had years of intense competition behind them. Both teams had been among the best in the league since the mid-1970s. The Yankees had defeated the Royals in the 1976 American League Championship Series (ALCS), and then repeated in 1977 and 1978, on their way to back-to-back World Series victories. The Royals had returned the favor in 1980, sweeping the Yankees in the ALCS before losing to the Philadelphia Phillies in the World Series.

So when they faced each other at Yankee Stadium in 1983, the two teams knew each other very well. In particular, the Yankees knew that the Royals rose or fell on the back of their superstar third baseman, George Brett. A consistent .300 hitter with power, Brett played the game with unparalleled fire and enthusiasm, seeming to be in the middle of the action in nearly every game.

So it was no surprise to find him stepping to the plate in the ninth inning of that July 24 game against the Yankees. There were two outs, a man on first, and the Royals trailed, 4–3. Brett was facing Yankee closer Goose Gossage, whom he'd faced in countless high-tension confrontations in the past.

Nor could anyone have been surprised when Brett smashed a two-run home run off Gossage, circling the bases to give the Royals a 5–4 lead.

But wait! As Brett crossed the plate, Yankee manager Billy Martin rushed out to confront the umpires. His contention: Brett had hit the home run while using an illegal bat. In particular, the bat violated Rule 1.10 (b), which dictated that pine tar not be allowed to extend more than 18 inches up from the bat handle.

The umpires studied the bat and measured the extent of the pine tar. Then, finding that the pine tar did, in fact, exceed the allowable 18 inches, umpire Tim McClelland raised his arm and signaled "out." Suddenly, shockingly, the game was over, and the Yankees were declared 4–3 winners.

Seeing his home run and the victory taken away, George Brett came exploding out of the dugout. He engaged in one of the most spectacular bursts of rage ever seen on the field, and only some quick-thinking teammates kept him from assaulting the umpires.

In the melee, Royals' pitcher Gaylord Perry tried to spirit the offending bat away, but Yankee Stadium security retrieved it before it could disappear.

The Royals protested the game, of course, and the whole matter went off to the American League office for judgment.

SPIRIT OF THE LAW

The Royals argued to A.L. President Lee MacPhail that the excess pine tar in no way helped Brett hit the home run. The Yankees, while not disputing this, argued that a rule was a rule.

Four days later, MacPhail reached his judgment. Citing the spirit, if not the letter, of the law, he decreed that the home run counted, the Royals once again led, 5–4, in the ninth inning, and the remainder of the game would be played at some future time.

In making the decision, MacPhail agreed with the Royals' point of view. The pine tar on the barrel of the bat was no aid to gripping the bat, and didn't help the ball travel farther. He also pointed out that the original meaning of the rule was to keep the ball in play from being discolored by pine tar on the bat—and that a discolored ball actually helped the *pitcher*, by making it harder to see. Therefore, it was silly to deny Brett his home run for having too much pine tar on his bat. As a result of the controversy, the original rule was rewritten and renumbered as rule 1.10 (c).

The Yankees screamed bloody murder, but MacPhail's ruling stood. A few weeks later, the two teams played out the rest of the game. The disgruntled Yankees went down in order in the bottom of the ninth, the final score was 5–4, Royals, and the whole matter was finally laid to rest.

AMERICAN LEAGUE PRESIDENT Lee MacPhail reversed the umpire's decision that nullified Brett's home run. The Royals and the Yankees had to face off in a single inning weeks later to decide the game; the Yankees lost.

THE THREE-THOUSAND HIT CLUB

No career total means more to a major league hitter than reaching 3,000 hits. It requires a superb mix of skill, single-minded intensity, and good health—which is why only 23 players have ever reached that pinnacle. The most recent superstars to join the club are Tony Gwynn and Wade Boggs, who made their major league debut three months apart in 1982, and who garnered their 3000th hits just a day apart in August 1999!

CAREER PINNACLE

From the moment that baseball records began to be kept in the late 1800s, fans and other players have distinguished between single-game and single-season records and those accumulated over a lifetime. For many, the most impressive achievements are those that are totaled up at the end of a great career.

As *Baseball Magazine*'s F. C. Lane put it more than 75 years ago: "A player's highest bid for fame must not rest upon the narrow foundation of a single season, still less upon the happenings of a single game. . . . Only the player who is great year after year and whose whole career is a masterpiece should properly rank among baseball's immortals."

Among lifetime achievements, perhaps the most coveted of all is to reach 3,000 hits. Throughout the

Tony Gwynn, who finished all but one of his 19 seasons to date batting above .300, hit a career milestone—his 3,000th hit—in August of 1999.

history of the Major Leagues, only 23 players have gotten there. Of those 23, 17 have reached the Hall of Fame. Pete Rose, the all-time hits leader, is not in the Hall because of his lifetime banishment from baseball. The other five (Dave Winfield, Paul Molitor, Tony Gwynn, Wade Boggs, and Eddie Murray) will likely march right in as soon as they become eligible.

By early in this century, players already considered 3,000 hits to be the finishing touch to a great career. Hall of Fame outfielder "Wahoo" Sam Crawford wrote a whole article in *Baseball Magazine* describing his struggle to reach the pinnacle. By 1916, Crawford was only 149 shy of 3,000—but then, suddenly, his skills eroded. Crawford got only 92 hits in 1916, and then he found himself playing only occasionally in 1917.

"I will admit that it has been my chief ambition for many years to make three thousand hits," Crawford wrote that year. "It is an unpleasant experience to think about that ambition now as I stand on the very verge and cannot see the certainty of its realization." Crawford got only 18 hits in 1917, his final season, and fell 39 hits shy of the grail.

For a pair of superstars who entered 1999 close to 3,000 hits, though, Sam Crawford's sad fate was never an issue. Almost from the moment they entered the Major Leagues, Tony Gwynn and Wade Boggs seemed destined to reach the exclusive club.

LOCKED-IN GWYNN

Tony Gwynn played his first game with the San Diego Padres in 1982, and from the start he was clearly something special. He got his first hit (a double to left-center) in that first game against the Philadelphia Phillies. As Gwynn stood on second base, the Phillies' Pete Rose (by then far past 3,000 hits himself) came up to him and said, "Congratulations. Don't catch me in one night."

By the end of 1984, when he was just 24 years old, it was obvious that Gwynn would have a career that could be matched up against any other great player's. He hit .351 that season, with 213 hits. "He's amazing," said his manager, Dick Williams. "He spots a hole and hits the ball through it."

Gwynn followed with a parade of other magnificent years. In 1987, for example, he hit .370 with 218 hits, and in 1997 (when he was 37 years old) he topped that, hitting .372. But perhaps his greatest year—and the biggest might-have-been of recent years—came in 1994, when labor-management strife shut down the baseball season in August. Gwynn was hitting .394 when the ballparks went dark. We'll never know if he might have become the first hitter since Ted Williams to reach .400.

WAITING FOR WADE

When Wade Boggs was asked how early in life he knew he would play professional baseball, he replied, "When I was six years old."

But some big league scouts seemed to think otherwise. Boggs kicked around the minors for six years, playing 662 minor league games before the Boston Red Sox called him up in 1982. He was already nearly 24 years old—late arriving for a true prospect.

Wade Boggs debuted with the Sox a little more than three months before Tony Gwynn

reached the Padres. It didn't take Boggs long to prove he belonged in the big leagues. He hit .349 in 338 at bats as a rookie, one of the highest rookie batting averages of all time. He followed that up by leading the league with a .361 batting average in 1983.

The 1983 season also began an astonishing string of seven straight years in which he exceeded 200 hits. Even Ty Cobb, perhaps the greatest hitter of all time, never maintained such a consistent level of hitting brilliance for so many seasons in a row.

Between 1982 and 1996, Wade Boggs hit over .300 14 times—every year but one. Though, unlike Gwynn, he never flirted with .400, he hit over .360 four times and over .330 nine times. During one stretch (1983–88), he led the American League in hitting five times in six years, a mark of a Hall of Fame ballplayer.

"The holy ground for a contact hitter is 3,000 hits," Tony Gwynn once said. In August 1999, both Gwynn and Boggs—contact hitters extraordinaire—reached that hallowed ground. In the game that he hit number 3,000, Gwynn also added hits number 3,001, 3,002, and 3,003. Wade Boggs' 3000th hit couldn't have been any more dramatic—it was a home run.

With the sense of drama and timing that have characterized the careers of these two great hitters, Tony Gwynn and Wade Boggs reached the pinnacle just one day apart. No two players have ever gotten to 3,000 in such close proximity before.

JUST ONE DAY AFTER Gwynn's 3,000th hit, Wade Boggs did the same. He made his 3,000th even sweeter by launching a home run. Boggs lifetime stats are as impressive as Gwynn's. For 14 of the 18 seasons he has spent in the Majors, Boggs has batted over .300.

CHARLIE HUSTLE

On September 11, 1985, Pete Rose lined a single off the Padres' Eric Show for hit number 4,192, to pass Ty Cobb as the all-time hit leader. The Reds fans gave their hometown hero a seven-minute standing ovation in recognition of his accomplishment. Rose had returned to Cincinnati after stints with the Phillies and Expos to serve as player-manager for the Reds.

Pete Rose Lifetime Stats

Games Played	3,562
At Bats	14,053
Runs	2,165
Hits	4,256
Doubles	746
Triples	135
Home Runs	160
RBI	1,314
Batting Average	.303
Stolen Bases	198

PETE ROSE'S SIGNATURE SLIDE, an explosive dive, headfirst into the base, exhibited his tremendous passion and exuberance for the game.

THE EAGER ROOKIE

From the moment he chose to pursue baseball as his career, Pete Rose got noticed.

It wasn't because he looked like such a spectacular athlete. While someone like Babe Ruth, Lou Gehrig, or Willie Mays might embody the strength and size we'd expect to see in a superstar, Rose was something far different: medium height (5 feet 11 inches), stocky (200 pounds), with sandy hair and the craggy face of an old-time ballplayer. Take a glance at Pete Rose, and you'd be forgiven for thinking you were looking at some scrappy middle infielder who would struggle to hit .260

But even from the start, Pete Rose was possessed by a passion for the game that set him apart. The *Geneva* (New York) *Times* noticed in 1960, when the 19-year-old Rose made his professional debut with the minor league Geneva Reds, a Cincinnati Reds farm team. "Rose is an aggressive and eager ballplayer at second base," the *Times* said. "He adds life to the infield."

Rose did this by treating every moment on the diamond as if it meant life or death. Instead of plodding down to first base after a walk, he would sprint. He would run the bases with complete abandon, hitting the ground as if he meant it, sliding on his face if that's what it took to get the job done. He studied every pitcher he faced, determined to use every edge he could muster.

In the history of organized baseball, there have been many ballplayers who were far better pure athletes than Pete Rose could ever dream of being. But none of them ever played for 24 seasons, appeared in 3,562 games (the most ever), hit .303 for his career, led the league in batting average three times, hit over .300 15 times, and got more than 200 hits in a season 10 times.

Oh, and none of them ever accumulated a total of 4,256 base hits in their careers. Pete Rose did, and that's why he holds the record for the most base hits ever.

WHEN IT COUNTED

"You play as hard as you can and you play to win every time out," was Pete Rose's baseball philosophy. Regardless of his personal goals, winning always came first for him. And, as a member of Cincinnati's famed Big Red Machine of the 1970s, he and his teammates did plenty of winning.

Rose, a Cincinnati native, made his debut with the Reds in 1963. ("It was like a boyhood dream come true, playing for the Cincinnati Reds," he said.) But for the first seven years of his career, the Reds didn't win anything. They were a good team in those years, but never quite good enough.

The Reds began to make their mark in the early 1970s. By now many of the components of the Big Red Machine were in place: Rose had been joined by future Hall of Famer Johnny Bench as well as Tony Perez, and the team was being piloted by the great manager Sparky Anderson.

In 1975, it all came together for the team. They swept the Pittsburgh Pirates in the NLCS (with Rose batting .357), and then went on to beat the Boston Red Sox in one of the greatest World Series of all time. The Reds had won their first World Series in 35 years, with Rose (10 hits in 27 at bats) a dominant force throughout the Series.

Pete Rose had finally accomplished what he'd been striving for ever since he decided he wanted to be a baseball player: To be part of the best team in baseball. Before his career was done, he helped lead the Reds and Philadelphia Phillies to three more World Series appearances and two more championships.

By the mid-1980s, Rose had just one more thing to prove: that he could capture the all-time record for most hits in a career.

THE RECORD

Ty Cobb's mark of 4,189 base hits had stood since 1928, the year he retired. No one had come close to it since.

But as Pete Rose continued to be a productive hitter (he hit .325 in 1981, the season he turned 40 years old), it began to become clear that he would be the man to break one of the towering records in the book. In 1984, he returned to the Reds as a player-manager, guaranteeing that the record-breaker would be with his hometown team.

As he approached the record in September of 1985, the attention from a huge media crowd became intense. "It's been like a long World Series," Rose said of the ongoing media frenzy. But he couldn't complain about having to answer questions for hours every day. "You guys have made me a lot of money," he said to the assembled reporters.

Rose tied Cobb's record in Chicago's Wrigley Field on September 9, then went hitless the following day. On September 11, the Reds came back home to Cincinnati to play against the San Diego Padres, in front of a huge crowd screaming for Rose to get the all-important hit.

Typically, Rose didn't keep them waiting long—but even at his moment of glory the team's fortunes loomed high in his mind. "When I got 4,192, it was in the first inning, and I scored a run," he recalled. "I got another hit in that game, a triple, and we won the game, 2–0. I scored both runs."

When Rose got his single in the first, the crowd rose in an unparalleled ovation that went on for minutes. "It was just overwhelming," he said. "There cannot be anything bigger that can happen to you in a baseball uniform."

AT CINCINNATI'S RIVERFRONT STADIUM, Pete Rose broke Ty Cobb's career record of 4,191 hits.

ACCEPTING ONE OF THE MANY OVATIONS he received throughout his career, Rose salutes his fans.

PUNCH 'EM OUT

*On April 29, 1986, Roger Clemens became more than New England's best kept secret. That night,
the Boston Red Sox hurler struck out 20 Seattle Mariners en route to a 3–1 victory. Clemens broke Tom Seaver's,
Steve Carlton's and Nolan Ryan's modern mark of 19 Ks in a game. (The 19-K record was also shared by
two pitchers in the late 1800s). From that night on, Clemens became the strikeout king of the American League.
Ten years later, on September 18, 1996, lightning struck again when he K'd 20 Tigers at Detroit.*

THE SURE THING

Some baseball stars sneak into the Majors, unheralded, and surprise everyone with their skill. The New York Mets' Mike Piazza, for example, was originally a sixty-second round draft pick by the Los Angeles Dodgers, signed primarily as a favor to then-manager Tommy Lasorda, Piazza's godfather. Very few sixty-second-round draft picks ever amount to anything, but Piazza may well be on his way to becoming one of the best-hitting catchers of all time.

On the other hand, over the course of baseball history, countless sure-thing prospects have fizzled in the big leagues—or even before they reach the Majors. Pitchers find that the hot young slugger can't hit a curveball. Or hitters discover that the fireballing college pitcher's fastball may clock in at 100 miles per hour, but stays straight, making it easy to hit. Either way, pretty soon it's goodbye, baseball.

Every once in a while, though, a sure thing lives up to his promise. Roger Clemens was one such prospect. He was chosen by the Boston Red Sox as the 19th player taken in the draft,

THE YOUNG ROGER CLEMENS proved himself quickly to the Boston Red Sox. Two years after joining Boston, he struck out 20 batters in a game against the Seattle Mariners, a feat he matched 10 years later in 1996 against the Detroit Tigers.

and immediately began to show that he should have been chosen even higher.

In his first taste of professional baseball, pitching in single and double A, Clemens was spectacular. His first 10 starts resulted in 73 innings pitched with 86 strikeouts and just six walks. He was also 6–2 with an ERA of about 1.50. It's difficult to pitch any better than that.

Clemens was called up to the Red Sox in 1984, when he was 21, and immediately began to show that his minor league record was no fluke. "He's about the most mature young pitcher I've ever seen come along," said Sox manager Ralph Houk. "He's one of those naturals a manager dreams about but rarely finds."

During his first two seasons with the Red Sox, Clemens showed flashes of brilliance. Then, at the end of the 1985 season, he underwent surgery on his right shoulder. It seemed that his career—full of such promise—might instead be over.

THE ROCKET'S BREAKTHROUGH

There was a dark cloud hanging over Roger Clemens as he came to spring training in 1986. Would he be able to pitch again? If so, would he ever be able to pitch effectively? The questions remained unanswered throughout spring training, as Clemens was battered in start after start.

But when the season began, he immediately shoved all doubts away. "I came out and started from game one," he recalled later. "I just spun off fourteen [straight wins], and everything just started happening."

On April 29, early in his streak, Clemens faced the Seattle Mariners in Boston. The day began badly for Clemens, as he got caught in a traffic jam and barely made it to Fenway Park before game time. Throwing on his uniform, he hurried to the bullpen to warm up. "I had nothing in the bullpen," he said. "I don't know if I threw a strike."

Plagued by a blinding headache, Clemens went to the mound to start the game. Then, suddenly, everything fell into place. He could place every pitch exactly where he wanted it—he didn't walk a batter the entire game. And his fastball seemed to have extra pop on it; Red Sox reliever Steve Crawford, standing in the distant bullpen, said Clemens' pitches made a sound like a gunshot when they slammed into the catcher's glove.

As the innings rolled on, one Seattle hitter after another went down on strikes. Some swung and missed, while others just watched as the ball caught a corner of the plate, then walked back to the dugout without saying a word. Homeplate umpire Vic Voltaggio later said that he had to ice down his right arm, which was aching from all the strikes he was calling.

After eight innings, with the Sox leading 3–1, Clemens knew that he had accumulated a host of strikeouts, but he wasn't aware of exactly how many. Fellow Sox pitcher Al Nipper came up to him in the dugout and said, "I don't think you know, but you've got eighteen strikeouts, you get two or three this inning and you set the all-time record." Clemens' response: "Wow."

In 1986, the record for most strikeouts in a nine-inning game was 19, shared by Steve Carlton, Tom Seaver, and Nolan Ryan. Clemens set out to claim the record for himself. "The ninth inning was all adrenaline," he said after the game. "I was just out there throwing."

And he did it, too, striking out Spike Owen swinging for number 19, and then Phil Bradley looking for number 20 and the record. After the game, even the losing team's players were overwhelmed by what they had just witnessed. "I think we should all be happy we were here," said the Mariners' Gorman Thomas. "We'll never see that again."

MATCHING THE BEST

Amazingly, 10 years later, Roger Clemens did it again. In a September 1996 game against the Detroit Tigers, he struck out 20 men—making him the only pitcher to do it twice.

When someone finally tied Clemens' record, it wasn't one of the expected candidates. It wasn't Randy Johnson or Pedro Martinez or David Cone.

No, the pitcher who finally tied Clemens' record was a 20-year-old Chicago Cubs rookie named Kerry Wood, making only his fifth major league start. Facing the Houston Astros at Wrigley Field on May 6, 1998, Wood had an overpowering fastball and untouchable curve. He allowed only one infield hit and one hit batsman in an overpowering performance that made the front pages of newspapers nationwide the next day.

"It felt like a game of catch out there," Wood said after the game. "It was one of those games where everything you throw was crossing the plate."

Roger Clemens knew exactly what he was talking about.

CLEMENS THREW FAST AND HARD throughout his career, accumulating 3,153 strikeouts, a record that places him 10th in the all-time strikeout roster.

ONE STRIKE AWAY

The 1986 postseason was one to remember—the Red Sox overcoming a three-games-to-one deficit against the Angels and the Mets' thrilling 16-inning victory over the Astros in the Astrodome to end the NLCS in six games. In addition, the Sixth Game of the World Series will be engraved forever in our memories. The Red Sox were one strike away from their first World Series title since 1918. The Mets staged a remarkable comeback, highlighted by the game-winning run crossing the plate when Mookie Wilson's grounder rolled through first baseman Bill Buckner's legs. As Yogi would say, "It ain't over till it's over."

PLAYOFF FEVER

The 1986 regular season was one of the least competitive in years, with the New York Mets and Houston Astros cruising to easy division championships in the National League, and the Boston Red Sox and California Angels doing the same in the A.L.

Lacking any exciting pennant races, baseball fans hoped that the playoffs and World Series might provide a more scintillating spectacle. In their wildest dreams, though, they never could have predicted that the 1986 postseason would be one of the most thrilling in baseball history.

The Angels began the '86 ALCS as if they intended to run roughshod over the Red Sox, winning two of the first three games. In Game Four, they scored three runs in the bottom of the ninth to tie the game and then won the game in the 11th. This gave them a three-games-to-one lead; all they needed was one more victory to make it to their first Series.

For eight innings, Game Five seemed like an easy win for the Angels. They led 5–2 going into the ninth with their ace, Mike Witt, on the mound. Then Bill Buckner singled and, with one out, Don Baylor hit a home run. Now it was 5–4.

TEAM SHOT OF THE BOSTON RED SOX, who matched up with the Mets in the 1986 World Series. They would lose Game Six dramatically in the bottom of the 10th inning, and would not be able to recover the Series in the final game.

With two outs, reliever Gary Lucas hit the Sox' Rich Gedman with a pitch. Manager Gene Mauch brought his closer, Donnie Moore, into the game. Moore got two strikes on the Sox' Dave Henderson—and then watched as Henderson slugged a home run. Shockingly, the Sox now led 6–5.

To their credit, the Angels tied the game in the bottom of the ninth. But that's as close as they'd get. The Sox won the game in the 11th and then went on to trounce the Angels in the next two games to capture the A.L. pennant—a pennant that had seemingly been within the Angels' grasp.

IN DOUBT TILL THE LAST OUT

The National League Championship Series was a tight, tense one from the start. The Mets were considered to be heavy favorites, but the Astros had Mike Scott, the game's single most unhittable pitcher. Possessing a devastating split-fingered fastball (which many opponents thought he scuffed), he was the Great Equalizer.

With Scott dominating Games One and Four, the Mets and Astros split the first four games. Game Five was thrilling, with the Mets capturing it in 12 innings, 2–1 to take a 3–2 series lead.

TEAM SHOT OF THE NEW YORK METS as 1986 World Series Champions. In Game Six, they came from a 3-2 game deficit to tie the Series against the Red Sox in a gripping extra-innings game.

THE CRUSHING BLOW against Boston in Game Six was a seemingly insignificant tap by Mets' outfielder Mookie Wilson that, due to an astonishing error by the Red Sox first baseman, drove in a run and won the game.

The Astros leaped out to a 3–0 lead in the first inning of Game Six in Houston, and as the innings rolled by and the Mets could barely get a hit off Bob Knepper, everyone began to realize what would happen if the Astros held on to win. It meant that the Series would be tied, and Met-killer Mike Scott would be pitching in Game Seven.

The Mets came to bat in the top of the ninth having gotten only two hits. But suddenly this dangerous team erupted for

three runs off Knepper and reliever Dave Smith, tying the game 3–3. When the Astros could not score in the bottom of the inning, the game headed into extra innings.

And there it stayed, through the 10th, 11th, 12th, and 13th. Finally, the Mets scored in the top of the 14th to take a 4–3 lead. But, quick as that, the Astros' Billy Hatcher homered in the bottom of the inning, tying the game once again.

In the 16th inning, the Mets scored three

runs. But again the Astros weren't done. They scored two runs off Mets closer Jesse Orosco before Orosco struck out Kevin Bass with two men on to preserve a thrilling 7–6 win.

The exhausted Mets then went off to face the Red Sox in the World Series.

ONE STRIKE AWAY

For the first five games, the 1986 World Series was interesting and exciting, but no classic. The big surprises were that neither ace, Dwight

Gooden or Roger Clemens, pitched well and that the Sox held a three-games-to-two lead over the heavily favored Mets going into Game Six.

Game Six was tight and tense all the way through. The Sox moved to a 2–0 lead, but then the Mets tied the game. The Sox regained the lead 3–2, only to see the Mets tie it again. At the end of nine, it was still 3–3.

The Sox went ahead in the 10th inning, 5–3, on another heroic home run by Dave Henderson, a double by Wade Boggs, and a single by Marty Barrett. In the bottom of the inning, the first two Mets went out, and suddenly the Sox were just an out away from their first World Series championship since 1918. The Shea Stadium crowd held its breath.

But then Gary Carter singled. Kevin Mitchell singled. The crowd began to stir.

The next hitter, Ray Knight, fell behind in the count 0–2, and now the Sox were just a strike away. But then Knight singled, driving home Carter and sending Mitchell to third. Now the score was 5–4, and the crowd was howling.

Mookie Wilson stepped to the plate against the Sox' Bob Stanley. The count went to 2–2, and again the Sox were a strike away. Wilson fouled one off, and then another. Then Stanley threw a wild pitch, scoring Mitchell and sending Knight to second. The game was tied 5–5.

Mookie Wilson fouled off two more pitches. Then Bob Stanley threw one more, and Wilson sent a little roller up the first base line. The Sox's Bill Buckner bent over to field the ball . . . and then watched as it rolled between his legs. Knight came racing around from second, and somehow, stunningly, the Mets had won the game and tied the Series, 3-3.

The general consensus was that the Red Sox could not recover from such a crushing loss. Though the Sox jumped to a 3–0 lead in Game Seven, the big Mets bats awoke and carried the Mets to an 8–5 victory and one of the most draining and surprising World Series championships in history.

SADLY, BOSTON'S first baseman Bill Buckner will forever be remembered for his error at the end of Game Six of the 1986 World Series. A timid tap of the ball by Mookie Wilson dribbled past him at first base and drove in the winning run for the Mets.

FIRST NIGHT

After Pearl Harbor, Cubs owner Phil Wrigley gave the steel, wire, and other material he purchased for lights at Wrigley Field to the war effort. Cub fans would have to wait almost 50 years to attend night games at Wrigley. The lights were designed to incorporate the charm, look, and feel of Wrigley. The Cubs held their first night game on August 8, 1988, but rain prevented the teams from finishing the game. Maybe Mother Nature preferred day games!

SPUTTERING

Almost from the moment when Thomas Edison unveiled the first light bulb in 1879, the owners of baseball teams sought to adapt the newfangled invention for use during games. As early as 1880, workers for two Boston companies met on a Massachusetts field for the first game ever played after sunset.

The game was played before 300 spectators, under the light cast by 36 lamps strung from poles. But though the teams made it through nine innings without major injury, the general consensus among observers was that night baseball had a ways to go. "The light was quite imperfect and there were lots of errors made," said one newspaper. "The players had to bat and throw with caution." The final verdict: "The showing was far from impressive."

Amazingly, that continued to be the verdict for the next half a century of repeated attempts to take advantage of what lights could bring: namely, more fans to the ballpark. It was a source of endless frustration that some of the largest potential fan bases—kids in school and working men and women—were unable to get to the ballpark during the week for day games.

But something always seemed to get in the way of successful night games. Either the lights were too dim, or they were harsh. Even a successful major league, regular season night game, played in Cincinnati in 1935, didn't cause teams to rush to install lights. Instead, they just kept trying a night game here, another there, usually with middling results.

A typical experience was that of the Philadelphia Phillies on June 1, 1939, soon after they spent $100,000 installing lights. The Phillies' first-ever night game drew just 8,000 fans on a cold night, a "bitter disappointment," according to *The Sporting News'* James Isaminger.

"It seems," Isaminger went on, "that the proper dates for night ball, when there is at least a certainty against chilly weather, would be one game in the last half of June, three in July, and three in August." In other words, a total of seven games—not exactly a ringing endorsement of baseball under the lights.

Still, led by the more aggressive actions of the Negro Leagues and many minor league teams, the Majors finally embraced night baseball soon after World War II.

A LEGENDARY BALL PARK, Wrigley Field in Chicago has housed the Cubs and their loyal fans from 1916 until today.

That is, all teams but one embraced lights. One team, the Chicago Cubs, said no.

WILTING IN THE SUN?

Soon after the Japanese attack on Pearl Harbor in December 1941, Cubs' owner Phil Wrigley did an altruistic deed. He had already bought steel, wire, and other materials, with the goal of installing lights in Wrigley Field. But instead he donated all the materials to the war effort, choosing to put off equipping his stadium for night games.

His delay lasted longer than even he may have predicted. After the war, when other teams were hurrying to install lights, Wrigley decided that he liked Wrigley Field the way it was. The Cubs, he decided, could play night games on the road, but every home game would be played (as it always had been) under the Sun.

With its ivy-covered walls, cozy dimensions, and neighborhood feel, Wrigley Field is one of baseball's most charming ballparks. It's a park to visit on a hot summer afternoon, to sit under the hot sun and work on your tan while cheering on the Cubs. Day baseball is an inherent part of the park's charm.

But the same day baseball that is so fan-friendly may also have contributed to the Cubs' history of frustration. As of 1999, the Cubs have not won a World Series since 1908, and some (though not all) Cubs fans believe that the team tends to wear down late in the season. They think that this may be because of all the games played in summer's heat, when other teams are playing in the cool of the evening.

Still, the Cubs' owners held out until 1988 before bowing to the inevitable and deciding to install lights. The team would play only 18 night games at Wrigley each season, they decided—but the first of those games would be a spectacle to remember.

FIRST LIGHT

The first night game was scheduled for August 8, 1988, against the Phillies. In the days leading up to the momentous evening, some residents of the streets surrounding Wrigley Field were worried about fan behavior at night. Signs reading "Stay Off the Grass" and "Beware of Dog, He Hates Lights" sprouted up on nearby lawns.

Weighing in, *Chicago Tribune* columnist Mike Royko quoted the poet T. B. Aldrich: "Night is a stealthy, evil raven, wrapt to the eyes in his black wings."

Most fans were excited, though. So many tried to get tickets for the long-sold-out game that Cubs' manager Don Zimmer added a message to his telephone answering machine: ". . . and I ain't got no tickets for the first night game." Added Zimmer, "I heard from people I ain't heard from in 10 years."

Finally, before a packed house, the much-hyped game began—only to be wiped out by rain after just four innings. One last time, a team installing lights had been disappointed by the results.

But the Cubs' disappointment was only temporary. Today, it feels as natural to sit at Wrigley at night as it does in any other stadium.

PHIL WRIGLEY, Chicago Cubs' owner, at an exhibition game at the beginning of the season in 1932.

AERIAL SHOT of Wrigley Field during its first night game on August 8, 1988.

BULLDOG

From August 30, 1988, through the end of that year, Los Angeles Dodger pitcher Orel Hershiser was unbeatable. He closed out the season with a scoreless streak of 59 innings, breaking fellow Dodger Don Drysdale's record by one, and with a 23–8 record was an easy choice for the Cy Young Award. In the streak, Hershiser threw five consecutive shutouts and earned a 10 inning no-decision against San Diego. Hershiser continued his hot pitching in the postseason, picking up three wins and the MVP award for both the N.L. Championship Series and the World Series.

THE ACE

From the beginning, Orel Leonard Hershiser IV looked like a throwback to another era. Long and lean, with a narrow face, unruly hair, and big smile, he would have looked right at home hurling for some scrappy team in the 1920s or '30s. But behind that country-boy exterior lay the soul of a fierce competitor—a man nicknamed "Bulldog" by Tommy Lasorda, his manager on the Los Angeles Dodgers.

Hershiser didn't make it to the Dodgers until he was 25 years old—testament to the fact that pitchers who don't throw the ball 100 miles per hour don't move up as fast as fireballers do. When he finally arrived, he already possessed a good fastball, excellent curve, and a devastating sinker. Even more importantly, he had brilliant control coupled with exceptional baseball intelligence. He could figure out a batter's weaknesses, and almost effortlessly put the ball wherever he wanted to.

During his first four years with the Dodgers, Hershiser was consistently one of the better pitchers in the National League. His best season among the four was 1985, when he went 19–3 with a 2.03 earned run average. Every season, as well as being a bulldog, he was a workhorse, ranking at or near the league lead in innings pitched.

Still, as 1988 arrived, Hershiser was already 29 years old, and he'd never had a 20-win season. He'd never won the Cy Young Award or led the league in either wins or ERA. He seemed destined to carve out a good, but not top-echelon, career.

Then came 1988, when Orel Hershiser took a step into baseball immortality.

GOOSE EGGS

It was obvious early in 1988 that Hershiser was on his way to his best season. He started off hot—winning the Pitcher of the Month award in April—and by the end of August he was 17–8. With the Dodgers looking like a playoff-bound team, it seemed clear that this was his best chance yet to win 20 games.

But no one could have predicted what Hershiser would do next. He became unhittable—as dominant as any pitcher ever.

On August 30, Hershiser shut out Atlanta, 3–0. He followed that with shutouts of Cincinnati, Atlanta again, Houston, and San Francisco. By September 28, he had pitched a total of 49 shutout innings in a row—and was only nine shutout innings away from tying the consecutive-shutout-inning streak set by former Dodger Don Drysdale in 1968.

On September 28, Hershiser took his streak to the mound against the San Diego Padres. Once again he was impossible to hit, and the scoreless innings rolled by. At the end of nine innings, Hershiser had tied the record . . . but the Dodgers hadn't scored either, sending the game to extra innings and giving Hershiser a chance to set the record that night.

OREL HERSHISER started with the Los Angeles Dodgers in 1983 and played with them for 12 years. By 1988, the season he broke Don Drysdale's record of 58 scoreless innings, he had established himself as a top pitcher in the National League.

"I wanted to stop," Hershiser said after the game. "I wanted me and Don to be together at the top." But when he suggested as much to his manager, Tommy Lasorda, Lasorda said, "No way. You're going all the way."

Drysdale, at the time a Dodger broadcaster, also rejected Hershiser's idea of sharing the record. "I'd have kicked him right in the rear if I'd known that," Drysdale said. "I'd have told him, 'Get your buns back out there and go as far as you can.'"

What made the streak far more special to Hershiser was that it continued through the last game of the regular season. He finished with a 23–8 record, a 2.26 ERA—and, most importantly, helped lead the Dodgers to the playoffs.

PITCHING FOR A RING

While the Dodgers were riding Hershiser's streak to the playoffs, the New York Mets were posting 100 wins and winning the Eastern Division easily. The Mets had dominated the season's series between the two teams, and were favorites to beat the Dodgers in the playoffs.

But the 1988 playoffs were yet another example of how one dominant pitcher can confound the conventional wisdom. It didn't start that way: In Game One, Hershiser pitched eight scoreless innings before the Mets scored three in the ninth against a reliever for a thrilling win. Then, in Game Three, Hershiser pitched well, but again the Mets pounded Dodgers' relievers.

Hershiser's moments in the spotlight began the next day. Though exhausted from pitching the day before, he came into the game in the 12th inning, with the Dodgers leading 5–4 and the bases full of Mets. He got Kevin McReynolds to fly out to end the game.

Hershiser was back out there for Game Seven, with the series tied 3–3. Reviving his late-season pyrotechnics, he shut out the Mets on five hits in the 6–0 victory that sent the Dodgers to the World Series.

Again, Los Angeles was deemed the underdog, this time against the powerful Oakland A's, led by Jose Canseco and Mark McGwire. Continuing his unparalleled run of brilliance, Hershiser shut out the A's on three hits in Game Two, giving the Dodgers a 2–0 lead in the Series.

It was only right that Hershiser's last appearance would be in Game Five, with the Dodgers up three games to one. Fans were surprised to see the A's score a pair of runs, but Hershiser gave up only four hits in the Dodgers' 5–2 victory, which capped off his stunning season and gave the Dodgers the World Championship.

SHOWING THE FORCE behind his pitch, this image reveals the reason why Hershiser was referred to as "Bulldog."

AS SEEN BY BATTERS facing him, Hershiser was a menacing force, one to be reckoned with.

HOLLYWOOD FINISH

*One swing of the bat can change a whole game, or even a whole series. In 1988, Dodgers' team leader
and MVP Kirk Gibson was sidelined in the World Series with a strained left hamstring and bruised right knee.
From the bench, he watched his teammates take on the highly favored Oakland A's. In Game One with his teammates
down by a run with two outs in the ninth and a runner on base, Gibson hobbled to the plate to pinch hit against
Oakland's relief ace Dennis Eckersley, who was all but unbeatable that year. Gibson rose to the occasion by
hitting a home run to right field, to win the game for the Dodgers. Watching Gibson limp around the bases, barely
making it back to home plate, somehow you knew the A's didn't have a chance.*

GIBSON, THE LEADER

Occasionally, professional sports will deliver a story that seems to be "made in Hollywood." When the story involves the Los Angeles Dodgers, it truly is: Dodger Stadium is just minutes from Hollywood.

And nothing better suited the description than a home run in the 1988 World Series, which took on legendary proportions the second it left Kirk Gibson's bat.

Kirk Gibson was no stranger to heroics. With the Detroit Tigers, he had hit two home runs in the final game of the 1984 World Series to finish off San Diego, and the photo of his arms raised in triumph had become a classic. But after the '87 season, he became a free agent, and the Dodgers signed him. He was expected to provide experience and leadership in addition to his multiple skills on the ballfield.

The Dodgers were not known for plunging into the free agent market, so there was some pressure on new general manager Fred Claire to make this move. But the team was well rewarded—Gibson came through with an inspiring season, hitting 25 homers, stealing 31 bases, and winning the league's MVP award, a rare feat in one's first year in a new league. While his statistics were not overwhelming, experience and leadership factors were indeed behind his award, as he helped the Dodgers to the N.L. pennant.

Their opponents were the Oakland Athletics. The A's had a potent line-up and strong starting pitching, but their real secret weapon was closer Dennis Eckersley, whom manager Tony LaRussa had used to virtually redefine the way a manager lays out his game plan.

Closers had been part of the game for several decades, but no one had crafted the role quite like LaRussa and Eck. Dennis was to be a one-inning pitcher, rarely more. He would pitch in almost every game in which the team had a lead, no matter how the preceding pitchers were doing. His control was so exceptional that the impact of Eckersley on a game virtually meant that the opponent had only eight innings to win. Between 1988 and 1992, Eck would hurl 360 innings and would allow only 26 unintentional walks, an average of about five a year.

Game One of the World Series, October 15, 1988, was played in Dodger Stadium.

KIRK GIBSON *joined the Dodgers in 1988, signed to the team after becoming a free agent. Dodger management was expecting a lot from him and he delivered.*

OAKLAND pitcher Dennis Eckersley faced off against the Dodgers in the 1988 World Series. He had met his match in Kirk Gibson.

in his aging and bleeding body to hit one miraculous home run. It was still on people's minds. Suddenly, Gibson emerged from the dugout, hoping to get in one swing against Eckersley. The crowd went wild at his very appearance. He had gone to manager Tommy Lasorda and said, "I'll give it my best shot."

IT DOESN'T GET BETTER THAN THIS

This was baseball at its best, the game's ultimate drama, our best pitcher against your best hitter, a World Series game on the line in the last of the ninth of a one-run contest. The winning run was at bat, but barely standing. A full count.

With each swing, futile or foul, Gibson nearly crumbled to the ground in pain. And then Eckersley delivered, and Gibson connected, the ball heading for the right field pavilion. Could it be?

It was! A home run to end all home runs! Gibson hobbled around the bases, pumping his arm, as Eckersley walked off, bound to get them another day. In the broadcast booth, Scully could not believe what he had seen. It was a moment to be frozen in time, a moment never to be forgotten by the millions who viewed it, nor by a couple of veterans named Gibson and Eckersley.

It was to be Gibson's only at bat in the Series, but, as with the regular season, it was the leadership and inspiration of that at bat that set the Dodgers off on a four-games-to-1 victory over the A's for the world championship.

DIRECTLY FROM THE CLUBHOUSE, where he was nursing a strained hamstring and a bruised knee, Gibson delivered with a home run. Following the homer, which won the first game of the Series for the Dodgers, Gibson circles the bases triumphantly.

Alas, the Dodgers would have to play without Gibson. He could barely walk.

Oakland led, 4–3, going to the last of the ninth, and Eckersley was summoned to pitch, just as he had been all season in such situations. And, as usual, he was masterful, getting Mike Scioscia on a pop-up and striking out Jeff Hamilton. It appeared to be another typical Oakland victory.

VIN SCULLY'S BROADCAST

In the clubhouse, Gibson listened to Vin Scully's play-by-play on television. Speculating on a pinch hitter in the one-run game, Scully noted that it clearly would not be Gibson, "who is not even on the bench!" Gibson picked up a bat and tried to swing. His leg almost collapsed under him. But, he thought, "if [pinch hitter] Mike Davis could get on . . ."

Davis drew a rare walk off Eckersley.

In 1984, in a popular baseball movie starring Robert Redford called *The Natural*, worn-out veteran Roy Hobbs finds enough

STRIKEOUT KING

When baseball fans ponder records that will stand the test of time, few go beyond Nolan Ryan's career strikeout mark. Ryan retired with 5,714 Ks, over 1,500 more than his nearest rival, Steve Carlton. Despite injuries that limited his innings late in his career, Ryan was re-energized by his service with the Texas Rangers between 1989 and 1993. Besides two no-hitters, Ryan's high point with the Rangers occurred on August 22, 1989, when he recorded his 5,000th strikeout against Rickey Henderson.

FROM THE BEGINNING

Nolan Ryan could always bring it. Even when he was still a green pea, a slightly built high school pitcher in the small town of Alvin, Texas, he could throw harder than anyone else.

Red Murff could see it. As a scout for the New York Mets in the early 1960s, Murff, scouting in Texas, decided to watch a high school baseball tournament in Alvin, just to pass the time. Without even knowing who was playing, he sat down to watch just as a new pitcher was warming up.

"This skinny, handsome right-hander threw two fastballs, and I was thunderstruck," Murff told sportswriter Jerome Holtzman later. "Then he threw an atrocious curveball, and the hitter doubled to right-center."

Another scout told Murff that the boy's name was Nolan Ryan, and that he didn't seem like much of a prospect. Murff, biting his tongue, admitted that Ryan didn't have much of a curveball, but didn't say anything about his amazing fastball. "That's the closest I've come to being a liar," he said.

Nolan Ryan began his 27-year career with the New York Mets in 1966.

That night, Murff went to see a major league game, Houston versus Cincinnati. The two starters, Turk Farrell and Jim Maloney, each could throw 95-mile-per-hour fastballs. "That young man I had seen threw harder than either of them," Murff said. "When I filled out my report for the Mets, I said that Ryan was in the 100-mile-an-hour range, that his fastball stayed level in flight, rose as it got to the plate, then exploded."

Not surprisingly, the Mets leaped to sign the skinny pitcher. And, after he made it to the Majors in 1966, he spent the next 27 years proving Red Murff right.

YEAR IN AND YEAR OUT

Ryan pitched with the Mets, California Angels, Houston Astros, and Texas Rangers, and he struck out hordes of opposing batters for all of them. His peak strikeout years were with the Angels, when he struck out more than 300 hitters five years out of six. (Most strikeout pitchers don't even reach 300 a single time in their careers.) In 1973, he set an all-time single-season record of 383 strikeouts, besting Sandy Koufax's 1965 record by one whiff.

During those peak years, batters hated to step to the plate against Ryan, who mixed his ferocious speed with a frightening lack of control. "If he ever hits me with a fastball, I'll have him arrested for manslaughter," said slugger Harmon

Killebrew. Added Reggie Jackson, "He's the only man in baseball that I'm afraid of."

According to sportswriter Arnold Hano, who had watched every pitcher from Bob Feller onward, Ryan in the early 1970s threw harder than anyone since Feller and "Koufax on his very greatest days only." He added, "Ryan throws like that all the time, more or less."

FIVE GRAND

The only way to set a career strikeout record is by pitching for a long time, and never losing your good stuff. No one has ever kept his good stuff longer than Nolan Ryan did. As Sandy Koufax said at the end of Ryan's career, "He got good genes, good mechanics—but there's been plenty of pitchers who have had good mechanics that have broken down after a year. . . . The fact that he's been a power pitcher for as long as he has has been amazing."

Ryan pitched during the administrations of seven different presidents: Johnson, Nixon, Ford, Carter, Reagan, Bush, and Clinton. In the early 1980s, arm woes seemed to threaten his career, but instead of packing it up he just ignored his injuries and kept on pitching. In 1989, when he was 42 years old, he struck out 301 batters for the Texas Rangers, one of the top 20 totals of all time. According to Hall of Fame pitcher Gaylord Perry, Ryan's secret was that "He got to be a better pitcher later. He kept learning his craft. . . . He's one of a kind."

In 1989, along with his 301 strikeouts, Ryan went 16–10 for the Rangers, holding opponents to a minuscule .187 batting average against him. The biggest moment of the year—and one of the biggest of Nolan Ryan's career—came on August 22, when he faced the Oakland A's.

In this game, Nolan Ryan became the first pitcher ever to strike out 5,000 batters in a career. (His closest competitor, Steve Carlton, retired with 4,136.)

Ryan's 5,000th victim was Rickey Henderson, baseball's all-time stolen base leader. Fittingly, Ryan struck out Henderson with a fastball. "It gave me no chance. He just blew it by me," Henderson said admiringly. "But it's an honor. I'll have another paragraph in all the baseball books."

Nolan Ryan retired in 1993, after striking out an astonishing total of 5,714 batters. In 1999, he was elected to the Hall of Fame on the first ballot.

RICKEY HENDERSON went down on strikes against Nolan Ryan on August 22, 1989. Henderson was honored to have been the casualty of Ryan's fastball. This strike-out counted in more ways than one: It was the 5,000th of Ryan's career.

HENDERSON'S SWING AND MISS AGAINST RYAN'S FASTBALL. This 5,000th strikeout would be followed by many more. Ryan retired in 1993 with 5,714 strikeouts to his name, a record no other pitcher has come close to.

Lifetime Strikeouts

Top Ten Pitchers

Pitchers	# of Strikeouts
Nolan Ryan	5,714
Steve Carlton	4,136
Bert Blyleven	3,701
Tom Seaver	3,640
Don Sutton	3,574
Gaylord Perry	3,534
Walter Johnson	3,509
Phil Niekro	3,342
Fergie Jenkins	3,192
Roger Clemens	3,316

THE LONGEST SERIES

The 1989 World Series was called the "Battle of the Bay," for San Francisco Bay rivals, the Athletics and the Giants. While the attention of the nation was focused on pre-game festivities for Game Three at Candlestick Park, the entire Bay Area was rocked by a major earthquake, measuring 7.1 on the Richter Scale, that claimed 62 lives. In the wake of this disaster, Commissioner Fay Vincent postponed the Series 10 days. Oakland native, starting pitcher, and eventual World Series MVP Dave Stewart worked diligently during the layoff to help his neighbors in the Bay Area return to normal. Two weeks after the opening game of the Series, the A's finished their four-game sweep.

OAKLAND'S JOSE CANSECO and his wife Esther wait out the tremors that shook Game Three of the 1989 World Series in Candlestick Park between Oakland and the San Francisco Giants.

DARK OMENS

The 1989 season was one where the biggest headlines seemed to be made off the field. Midway through spring training, word got out that Cincinnati manager Pete Rose, the all-time hits leader and one of the most popular men in the game, was suspected of using a bookmaker to bet on

sports. There were even allegations that he bet on baseball.

The matter consumed the public's attention for weeks. Finally, after much public wrangling, Rose was suspended from baseball for life by Commissioner Bart Giamatti. Soon after, Giamatti died suddenly of a heart attack. The events cast a pall over the rest of the season.

Fans turned to the game itself to distract them from the seamy reality. And there were some bright spots along the way. San Diego's Tony Gwynn and Minnesota's Kirby Puckett, two beloved superstars, led their respective leagues in batting. Young Bret Saberhagen won 23 games for the Kansas City Royals, while Mike Scott reached 20 victories for Houston. Nolan Ryan struck out his 5,000th batter.

The pennant races were enjoyable as well. In the N.L. East, the Chicago Cubs held off the declining New York Mets, while in the West, San Francisco barely staved off a determined challenge from San Diego. One of the A.L. races was even closer: Toronto nipped Baltimore by only two games for its first-ever division championship in the East, while Oakland won 99 games on its way to an easy victory in the West.

Unfortunately, neither Championship Series provided much drama. The Giants got powerful hitting from Kevin Mitchell, Will Clark, Matt Williams, and others, and rolled to a 4–1 series victory over the Cubs. And Oakland's pitching ace Dave Stewart, backed by stars Rickey Henderson, Mark McGwire, and Jose Canseco, led the A's to an easy five-game victory over the Blue Jays.

So San Francisco and Oakland, neighboring cities, were slated to play each other in the World Series for the first time. The press dubbed the Series "The Battle of the Bay," and fans hoped for more than the season had yet provided.

But who was to know that the 1989 World Series would be famous for all the wrong reasons?

DENNIS ECKERSLEY, Oakland's flamethrower, finished the fourth game of the World Series, which was played 10 days after the quake shook Game Three to a close. He put the period on Oakland's four-game sweep against the Giants.

THE BIG ONE

The first two games of the World Series made it apparent that this was unlikely to be a Series for the ages. In Game One, Dave Stewart stifled the Giants, winning 5–0. The A's Mike Moore was almost as effective in Game Two, an easy 5–1 win for the A's.

Then, minutes before Game Three was about to start in San Francisco's Candlestick Park, disaster struck. A devastating earthquake—measuring 7.1 on the Richter Scale—shook San Francisco and its environs. Dozens of people died in the area, portions of bridges and freeways collapsed, and fires raged out of control.

At Candlestick, packed with fans, media, and players, the full extent of the quake wasn't known immediately. But everyone knew it was a big one. "I thought it was jets flying overhead that were causing the vibration," said Commissioner Fay Vincent. "Then my wife turned and said, 'Honey, I think it's an earthquake.'"

As fans held on for dear life, the upper decks swayed as the earth shook. Players, sometimes with their loved ones in tow, gathered in the middle of the field. "There's a lot of praying going on right now," said Giants' pitcher Mike Krukow, holding his two-year-old son.

It was clear from the start that no baseball would be played that day. As soon as the immediate danger was past, the ballpark emptied and people made their way home as best they could. The next day, in the ballroom of a hotel whose power had been disrupted by the quake, Fay Vincent announced that the Series was being postponed indefinitely.

A Refuge

As the area picked up the pieces, there was continuous debate as to whether the rest of the World Series should be played. Fans, players, and the media were divided, but as time went on a consensus built that the Series should go on. "We can't do anything to bring people back," said Oakland's Dave Henderson. "What we can do is alter people's thought patterns for three hours—get their thoughts on something other than gloom and doom and show signs of resuming life."

Game Three was slated for October 27, 10 days after the earthquake. It seemed only right that Oakland ace Dave Stewart would start the game. Stewart, an Oakland native, had long been deeply involved in local charities. In the days following the earthquake, he had seemingly been everywhere, visiting damaged neighborhoods, listening to people's stories, trying to help any way he could.

Stewart pitched strongly and his teammates hit five home runs in Game Three, which ended in a 13–7 victory for the A's. The next day, Mike Moore pitched well and the A's ace closer, Eckersley, finished the game, giving the A's a Series sweep with a 9–6 win.

After the Series was over, the teams voted to donate portions of their World Series shares to the people of the Bay Area who had been affected by the earthquake.

PLAYERS, MANAGERS, AND FANS seek safety on the field during the earthquake that hit the San Francisco Bay Area and shut down Game Three of the 1989 World Series.

LIKE FATHER, LIKE SON

Kids get their love of baseball from their parents. Many players have followed their dad's lead: Bret Boone and Barry Bonds to name two, and one player, Casey Candaele, followed his mom, a player in the old AAGPBL. But only Ken Griffey Sr. and Jr. ever played in the Major Leagues at the same time. In 1990 and 1991, Seattle had both Griffeys on their roster. Their highlight was hitting back to back home runs at Anaheim on September 14, 1990. The Griffeys were born in the Pennsylvania steel town of Donora, the birthplace of another ball player of some repute . . . Stan Musial.

TRADITION

Baseball has a long tradition of sons following their fathers into the major leagues. Growing up, the sons of big leaguers often spend a lot of time in the clubhouse and dugout, hanging out with the other players, watching the game close up, playing it themselves in school. It's easy to see why they would be drawn to the excitement and potential glory of playing before huge crowds, getting a crucial hit, or winning the World Series.

Of course, not every ballplayer's son has the tools to follow in his father's footsteps. But a surprising number of them do. For example, Dick Schofield and Dick Schofield, his son, both had substantial major league careers. Randy Hundley was a catcher; so is his son, Todd. Julian Javier and his son, Stan, both made their marks in the Majors. Casey Candaele wrung a new variation from the theme: He followed his *mother*, who played in the All-American Girls Professional Baseball League in the 1940s.

In one case, three generations in one family have made it to the majors. Ray Boone was a good-hitting infielder during a career that lasted from 1948 to 1960. His son, Bob, chose to be a catcher, playing 2,225 games at the position during a 19-year career. As of

Bobby Bonds (above) played from 1968 to 1981 and performed impressively in nearly all categories. But his son Barry (right) surpassed his father at the plate and on the field, winning multiple MVPs and Golden Gloves.

1999, *two* of Bob Boone's sons—Bret, a second baseman, and Aaron, a third baseman—were in the midst of productive major league careers as well.

But perhaps the most stunning father-son combinations of all time are a pair whose stories are still unfolding. In both cases, the father was a fine player. In both cases, the son may well be among the 100 greatest baseball players of all time.

You've probably heard of these superstar offspring. One is named Barry Bonds. The other is known as Junior, but his full name is Ken Griffey, Jr.

A FAMILY BASEBALL DYNASTY, Ken Griffey, Sr., Ken Griffey, Jr., and Craig Griffey, Junior's younger brother and a minor league player, enjoying each other's company on the field.

GOLD-PLATED BONDS

During his 14-year career (1968–81), Bobby Bonds was one of the most dangerous hitters in baseball. He possessed a devastating combination of speed and power. In 1969, he hit just .259 and struck out 187 times—but he also walked 81 times, hit 25 doubles and 32 home runs, and stole 45 bases, resulting in a league-leading 120 runs scored.

And 1969 was a typical year for Bobby. It began a string of five straight seasons in which he scored more than 100 runs, seven consecutive seasons with more than 20 home runs, and years in which he stole 48, 44, 43, and 41 bases. Bobby Bonds ended his career with 332 home runs and 461 stolen bases. It was hard to imagine that his son could do any better.

But Barry Bonds has outstripped his father in nearly every category. Playing with Pittsburgh and San Francisco, Barry has compiled spectacular offensive numbers: Through 1999, he had 445 home runs, 460 stolen bases, 1,299 RBI, and 1,455 runs scored. He has already won three Most Valuable Player awards and may be on his way to 3,000 hits, and perhaps 500 home runs. He is also a superb outfielder and a winner of multiple Gold Gloves.

Amazingly, though, another son of a famous major leaguer is likely to post even more spectacular numbers before he is done. That player, of course, is Ken Griffey, Jr., who also holds another record: He is the only baseball son to play on the same major league team, at the same time, as his father.

TWO OF A KIND

Ken Griffey, Sr., was an integral part of Cincinnati's Big Red Machine in the 1970s.

He consistently hit close to .300, with a high of .336 in 1976. Like his teammates Pete Rose, Johnny Bench, and Tony Perez, he made postseason visits a regular occasion, taking home World Series rings in 1975 and 1976.

But when Ken Griffey, Jr., came to the Majors as a 19-year-old in 1989, onlookers saw that he might be just as good as his father. And Dad agreed, saying, "He reminds me of myself. He has power and speed—even more than I had."

Junior appreciated his father's support in those early days. "It's a great compliment when people compare me to him," he said. "I sure wouldn't mind being compared to him after my career is over, too."

During Junior's rookie year (1989), his father was playing for the Reds. Midway through 1990, though, Cincinnati waived the elder Griffey, allowing him to sign with the Mariners, so he could end his career on the same team with his son.

On August 31, 1990, Ken Griffey, Sr., batted second and played left field in a game against Kansas City. Junior played center field and batted third. During that game, they hit back-to-back singles. Afterwards, they both called the experience the greatest of their careers.

But they went one better in a September 14 game against the California Angels. Hitting against Kirk McCaskill, Senior slugged a home run. Then Junior followed with one of his own. They hugged in the dugout, and then went back to work, just as a pair of professionals should.

Ken Griffey, Sr., hit .377 playing beside and hitting in front of his son during their weeks together. Afterward, Junior couldn't have been more proud. "He protected me for the first 17 years of my life," he said of his father. "Now I can always say I protected him for a month and a half."

JACK MORRIS'S MOMENT

*For sheer Hollywood value, few World Series could match 1991 in surprise and excitement.
Both teams, Atlanta and Minnesota, had finished in last place the year before. The seven-game Series was close,
with four of the games decided in the last at bat. Twins star outfielder Kirby Puckett hit the game-winning
home run in the bottom of the 11th inning of Game Six. The Seventh Game was a World Series classic, as the Twins'
Jack Morris pitched 10 innings of shutout baseball to give the game, and the Series, to the Twins.*

WORST TO FIRST

More than a century ago, a major league team called the Louisville Colonels, in a league called the American Association, accomplished something amazing: They finished last in the league in 1889 and rebounded to finish first just one year later.

The Colonels are largely forgotten today, but their worst-to-first dash remained an unmatched record for more than a century. Then, in 1991, the record was broken—and not by one team, but by two.

In 1990, the Atlanta Braves were dreadful, going 65–97. Over in the American League, the Minnesota Twins were little better. Though featuring All-Star Kirby Puckett, they had little else to offer, and limped home with a 74–88 record.

Then, in 1991, everything was different for both teams. Under the leadership of manager Bobby Cox, the Braves soared to a 94–68 record. Ron Gant hit 32 home runs, and Terry Pendleton and David Justice chipped in with more than 20 as well. But it was the Braves' young pitchers that made all the difference. Tom Glavine, John Smoltz, and Steve Avery all won in double-digits, and were backed by strong relief pitching. The Braves nipped the Dodgers by just one game in the Western Division.

The Twins, managed by Tom Kelly, were even better, winning the A.L. West easily with a 95–67 record. Kirby Puckett hit .319, Chili Davis slugged 29 home runs, and starting pitchers Scott Erickson, Jack Morris, and Kevin Tapani were stellar.

Somehow, amazingly, as the season ended, these two teams—doormats just a year earlier—were headed to the playoffs.

A SERIES FOR ALL TIME

The Twins were slated to face the Toronto Blue Jays, easy winners in the A.L. East, in the ALCS. But though the Blue Jays, led by All-Stars Roberto Alomar, Joe Carter, and Jimmy Key, appeared formidable on paper, on the field the series was all Twins. Kirby Puckett hit .429, slammed two home runs, and drove in six runs, Jack Morris won two games, and the Twins cruised to a 4–1 series victory.

The Braves' challenger, the Pittsburgh Pirates, presented a far tougher fight. The Pirates' Barry Bonds and Bobby Bonilla were formidable hitters, and Doug Drabek, John Smiley, and Zane Smith were solid pitchers. Clearly, the Braves were facing all they could handle.

But somehow they did it. Trailing three games to two, the Braves' Steve Avery and Alejandro Pena combined on a four-hit shutout and a 1–0 victory. Then, in the climactic Game Seven, John Smoltz shut down the Pirates' sluggers, winning 4–0 and pitting the

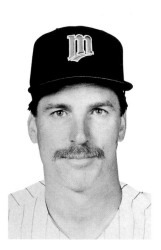

MINNESOTA'S PITCHER, JACK MORRIS, delivered on the promise of his career with 10 shutout innings of baseball against the Atlanta Braves in Game Seven of the 1991 World Series.

improbable Braves against the equally improbable Twins in the World Series.

The 1991 World Series will always rank as one of the best of all time. Three games went to extra innings, and four weren't decided until the last at bat. And the Series itself wasn't decided until the very last swing of Game Seven.

Early on, it seemed as if the Series might end quickly, as the Twins won the first two games. But the Braves plated a run in the bottom of the 12th inning of Game Three to earn a crucial first win. Then, in Game Four, a ninth-inning sacrifice fly gave the Braves another win, tying the Series. In Game Six, it was the Twins' turn: Trailing in the Series, 3–2, Puckett slammed a home run in the bottom of the eleventh, knotting the score at three games apiece.

Any one of these games could be called a classic. But they all paled beside Game Seven, perhaps the most excruciatingly suspenseful and climactic World Series game in baseball history.

MORRIS THE MASTER

Leaving the Detroit Tigers after 14 high-quality seasons to sign with the Twins in 1991, Jack Morris had provided his new team with both maturity and fine pitching. He'd gone 18–12 during the regular season, added two wins in the playoffs, and pitched superbly to win Game One of the Series.

When manager Tom Kelly told him that he was to pitch Game Seven, the 36-year-old Morris felt as if it was the culmination of his whole career. "There was a calmness that came over me," he said later. "It's crazy, I can't explain why—it's almost like it had been planned or that I had dreamed it so many times as a little boy. . . . I'd almost planned it my whole life."

The game was played before a packed, apprehensive crowd in Minneapolis. As the innings passed, it became obvious that both Morris and the Braves' 24-year-old John Smoltz were pitching the games of their lives. Afterward, Morris called the young Smoltz'

ANOTHER TWINS' STAR, Kirby Puckett, knocked the Braves out of Game Six with a home run in the bottom of the 11th inning.

effort "one of the greatest games a pitcher has thrown in modern baseball."

Neither team scored—neither team could even mount a decent threat—through the first seven innings. Then, in the top of the eighth, the Braves loaded the bases with one out, but could not score. The Twins reciprocated in the bottom of the inning, sending Smoltz to the showers as they loaded the bases. But when Kent Hrbek lined into a double play, the game stayed 0–0.

After nine innings, manager Tom Kelly turned to Morris and said, "That's it, you did a hell of a job. I couldn't ask for anything more." Morris' reply: "I'm not going anywhere."

Morris retired the Braves in the top of the 10th. In the bottom of the inning, the Twins loaded the bases again on a double by Dan Gladden and two intentional walks. This time they didn't waste their opportunity. Pinch hitter Gene Larkin lifted a long fly ball over the outfield (which was drawn in to try to throw out the winning run at home), sending Gladden to the plate and setting off a wild celebration among both players and fans.

"It was absolute ecstasy and chaos when we scored," said Morris, who was named the Series' Most Valuable Player. "It was just such a relief."

DAN GLADDEN was the first and last to score in the final game of the 1991 Series. His double put him in scoring position and teammate Gene Larkin drove him home. He is all smiles as his teammates congratulate him in the center of the field.

THE NEW ELYSIAN FIELDS

Fans of baseball in Baltimore had a great reason to go the ballpark in 1992. With the opening of Oriole Park at Camden Yards, Baltimore had arguably the most beautiful ballpark built since the 1920s. Designed by the Hellmuth, Obata and Kassabaum (HOK) architecture firm, the stadium was a throwback to older parks and created an enjoyable experience for the fans in and of itself. Camden Yards is a jewel in baseball's crown, and has served as the model for other new ballparks.

HUMBLE BEGINNINGS

In the late 1800s, the average ballpark was little more than a few bleachers made of splintery wood, a rickety wooden fence, and a diamond sketched in the dirt. For important games, fans would line the bleachers and spill out onto the field, even standing behind ropes in the outfield. These ballparks had a short lifespan. Those that didn't burn down (and many did) would collapse or rot out in just a few years.

In the early decades of the 20th century, progressive team owners began to build the first ballparks worthy of the name—parks that teams would play in for decades, through what many consider the "Golden Age" of baseball. Shibe Park in Philadelphia, which seated 20,000 fans and opened in 1909, inaugurated "a new era in base ball," according to *The Sporting News*. It was soon followed by Forbes Field in Pittsburgh, Chicago's Comiskey Park, Brooklyn's Ebbets Field, and many other famous parks.

Today, these shrines—all long gone—are recalled with deep nostalgia by fans lucky enough to have seen them. But the fact was that by the 1960s and '70s many of them were ramshackle old places, ripe for replacement.

What they were replaced by, however, was no improvement.

THE DARK AGES

By the 1970s, half of the major league teams were playing in ballparks that were cold and windy, had terrible sightlines, or in some other way were not conducive to watching a ballgame. For example, while Dodger Stadium in Los Angeles was an attractive ballpark, San Francisco's Candlestick Park required fans to wear parkas even in summertime.

But perhaps the most powerful trend of this era was the arrival of the "multipurpose stadium." These parks (Pittsburgh's Three Rivers Stadium, Cincinnati's Riverfront, and Philadelphia's Veterans Stadium were prime examples) were virtually identical concrete doughnuts, often situated far from the city center. They weren't designed primarily for the watching of baseball, but for year-round use including football, rock concerts, rodeos, and whatever other events the owners could schedule. Many had artificial turf, and they all

CAMDEN YARDS in Baltimore became a Mecca for baseball fans when it was competed in 1992. Designed to evoke the traditional beauty of ballparks of the past, it has beckoned many baseball followers to its stands.

featured thousands of seats set a long way from the field itself.

By the 1990s, fans had grown tired of these anonymous ballparks. They craved real grass, seats set close to the action, the feel of the ballparks their parents used to tell them about.

In answer to these desires, Baltimore gave baseball Oriole Park at Camden Yards—one of the most beautiful parks of all time, and by far the most influential.

A BALLPARK FOR THE AGES

"It seems like only yesterday that baseball fans were decrying the advent of giant, cookie-cutter stadiums, equally suitable for football, Stones concerts and tractor pulls," wrote *Newsweek*'s Mark Starr in 1994. But then came Camden Yards, "an old-fashioned park smack-dab in the heart of the city—brick on the outside, cozy, grassy and redolent of Italian sausage on the inside. On the field it features nooks and crannies; from the stands the sightlines bisect home plate."

In other words, with its slatted seats, asymmetrical dimensions, and brick facade, Camden Yards is an almost perfect ballpark—exactly what baseball needed and deserved after the artificial turf years. And fans have responded: The park drew 3,567,819 fans in 1992, its first year, and has continued to sell out ever since.

If imitation is the highest form of flattery, then Camden Yards' has been flattered over and over. Over the course of a handful of years, one new ballpark after another has opened—and every one has either modeled itself after Camden Yards or looked back to baseball's classic ballparks for inspiration. Jacobs Field in Cleveland, the Ballpark at Arlington, Atlanta's Turner Field, and Coors Field in Denver all follow this pattern—and more are on the way. The New York Mets are even planning to build a park that duplicates many of the features of beloved Ebbets Field.

It seems clear that we are in the midst of a new Golden Age of the American Ballpark.

ORIOLE PARK AT CAMDEN YARDS has pleased observers since 1992. The harmonious way it blends into the surrounding city makes it a jewel in the urban landscape of Baltimore.

EVERY BALLPLAYER'S DREAM

The 1993 World Series was a see-saw affair between two strong offensive teams, the Phillies and the defending champion Blue Jays. Philadelphia trailed Toronto three games to two after five games. In Game Six, the Phillies were up by one run in the bottom of the ninth inning. Toronto's star right fielder Joe Carter crushed a three-run home run off Phillies stopper Mitch Williams, winning the Series for Toronto.

OPPOSITES ATTRACT

From the start, the 1993 World Series was a study in contrasts. Representing the National League were the Philadelphia Phillies, a scrappy, rough-and-tumble team filled with players who were always getting their uniforms dirty. Its long-haired, usually unshaven stars included center fielder Lenny Dykstra; Mitch Williams, the closer known as "Wild Thing"; Curt Schilling; and such blue-collar overachievers as Darren

IN THE BOTTOM OF THE NINTH inning in Game Six of the 1993 World Series, Joe Carter hit a home run with two men on base to give his Toronto Blue Jays the series win over the Philadelphia Phillies. Carter's teammates leaped out of the dugout to see the ball clear the left field fence.

Daulton, Jack Kruk, and Dave Hollins.

The Phillies were facing the Toronto Blue Jays, a team epitomized by the steady professionalism of Paul Molitor, pitching ace Dave Stewart, and slugger Joe Carter. Where the Phillies had chubby, talkative Kruk at first base, the Blue Jays had John Olerud, who had managed to hit .363 during the season while remaining so silent that he often seemed, in his own words, "just north of comatose."

To make the contrast even starker, the Jays had won the World Series in 1992, while the Phillies hadn't won a thing in a decade. No one had expected them to either capture their division or defeat the Atlanta Braves in the National League Championship Series (NLCS). Going in, said Phillies pitcher Larry Anderson, the confrontation resembled nothing so much as "the ugly stepsister being invited to the prom by the best-looking guy in class."

ONE WILD GAME

As the Series began, onlookers were curious to see which style of play would prevail. The answer wasn't long in coming: The Phillies scored two runs in the top of the first inning of Game One, only to see the Jays come back for a messy 8–5 win. The ugly stepsister was setting the tone.

CARTER (and his bat) leap for joy.

Series. He'd hit just one homer, in a losing cause in Game Two, while his teammate Paul Molitor had dominated the box scores in Toronto's three victories.

Early in Game Six, it looked as if Molitor would again have the next day's headlines to himself. The Jays were poised to cruise to their second consecutive Series win.

But then came the seventh inning. Lenny Dykstra hit a three-run home run to bring the Phillies back to within a run. Dave Hollins' RBI single tied the game. And Pete Incaviglia hit a sacrifice fly to give the Phillies their first lead of the game, 6–5. Suddenly, shockingly, the Series seemed likely to go to Game Seven.

Entering the bottom of the ninth, the score still stood at 6-5, Phillies. On the mound was Mitch Williams. He'd been masterful in the Phillies' NLCS victory over Atlanta, but he'd been both wild and hittable in the World Series. And now he was facing the top of the Blue Jays' batting order.

Leading off, Rickey Henderson walked. Williams got Devon White to fly out, but then Molitor came through again with a single. The tying and winning runs were on base, and Joe Carter, the Jays' clean-up hitter, came to bat.

Williams pitched Carter carefully, bringing the count to 2–2. But he couldn't get the third strike. Carter reached out for a low fastball and hit a hard, high line drive that headed for the left field fence. As the ball cleared the wall, the fans—along with the city of Toronto and the rest of Ontario— erupted in celebration. The final score was 8–6, and the Blue Jays had their back-to-back championships.

AN ECSTATIC CARTER rounds the bases after a home run shot that gave the Blue Jays their second World Series in two years. "Everyone who has ever played baseball has probably dreamed of hitting a home run in the bottom of the ninth to win a World Series," Carter said. "I can tell you what it feels like to actually do it. It feels incredible— really incredible."

CARTER IS HOISTED by a throng of teammates and surrounded by the press.

After three high-scoring games, Toronto held a 2–1 Series lead. Then came Game Four in Philadelphia. After seven innings, the Phillies held a seemingly insurmountable 14–9 lead, thanks largely to Lenny Dykstra's two home runs. But no lead was safe. In the eighth, the Blue Jays put together six runs for a 15–14 lead. Toronto pitchers retired the last seven Phillies in order, and the Blue Jays had taken both the game and a 3–1 Series edge.

Facing steep odds, the Phillies won Game Five behind the shutout pitching of Curt Schilling. Then came Game Six, back in Toronto. It was the game that finally gave Joe Carter his moment in the spotlight.

JOLTIN' JOE

Carter had been one of the most consistent sluggers in baseball for almost a decade. But after slamming 33 home runs and driving in 121 runs during the regular season, he had had a quiet

IRON HORSE, JR.

On May 30, 1982, Oriole manager Earl Weaver penciled into his lineup a young infielder named Cal Ripken. The rest is history. On September 6, 1995, Ripken played in his 2,131st consecutive game, surpassing Hall of Fame great Lou Gehrig. When the game became official in the middle of the fifth inning, the sell-out crowd, and millions of television viewers, celebrated Baltimore's finest as he took a lap around the stadium, giving "high fives" to all fans within his reach.

IN GEHRIG'S FOOTSTEPS

In baseball's olden days, players were expected to play every day. Sore arms? Pulled muscles? Broken bones? Walk it off and get out on the field! And who cared if you were putting your career in jeopardy in doing so!

Even in that more rough-and-tumble era, though, what Lou Gehrig, the "Iron Horse," accomplished was extraordinary. He went out every day for more than 14 seasons, fighting through injury and illness and bone-weariness to play in 2,130 consecutive games. This was over 800 games (or five seasons of everyday play) more than the previous record of 1,307, held by Everett Scott. Said sportswriter

"JUST ONE MORE GAME, MOM."

THE SIGN HUNG OUTSIDE Oriole Park proclaimed Cal Ripken, Jr.'s achievement—the tying of Lou Gehrig's record 2,130 consecutive games played.

Jim Murray of Gehrig: "He was a symbol of indestructibility—a Gibraltar in cleats."

After Gehrig's streak came to an end with the tragedy of his incurable and quickly fatal illness, no one came close to matching it for decades. In many ways, Gehrig's consecutive games streak was the most spectacular record in baseball, standing like a colossus above anyone who attempted to assault it.

Steve Garvey, the great first baseman with the Los Angeles Dodgers, came closest, playing 1,207 consecutive games between 1975 and 1983. Garvey's problem wasn't stamina, but opportunity: He didn't become a regular player and begin his streak until he was 26 years old (Gehrig was only 21), and simply got old before he could dream of approaching the Iron Horse's record.

On May 29, 1982, a season before Steve Garvey's streak came to an end, Baltimore Orioles manager Earl Weaver rested a rookie named Cal Ripken in the second game of a double-header. The next day, Ripken was back in the lineup.

Who would have guessed that he wouldn't miss another game for more than 16 years?

LOVE OF THE GAME

"I wish I had a nickel for every time I heard 'Just one more game, Mom,'" said Vi Ripken, describing life with Cal when he was a child.

CAL RIPKEN, JR.'S reaction to the tribute by teammates and fans after he broke Gehrig's record. (right).

It was this drive and determination that carried Cal Ripken to the Major Leagues—and made sure that, once he joined the starting lineup, he would never leave.

Ripken won the Rookie of the Year award in 1982, and followed that up with an outstanding season in 1983. He hit .318, with 211 hits, 47 doubles, and 27 home runs, won the Most Valuable Player award and helped lead the Orioles to a World Series victory over the Philadelphia Phillies. After that, he was

guaranteed to be in the lineup for as long as his health allowed.

It's mostly forgotten today, but early in his streak Ripken didn't miss a single *inning* for 904 consecutive games between 1982 and 1987. When his father, Cal Sr., then the Orioles' manager, chose to rest his son late in a game, Ripken accepted the decision gracefully, but felt painfully at loose ends. "I didn't know what to do with myself," he said of sitting on the bench. "It was the strangest feeling

RIPKEN AT BAT on September 6, 1995. This was the 2,131st game he had played in without a break. Ripken would go on to play in a total of 2,632 consecutive games, beating Gehrig's record by more than 500.

that I was over here and not playing."

As the years went on, fans and reporters began to notice that Ripken was gradually playing a significant number of consecutive games—and that he showed no sign of stopping anytime soon. With the realization came the beginning of intense media scrutiny that lasted for years.

As he approached Gehrig's record, the prematurely gray-haired Ripken could still laugh about the attention he'd received. Asked

when his hair had turned gray, he joked, "The first time I answered a question about the streak. All at once."

Ripken must have been asked 10,000 questions during the 1995 season. But he answered every one of them, while the calendar drew closer and closer to the day he would finally surpass Gehrig's record: September 6, 1995.

THE BIG DAY

In an evocative article for *Time* magazine, Steve Wulf and Brian Doyle lamented the use of the word "streak" to describe Cal Ripken's feat. "If you pitch 59 consecutive shutout innings or hit in 56 innings, you are on a streak," they wrote. "But if you play so long that 3,695 other major leaguers have gone on the disabled list since the last time you spent an entire game on the bench, so continuously that more than 50 million fans have seen nobody but you start the game at your position, you are not on a streak. You are on a river, a long, meandering river . . ."

On September 5, that river carried Ripken to Camden Yards, where the Orioles beat California and Ripken tied Gehrig. At the time, some observers suggested that Ripken take the next day off, and go down in the record books forever tied with the Iron Horse.

But Ripken rightly rejected any such suggestions. In his 1997 autobiography, *The Only Way I Know*, he wrote that sitting down would dishonor both Gehrig and himself "by implying that the record was a purpose and not a by-product of my simple desire to go out and play every day, which had been Gehrig's desire, too. Lou Gehrig would *not* have wanted me to sit out a game as a show of honor. No athlete would."

On September 6, Cal Ripken went out to his usual position at shortstop and played in his record-setting 2,131st straight game. By the time he finally took himself out of the lineup more than three years later, on September 20, 1998, his streak had hit 2,632 consecutive games.

This truly is a record that may never be broken.

Most Consecutive Games Played Top 10	
Player	# of Games
Cal Ripken, Jr.	2632
Lou Gehrig	2130
Everett Scott	1307
Steve Garvey	1207
Billy Williams	1117
Joe Sewell	1103
Stan Musial	895
Eddie Yost	829
Gus Suhr	822
Nellie Fox	798

THE QUIET ACE

Off the field, Greg Maddux could be mistaken for a regular guy. But on the mound, there is no doubt that he is one of the best pitchers of his generation. Maddux won the Cy Young Award four consecutive years, from 1992 to 1995. Only four pitchers, Sandy Koufax, Denny McLain, Jim Palmer, and Roger Clemens, ever won the award in back-to-back seasons.

THE ARTIST

Baseball fans always gravitate toward the pitcher who can throw hard. They like the ace of their team's pitching staff to just rear back and throw the ball 100 miles per hour. There's something awe-inspiring about the physical tools needed to throw a ball so hard that it whistles as it flies and slams into the catcher's glove with a sound like a small grenade going off. Walter Johnson, Bob Feller, Sandy Koufax, Nolan Ryan, Randy Johnson—these are the flamethrowers that fans have flocked to see.

Greg Maddux doesn't fit that mold. He is quiet and unassuming. He often goes unrecognized even in Atlanta, where he pitches for the Braves. Worse, he possesses a modest fastball that tops out at only about 85 miles per hour. He's the furthest thing from the dazzling fastball artist.

But all Greg Maddux has done with his seemingly unimpressive tools is put together the most magnificent stretch of brilliant seasons since Sandy Koufax.

THE CONTROL ARTIST

"The secret of pitching," says Greg Maddux, "is to make your strikes look like balls and your balls look like strikes."

Sounds simple, and in watching Maddux pitch it's easy to see what he means. He'll start a hitter out with one of his medium fastballs. For about 59 feet it looks like it's going to ride outside for a ball, but at the last second it drifts over the outside edge of the plate. Strike one!

Then, on the next pitch, he'll throw a curveball that drops away as it reaches the plate. It ends up in the dirt, but the batter swings at it, because right before it dropped it looked like a good pitch. Strike two!

By pitch number three, the batter won't know what to look for, or what he's seeing when it arrives. He'll take a weak, defensive swing and hit an easy grounder or popup for an out.

Multiply this pitch sequence—and dozens of others, each designed to mess with the batter's self-confidence—and you have a typical Greg Maddux pitching gem. Batters never feel overmatched, but they rarely seem to get a hit.

Greg Maddux has possessed great baseball intelligence and iron nerves from the moment he made the Majors with the Chicago Cubs in 1986. But at first these skills weren't apparent on the field. During 1987, his first full season, Maddux went just 6–14, with an earned run average of 5.61 and a high walk total.

His problem, Maddux said later, was an inability to throw his changeup for strikes. Maddux uses this pitch, which looks like a fastball leaving the pitcher's hand but floats to the plate at an unpredictable speed, to confuse batters and keep them off-balance. "In my first year, I pitched fast okay, but I didn't know how to pitch slow," he told *Sport Magazine* later. "I had a good changeup in

GREG MADDUX joined the pitching staff of the Atlanta Braves in 1993, the year following his first Cy Young Award earned with the Cubs. His initial year with Atlanta, he won it again...and then again, and then again, becoming the first pitcher to win four consecutive Cy Young Awards.

the minors, but when I got to the majors I forgot how to throw it. . . . Forgot how to grip it. Forgot what it feels like to throw it."

Maddux remembered how to throw his changeup in 1988, though, going 18–8 with a 3.18 ERA—great numbers for any pitcher who has to pitch half his games in Chicago's hitter-friendly Wrigley Field. He followed this up with an even better year in 1989 (19–12, with a 2.95 ERA), and two more good seasons after that.

But it wasn't until 1992 that Greg Maddux took the next step.

INCOMPARABLE

In 1992, his last season with the Cubs, Greg Maddux won 20 games for the first time, going 20–11. He started 35 games, threw four shutouts, and finished the year with a spectacular 2.18 ERA. For these achievements he was given the Cy Young Award.

Then he went out and did it again in 1993, this time for his new team, the Atlanta Braves: 20–10, with a league-leading 2.36 ERA. He was voted his second Cy Young Award for this performance.

But if he'd been superb in 1992–93, in 1994–95 Maddux turned in a performance that was virtually unbelievable. In the strike-shortened 1994 season, he went 16–6, with 10 complete games, three shutouts, and a dazzling 1.56 ERA. He followed that up with a 19–2 mark in '95, with a 1.63 ERA. He received the Cy Young Award for both seasons, of course, by unanimous vote, making him the only pitcher ever to win the award four years in a row.

Maddux' 1.56 and 1.63 ERAs were the first time a pitcher had posted back-to-back ERAs under 1.80 since Walter Johnson did it in 1918 and 1919. But Johnson pitched during a pitchers' era, when the league earned run average was only about 3.00. Maddux posted his numbers in the midst of one of the greatest hitters' era of all time.

GREG MADDUX, the quiet, reliable pitcher of the Atlanta Braves, who has amassed four Cy Young Awards to date.

In 1995, for example, the National League average ERA was 4.18—which meant that Maddux' 1.63 was an incredible 2.55 runs below the league average. This is the widest disparity of all time—meaning that Maddux was comparatively more dominant than Sandy Koufax during his great years in the 1960s.

Since 1995, Maddux hasn't pitched quite as well as he did during those spectacular two seasons. But he's still one of the best pitchers in baseball. In 1998, for example, when Mark McGwire and Sammy Sosa were crashing home runs all over the ballpark, Maddux finished with an 18–9 record and a 2.22 ERA (compared to a league average of 4.23). Then, in 1999, he won 19 games.

Quietly, unassumingly, Greg Maddux has put together a signature career.

Unanimous Cy Young Awards

Player	Year
Sandy Koufax (N)	1963, 1965, 1966
Bob Gibson (N)	1968
Denny McLain (A)	1968
Steve Carlton (N)	1972
Ron Guidry (A)	1978
Rick Sutcliffe (N)	1984
Dwight Gooden (N)	1985
Roger Clemens (A)	1986, 1998
Orel Hershiser (N)	1988
Greg Maddux (N)	1994, 1995
Pedro Martinez (A)	1999

TWIN TITANS

*In 1961, New York Yankee teammates Roger Maris and Mickey Mantle engaged in a breathless
home run chase, which ended with Maris hitting 61 home runs, breaking Babe Ruth's hallowed record. After that,
no one made a real run at Maris' record—until 1998. In the most spectacular single-season chase of all time,
the St. Louis Cardinals' Mark McGwire and the Chicago Cubs' Sammy Sosa battled neck and neck throughout
the entire season, slamming round-trippers at an amazing rate. The great year ended with both men shattering
Maris' 37-year-old record: Sosa with 66 home runs, and McGwire with an awe-inspiring 70.*

NEVER BEFORE

Baseball had never seen anything like it. When Mark McGwire and Sammy Sosa engaged in their thrilling home run race in 1998, they broke new ground.

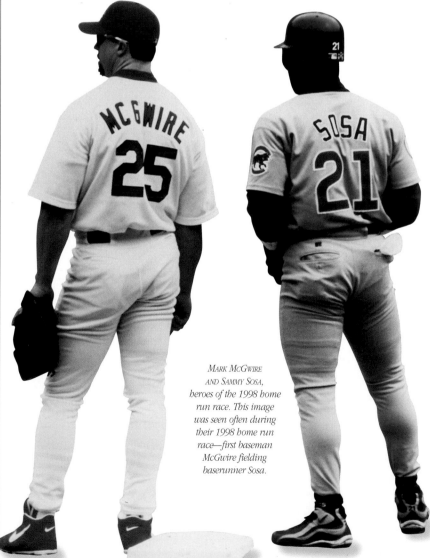

*MARK MCGWIRE
AND SAMMY SOSA,
heroes of the 1998 home
run race. This image
was seen often during
their 1998 home run
race—first baseman
McGwire fielding
baserunner Sosa.*

Never before had two different sluggers chased the record with such ferocity in the same season.

When Babe Ruth hit 54 home runs in 1920, and followed it with 59 in 1921, he was competing only with himself. When he slugged 60 in 1927, he got some competition from Lou Gehrig, who finished the year with 47. But in general, the Babe was in a class by himself, hitting more round-trippers in a season than many teams. No other individual hitter was going to approach his lofty home run totals.

In the decades following Ruth's 60-homer year, a few other hitters made a run at matching his feat. Jimmie Foxx slammed 58 home runs in 1932, and then Hank Greenberg followed with 58 in 1938—but both Foxx and Greenberg were also competing against themselves . . . and the ghost of Babe Ruth.

The closest equivalent to the McGwire-Sosa race took place in 1961, when teammates Mickey Mantle and Roger Maris of the New York Yankees both set out to topple Ruth's record. Unfortunately, as Maris hit nine home runs in September to reach 60 and then added one on October 1 to set a new record, Mantle struggled with injuries and finished with just 54.

After that, no one truly challenged what was now Maris' record for more than 30 years. In 1994, though, it looked as if the record

might finally fall, as Matt Williams, Ken Griffey, Jr., and others were close to the pace in early August—when the season came to a crashing halt due to labor strife, and never resumed.

Mark McGwire, already a feared slugger, barely played in 1994 due to injuries, hitting just nine home runs. Sammy Sosa had a somewhat better season with 25 round-trippers. At that time, no one would ever have predicted that four years later they would be neck and neck in a race for the record, taking the art of slugging to heights never before seen.

EVERY DAY EVENT

In 1997, Mark McGwire had announced in no uncertain terms that he was a candidate to set a new home run record. Shrugging off the disruption of a mid-season trade from Oakland to St. Louis, he'd fallen only three short of Maris' mark, hitting 58 home runs. Even more impressively, he'd hit 24 of those home runs

in only 174 at bats with the Cardinals. Clearly, he found St. Louis and the rest of the National League a good place to hit.

Sammy Sosa was a less likely candidate for immortality. His previous high was 40 home runs, and in 1997 he'd managed just 36. Critics said he struck out too much to ever be a top-echelon slugger.

As the 1998 season got underway, it seemed that the critics were right. McGwire started out with a bang, hitting a grand slam on Opening Day and following with a home run in each of the next three games. Sosa, on the other hand, got off to a slow start. By May 22, when each hit a homer, McGwire had 21 round-trippers, while Sosa had only nine.

But then Sammy went on a tear. He slugged two on May 25, two more on May 27—then he proceeded to hit an astounding 20 home runs in the month of June. By the end of the month, McGwire had 37

SOSA NAILS HIS 62ND HOME RUN, surpassing Maris' single-season record of 61. The race between him and McGwire, however, didn't end at 62 home runs.

McGwire's home run swing that tied Maris' record 61 single-season homers (right).

round-trippers and Sosa had 33, and every baseball fan knew that both men had a shot at the record.

After that it was a matter of Sosa always threatening to catch McGwire, and McGwire then pulling away. Only twice did Sosa gain the lead, and both times McGwire matched him within an hour and went ahead soon thereafter. It was clear that these two men were bound together—they were simultaneously competitors and friends, each cheering the other on. But it was also clear that McGwire was not to be denied the record.

SIXTY-TWO AND BEYOND

On September 7, 1998, Mark McGwire hit his 61st home run, tying Roger Maris' 37-year-old record. Maris died in 1985, but as McGwire approached the record he grew close to Maris' children.

Before the game on September 8, McGwire held the bat that Maris had used to hit home run number 61. "I touched it with my heart," he said later. "When I did it, I knew tonight was going to be the night."

McGwire's heart did not lie. Coming to bat in the bottom of the fourth inning against the Cubs' Steve Trachsel (and with Sammy Sosa playing the outfield), McGwire ripped a low line drive that disappeared over the left field fence in an eyeblink. He'd done it, broken the record, with an amazing 18 games left to play. "It was a sweet, sweet run around the bases," said McGwire, who hugged Maris' children after touching home plate.

Just five days later, Sammy Sosa broke Maris's record as well, hitting a home run off of Milwaukee's Eric Plunk. Then, remarkably, Sosa went on another homer splurge, reaching 66 on September 25 and

McGwire hugs his son Matt after his blast that tied Maris' record. Both are bursting with pride.

briefly pulling ahead of McGwire. "I'm not going to lie to you," Sosa said. "This season is like a gift to me."

But number 66 was the last home run that Sosa would hit in 1998. On the same day, Mark McGwire slugged his 66th, to catch his rival once again. He hit two more on September 26 and two *more* on September 27, to finish with the nearly legendary total of 70.

"I can't believe I did it," McGwire said after his final flourish. "I'm in awe of myself right now."

He wasn't the only one.

TEAMMATES CONGRATULATE MCGWIRE following his 70th home run of the season.

THE TWO PRINCIPAL ACTORS in one of the most exciting stories in baseball history were never antagonists. They celebrated each other's talents and achievements in a way that defined sportsmanship.

MCGWIRE RIDES THE BASES triumphantly. His 70th home run, in 1998, set a new single-season home run record. Who will be the next to match and top his achievement? And when it will happen?

INDEX

Page number in *italic* type indicates separate illustration caption. Page number followed by *t* indicates a table.

PHOTO CREDITS

National Baseball Hall of Fame: 14, 15, 18, 19t, 19b, 20, 21, 22, 23tr, 23bl, 24, 25b, 26tl, 27, 28c, 28bl, 29tc, 29br, 31tr, 31bl, 32, 33tr, 33br, 34, 35tr, 35br, 36, 37tr, 37br, 38, 39, 40, 42, 43, 44tc, 44c, 44bc, 45tl, 45br, 50, 51tr, 51br, 52, 53tr, 53b, 54b, 55tr, 55br, 56, 57tl, 57br, 58, 59, 60l, 60br, 61, 62, 63tr, 63bl, 64, 65br, 66, 67, 68l, 68-69c, 69tr, 70, 71, 72, 73, 75r (top), 75r (second from top), 75r (center), 75r (second from bottom), 75r (bottom), 81tr, 81br, 84, 85br, 88tr, 88b, 89, 90tl (courtesy of **Homer Osterhoudt**), 90bl, 91, 92 (courtesy of **Homer Osterhoudt**), 95br, 97br, 98, 104bl, 104-105c, 105tr, 106, 107tr, 108, 109tr, 110, 111, 112, 113tr, 116, 117tr, 122, 124bl, 130 (courtesy of **Don Wingfield**), 131, 132, 133tr, 133bc, 135, 138, 141tr, 141bl, 145br, 147tr, 147br, 148bc (courtesy of **Bernard Peselow**), 149b, 150cl, 152, 164, 165tr, 165br, 166cl, 166bc, 167tr, 167br, 168, 169br, 170bl, 171tr, 172, 177tr, 177bl, 177br, 178, 179, 184-185c, 187br, 188, 189br, 190, 191, 199b, 202, 204cl, 204br, 210, 211, 212, 213, 214 (courtesy of **Baltimore Orioles**), 216 (courtesy of **Don Wingfield**), 217, 218-219 (courtesy of **Les Banos**), 220cl, 220-221c, 221tr, 224t (courtesy of **Texas Rangers**), 224bl (courtesy of **Texas Rangers**), 225br (courtesy of **Texas Rangers**), 230tl, 231, 244, 245br, 246, 254, 255tl, 256, 264, 265tr (courtesy of **Marilou Crow Leigh**), 266, 268-269b, 269tr, 270-271bl (courtesy of **Tom Heitz**), 271tr, 272, 273tr, 273br (co-owned by **Chicago Cubs**), 274, 276, 276-277tc, 284cl, 288, 291, 298.

Agencies and Photographers:

John Albert: 114. **Carlo Allegri**: 293b. **AP Photos**: 32bl, 82-83c, 83tr, 85tl, 86bl, 94, 95t, 107b, 109b, 117bl, 118-119, 120, 121, 123tr, 123br, 127br, 129, 134, 136, 137, 139, 140, 143tl, 150-151c, 153tr, 153br, 154, 155tr, 155br, 160, 163tr, 169tr, 175tr, 176, 183, 184, 186, 187, 192-193, 198, 203tr, 242tl, 247, 248, 249, 277br. **Barry Halper Collection**: 196-197. **Robert Bartosz**: 258. **Bettmann/Corbis**: 46, 47, 102, 103, 156, 157, 158, 159. **Mike Blake/*Reuters***: 292. **Jonathon Busser**: 290. **Corbis**: 11 (**Underwood & Underwood**), 13 (**Lewis W. Hine**), 48 (**George W. Ackerman**), 232 (**Dave G. Houser**), 233 (**Owen Franken**), 234 (**Sandy Felsenthal**). **Corbis/Bettmann Photos**: 10, 12, 31t, 74, 78-79, 80, 83br, 86-87, 99t, 113br, 125, 126-127t, 128, 142, 143br, 144, 145t, 146, 148t, 149tr, 151tr, 151br, 170cr, 171br, 174, 175br, 182, 193, 200, 201tr, 201bl, 203br, 205tr, 205c, 206, 207 (all), 208-209, 215, 220cl, 222, 223, 226tr, 226bl, 227tr, 229, 230br, 237tr, 239, 240, 241, 242-243, 245tl, 250, 251, 252, 253, 255br, 257tl, 257br, 259br, 260, 261. **Tom Cruze**: 289tr. *Detroit Free Press*: 189br. **Rick Eglinton**: 293tl. **Nate Fein**: 115tr, 115br. **Karl Merton Ferron**: 295. **Ted Fink**: 280. **Ray Gallo**: 195. **Andy Hoyt/*Sports Illustrated***: 275br. **Heinz Kluetmeir/*Sports Illustrated***: 289br. **Ron Kuntz**: 282-283. **Richard Lasner**: 294, 296-297. *Life Magazine*: 180-181. **Jim McMillan**: 293tr. **J. Howard Miller/Corbis**: 100. **Minnesota Historical Society/Corbis**: 49, 101. **Tim Parker**: 304bl. **Earl Payne**: 76, 77tl, 77-78. **Rich Pilling/MLB**: 302-303. **Michael Ponzini**: 16. **Photo File Photos**: 17, 194bl, 228, 262, 263, 265tr, 267, 275tr, 278, 279tr, 279b, 284r, 299. **Russ Reed/*Oakland Tribune***: 217br. *Reuters Newsmedia Inc./Corbis*: 235. **Eric Risberg**: 281. *St. Louis Post-Dispatch*: 172, 173tr. **Steven Schwab**: 301. **Herb Sharfman/*Sports Illustrated***: 161, 162-163. **Charles Shoup**: 65br, 81tr, 96. *The Sporting News*: 25tr. **Kurt Smith**: 285. **Harley Soltes**: 286-287. **Brian Spurlock**: 302l, 304tr, 305. **William J. Taylor**: 300.

every